iOS 5 Recipes

A Problem-Solution Approach

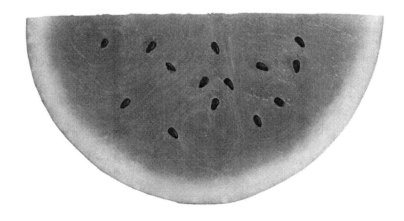

Shawn Grimes
Colin Francis

Apress®

iOS 5 Recipes: A Problem-Solution Approach

Copyright © 2012 by Shawn Grimes and Colin Francis

ISBN-13 (pbk): 978-1-4302-4005-1

ISBN-13 (electronic): 978-1-4302-4006-8

Trademarked names, logos, and images may appear in this book. Rather than use a trademark symbol with every occurrence of a trademarked name, logo, or image we use the names, logos, and images only in an editorial fashion and to the benefit of the trademark owner, with no intention of infringement of the trademark.

The use in this publication of trade names, trademarks, service marks, and similar terms, even if they are not identified as such, is not to be taken as an expression of opinion as to whether or not they are subject to proprietary rights.

President and Publisher: Paul Manning
Lead Editor: Michelle Lowman
Development Editor: Ralph Moore
Technical Reviewer: Anselm Bradford
Editorial Board: Steve Anglin, Mark Beckner, Ewan Buckingham, Gary Cornell, Morgan Ertel, Jonathan Gennick, Jonathan Hassell, Robert Hutchinson, Michelle Lowman, James Markham, Matthew Moodie, Jeff Olson, Jeffrey Pepper, Douglas Pundick, Ben Renow-Clarke, Dominic Shakeshaft, Gwenan Spearing, Matt Wade, Tom Welsh
Coordinating Editor: Anita Castro
Copy Editor: Mary Ann Fugate
Compositor: MacPS, LLC
Indexer: SPi Global
Artist: SPi Global
Cover Designer: Anna Ishchenko

Distributed to the book trade worldwide by Springer Science+Business Media, LLC., 233 Spring Street, 6th Floor, New York, NY 10013. Phone 1-800-SPRINGER, fax (201) 348-4505, e-mail orders-ny@springer-sbm.com, or visit www.springeronline.com.

For information on translations, please e-mail rights@apress.com, or visit www.apress.com.

Apress and friends of ED books may be purchased in bulk for academic, corporate, or promotional use. eBook versions and licenses are also available for most titles. For more information, reference our Special Bulk Sales–eBook Licensing web page at www.apress.com/bulk-sales.

The information in this book is distributed on an "as is" basis, without warranty. Although every precaution has been taken in the preparation of this work, neither the author(s) nor Apress shall have any liability to any person or entity with respect to any loss or damage caused or alleged to be caused directly or indirectly by the information contained in this work.

The source code for this book is available to readers at www.apress.com. You will need to answer questions pertaining to this book in order to successfully download the code.

I dedicate this book to my wife, Stephanie, and my family, who have always supported me and encouraged me.

—Shawn Grimes

This work is dedicated to my grandfather, Larry Cohan.

—Colin Francis

Contents at a Glance

Contents

About the Authors

In 2010, **Shawn Grimes** taught himself Objective-C and iOS development and wrote his first iOS app for the iPad. From Baltimore, Maryland, Shawn attended Capitol College in Laurel, Maryland and graduated in 2003 with a bachelor's degree in software and Internet applications. He founded Shawn's Bits, LLC to create additional apps and present workshops for other aspiring iOS developers. To help local developers, he co-runs the Baltimore Mobile Developers group with Chris Stone. Shawn and his wife, Stephanie, run Campfire Apps, LLC, a mobile app development company focused on children's apps.

Colin Francis is an iOS developer from Gaithersburg, Maryland. After extensively studying computer science, he trained himself in iOS development and worked with Shawn Grimes in Baltimore. Now he lives in Miami, developing iOS apps independently with a focus on utilities and audio-focused software applications.

About the Technical Reviewer

 **Anselm Bradford** is a lecturer in digital media at the Auckland University of Technology (AUT) in New Zealand, where he researches interactive media, web media, and visual communication. His experience with Internet-related development stretches back to 1996, when he hand-coded his first web site. He may be found at @anselmbradford on Twitter and occasionally blogs at AnselmBradford.com.

Acknowledgments

First, I would like to thank Colin, who took on this project with me and led the way to getting it completed. It has always been a pleasure working with him, and his appetite for knowledge is an inspiration to me.

I would also like to thank my wonderful family, who has inspired me and always supported me: Terri, Larry, Amber, Gloria, Wayne, Kelly, Debbi, Billy, Tom, Mark, Derek, Devin, Bethany, Lauren, Kelsie, Matt, Pam, Mike, Jackie, Gus, Chris, Sam, Brynn, and Courtney.

Finally, I would like to thank my friends, who put up with me taking my laptop everywhere with me so I could work on the book and kept Stephanie company while I was working on this book. Special thanks to Jessop, Lauren, and Henry.

Shawn Grimes

Working on this book has been an immense pleasure, but it was a task that I could not have faced without the full support of my family. I thank every one of them for supporting me and providing suggestions when I was stuck. A huge "thank you" as well goes to my mother, for all her help and support, no matter the occasion.

It has been a terrific experience working with Shawn. Ever since I met him and his wonderful wife, Stephanie, I have particularly enjoyed working on a huge variety of iOS projects with them both. Shawn's technical experience has helped guide me through many tasks with ease, and his generous nature makes him incredibly easy to work with. When he originally brought the project of writing this book to me, I was apprehensive, but with his assistance it was easily turned into the completed product that you see today.

I would like to thank everyone I have worked with in writing this book. Anselm, Ralph, and Mary have been fantastic reviewers, and it was through their intense and dedicated focus that this book has turned out so well. This book also would never have seen the light of day if not for the incredible organizational efforts of both Mark and Anita, as well as the multitude of other individuals at Apress.

Finally, I would like to especially thank all of my friends, of whom there are too many to name individually, who have helped me throughout the process of writing this book. Through my countless hours spent writing, they have constantly been a source of support, providing constant and often incredible suggestions, even if they could not decipher the subject. If not for their original insistence and encouragement to take on such a project, I would never have reached this point.

Colin Francis

Introduction

Once you have already acquired an understanding of the syntax structure of programming in Objective-C for iOS development, the most important part of creating applications is learning to work with the various tools and frameworks provided by Apple. In order to fully develop iPhone and iPad applications, you must have a detailed understanding not only of your development environment, but also of the various elements and functionalities that you are able to use. Regardless of whether your application is playing music, taking pictures, printing documents, or filtering images, this book will help guide you through the setup and building of your functionality.

What to Expect from This Book

The first few chapters of this book are devoted to acquiring a basic understanding of your development environment. You will learn a variety of ways to work within Xcode and Interface Builder, as well as the various standard user interface elements with which you can build your application. The remaining 13 chapters focus on specific examples, or recipes, of a variety of different applications, in order to demonstrate exactly how to implement each functionality from start to finish.

How This Book Is Organized

The example-based chapters of this book do not particularly build off of one another, in the hope that you can simply open up to any chapter of specific interest and start building a certain type of application. However, it is highly recommended that you read the first three chapters in order to acquire a solid understanding of working with Xcode and Interface Builder, if you have not already. Some of the methods used in these early chapters, such as those used to create properties, are referenced throughout the text and should be fully understood.

Throughout this book, it is assumed that you are developing in the latest versions of iOS (5.0) and Xcode (4.2) at the time of writing. This means that every recipe in this text assumes that you will be using ARC (Automatic Reference Counting), and as such does not include significant memory management. This also means that depending on when you are reading this, your results may look slightly different, though the basic functionality should remain similar.

Many of the recipes in this book cannot be fully tested on the iOS simulator, and as such will require both an Apple device and a provisioning profile, which can be acquired when you subscribe to Apple's iOS Developer Program. Each recipe that cannot be tested in the simulator will mention this fact.

Source Code and Errata

All the source code used in this book is available online for download at www.apress.com, and it is entirely free for use in any application, whether commercial or personal. A number of people have worked hard to keep this code as perfect and error-free as possible, but a few typos or bugs may become apparent with extensive use. Any corrections to the text or code are available in this book's "Errata" section, also at www.apress.com.

Contact Information

If you have any questions or comments regarding the book or its source code, we would be happy to assist. You can contact either author:

Colin Francis:
E-mail: cmfrancis24@gmail.com

Shawn Grimes:
E-Mail: shawn@shawnsbits.com
Web: www.shawnsbits.com

Xcode 4 Tips and Tricks

Xcode 4 brought forth a number of changes to the look and feel of Xcode as well as changes in functionality. As with any major change to the way people do things, it was met with mixed reviews and some complaints. In this chapter, we'll steer clear of the shortcomings of Xcode 4 and insted focus on its strengths and improvements, which are many.

Xcode 4: An Introduction

The very first thing you'll notice about Xcode 4 is its unified interface window. Everything has been brought into one window, and the new interface has introduced the common interface element of tabs instead of multiple windows.

Figure 1–1 shows an example of the Xcode user interface, including its various display panes. These panels help you to navigate, build, and debug your application. Their visibility can be adjusted easily using the View buttons in the upper right-hand corner in order to provide more viewing space for the Editor.

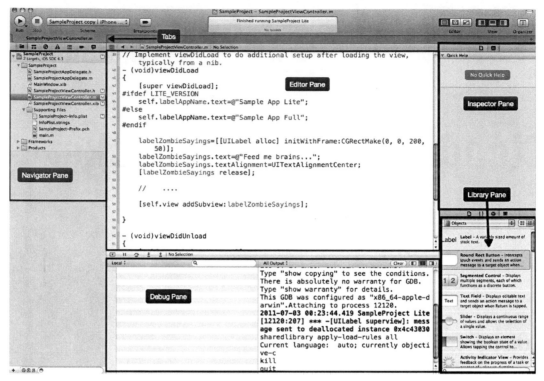

Figure 1–1. *The Xcode interface*

Even Interface Builder has been included in the single window interface of Xcode 4. With the inclusion of Interface Builder, Apple has built some swift functionality to help you go from visual interface to functioning code. Figure 1–2 shows Interface Builder being used to construct an application's user interface. This will be covered more in Chapter 2.

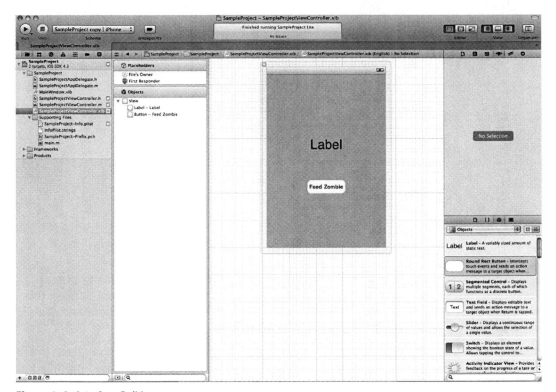

Figure 1–2. *Interface Builder*

With the Assistant Editor, you can easily see two related files side by side. This is very useful when working with class headers and implementation files because you can easily modify both files in a single view. By using the small navigation area at the top of each pane, you can either select specific files to show together, or specify "Counterparts" to automatically show the related header or implementation file, as shown in Figure 1–3.

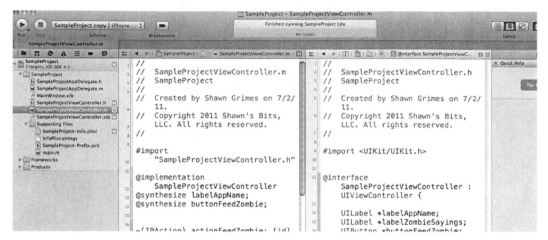

Figure 1–3. *The Assistant Editor*

A feature of Xcode 4 that is sure to save you time is Fix-It. This feature tries to detect common programming mistakes and offers suggestions on how to fix them. It does this while you are writing the code rather than waiting for you to run a build command. This makes it a great time saver for common mistakes.

Xcode 4 also features better source control integration with Git. You are now given the option to create a local Git repository every time you start a new project, and modified files are clearly marked in the Navigator pane. The Timeline Editor view will even show you changes that you've made since the last check-in or compare your current file to any past file version in the repository. This view back in time is very similar to the Time Machine backup interface in Snow Leopard, as shown in Figure 1–4.

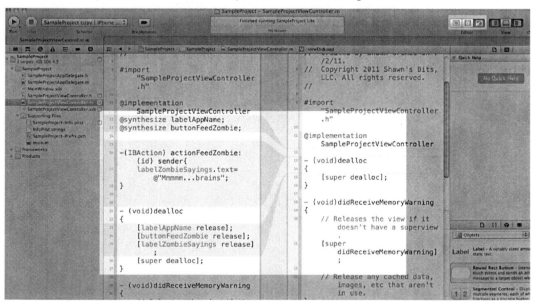

Figure 1–4. *Timeline Editor displaying recent revisions*

Build a Lite and Full Version in One Xcode Project

Offering a lite version of your app is a great way to give customers a chance to try your app before buying it. Maintaining two code bases, however, can be quite tiresome and get out of hand as you implement new features into your app. While the ability to maintain two build targets was available in Xcode 3, Xcode 4 has made it even easier.

Select your project file in the Navigator area, and then select the build target for your project. Now press ⌘D to duplicate the target. You will be prompted to "Duplicate Only" or "Duplicate and Transition to iPad." Click Duplicate Only to create a new target that will be used for your Lite build, as shown in Figure 1–5. This will result in a separate build target with which you can implement a second version.

Figure 1–5. *Project duplication options*

Rename the new target with an appending "Lite". You will also want to go to the Build Settings tab and find the Product Name attribute under the Packaging heading in order to append "Lite" to the app name. Now that the build name is set, you need a way to differentiate between the two builds in your source code. For that, scroll down and find the Preprocessor Macros, and add a new macro named LITE_VERSION. Make sure to add the new macro for the Debug and Release build settings. Figure 1–6 shows an example of these changes.

Private Headers Folder Path	SampleProject Lite.app/Priv...		.app/PrivateHeaders
Product Name	SampleProject Lite	**SampleProject Lite**	
Property List Output Encoding	binary :		binary :
Public Headers Folder Path	SampleProject Lite.app/Hea...		.app/Headers
Strings file Output Encoding	binary :		binary :
Wrapper Extension	app	**app**	app
▶ Search Paths			
▶ Unit Testing			
▶ Versioning			
▶ Interface Builder XIB Compiler – Options			
▶ LLVM GCC 4.2 – Code Generation			
▶ LLVM GCC 4.2 – Language			
▼ LLVM GCC 4.2 – Preprocessing			
▼ Preprocessor Macros	‹Multiple values›	‹Multiple values›	‹Multiple values›
Debug	DEBUG	**DEBUG**	**DEBUG**
Any Architecture | Any SDK :	LITE_VERSION	**LITE_VERSION**	
Release			
Any Architecture | Any SDK : ○	LITE_VERSION	**LITE_VERSION**	
Preprocessor Macros Not Used In Preco...			
▶ LLVM GCC 4.2 – Warnings			

Figure 1–6. *"Lite" application configuration*

If you build and run that now, you will end up with a second app on your device with the name "SampleApp Lite" as the title, but it runs the same code as the regular version of the app, as demonstrated in Figure 1–7. Keep in mind that the two targets must have separate bundle identifiers in order to show up as separate apps. This is the default setting, but be careful when making changes.

Figure 1–7. *Two versions of the same application*

To build different features into your app, you will need to utilize that preprocessor macro you created. Anywhere in your code that you want to specify different code for your lite version vs. the full version, use the following #ifdef directive:

```
#ifdef LITE_VERSION
//Stuff for Lite version
Self.labelAppName.text=@"Sample App Lite";
#else
//Stuff for Full version
Self.labelAppName.text=@"Sample App Full";
#endif
```

Build and compile the two apps on the simulator, and you will see that the apps change the code they compile and run based on the preprocessor macro and the power of the #ifdef directive. Figure 1–8 demonstrates the result of this configuration.

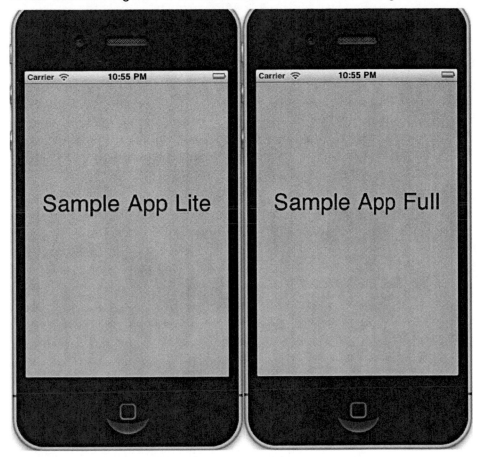

Figure 1–8. *Full and "lite" applications*

> **NOTE:** You can also control what files are included in each build. For instance, you may not need to include the full version artwork in the lite version. Click your Lite project target and go to the Build Phases tab. Now expand the Copy Bundle Resources ribbon, and remove or add any files that are specific to the lite version.

Zombie Hunter

Occasionally, you will run into an error described only as "EXC_BAD_ACCESS," and unfortunately, it doesn't tell you in which line the bad access is occurring. This is caused when you have released a variable and then tried to access that freed object. When an object is no longer there and you try to access it, the term is a zombie object. Enter the zombie hunter, the NSZombieEnabled flag. This is not new to Xcode 4, but where you set the flag can be difficult to find in Xcode 4. Go to the Product menu and select "Edit Scheme…". Now select the Run step and click the Arguments tab. Under the Environment Variables section, add NSZombieEnabled and set the value equal to YES, as shown in Figure 1–9.

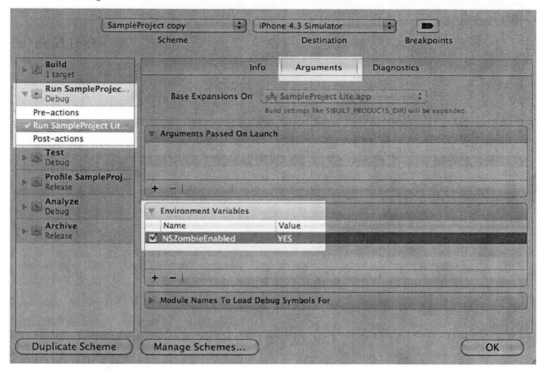

Figure 1–9. *Enabling* NSZombieEnabled

The next time you run your code, the zombies will be identified in the Debug window. Figure 1–10 displays an example of a zombie caught by Xcode.

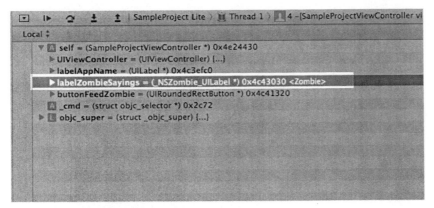

Figure 1–10. *A zombie identified*

Version Control with Xcode 4

Version control can be a daunting concept to new developers, but it is something worth learning. Once you have started using version control, you will wonder how you ever got along without it. Its benefits for teams of developers are fairly obvious. Individual team members can work on different parts of an app without stepping on each other's code.

Single developers can benefit from version control as well. With multiple branches, you can add features to your app without disturbing the previous released version. If a bug is discovered in your released version, you can switch branches and fix the bug without impacting the future version of your app. Then you can merge the two versions and have a new version that contains the bug fixes and the new features. All the while, you can reach back to any point in time and see changes that were made to your code.

Xcode 4 introduced version control into the Xcode environment. Initially, it supported only local Git repositories, but Xcode 4.2 has brought remote repositories to the environment. This is great news if you are part of a development team or if you work on multiple machines. Remote repositories also provide a safe place for your code in case of computer failure or loss.

Creating a Local Repository

Whenever you start a new project in Xcode 4, you are given the option to create a local Git repository, as shown in Figure 1–11. If you select this box, Xcode will create the local repository and automatically add the project files it thinks are necessary.

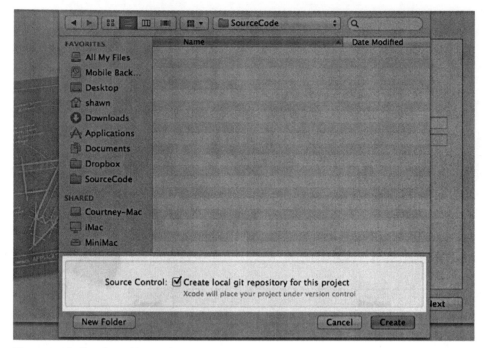

Figure 1–11. *Creating a Git repository*

As you make changes to your project and its files, their source control status will be displayed in the navigator window. "A" is for when a file has been added to your project, and "M" is for when it has been modified since the last check-in. Figure 1–12 shows a navigation pane with multiple files with these statuses.

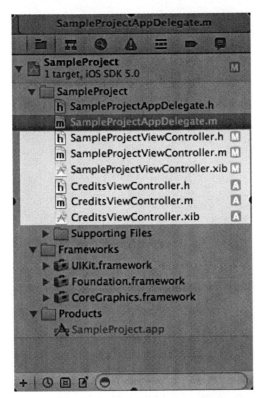

Figure 1–12. *Modified and added project files*

You can filter the navigator contents so that you see only the files that are pending changes to the source control repository by clicking the middle icon in the bottom of the navigator pane, as shown in Figure 1–13.

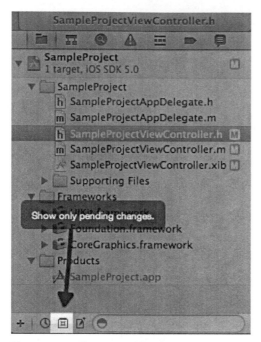

Figure 1–13. *Filtered modified files*

To commit your changes back into your local repository, go to **File ➤ Source Control ➤ Commit** or ⌥⌘C. The Commit window will be presented. By clicking a modified file, you will see your edited version in the left pane and the current version in the repository in the right pane. All of your changes will be highlighted so that you can easily see the differences between the two files. Figure 1–14 displays such a window with highlighted changes.

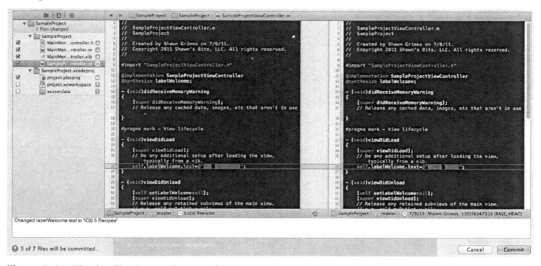

Figure 1–14. *Viewing file changes for committal*

Worth mentioning is the fact that the left pane is a live editor, so if you see something that should not be committed, such as an NSLog statement, this is your chance to comment it out or make the necessary changes.

Xcode does a good job of suggesting which files should be committed. You do not want to version control your workspace file (*.xcworkspace) or your userdata directory (xcuserdata). Generally Xcode will not check those files, and you will note the "?" mark icon next to the files. This means they are not currently under version control, nor should they be. Figure 1–15 shows these non-version-controlled files/directories.

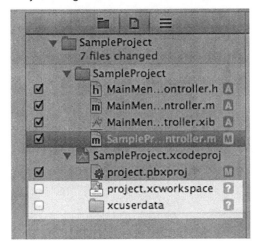

Figure 1–15. *Disabled version control for certain directories*

At the bottom of the commit window, as shown in Figure 1–16, is where you need to enter a message about the changes you have made before committing. Your commit message should be a descriptive summary of the changes you have made to your code, such as "added such and such feature."

Figure 1–16. *Commit message*

Branching and Merging

Branches are copies of your project that you can work on without disturbing the main branch, also known as the master branch. They allow you to add features and fixes without affecting the main build.

To manage your repository, you can go to **Window Organizer** or ⇧⌘2 and click the Repositories tab. In this view, you will see a list of repositories that Xcode knows about.

As shown in Figure 1–17, you can click the Branches folder under a repository to see a list of branches available to Xcode for this repository.

Figure 1–17. *Repositories tab in Organizer*

When you select a branch, you will see a list of the latest commits to that branch. The information includes who made the commit and their commit message.

Create a new branch to start adding a main menu to your app. Click the Add Branch button at the bottom of the Organizer window. In the window shown in Figure 1–18, type a branch name and click the check box next to "Automatically switch to this branch". This will duplicate the code in the master branch into a new branch called "MainMenu," and then it will switch you to that branch.

Figure 1–18. *Creating a branch*

Now that you are working in the MainMenu branch, you can add a new view controller for the main menu without affecting the rest of the app source code. After adding the view controller and coding it up, you can commit this back to the source code repository. Again, this will affect only the MainMenu branch and not make any changes to the master branch.

To merge the two branches, you want to switch to the branch that you want to merge the changes into. You are done coding up the MainMenu, and you want to put it into the master branch, so you are going to switch to the master branch. This is done from the Organizer window, so press ⇧⌘2.

Click the project folder, and then click the Switch Branch button on the bottom right. Select the branch you want to switch to—master in this case—and click OK. This will switch your active branch back to the master branch, and now you can merge the two branches together. Figure 1–19 highlights these steps.

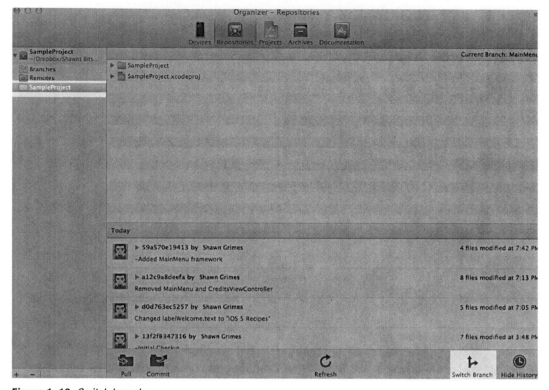

Figure 1–19. *Switch branch*

Go back to the Xcode window and click **File ➤ Source Control ➤ Merge**. You will be prompted to select which branch you want to merge into the current branch (master), as shown in Figure 1–20. When you click Choose, you will see the commit changes window.

Figure 1–20. *Merging a branch with the current branch*

This commit changes window is very similar to the one you saw before with one minor change: at the bottom of the code review panes, you will see four icons. If each branch contains a file that has been modified in both branches, these icons will allow you to decide which one takes precedence. The icons are, in order from left to right, "Merge the left file first and then the right," "Keep the left file changes only," "Keep the right file changes only," and "Merge the right file first and then the left." These icons are shown in Figure 1–21. This is very useful for resolving conflicts if two people have made changes to the same file or if a file has been modified in both branches.

Figure 1–21. *Specify the change precedence for merging*

Clicking the Merge button will combine the MainMenu branch into the master branch. If you look at the master branches commit history in the Organizer view (⇧⌘2), you will see that the commits from the MainMenu branch have been combined with the master branch commits.

Remote Repositories

Up until this point, you have been working with local repositories. In Xcode 4.2, support for remote repositories was added. This allows you to store your code online where you can get to it from any computer and allows multiple users to access your code. Another benefit of remote repositories is storing your source code offsite in case of sudden device failure or worse.

To add a remote repository, go to the Organizer view (⇧⌘2) on the Repositories tab and select the repository you want to add a remote option to. Click the Remotes folder under the project repository, and click Add Remote at the bottom. This will bring up a view similar to Figure 1–22. Enter a name for your remote repository and the location, and then click Create.

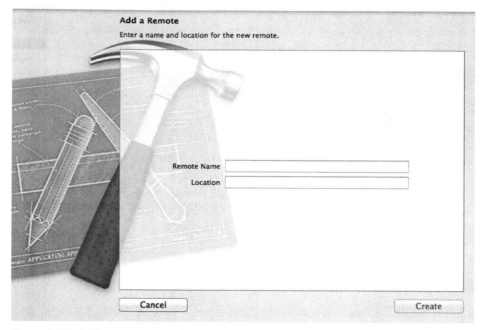

Figure 1–22. *Adding a remote repository*

Now that you have a remote repository, you can push and pull your code from the remote repository to keep things up to date. This is not the same as a commit. A commit or merge affects only your local copy. You need to then push your code to the remote repository to update the remote repository.

GitHub

A very popular online repository for Git projects is GitHub, found at www.github.com. GitHub offers the ability to remotely store your code in either a public or private repository. This allows small teams of developers to work on one project together or individual developers to remotely store their code repository. Up until now, you had to use third-party software or the command-line version of Git to push your changes to a remote repository. With the inclusion of remote repositories in Xcode, it's easy to work with GitHub and to store your source code remotely.

Before you add the project to Xcode, you should create a repository on GitHub. You'll need an account on GitHub to do this; follow the very detailed instructions to set up your account. Once you've created a repository on GitHub, copy the entire HTTP access path on the Source tab, as shown in Figure 1–23. This will be the remote location of your repository.

Figure 1–23. *Finding the HTTP access path of a repository*

Setting up GitHub in Xcode is very similar to setting up any remote repository. Go to the Organizer view (⇧⌘2) on the Repositories tab, and select the Remotes folder beneath the repository you want to add to your GitHub repository. Now click Add Remote at the bottom of the window, paste the HTTP location into the location field (as is done in Figure 1–24), add a name, and click Create.

Figure 1–24. *Configuring a Git repository*

After clicking Create, you will see a place to enter your GitHub credentials at the bottom of the Organizer window. Your username should already be filled in, so all you need to enter is your password. Now go back to your main Xcode window, and use File ➤ Source Control ➤ Push. In a window reflecting Figure 1–25, you will be prompted to select the remote repository to push the code to. Select the GitHub repository, and click Push. Xcode will now send your code to your GitHub project repository. Using the GitHub web interface, verify that your changes and changelog have been uploaded properly. Now other developers can check this code out using their own GitHub accounts and the File ➤ Source Control ➤ Pull… menu option.

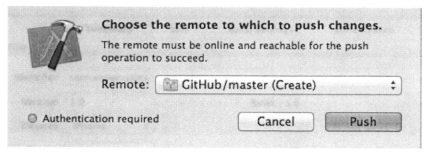

Figure 1–25. *Specifying a GitHub repository*

Source Control Best Practices

These are some tips for working with source control repositories:

1. Try not to work on the master branch directly. Instead, work on branches that you can then merge back into the master branch when you are ready.

2. When working with remote branches, always perform a pull on your working branch before starting to code. This will ensure that you are working on the most recent code revision.

3. Try not to push code to the remote repository that does not compile. While you want to check in often to ensure availability, it is always best if your code at least builds without errors before pushing it to a remote repository.

4. Use commit messages that are descriptive about the changes you made. Not only will this help you to manage your code, but also you can easily see what features you have added and list them when you submit your app for review.

Steve and the ARC

Xcode 4.2 introduced Automatic Reference Counting (ARC) as a way to help developers focus more on writing great apps and spend less time on memory management. As any developer new to Objective-C, and some who have been at it for a while, you will likely struggle with memory management concepts. Retain this, release that, autorelease what? If those three methods baffle you, then fear not, Xcode 4.2 is for you! Even if you are comfortable with memory management, you will see benefits from migrating your code to using ARC.

ARC is a compile time memory management method. It does not add performance overhead to your running apps because it is compiled into the code before you build it. This is a different concept than garbage collection, a method of memory management that Java developers are familiar with. With ARC, the compiler (LLVM version 3.0) automatically adds retain and release calls by analyzing your objects and determining when objects are no longer referenced. While a pointer to an object exists, the object will exist. After it has synthetically added the memory management methods, it compiles the binary for running and deployment.

Without ARC, the following code would produce a memory leak because the return value is not autoreleased:

```
-(NSString *) cityStateZip {
    return [[NSString alloc] initWithFormat:@"%@, %@ %@", self.city, self.state,
self.zip];
}
```

Without any changes to the code, ARC will compile this method and add the autorelease at compile time to remediate the memory leak.

ARC Rules

The following are some rules to follow while working with an ARC-enabled project:

1. You cannot call retain, release, or autorelease in your code. You cannot override or implement these methods either.

2. Because release statements are no longer needed, you must no longer implement a dealloc method in your classes.

3. You cannot create structs anymore. Instead, you must utilize custom Objective-C subclasses.

4. You cannot use casual casting such as the following:
   NSString *B = (NSString *)A;
   The solution is to use the __bridge directive:
   NSString *B = (__bridge NSString *)b;

5. You cannot use NSAutoreleasePool; instead you can use @autoreleasepool.

Using ARC

Every new project template in Xcode 4.2 uses ARC and the LLVM v3.0 compiler by default. There is nothing special that you need to do. ARC-enabled projects are also compatible with iOS 4.

Converting Older Projects to ARC

One day, we will look back and not even remember writing code with retain, release, and autorelease calls. Until that day, we'll need to work on existing projects and migrate to the ARC method of memory management to keep them current and to also take advantage of the performance improvements. Apple highly encourages that all projects move to LLVM 3.0 and ARC. They have provided a way to convert your old projects to use ARC.

Open your old project and make sure it builds correctly before you make any changes.

> **NOTE:** This might also be a good time to commit your changes to your Git repository and push your changes to a remote repository for safekeeping.

Next go to **Edit ➤ Refactor ➤ Convert to Objective-C ARC**. Xcode will ask you which targets to convert. Select your targets and click Precheck. Figure 1–26 shows a sample target selection.

> **NOTE:** Make sure you are set to build for device and not the simulator.

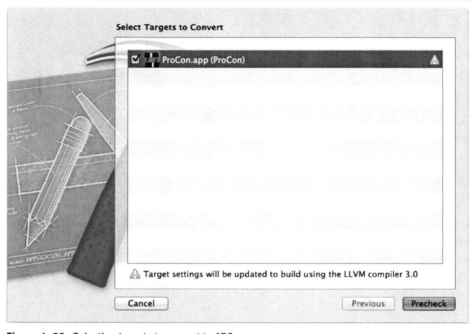

Figure 1–26. *Selecting targets to convert to ARC*

The precheck will begin and analyze your code to see what changes need to be made to your project before the conversion can begin. A notification will be displayed if there are issues, as shown in Figure 1–27; you can see them in the navigator pane under build results, an example of which is shown in Figure 1–28.

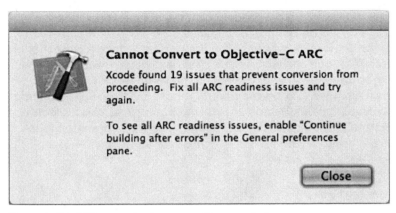

Cannot Convert to Objective-C ARC

Xcode found 19 issues that prevent conversion from proceeding. Fix all ARC readiness issues and try again.

To see all ARC readiness issues, enable "Continue building after errors" in the General preferences pane.

Close

Figure 1–27. *ARC conversion issues must be corrected.*

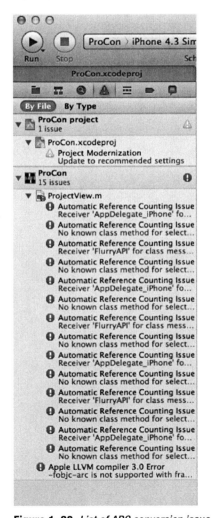

Figure 1–28. *List of ARC conversion issues*

You will need to correct any issues before proceeding with the conversion. Once the issues have been corrected, you will be prompted to start the conversion. Figure 1–29 shows a window detailing the conversion process. The first step is to take a snapshot of your application's source code so you can revert back. The next window will show you any changes that are going to be made to your code. It is the same window that you have seen when you commit changes to a source control repository. The most common changes include removing `dealloc` methods and `autorelease` and `retain` statements. Properties are also specified to be either "strong" or "weak." "Strong" corresponds to the former "retain" statement, while "weak" results in immediate de-allocation of an object as soon as no other strong pointers refer to it.

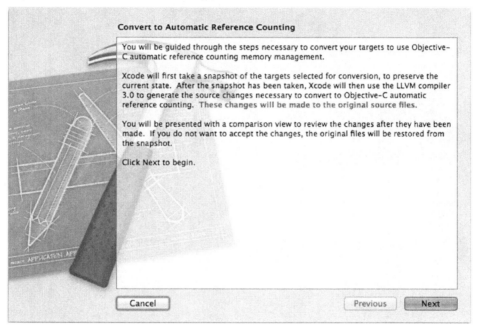

Figure 1–29. *Conversion to ARC*

After you have reviewed the changes, you can click Accept, and Xcode will make the necessary changes. Build your project, and make sure it builds correctly after the changes have been made.

You can verify that your project is using the LLVM 3.0 compiler by checking your target compiler settings, as shown in Figure 1–30.

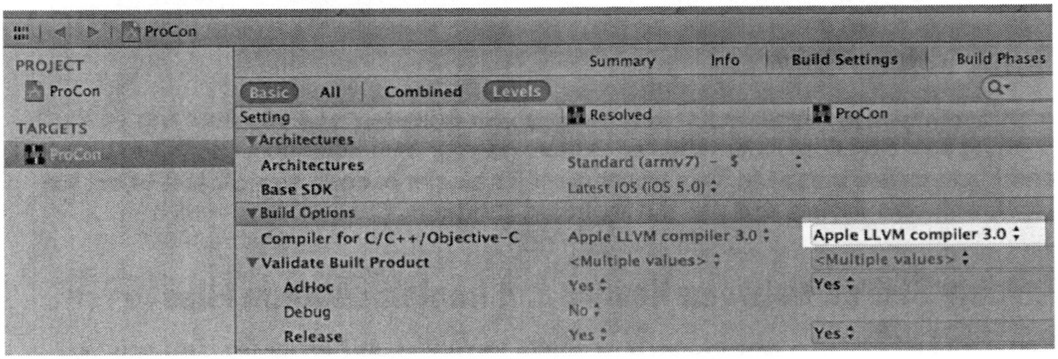

Figure 1–30. *Verifying the LLVM 3.0 compiler*

To verify that you are using ARC in your project, navigate to your target Build Settings and go to the "Apple LLVM compiler 3.0 – Language" section. You should now see the Objective-C Automatic Reference Counting setting is equal to Yes. Figure 1–31 demonstrates this verification.

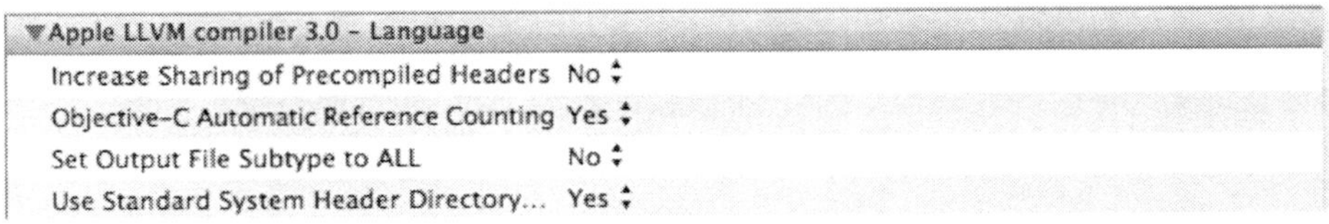

Figure 1–31. *Verifying ARC*

Quick Tips

Xcode has a variety of intricacies built into it that can greatly improve your development experience. Listed in this section are a few shortcuts meant to expedite common tasks and make building applications a simpler process.

Comments

To quickly comment out a block of code, select the code with your mouse and then press ⌘/ on the keyboard; each line will be commented out. Need to turn the comment off? Just repeat the procedure and the lines will be uncommented.

Autocomplete

Xcode 4 improved greatly upon the previous autocompletion functionality that works as you type. This is a big help to let you know what methods are available and to increase your coding efficiency. If the autocomplete isn't showing up or you want to know what is available for an object, hit the Esc key to bring up a list of available methods.

Quick Indent/Unindent

Xcode 4 does a pretty good job of managing your indents, but if you ever find yourself needing some custom indentation or to manage your own indenting, use ⌘[to unindent and ⌘] to indent manually. This works great for blocks of code as well; just select the block with your mouse and use the keyboard shortcuts.

Quickly Switch Between Header and Implementation Files

You have just added a new property or object to your class header file, and now you want to switch to the implementation file to start writing the code for that object. Pressing ^⌘+Up/Down will switch you between the two files. Figure 1–32 displays a common use of the Assistant Editor.

Xcode 4 also offers a new split pane view that will show related files, called the Assistant view. To enable this view, you can click the Assistant view icon at the top of the screen, or press ⌥⌘+,(option+command+comma) to load the Assistant view.

> **NOTE:** The keyboard shortcut works best if you are looking at the implementation file; execute the command, and it will automatically load the header file in the right pane.

Figure 1–32. *Selecting the Assistant Editor*

Class Documentation

Can't remember all the properties or methods of a class? You can get a reminder with a ⌥-click of an object type, and a pop-up will be displayed with a description of the object, as shown in Figure 1–33. From this pop-up, you can also view the object's documentation or the header file.

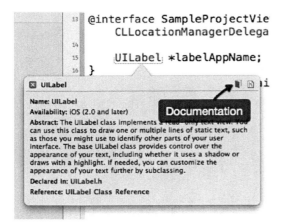

Figure 1–33. *Accessing class documentation*

A similar shortcut is to ⌘-click any object or class to jump to its definition.

Open File in Assistant Editor

You can ⌥-click any file in the navigator pane to open it in the Assistant Editor. You can also ⇧⌥-click any file, and a diagram, such as that shown in Figure 1–34, resembling the Xcode interface will pop up. Select a region in the diagram to open the file in the corresponding pane in Xcode.

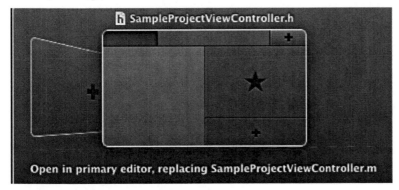

Figure 1–34. *Configuring the Assistant Editor*

Behaviors

Xcode 4 introduced behaviors to the editing interface. These allow you to run custom commands or scripts when performing actions in Xcode. Access behaviors by going to **Xcode ➤ Behaviors ➤ Edit Behaviors**. Figure 1–35 shows the resulting opened window.

You can customize the actions available on the left side of the pane with behaviors found on the right pane. For instance, one behavior that I like to use is to open a separate tab that contains build errors. This preserves my editing tab and allows me to pick up where I left off after the build succeeds, or fails, as is usually the case. The behavior in Figure 1–35 will create or show the tab named Build Results, show the Issue navigator, show the debugger pane, and navigate to the first issue found (if any).

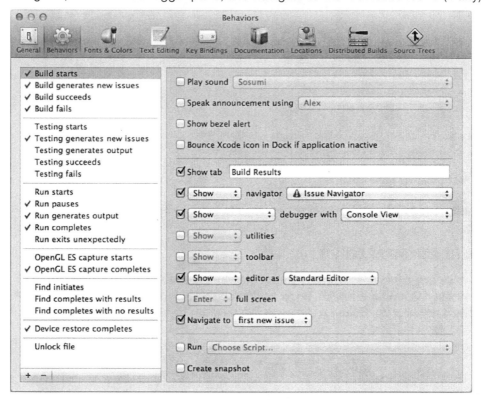

Figure 1–35. *Configuring behaviors*

You can also add custom behaviors that are performed with a shortcut key. Click the + at the bottom of the behaviors pane, and set a name for your custom behavior. Now click the command key symbol (⌘) at the end of the line to set your keyboard shortcut.

Summary

Apple has provided iOS developers with an updated application development environment in Xcode 4. While not perfect, it does offer many improvements over previous versions and is worthy of some praise. The transition between Xcode 3 and 4 may be difficult and time-consuming, but once you have been converted, you will be writing code more efficiently and easily in the new interface.

New enhancements, such as source control with remote repositories, will make your project development with teams more seamless and provide independent developers with the ability to remotely store source code for safekeeping.

Chapter 2

Introduction to Interface Builder

One of the many changes introduced in Xcode 4 was the consumption of Interface Builder into the main Xcode application. Interface Builder became a core component of Xcode and was able to run in the same windows and tabs as Xcode. The change was more than just a simple embedding of one application into another. As you will see in this chapter, the way that Interface Builder interacts with your source code makes it more of a well-intentioned integration into Xcode.

Interface Builder Walkthrough

When you click on a `.xib` (user interface) file in the navigator pane of Xcode, Interface Builder will seamlessly load into the editor pane. Generally, when I'm working with `.xib` files, I will close the navigator pane and show the utility area on the right. This gives me the most screen real estate for visually creating the interfaces, as shown in Figure 2–1.

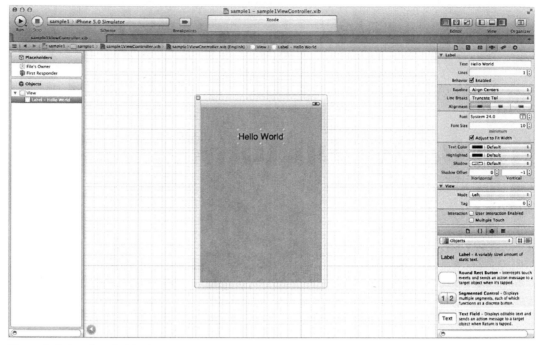

Figure 2–1. *Interface Builder in use*

By clicking an object in the outline view dock on the left side, you can see the object's attributes and settings in the inspector pane on the right side. The inspector pane should be very familiar to anyone who has worked with Interface Builder before. The object browser has also been integrated into the library pane below the inspector pane. This creates one-stop shopping for your `.xib` design needs.

Our Forces Combined...

With the integration of Interface Builder into Xcode, it extends beyond just two tools in one. Just as in the cartoon Voltron, when the combination of individual tiger robots resulted in an incredible defender of the galaxy, Interface Builder when combined with the Assistant Editor view creates a super tool for source code. Figure 2–2 shows a prime example of this useful combination.

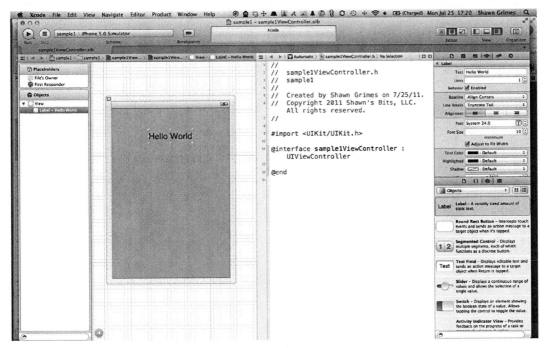

Figure 2–2. *Using Interface Builder with the Assistant Editor*

When the Assistant Editor is visible and you select one of the objects in the .xib's object browser on the left, any existing header file for the associated view controller is loaded. At first this appears to be minimally useful. You can see your code and the .xib file. The real magic comes when you ^-click-drag one of those objects to the interface (.h) file. As Figure 2–3 shows, a blue line will extend into the code, and when you release it in the right pane of the Assistant Editor, you will be prompted to create an outlet.

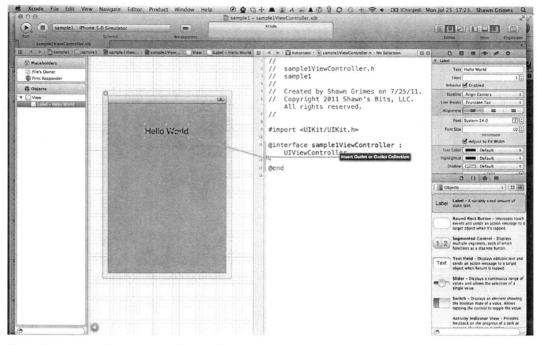

Figure 2–3. *Connecting an outlet automatically*

When you release the mouse button, Xcode will prompt you for the name of this outlet connection, as shown in Figure 2–4. After you specify a name and click Connect, Xcode will create all the necessary code to connect the .xib's object to your interface (.h) file and implementation (.m) file.

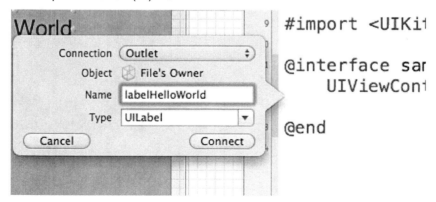

Figure 2–4. *Configuring an outlet's creation*

The header file now looks like this:

```
//
//  sample1ViewController.h
#import <UIKit/UIKit.h>
```

```
@interface sample1ViewController : UIViewController {
    UILabel *labelHelloWorld;
}

@property (strong, nonatomic) IBOutlet UILabel *labelHelloWorld;

@end
```

And the relevant code from the implementation (.m) file now looks like this:

```
//
//   sample1ViewController.m
#import "sample1ViewController.h"

@implementation sample1ViewController
@synthesize labelHelloWorld;

- (void)viewDidUnload
{
    [self setLabelHelloWorld:nil];
    [super viewDidUnload];
    // Release any retained subviews of the main view.
    // e.g. self.myOutlet = nil;
}

@end
```

You can use the same steps to create IBActions for buttons and other objects. ^-click-drag from a button or similar object in the .xib to the implementation (.h) file and release. This time, change the drop-down menu for Connection from Outlet to Action. If this option does not appear, the wrong type of object was selected. Figures 2–5 and 2–6 detail the process of configuring an action in this way.

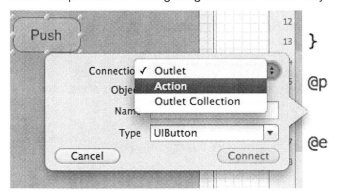

Figure 2–5. *Creating an action*

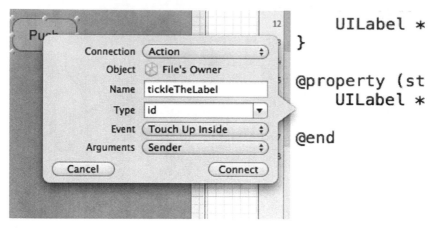

Figure 2–6. *Configuring an action*

You can specify the name of the action, the type, the event to trigger the action on, and the arguments to send. Just like the Outlet connection, the code will be updated with placeholders to support your new action.

The interface (.h) file now includes the IBAction declaration:

```
//
//  sample1ViewController.h
#import <UIKit/UIKit.h>

@interface sample1ViewController : UIViewController {
    UILabel *labelHelloWorld;
}

@property (strong, nonatomic) IBOutlet UILabel *labelHelloWorld;
- (IBAction)tickleTheLabel:(id)sender;

@end
```

And the implementation (.m) file includes a method placeholder for you to complete:

```
- (IBAction)tickleTheLabel:(id)sender {
}
```

I'm going to complete the tickleTheLabel method with the following code:

```
- (IBAction)tickleTheLabel:(id)sender {
    self.labelHelloWorld.text=@"That tickled";
}
```

Figures 2–7 and 2–8 show that now, when the app is run and the button touched, the labelHelloWorld is updated.

Figure 2–7. *Original view*

Figure 2–8. *View after action performed*

Touches Too

One of the new features implemented into Interface Builder is the ability to assign touch gesture recognizers to objects directly in Interface Builder. The various gestures are available in the lower right section of Xcode, resembling the pane shown in Figure 2–9.

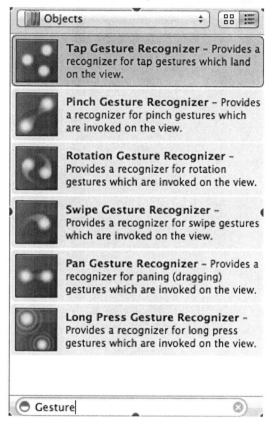

Figure 2–9. *Available gesture recognizers*

To add a gesture recognizer to an object in a `.xib`, just drag and drop the gesture recognizer from the object browser onto the object you want to add it to, similarly to that shown in Figure 2–10. This will add the gesture recognizer to the Objects list in the `.xib` project file, as shown in Figure 2–11.

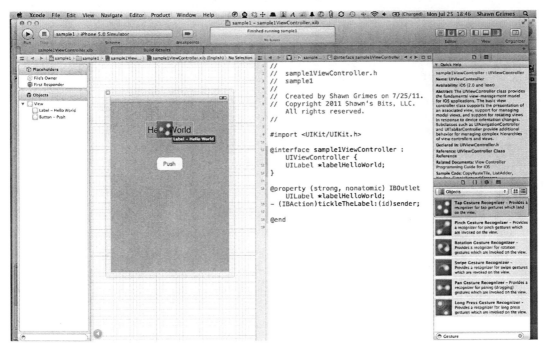

Figure 2–10. *Adding a gesture recognizer to an element*

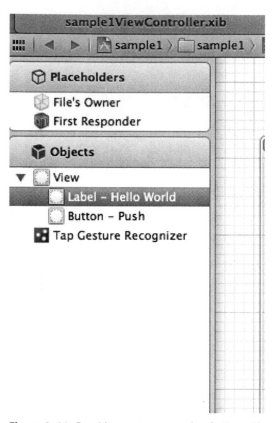

Figure 2–11. *Resulting gesture recognizer in the outline view*

Before you proceed, it's important that user interaction is enabled for the object that you want to add the gesture recognizer to. In this case, you attached it to the Hello World label, and you can set user interaction to true by clicking the label and going to the Attributes inspector tab. Under the View options, click the check box next to User Interaction Enabled, as shown in Figure 2–12. This will ensure that the object responds to gesture recognizers.

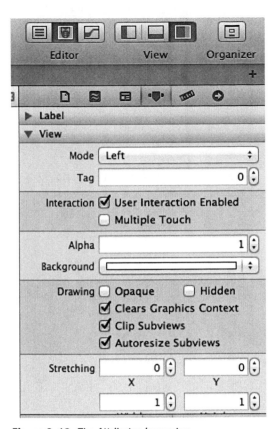

Figure 2–12. *The Attributes inspector*

By clicking the gesture recognizer in the `.xib`'s dock outline view, you can set the settings for the gesture recognizer in the Attributes inspector pane. Figure 2–13 demonstrates the various configurations that can be applied to this recognizer.

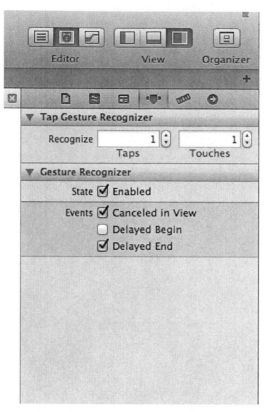

Figure 2–13. *Adjusting attributes of gesture recognizer*

Now that the settings have been enabled, you can connect the gesture to an IBAction by following the same procedures as ^-click-drag from the gesture recognizer object to the interface (.h) file in the Assistant Editor pane. In the resulting pop-up, resembling Figure 2–14, specify a name and click Connect. The placeholders for that action will be added to your code just as before.

Figure 2–14. *Connecting an action to the label*

Now your interface file looks like this:

```
//
//   sample1ViewController.h
```

```
#import <UIKit/UIKit.h>

@interface sample1ViewController : UIViewController {
    UILabel *labelHelloWorld;
    UITapGestureRecognizer *tapTheLabel;
}

@property (strong, nonatomic) IBOutlet UILabel *labelHelloWorld;
- (IBAction)tickleTheLabel:(id)sender;
- (IBAction)tapTheLabel:(id)sender;

@end
```

And I've made the new "tapTheLabel" action in the implementation (.m) file look like this:

```
- (IBAction)tapTheLabel:(id)sender {
    self.labelHelloWorld.text=@"Tap Tap Tap";
}
```

Now when the app is run and the label is tapped, you get the following two screens in Figures 2–15 and 2–16.

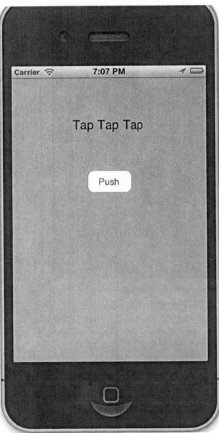

Figure 2–15. *Application's starting view*   **Figure 2–16.** *View after label tapped*

Adjusting Tint

If you wanted to give your app a different look and feel by customizing the navigation bar or tool bar, you used to have to create your own custom classes; but in Xcode 4.2, you can now customize certain design elements with the new tint property. `UINavigationBar`, `UIToolBar`, `UISearchBar`, and `UISegmentedControl` all respond to this setting and are available in Interface Builder. Other controls respond to tinting as well, but the property is not available in Xcode and must be changed with code. To update the tint, select an object in your `.xib` that supports the tint property, and in the inspector pane you should see the Tint control, as shown in Figure 2–18. Figure 2–17 demonstrates a view with drastically altered tint on several elements.

Figure 2–17. *A view with tint*

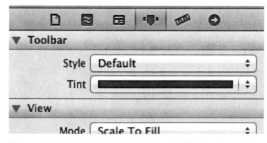

Figure 2–18. *Adjusting tint in the Attributes inspector*

> **NOTE:** The `UISegmentedControl` supports tint in Xcode only in the Bar or Bezeled style.

Rapid App Development with Storyboarding

Remember the days when you had to use paper and pen to sketch out design flows for your apps? Then came flowcharting software, in which you could digitally record your workflows and processes, but it was a manual process to convert those workflows into source code. Apple has provided a new tool called Storyboards that provides a visual representation of an app's workflow and can then produce a working framework for your app.

So What's in a Story(board)?

A storyboard is a collection of `.xib` files packaged together along with some metadata about the views and their relationships to each other. It is the ultimate separation of views from models and controllers that you have been hearing about since the early days of Model-View-Controller (MVC) programming. The storyboard has two main components: scenes and segues.

Scenes

Scenes are any view that fills the screen of the device. They contain UI objects and are controlled by view controllers (or subclasses of view controllers). This is almost exactly like the `.xib` files that you are familiar with editing in Interface Builder. Figure 2–19 displays three different scenes in a storyboard that you will soon build.

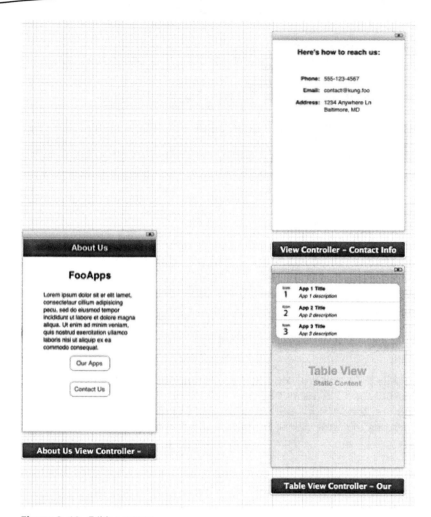

Figure 2–19. *Editing scenes*

Segues

Segues are the transitions that present subsequent views in a storyboard. The segue can present a view with a push, as a modal view, as a pop-over, or with a custom transition. A segue is of the class UIStoryboardSegue and contains three properties: sourceViewController, destinationViewController, and identifier. The identifier is an NSString that can be used to validate that a segue is the segue you are expecting.

You would normally initiate a segue based on an action from the user. This can be the touching of a button or tableview cell, or it could be the result of a gesture recognizer. Segues are represented on the storyboard by a line connecting two scenes, as shown in Figure 2–20.

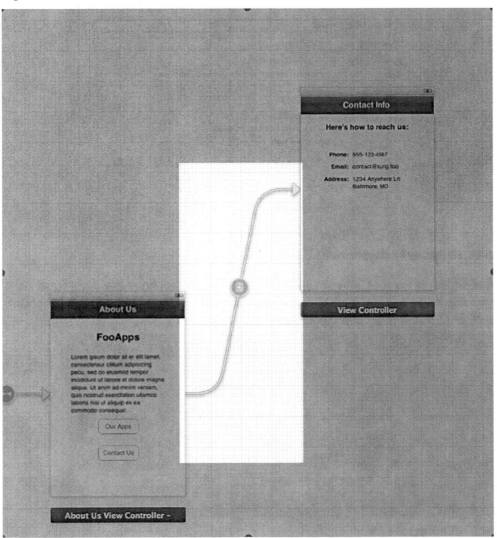

Figure 2–20. *A segue connecting two scenes*

Telling a Story

Storyboards are available in all of the application templates in Xcode 4.2 with the exception of the empty project template. When creating a new project, just select the option to "Use storyboard" when setting the options for the new project. In this case, you will name the project "aboutUs", as demonstrated in Figure 2–21.

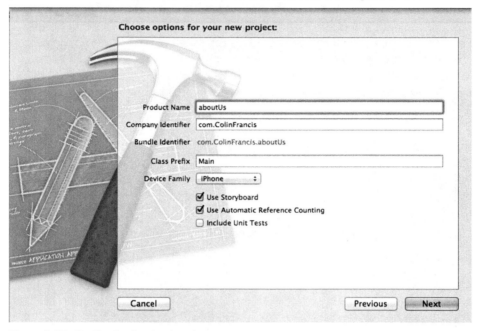

Figure 2–21. *Configuring for storyboard use*

Once the project is created, you will see the storyboard option has been populated on the target Summary tab and an additional field has been added to the Info tab (as shown in Figures 2–22 and 2–23), "Main storyboard file base name".

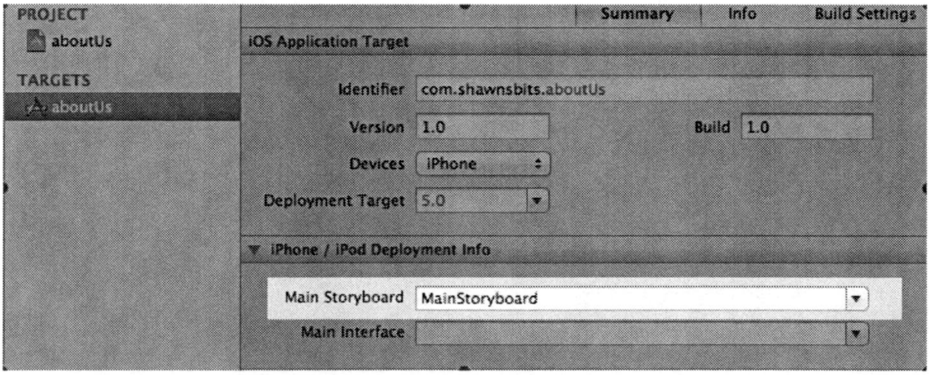

Figure 2–22. *Main storyboard info*

		Summary	Info	Build Settings	Build
PROJECT	▼ Custom iOS Target Properties				
aboutUs	Key	Type	Value		
	Bundle versions string, short	String	1.0		
TARGETS	Bundle identifier	String			$(PRODUCT_NAME:rfc1034
aboutUs	InfoDictionary version	String	6.0		
	Main storyboard file base name	String	MainStoryboard		
	Bundle version	String	1.0		
	Executable file	String	${EXECUTABLE_NAME}		
	Application requires iPhone environmer	Boolean	YES		
	▶ Icon files	Array	(0 items)		
	▶ Supported interface orientations	Array	(3 items)		
	Bundle display name	String	${PRODUCT_NAME}		
	Bundle OS Type code	String	APPL		
	Bundle creator OS Type code	String	????		
	Localization native development region	String	en		
	Bundle name	String	${PRODUCT_NAME}		
	▶ Document Types (0)				
	▶ Exported UTIs (0)				
	▶ Imported UTIs (0)				
	▶ URL Types (0)				

Figure 2–23. *Storyboard target settings*

Finally, in the project navigator pane, you will see the MainStoryboard.storyboard file, as Figure 2–24 demonstrates. Click on this file to load it into Interface Builder and start building your storyboard.

Figure 2–24. *Storyboard file*

In this example, you are going to build a simple project that displays information about your company. The storyboard starts off with a view that is controlled by the aboutUsViewController it created as part of the project. I'm going to add some objects

(UILabel, UITextView, and two UIButtons) to the view to make it a little more informative to the user. Refer to Figure 2–25 for the view to build.

Figure 2–25. *aboutUsViewController view*

Now I want to embed this view into a navigation controller, and Xcode 4.2 makes this an easy task. As shown in Figure 2–26, select the view and go to the menu option **Editor ➤ Embed In ➤ Navigation Controller**. This will create a navigation controller and add it to your storyboard as well as create a segue between the navigation view and your aboutUsView. The resulting segue will be represented with an arrow, as in Figure 2–27.

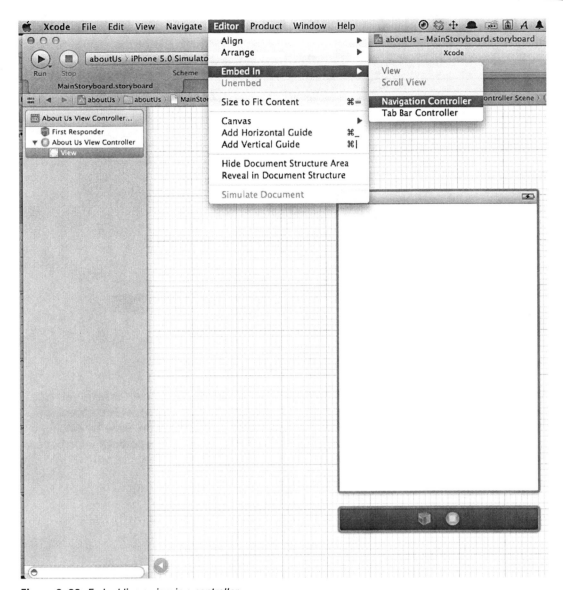

Figure 2–26. *Embedding a view in a controller*

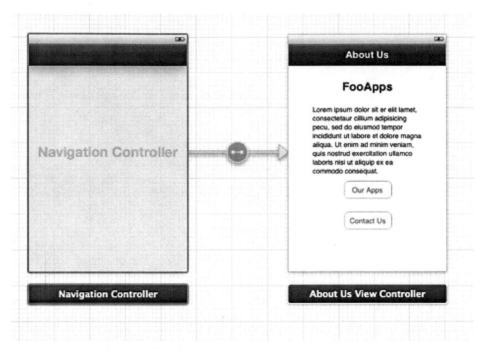

Figure 2–27. *Resulting embedded view display*

Now I'm going to add a new UIViewController object to the storyboard where you can put your contact information. It's as simple as dragging a UIViewController object, as well as a UIView, from the object library to the storyboard. I set up the view by adding a UILabel as the heading, and then I add a few more UILabels for the contact information. Figure 2–28 displays the result of these additions.

Figure 2–28. *Configured scenes*

In order to connect the new contact information view to the About Us view, you are going to click on the "Contact Us" UIButton on the About Us view and ^-click-drag to the Contact Info view. This is the same action used to connect outlets and actions, and that is exactly what you are going to do. You are going to connect the Contact Us button to the performSegueWithIdentifier action. When you release the mouse button, a pop-up will display, asking which action you want to connect to, and you can select performSegueWithIdentifier:sender. These steps, along with the resulting segue, are demonstrated in Figures 2–29 and 2–30.

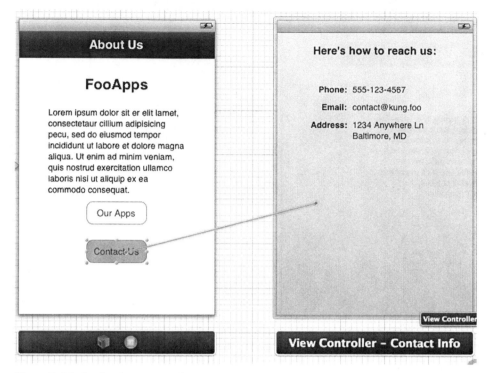

Figure 2–29. *Configuring segue action*

Figure 2–30. *Perform segue pop-up*

When the connection is made, the UINavigationBar is automatically added to the view. If you specify titles for each one, the result will resemble Figure 2–31.

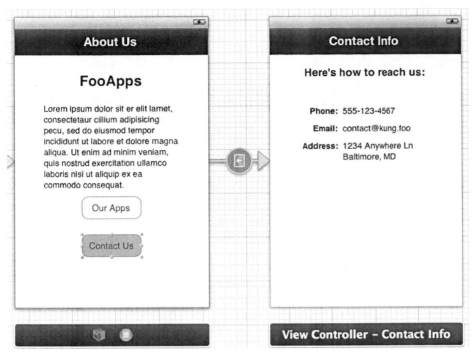

Figure 2–31. *Connected scenes with segue*

One habit to get into is providing your segues with an identifier. This will help future-proof your apps if you end up connecting multiple segues to one view. You will be able to check the identifier of the calling segue to see the path the user took to reach that view and respond accordingly. You can set the identifier of a segue by selecting it in the storyboard and viewing its properties in the inspector pane, as shown in Figure 2–32.

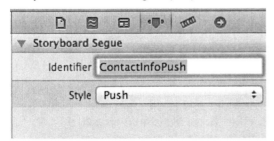

Figure 2–32. *Setting segue identifiers*

If you run this app now, Figures 2–33 and 2–34 show you that the Contact Us button will work and will load the Contact Info view without having written any code whatsoever.

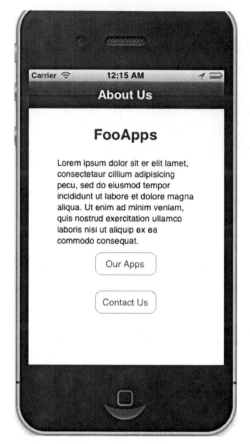

Figure 2-33. *Main simulated view*

Figure 2-34. *Resulting segue performed*

What about the other button, "Our Apps"? You want to create a new view that lists your other apps so you can get some cross promotion. The first thing I think of when I hear the word "list" is UITableViewController. And storyboarding takes UITableViewController to a whole new level of convenience.

I'm going to drag a UITableViewController to the storyboard, creating an Apps Table view. The first thing that you will notice is that this looks a little different than the regular UITableViewController available in Interface Builder. There is something called Prototype Cells at the top, as in Figure 2-35. With storyboards, you can customize the layout and objects of a UITableViewCell with something called a prototype. We'll go into this further later on.

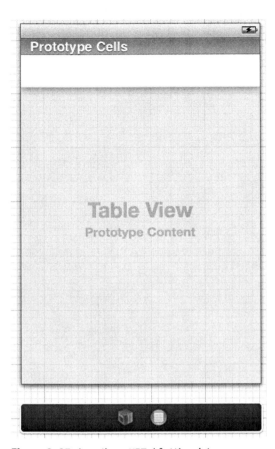

Figure 2–35. *Inserting a* `UITableView` *into a scene*

Select the Table View, and in the Attributes inspector, change Content from Dynamic Prototypes to Static Cells. I'm also going to change the style to Grouped because I like the look of the rounded edges of the cells. Figures 2–36 and 2–37 show these steps and their result.

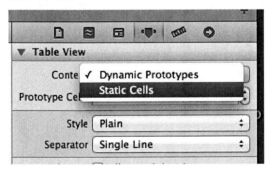

Figure 2–36. *Static Cells configuration*

Figure 2–37. *Grouped cells*

Since every cell is going to have the same layout, I'm going to delete the bottom two cells so that I can quickly duplicate the top cell. Now I will customize the remaining cell with a UIImageView to hold the app icon and two UILabels for the app name and description, as shown in Figure 2–38.

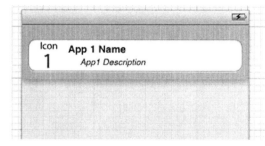

Figure 2–38. *Customized cell*

Select the remaining cell now that it has been designed to your specifications, and ⌥-click-drag to duplicate it below. Repeat again to add a third row to the UITableView, as demonstrated in Figure 2–39.

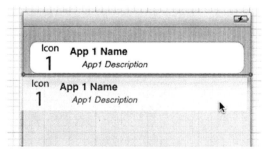

Figure 2–39. *Duplicating cells*

Now you can customize each image and label in the UITableView to list the three apps you'll be displaying, resulting in a view resembling Figure 2–40.

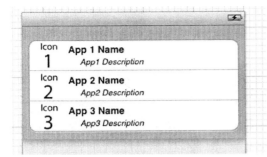

Figure 2–40. *Customizing duplicated cells*

All that is left is to connect your button in the About Us view to this new view. Select the button in the About Us view, and ^-click-drag to the UITableView you just created. Your storyboard now looks something like that shown in Figure 2–41.

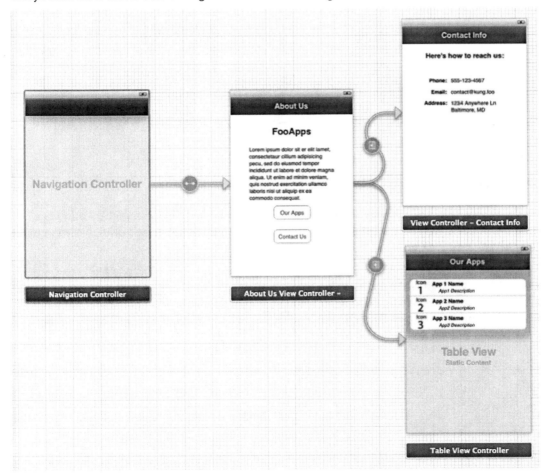

Figure 2–41. *Newly connected table controller*

And when you run the application, both buttons on the About Us view will now work, demonstrated in Figure 2–42. And you can load the pages without ever having written a bit of code.

Figure 2–42. *The three resulting views of your application*

Passing Data Between Scenes

The previous app segment works well enough without any code, but just by adding a little bit of code behind the scenes, you can create an even more powerful interface in a very short period of time.

When you see a UITableView, you almost instinctively know that there is likely to be a detailed view attached to it when you touch one of the cells. Let us add that detail view now. Drag and drop a new UIViewController object named AppDetailsViewController onto the storyboard, and add a UIImage, UILabel, UITextView, and two UIButtons to it, resembling Figure 2–43.

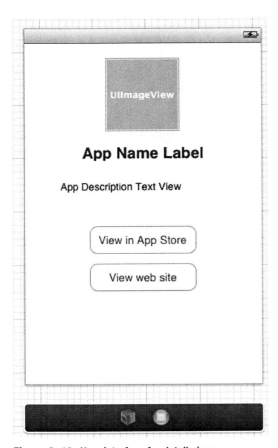

Figure 2–43. *User interface for detail view*

You want each of the UITableViewCells to segue to this App Details view when touched, so ^-click-drag from the UITableViewCell to the detail view. Just as before, a pop-up will display the available actions, and you should select "performSegueWithIdentifier:selector:", as demonstrated in Figures 2–44 and 2–45.

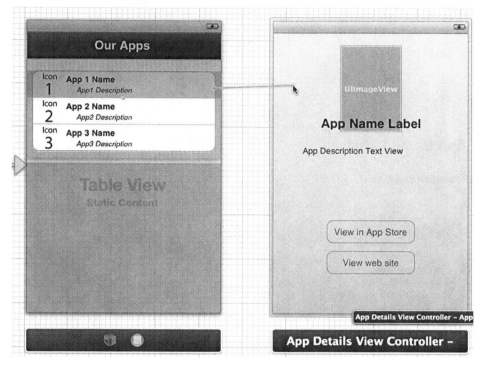

Figure 2–44. *Connecting a cell to the detail view*

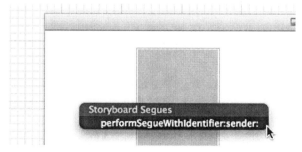

Figure 2–45. *Selecting a segue action*

You will see the segue connecting the table to the App Details view controller. Just as is shown in Figure 2–46, select the segue and enter an identifier for it in the Attributes inspector.

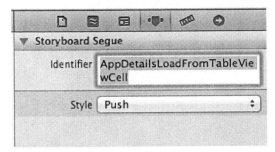

Figure 2–46. *Configuring detail segue identifier*

Repeat the process for the other two UITableViewCells, and use the same segue identifier for each connection since you are going to execute the same code for each segue. You should now see three segues linking the two views, similar to Figure 2–47.

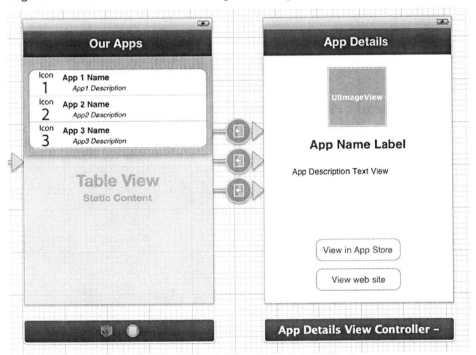

Figure 2–47. *Multiple segues connecting a* UITableView *to a view controller*

You've gotten this far without using any code, but that convenience is about to end. You need to start generating some dynamic content on the App Details view controller, and you are going to need to dive into some code for that.

First you are going to create a custom class to hold information about your apps. Since this is a static list of apps at the moment, I'm going to create a very basic subclass of NSObject to hold the data. Use the menu option File➤➤ New ➤ New File…, and select "Objective-C class" from the Cocoa Touch templates, as demonstrated in Figure 2–48.

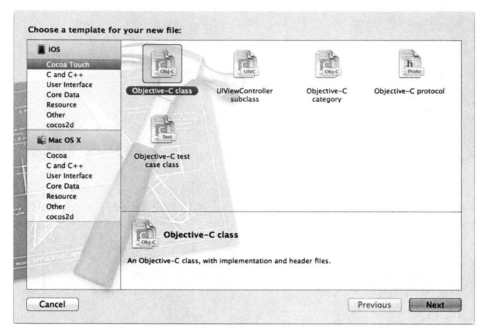

Figure 2–48. *Selecting the "Objective-C class" template to make a new basic class*

Now, as shown in Figure 2–49, select NSObject from the "Subclass of" drop-down if it is not already specified.

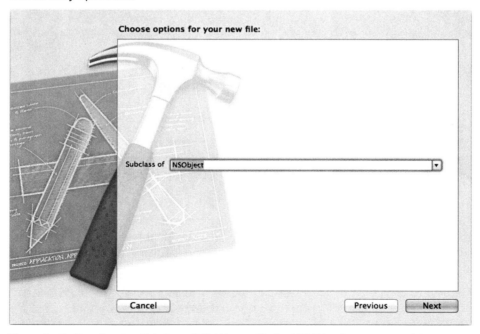

Figure 2–49. *Ensuring the "Subclass of" field is specified to "NSObject" to create an* Object *subclass*

And finally, set the class name to MyAppClass. This is shown in Figure 2–50, but just as before, newer versions of Xcode may have this combined with the previous step of specifying the "Subclass of" field.

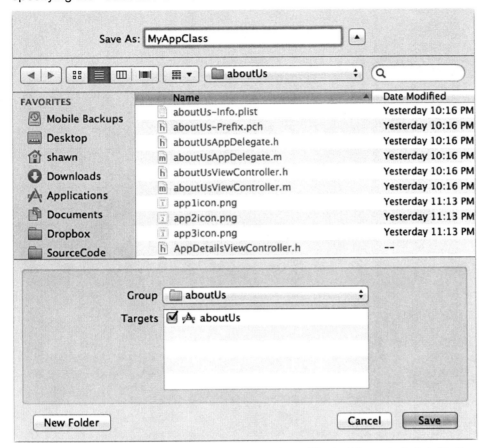

Figure 2–50. *Specifying the class name—on newer versions of Xcode, this may be included in the previous screen.*

You want this class to have the following interface (.h):

```
//  MyAppClass.h
#import <Foundation/Foundation.h>

@interface MyAppClass : NSObject

@property(strong, nonatomic) NSString *appName;
@property(strong, nonatomic) UIImage *iconImage;
@property(strong, nonatomic) NSString *appDescription;
@property(strong, nonatomic) NSURL *appStoreURL;
@property(strong, nonatomic) NSURL *webSiteURL;

+(MyAppClass *)appWithAppID:(int)appID;

@end
```

And the implementation file (.m) should look like this:

```
#import "MyAppClass.h"

@implementation MyAppClass

@synthesize appName;
@synthesize iconImage;
@synthesize appDescription;
@synthesize appStoreURL;
@synthesize webSiteURL;

+(MyAppClass *)appWithAppID:(int)appID{
    MyAppClass *newApp=[[MyAppClass alloc] init];
    newApp.appName=[NSString stringWithFormat:@"App %i Name", appID];
    newApp.iconImage=[UIImage imageNamed:[NSString stringWithFormat:@"app%iicon.png",
appID]];
    newApp.appDescription=[NSString stringWithFormat:@"This is the description for App
%i", appID];
    newApp.appStoreURL=[NSURL URLWithString:[NSString stringWithFormat:@"itms-
apps://itunes.com/apps/%iappName", appID]];
    newApp.webSiteURL=[NSURL URLWithString:[NSString
stringWithFormat:@"http://www.shawnsbits.com/apps/%iappName", appID]];
    return newApp;
}

- (id)init
{
    self = [super init];
    if (self) {
        // Initialization code here.
    }

    return self;
}

@end
```

> **NOTE:** If you are wondering where all the memory management has gone, see the section on Automatic Reference Counting, called "Steve and the ARC," in Chapter 1.

So that sets up your data object, but now you need to code up your detail view controller to display the attributes of the MyAppClass object. You will need a custom view controller class to control the view. Create a new file with File➤➤ New➤➤ New File…, and select "UIViewController subclass" from the Cocoa Touch templates, as Figure 2–51 demonstrates.

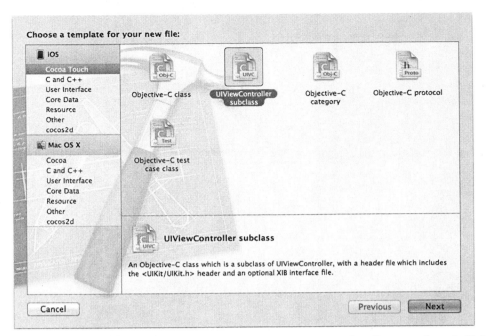

Figure 2–51. *Selecting the "UIViewController subclass" template to create a file pre-configured with important* UIViewController *methods*

Now, as in Figure 2–52, make it a subclass of UIViewController (if not specified by default), and make sure that the check box for "With XIB for user interface" is *not* selected. You will be using your storyboard for the XIB.

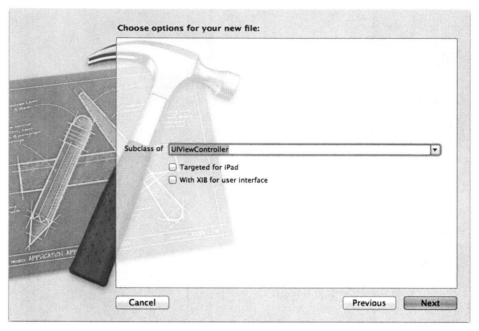

Figure 2–52. *Configuring a* `UIViewController` *subclass*

Name the new class `AppDetailsViewController`, and use the following interface (`.h`) file definition:

```
// AppDetailsViewController.h

#import <UIKit/UIKit.h>
#import "MyAppClass.h"

@interface AppDetailsViewController : UIViewController

@property (strong, nonatomic) MyAppClass *selectedApp;
@property (strong, nonatomic) IBOutlet UILabel *labelAppName;
@property (strong, nonatomic) IBOutlet UIImageView *imageAppIcon;
@property (strong, nonatomic) IBOutlet UITextView *textViewAppDescription;
@property (strong, nonatomic) IBOutlet UIButton *buttonAppStore;
@property (strong, nonatomic) IBOutlet UIButton *buttonWebSite;

-(IBAction) loadAppStore:(id) sender;
-(IBAction) loadWebSite:(id)sender;

@end
```

This interface file will create the outlets that you need for your view and also create the two `IBActions` that will be assigned to your `UIButtons`. The implementation file (`.m`) looks like this:

```
// AppDetailsViewController.m

#import "AppDetailsViewController.h"
```

```
@implementation AppDetailsViewController

@synthesize selectedApp;
@synthesize labelAppName;
@synthesize imageAppIcon;
@synthesize textViewAppDescription;
@synthesize buttonAppStore;
@synthesize buttonWebSite;

-(IBAction) loadAppStore:(id) sender{
    [[UIApplication sharedApplication] openURL:self.selectedApp.appStoreURL];
}
-(IBAction) loadWebSite:(id)sender{
    [[UIApplication sharedApplication] openURL:self.selectedApp.webSiteURL];
}

- (void)viewDidLoad
{
    [super viewDidLoad];
    self.labelAppName.text=selectedApp.appName;
    self.imageAppIcon.image=selectedApp.iconImage;
    self.textViewAppDescription.text=selectedApp.appDescription;
}


- (id)initWithNibName:(NSString *)nibNameOrNil bundle:(NSBundle *)nibBundleOrNil
{
    self = [super initWithNibName:nibNameOrNil bundle:nibBundleOrNil];
    if (self) {
        // Custom initialization
    }
    return self;
}

- (void)didReceiveMemoryWarning
{
    // Releases the view if it doesn't have a superview.
    [super didReceiveMemoryWarning];

    // Release any cached data, images, etc. that aren't in use.
}

- (void)viewDidUnload
{
    [super viewDidUnload];
    self.labelAppName = nil;
    self.imageAppIcon = nil;
    self.textViewAppDescription = nil;
    self.buttonAppStore = nil;
    self.buttonWebSite = nil;
}

-
(BOOL)shouldAutorotateToInterfaceOrientation:(UIInterfaceOrientation)interfaceOrientatio
n
{
    // Return YES for supported orientations
```

```
    return (interfaceOrientation == UIInterfaceOrientationPortrait);
}
```

@end

This controller class will populate the view with the properties of the MyAppClass object "selectedApp". Now you need to attach this view controller to the view and connect the outlets and IBActions. Go back to the storyboard editor, and select the view controller object at the bottom of the App Details view, as shown in Figure 2–53.

Figure 2–53. *Selecting a view controller*

Now you can select the Identity inspector in the inspector tab and set the class to your new custom AppDetailsViewController class. Figure 2–54 demonstrates how to do this.

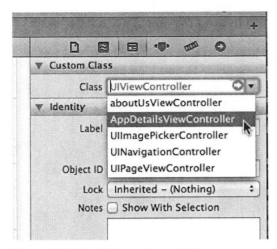

Figure 2–54. *Specifying a view controller*

Connect all of the objects to their corresponding outlets, following Figure 2–55.

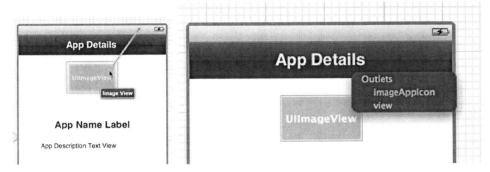

Figure 2–55. *Configuring elements to properties*

To connect the actions, you reverse the process. You ^-click-drag from the UIButtons to the view or view controller object and select the corresponding IBAction from the pop-up, as in Figure 2–56.

Figure 2–56. *Connecting actions*

You can now accept a MyAppClass object and display it properly on the App Details view, but now you need to send this object when you load this view. To do this, you will configure the previous view (Apps Table View list) to send the object when it performs the segue. It turns out that there is a method for this; it is called -(void)prepareForSegue:(UIStoryboardSegue *)segue sender:(id)sender;. You can override this method in a custom UITableViewController to send the selected object.

First, you will need a new custom UITableViewController class. Create a new file with File ➤ New ➤ New File..., and select "UIViewController class" from the Cocoa Touch templates, as shown in Figure 2–57.

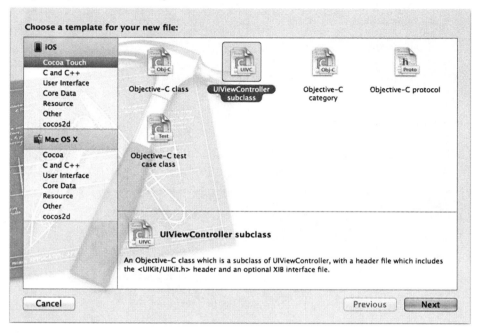

Figure 2–57. *Specifying a UIViewController subclass file*

This time, you want it to be a subclass of UITableViewController, and again, make sure that you do not create a XIB for the new class, as in Figure 2–58.

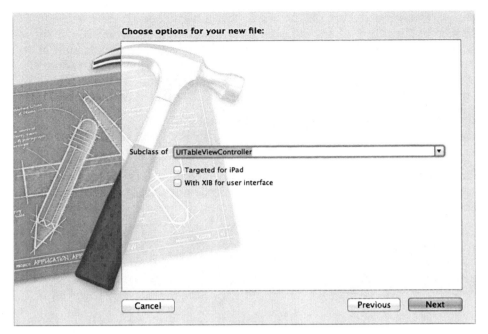

Figure 2–58. *Configuring a* `UITableViewController` *subclass*

Name the class "AppListTableViewController". There are no changes needed for the interface file (.h), so you will jump straight to the implementation file (.m). The first thing you want to do is clear out the methods for the `tableView` data source and `tableView` delegate because you are using statically defined `UITableViewCells` in your storyboard. So delete or comment out the following methods:

```
- (NSInteger)numberOfSectionsInTableView:(UITableView *)tableView
- (NSInteger)tableView:(UITableView *)tableView numberOfRowsInSection:(NSInteger)section
- (UITableViewCell *)tableView:(UITableView *)tableView
cellForRowAtIndexPath:(NSIndexPath *)indexPath
- (void)tableView:(UITableView *)tableView didSelectRowAtIndexPath:(NSIndexPath
*)indexPath
```

At the top of your implementation file, import the two custom classes you created:

```
#import "AppDetailsViewController.h"
#import "MyAppClass.h"
```

Now override the `prepareForSegue` method with the following code:

```
- (void)prepareForSegue:(UIStoryboardSegue *)segue sender:(id)sender{
    if([segue.identifier isEqualToString:@"AppDetailsLoadFromTableViewCell"]){
        AppDetailsViewController *appDetailsVC = segue.destinationViewController;
        appDetailsVC.selectedApp=[MyAppClass appWithAppID:[[self.tableView
indexPathForSelectedRow] row]+1];
    }
}
```

This code checks to ensure you are responding to the correct segue in case you add additional segues in the future. Afterward, it acquires the currently selected row of the tableView and adds 1 to it (because your apps start at 1 but your row counts start at 0). It then creates an object of class MyAppClass using that appID and the convenience method appWithAppID: that you created. This new object is assigned to the selectedApp property of the destinationViewController (an instance of AppDetailsViewController).

Before proceeding to test this application, make sure that the AppListTableViewController has been set as the class for the App List table view controller.

If you run your app now, you'll see that each of the UITableViewCells will load a different app detail into the detailsViewController. Figure 2–59 demonstrates a simulated result of this application.

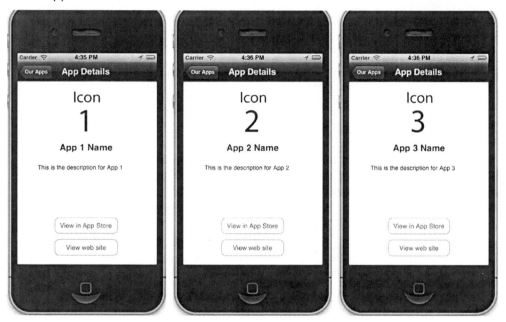

Figure 2–59. *Resulting detail views in your simulated application*

UITableViewCell Prototypes

The app is working as intended up to this point, but what if you add new apps to your inventory? With your current app layout, it would mean having to update your UITableView with new cells for each new app item. Wouldn't it be easier if you loaded the UITableView dynamically so you didn't have to update the storyboard XIB each time you had a new app?

First, you'll create a custom UITableViewCell class that has outlets that model your existing UITableViewCells. Use the menu option **File ► New ► New File...**, and select

"Objective-C class" from the Cocoa Touch templates. Create a subclass of UITableViewCell, and name it "AppUITableViewCellClass", as in Figure 2–60.

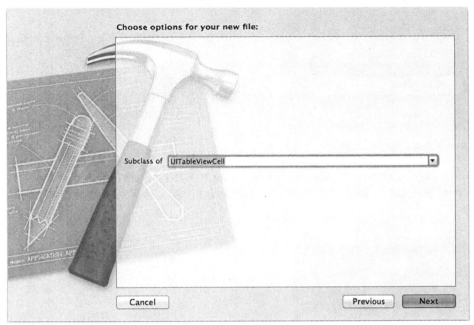

Figure 2–60. *Configuring a* UITableViewCell *subclass*

In the interface file (.h), create two UILabel outlet properties and a UIImage outlet property. It should look like this:

```
// AppUITableViewCellClass.h

#import <UIKit/UIKit.h>

@interface AppUITableViewCellClass : UITableViewCell

@property (strong, nonatomic) IBOutlet UILabel *labelAppName;
@property (strong, nonatomic) IBOutlet UIImageView *imageAppIcon;
@property (strong, nonatomic) IBOutlet UILabel *labelAppDescription;

@end
```

All that's left to do is synthesize those properties in the implementation file (.m):

```
// AppUITableViewCellClass.m

#import "AppUITableViewCellClass.h"

@implementation AppUITableViewCellClass

@synthesize labelAppName;
@synthesize imageAppIcon;
@synthesize labelAppDescription;

@end
```

Switch back to your storyboard view, and switch the UITableView content mode to Dynamic Prototypes using the Attributes inspector, just as in Figure 2–61.

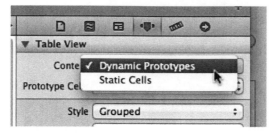

Figure 2–61. *Reselecting Dynamic Prototypes*

Your table view should now look something like Figure 2–62. You will notice that the segues you had created to the App Detail view are now gone, along with your static cell layouts.

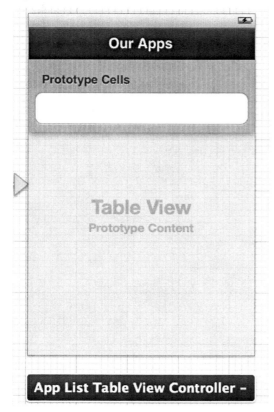

Figure 2–62. *Your new table view*

Drag the UIImageView and UILabel objects to the UITableViewCell prototype, along with their contents "App Name Label" and "App Description", as shown in Figure 2–63. Then set the class on the UITableViewCell to your custom AppUITableViewCellClass in the Identity inspector pane.

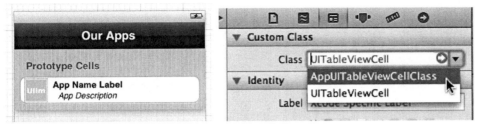

Figure 2–63. *Configuring cells as a custom subclass of* UITableViewCell

Now ^-click-drag from the UITableViewCell to the App Name label, and when you release the mouse button, the pop-up with the list of outlets should be displayed. Select the labelAppName outlet. Connect the other objects in the UITableViewCell. Figure 2–64 demonstrates the first of these steps.

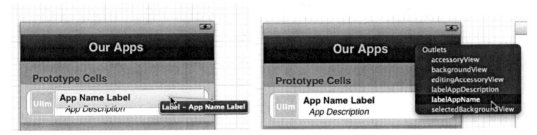

Figure 2–64. *Connecting cell elements to outlets*

You also need to set the Table View Cell Identifier field in the Attributes inspector, as shown in Figure 2–65.

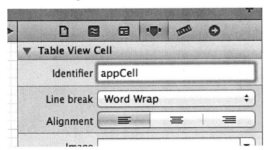

Figure 2–65. *Setting the cell identifier*

Now ^-click-drag from the UITableViewCell to the App Detail view controller to create the segue, as shown in Figure 2–66.

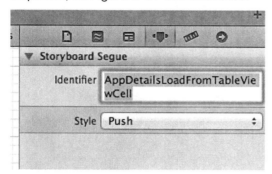

Figure 2–66. *Reconfiguring detail view segues*

And set the identifier for the segue by selecting the segue and setting it in the Attributes inspector, as Figure 2–67 demonstrates.

Figure 2–67. *Setting the new segue identifier*

Now you need to add the `AppUITableViewCellClass` and the datasource methods to the `AppListTableViewController` implementation file (.m).

```objc
//  AppListTableViewController.m

#import "AppListTableViewController.h"
#import "AppDetailsViewController.h"
#import "MyAppClass.h"
#import "AppUITableViewCellClass.h"

@implementation AppListTableViewController

- (void)prepareForSegue:(UIStoryboardSegue *)segue sender:(id)sender{
    if([segue.identifier isEqualToString:@"AppDetailsLoadFromTableViewCell"]){
        AppDetailsViewController *appDetailsVC = segue.destinationViewController;
        appDetailsVC.selectedApp=[MyAppClass appWithAppID:[[self.tableView
indexPathForSelectedRow] row]+1];
    }
}

#pragma mark - Table view data source
- (NSInteger)numberOfSectionsInTableView:(UITableView *)tableView
{
    return 1;
}
```

```
- (NSInteger)tableView:(UITableView *)tableView numberOfRowsInSection:(NSInteger)section
{
    return 3;
}

- (UITableViewCell *)tableView:(UITableView *)tableView
cellForRowAtIndexPath:(NSIndexPath *)indexPath
{
    //Set the CellIdentifier that you set in the storyboard
    static NSString *CellIdentifier = @"appCell";

    AppUITableViewCellClass *cell = [tableView
dequeueReusableCellWithIdentifier:CellIdentifier];
    if (cell == nil) {
        cell = [[AppUITableViewCellClass alloc]
initWithStyle:UITableViewCellStyleDefault reuseIdentifier:CellIdentifier];
    }

    //Configure the cell
    MyAppClass *appForCell=[MyAppClass appWithAppID:indexPath.row+1];
    cell.labelAppName.text=appForCell.appName;
    cell.labelAppDescription.text=appForCell.appDescription;
    cell.imageAppIcon.image=appForCell.iconImage;

    return cell;
}
```

Now when you run the app, the app UITableView will load as before using the one prototype cell and the datasource. Figure 2–68 shows the simulated result of your newest updates to your application. In this instance, you are still using static data for the MyAppClass, but this app could easily be extended to use a core data object model or even pull a list of apps from a remote XML file on your server so that it is truly dynamic. Those features will be covered more in Chapters 10 (Data Storage Recipes) and 11 (Core Data Recipes).

Figure 2–68. *New application's views after the latest changes*

Adding a Storyboard to an Existing Project

You've created this "About Us" app, which works well, but it is pretty unimpressive on its own. It is meant to be included in your other apps so that you can easily show information about your company in any of your apps and also cross-promote your app library easily.

Apple has provided an API for storyboards so that they can easily be included in existing apps that may not leverage storyboards yet. The UIStoryboard class provides the method +storyboardWithName:bundle: that will load a storyboard with the given name. You can then load the initial view controller in the storyboard with the method -instantiateInitialViewController.

Let's create a new project called "Chapter2Project" without storyboards. Use the menu option **File ► New ► New Project...** to create a new single view application. The window in which you do this will resemble Figure 2–69.

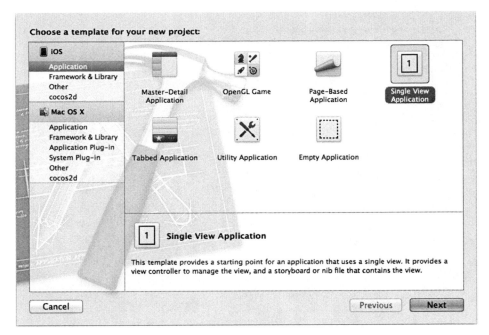

Figure 2–69. *Selecting a single view application*

And this time, you will call the project "Chapter2Project" and make sure that Use Storyboard is not selected, just as in Figure 2–70. If your version of Xcode includes it, make sure the Use Automatic Reference Counting box is checked as well. If your version also includes a field for Class Prefix, set this to Chapter2Project.

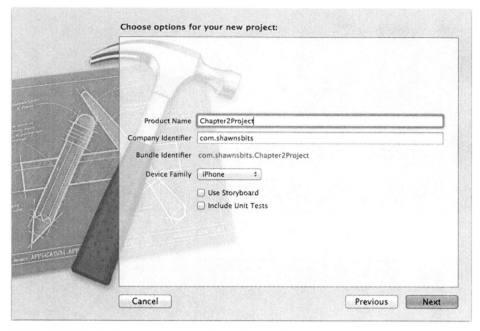

Figure 2–70. *Configuring a new project without storyboards*

Using the navigation pane of this new project, create a new group under the project named "AboutUsStoryBoard", the result of which is shown in Figure 2–71.

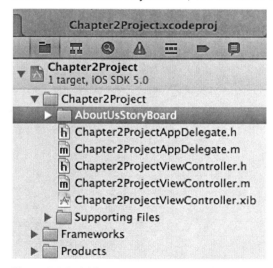

Figure 2–71. *Adding a subgroup to the project*

Now select `Chapter2ProjectViewController.xib`, and add a `UIButton` that will launch your About Us view when you touch it. Your view should resemble that shown in Figure 2–72.

Figure 2–72. *Configured view controller's interface*

Let's go ahead and connect that About Us button to an IBAction by using the Assistant Editor and doing a ^-click-drag from the UIButton to the Chapter2ProjectViewController interface file (.h). Change the connection type to Action, and enter **showAboutUsView** for the Name, as shown in Figure 2–73.

Figure 2–73. *Configuring the UIButton's action*

Before you can complete that method placeholder, you need to copy your About Us files to this project. Switch to the About Us project, and, so you don't get the About Us storyboard confused with any future storyboards you might add to projects, you should rename the storyboard. In the project navigator pane, change the name of MainStoryboard.storyboard to AboutUs.storyboard. If you have opted to create a universal app, this will initially be called MainStoryboard_iPhone.storyboard instead. In Figure 2–74, you can see the storyboard file renamed to the new name.

Figure 2–74. *Renaming the storyboard file for the new project*

Now select all the files in the AboutUs group except the aboutUsAppDelegate.h/.m files, and copy them to the Chapter2Project project in the AboutUs group you created previously. If you move these files via "drag and drop," make sure that the box marked "Copy items into destination group's folder" is checked in the resulting transfer window. Figure 2–75 shows the resulting navigator pane with your files copied from your previous project.

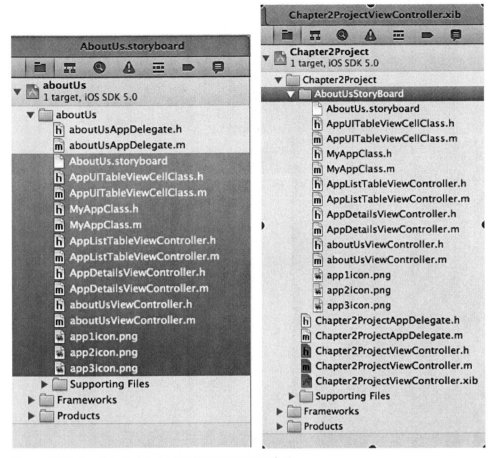

Figure 2–75. *Copying storyboard files into your new project*

Now you can complete that IBAction you created in the
Chapter2ProjectViewController implementation file (.m). Select
Chapter2ProjectViewController.m in the project navigator pane, and import the
aboutUsViewController.h header file. Then scroll down to the bottom of the code where
the IBAction method placeholder is, and complete it so the file looks like this:

```
// Chapter2ProjectViewController.m

#import "Chapter2ProjectViewController.h"
#import "aboutUsViewController.h"

@implementation Chapter2ProjectViewController
…
- (IBAction)showAboutUsView:(id)sender {
    UIStoryboard *aboutUsStoryboard=[UIStoryboard storyboardWithName:@"AboutUs"
bundle:nil];
    aboutUsViewController *aboutUsVC=[aboutUsStoryboard
instantiateInitialViewController];
    [self presentViewController:aboutUsVC animated:YES completion:nil];
```

```
}
@end
```

When the project is run and the button is touched, your storyboard will load and all the subsequent views will load, resulting in a view resembling those shown in Figure 2–76.

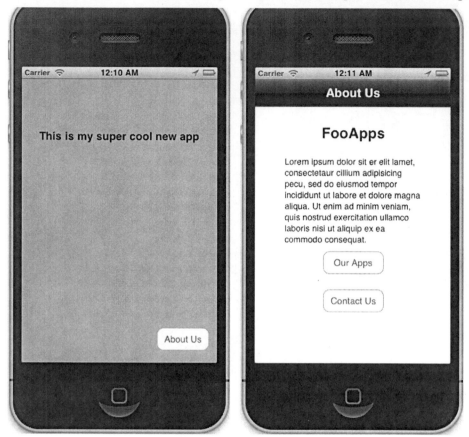

Figure 2–76. *Resulting application with storyboard loaded*

But there is a problem. There is no way to close your About Us view controller when you are done. The easiest method would be to add a Back button to the view in your storyboard that dismisses the view.

First you define the IBAction that your Back button is going to trigger in your aboutUsViewController interface file (.h):

```
//  aboutUsViewController.h

#import <UIKit/UIKit.h>

@interface aboutUsViewController : UIViewController

-(IBAction)closeAboutUs:(id)sender;

@end
```

Then implement the method in the `aboutUsViewController` implementation file (`.m`):

```
// aboutUsViewController.m

#import "aboutUsViewController.h"

@implementation aboutUsViewController

-(IBAction)closeAboutUs:(id)sender{
    [self dismissViewControllerAnimated:YES completion:nil];
}
```

Open `AboutUs.storyboard`, and add a `UIBarButtonItem` object with a title of "Back" to the `UINavigationBar` in the About Us view. Then connect this `UIBarButtonItem` to the IBAction `closeAboutUs` by doing a ^-click-drag from the `UIBarButtonItem` to the View Controller status bar and then selecting the `closeAboutUs` event from the pop-up. These steps are demonstrated in Figure 2–77.

Figure 2–77. *Connecting the bar button to a segue action*

Now when you run the application, you will be able to launch the About Us story board and get back to your main app. Don't forget that you should add this `UIBarButtonItem` and method to the main About Us project so that when you copy it to future projects, you don't run into the same issue.

Summary

The first thing you will notice in Xcode 4 is that Interface Builder is no longer a separate application. The changes, however, go much deeper and represent a truly integrated experience. Interface Builder has extended the ease of drag-and-drop interface building into code generation when combined with the Assistant Editor view.

The Storyboards tool takes your interface building even further and allows you to rapidly build working prototypes of your applications. Your storyboard diagrams are no longer thrown away when the coding starts but are an integral part of the application development process and can be utilized by controllers. This new feature takes the Model-View-Controller from an abstract best practice and makes it a tangible application development process.

Chapter 3

Application Design Elements

Every occupation has its own specific set of materials, tools, and methods, and aperson's skill and understanding of this equipment arealmost always what definehis or hersuccess in the given field. In iOS development, you are given a great many components and functionalities from which you can assemble your applications. Having a full and practical understanding of these tools allows any developer to considerably improve the quality of any work he or shecontributes to.

In this chapter, you will systematically go through the design elements that iOS developers are initially given, discussing their purpose, use, implementation, functionality, and general guidelines for acquiring the best possible result from each item. Through this approach, you can acquire a better understanding of how best to utilize the tools given to youto create higher-quality applications.

Cocoa Touch Controls

Cocoa Touch includes a nice variety of items known as "controls," which are the main objects used by an application to interact with the user. All of these elements, some of which are entirely new to iOS 5.0, allow you to build a more advanced yet simpler user interface with which to operate your applications.

UILabel

The UILabel class is easily one of the most basic and fundamental controls with which you can interact with your user by displaying information. A variety of other elements make use of UILabels, making them the foundation of nearly any user interface. Figure 3–1 is the simplest example of a UILabel.

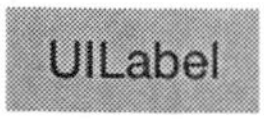

Figure 3–1. *A simple* UILabel

The primary way that you deal with a UILabel is simply by setting its text using either the -setText: method or, more simply, the text property. However, the class also has a variety of other properties you can set to customize your display even more, including the following:

- font

- textColor

- textAlignment

- enabled: You can easily dim or undim labels with this property, as a disabled UILabel is displayed dimmed out.

For a more precise control of a text display, you can also create a drop shadow using the shadowColorandshadowOffsetproperties. The shadowOffset property takes a CGSize type, which you can create using the CGSizeMake() function. This function takes two parameters, a width and a height, which specify where your shadow is placed in reference to the label. For example, if you configure a shadow with the following code, then the resulting UILabel will resemble Figure 3–2.

```
myLabel.shadowColor = [UIColor blackColor];
myLabel.shadowOffset = CGSizeMake(2.0, 2.0);
```

Figure 3–2. *Heavily shadowed text*

Compare this to a UILabel with no shadow, as in Figure 3–3.

Figure 3–3. *A label with no shadow*

As you can see, by specifying shadowOffset width of 2.0 and a height of 2.0, you made your label's shadow appear shifted 2 points to the right and 2 points down from the original text. As you can guess, negative values for these will cause a shadow to move left and up respectively.

It is often helpful to an application's graphic design to make use of the UILabel's shadow, but it is often difficult to determine the ideal specifications to use. In general, it is safe to say that less is more, and a very subtle change, such as a gray shadow with an offset of (1.0, 1.0), will help improve the visual quality of an application. Figure 3–4 features one UILabel without a shadow compared to one with a gray shadow and an offset of (1.0, 1.0), in order to demonstrate the difference in visual appeal.

No Shadow

Subtle Shadow

Figure 3–4. *A label with no shadow compared with a one square point shadow*

The UILabel also has properties highlightedTextColor, which you can specify, andhighlighted, which allows you to specifically highlight a label. However, no highlighting color will be applied unless one is specified with the highlightedTextColor property.

The UILabel, like many other elements you deal with, has a property called userInteractionEnabled. This property must be set to YES in order for any kind of gestures, such as a tap, to have any effect with a UILabel.

UIButton

As the cornerstone of two-way user interaction, the UIButton allows you to actively give your users clear options in their abilities within an application.

There are a variety of pre-defined types of UIButtons that you can very easily use. You can set the type of a button by way of the class method +buttonWithType:, which takes the following possible pre-defined values.

- UIButtonTypeCustom

- UIButtonTypeRoundedRect

- UIButtonTypeDetailDisclosure

- UIButtonTypeInfoLight

- UIButtonTypeInfoDark

- UIButtonTypeContactAdd

If no value is specified for the property, the Custom type is assumed, giving you the most freedom in customizing the view of your button.

In general, you will probably use a UIButtonTypeRoundedRect button if you simply want to give a simple button with text, but if you have a more complex button, including one that is image-based, you will probably use the UIButtonTypeCustom option. This way, you can more easily control the background settings of the button to ensure your visual theme stays well maintained.

Whenever you are dealing with a UIButton, you must always consider the possible "state" of the button, whether it is currently being selected. For this reason, most of the UIButton methods include a parameter for a UIControlState. For example, in order to set a UIButton's text, rather than accessing the titleLabel property, you should use the -setTitle:forState: property. For example, you may configure a UIButton like so:

```
UIButton *button = [UIButton buttonWithType:UIButtonTypeRoundedRect];
[button setTitle:@"Test" forState:UIControlStateNormal];
[button setTitle:@"Selected" forState:UIControlStateHighlighted];
```

Remember that whenever you create a view element programmatically, you should set its frame to specify the location, and then add it as a subview of whichever view it belongs in.

```
[button setFrame:CGRectMake(10, 10, 100, 44)];
[self.view addSubview:button];
```

The button title on a UIButton is simply a UILabel, so you can customize fonts and shadows quite easily with such methods as -titleColorForState: and -titleShadowColorForState:.

A UIButton also allows quite easily for two different images to be placed inside of it: a background image and a foreground image. You can easily set these with the -setBackgroundImage:forState:and setImage:forState: methods.

In order to programmatically add actions for a UIButton to perform, use the -addTarget:action:forControlEvents:method.

```
[button addTarget:self action:@selector(buttonPressed:)
forControlEvents:UIControlEventTouchUpInside];
```

From here, you can define your -buttonPressed: method to do whatever you prefer. If you implement your action in this manner, a reference to the UIButton will be passed to the method as the first parameter. This allows you a great deal of power in reacting to a multitude of different events with a single method by simply checking the properties of the "sender" element and acting accordingly. As a simple example, the following implementation will display in the log the text of whichever button was pressed.

```
-(void)buttonPressed:(UIButton *)sender
{
NSLog(@"%@", sender.titleLabel.text);
}
```

UISegmentedControl

The UISegmentedControl class is essentially an extension of the UIButton. It allows you to not only make selections, but alsopreserve those selections indefinitely, until another selection is made. They are particularly designed for situations in which one of multiple options will always be selected, such as choosing the type of display in a Maps application, or simply for configuring settings in a game.

UISegmentedControl elements are made up of multiple "segments," with each one having either a string or an image inside them, as in Figure 3–5.

Figure 3–5. *A simple* UISegmentedControl

Each segment has an index referring to it, starting with the first segment having index 0.

Just like with the UIButton, you can add actions to a UISegmentedControl to be performed any time the selected segment is changed using the -addTarget:action:forControlEvents:method, like so:

```
[self.segConaddTarget:self action:@selector(segmentChanged:)
forControlEvents:UIControlEventValueChanged];
```

When building instances of UISegmentedControl, you can specify an initial set of items to display using the -initWithItems: method after allocating the object. From there, you can add segments using the -insertSegmentWithImage:atIndex:animated:and-insertSegmentWithTitle:atIndex:animated: methods, and remove them using -removeSegmentAtIndex:animated: or -removeAllSegments:.

At any point, you can always access the current number of items in the control using the numberOfSegments property, and access the currently selected index with selectedSegmentIndex.

Once you have a specific index you want to access, you can use -setImage:forSegmentAtIndex:, imageForSegmentAtIndex:, setTitle:forSegmentAtIndex:, and titleForSegmentAtIndex: to modify or utilize your UISegmentedControl as needed! The following is an example of an action for the UISegmentedControl, which replaces the text of a newly selected segment with the square of its previous value.

```
-(void)segmentChanged:(UISegmentedControl *)sender
{
int index = sender.selectedSegmentIndex;
NSString *title = [sender titleForSegmentAtIndex:index];
int x = [title intValue]*[title intValue];
NSString *newTitle = [[NSNumber numberWithInt:x] stringValue];
    [sender setTitle:newTitle forSegmentAtIndex:index];
}
```

UITextField

The UITextField is easily the most customizable form of user input, as well as the most heavily used, as it allows you to easily take input from a user to be processed. You even have the ability to apply auto-correct to the user input, though this should be used sparingly to avoid unwanted corrections.

If you want to add a UITextField to a view, the easiest way to do it is to place it in the view in your XIBfile, as in Figure 3–6. You can then connect it to your header file as a property, and configure it in your -viewDidLoad method.

One of the absolutely most important things to remember whenever you are dealing with a UITextField (or other text-based inputs that you will deal with later) is that at some point, a keyboard will likely end up covering half of your screen. You need to plan for this as a designer by making sure your UITextField is in the top half of the screen or moves up to the top half of the screen when the keyboard appears. You can set up actions to be performed when the keyboard appears or disappears by registering for the following notifications:

- `UIKeyboardWillShowNotification`

- `UIKeyboardDidShowNotification`

- `UIKeyboardWillHideNotification`

- `UIKeyboardDidHideNotification`

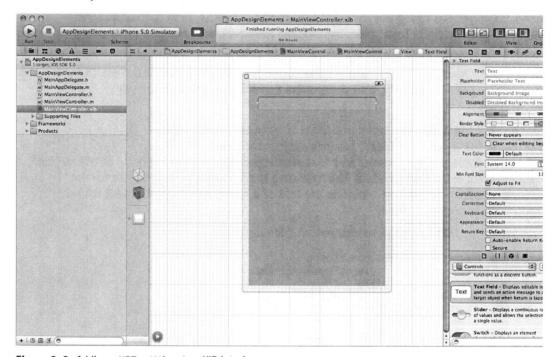

Figure 3–6. *Adding a* `UITextView` *to a XIB interface*

While in Interface Builder, you can also do some easy configuration of your `UITextField`. You can make all these changes programmatically using `UITextField` properties, but Interface Builder makes them a great deal easier, especially the keyboard settings such as Capitalization and Auto-Correction. Figure 3–7 is a view of the Attribute inspector containing these settings. As shown, the "Correction" type defaults to "Default", resulting in the general response you often see when typing messages.

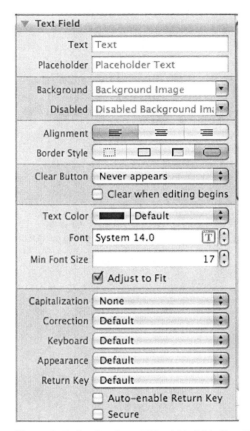

Figure 3–7. *Configuring a* UITextField *in the utilities pane*

It is also very easy to programmatically customize the view of a UITextField through the use of the leftView, rightView, inputView, and inputAccessoryView properties.

One of the most important properties of a UITextField is the delegate property, which receives a variety of method calls relating to the actions of a UITextField. Whichever object is set as the delegate (usually the view controller in whose view the UITextField is shown) must conform to the UITextFieldDelegate protocol.

The UITextFieldDelegate protocol specifies a variety of methods to manage the editing of a UITextField. You can use the -textFieldShouldBeginEditing:and-textFieldShouldEndEditing: methods to either enable or disable the beginning or ending of editing. (Return NO in either of these to disable the given action.)

You can also use -textFieldDidBeginEditing:and-textFieldDidEndEditing: to do any movement of elements around to make sure that the keyboard does not block your UITextField.

In terms of editing the UITextField's text, the UITextFieldDelegate offers a few methods to help customize the actions of your text field. -textField:shouldChangeCharactersInRange:replacementString: is useful for actively parsing text as it is entered. The `-textFieldShouldClear:`method also allows you a voice in whether a `UITextField` clears.

Quite possibly the most useful `UITextFieldDelegate` protocol method is the `-textFieldShouldReturn:` method, as it often serves as the main method by which you can implement the dismissing of the keyboard. Most users are used to pressing the return key to finish editing a `UITextField`, so you can simply implement this method like so:

```
-(BOOL)textFieldShouldReturn:(UITextField *)textField
{
    [textField resignFirstResponder];
return YES;
}
```

By using the `-resignFirstResponder` method, your `UITextField` gives up its role as the current key element, dismissing the keyboard.Yourresulting app, as simulated in Figure 3–8, will allow you to dismiss a keyboard with the pressing of the return key.

Figure 3–8. *An app with enabled functionality for dismissing the keyboard*

UISlider

The UISlider provides a very nice and simple UI element for allowing a user to smoothly adjust values, as shown in Figure 3–9.

Figure 3–9. *A simple* UISlider

These sliders are fairly easy to set up and configure. You can use Interface Builder to do most of the value setup, or you can set values programmatically. The most important properties to configure are the minimumValue, maximumValue, and initial value. You can set the initial value when you set up your XIB file, or in code by simply setting the value of the slider in your -viewDidLoad.

Beyond these essential properties, you can also greatly customize the appearance of the slider, including specifying customized track images and thumb images. You can also specify images to place on either end of the UISlider to help represent your maximum and minimum values using the minimumValueImage and maximumValueImage properties. For example, if your UISlider deals with an audio player's volume, your minimum value image may be an image of a speaker, and the maximum value image might be the same speaker but with sound waves emanating from it.

You can create actions to be performed upon the changing of a UISlider's value through two methods:

1. Declare a method of return type (IBAction) in your header file, and then connect the UISlider in your XIB file to this method by holding ⌘ and dragging from the slider to the method header.

2. Use the -addTarget:action:forControlEvents: method, as shown here:

```
[self.mySlider addTarget:self action:@selector(valueChanged:)
forControlEvents:UIControlEventValueChanged];
```

The UISlider also has a property called continuous, which determines whether the value changes are reported continuously. If not, whichever action you have associated with the slider will be called only when users finish adjusting the value, rather than repeatedly as they move the thumb.

If you wish to cause the value of your slider to change programmatically, rather than having the user adjust it (possibly due to some other event), you should use the -setValue:animated: method, rather than simply setting the value property, in order to provide a smoother transition to the user.

UISwitch

The UISwitch acts very similarly to the UISlider, but allows the user to choose only a Boolean value, either "On" (as in Figure 3–10) or "Off". These are very often used in Settings areas of applications to allow users to easily customize their preferences.

Figure 3–10. *An enabled* UISwitch

The UISwitch works the exact same way as the UISlider in terms of adding actions to be performed upon the changing of the value, though significantly simplified due to the Boolean nature of the switch. Just as before, -addTarget:action:forControlEvents: is used to connect a method to the switch. You can also access the value of the switch using the onproperty, and animate the changing of its value using the -setOn:animated: method.

UIActivityIndicatorView

Often an application may be currently working on a task that does not happen immediately. This could be a process of downloading files from a server or even simply a task dealing with a large amount of data requiring some significant amount of time to complete. As the developer, you should always strive to keep your user informed of such activities. For this, you have the UIActivityIndicatorView, shown in Figure 3–11.

A UIActivityIndicatorView is a simple element that is used to display whether an activity is going on in the background. However, it allows for only two states: in progress, and not in progress. To switch between these, you can use the -startAnimating and -stopAnimatingmethods. You can also access whether the indicator is currently animating through the –isAnimating method. If you do not have any particular use of the indicator once your task is finished, you can use the hidesWhenStopped property.

Figure 3–11. *A* UIActivityIndicatorView *element*

For this element, you are fairly limited in your customization options in that you are given only properties to adjust the color and size. First, you have the activityIndicatorViewStyle property, which takes three possible values:

- UIActivityIndicatorViewStyleWhiteLarge

- UIActivityIndicatorViewStyleWhite

- UIActivityIndicatorViewStyleGray

These three values differ only in size and color, and should be chosen from to maximize visual display quality.

If none of the foregoingstyles fit your application's design very well, you can also specify a different color, through the UIColor class, using the color property.

UIProgressView

Following along the lines of the UIActivityIndicatorView, you have the UIProgressView. This acts very similarly to a UISlider in that it displays a value (although limited to scaling between 0 and 1), but does not allow for any user input. This element is most often used for displaying some amount of progress of a task completed, as in Figure 3–12, as an alternative to simply using a UIActivityIndicatorView to show that progress is occurring.

Figure 3–12. *A UIProgressView in use*

Just like the UIActivityIndicatorView, UIProgressViews can be created with a style, accessed through the progressViewStyle property, which has the following possible values:

- UIProgressViewStyleDefault:Standard style chosen for UIProgressViews

- UIProgressViewStyleBar:Style often used inside of a toolbar

The most important property of the UIProgressView is, naturally, the amount of progress. This value, which ranges between 0.0 and 1.0, can be accessed through the progress property. You can also set this property using the -setProgress:animated: method to improve your application's visual quality.

Aside from the progressViewStyle, the UIProgressView allows for decent appearance customization of the tint color and image for both the progress displayed, as well as the track upon which it rests. These are all respectively accessed through the progressTintColor, progressImage, trackTintColor, and trackImage properties.

UIPageControl

For dealing with applications with "paging," a very useful little UI element is the UIPageControl, shown in Figure 3–13. This device acts mainly as an indicator to users as to which page they are currently on, though it can also be used to directly manipulate an application, usually by changing the current page. For an excellent example of this utility, look at the bottom of your device's Weather app.

Figure 3–13. *A UIPageControl*

When using a UIPageControl, you can easily access multiple values associated with it through such properties as currentPage and numberOfPages. If your application happens to have a possibility of havingonlyone page at some point, you may also make use of the hidesForSinglePage property.

Just as with the UISlider and UISwitch, you can add actions to a UIPageControl to be performed on the changing of the currentPage value using the -addTarget:selector:forControlEvents: method in conjunction with the UIControlEventValueChanged event. This method would ideally handle the actual changing of your application's display to display the newly selected page.

If, upon the changing of the currentPage, you decide there might be some reason to not have the display of the UIPageControl update immediately, you can set the defersCurrentPageDisplayproperty to YES, causing it to wait until the -updateCurrentPageDisplay method is called before adjusting the display. This property defaults to NO otherwise.

Unfortunately, you are incredibly limited in terms of customizing the appearance of a UIPageControl. However, you are given a very useful method called -sizeForNumberOfPages:,which allows you to easily find the minimum size needed to display a UIPageControl with any given number of pages.

Anytime you make use of a UIPageControl element, you want to make sure the indicator does not at all interfere visually with the pages that it manages. The element should therefore, according to Apple's Interface Guidelines, be centered between the bottom of the "pages" and the bottom of the screen.

UIStepper

The UIStepper is an element entirely new in iOS 5.0,intended to streamline an application's use of incremental values. It is equipped with "+" and "-" buttons for the user, but does not actually display its associated value, as in Figure 3–14. This task is left up to the developer to implement as is appropriate for each application.

Figure 3–14. *The new* UIStepper

The main property of the UIStepper is its value property, which you can access in order to update your display accordingly. This value can be easily configured with a variety of properties:

- minimumValue: The minimum number that the value can reach

- maximumValue: The maximum value

- stepValue: The amount by which value is incremented upon the use of the stepping buttons

- **wraps:** If this property is set to YES, your minimum and maximum values will wrap together. Thus, if your value is incremented to exceed the maximumValue, it will wrap around to the minimumValue, and vice versa.

- **autorepeat:** This property allows the UIStepper buttons to be held in order to repeatedly increment the value without having to repeatedly tap the element.

- **continuous:** Specifies whether value change events are sent every time the valueproperty changes or only if the user has finished changing the value, as used with the autorepeatproperty

As before, you can assign actions to be performed upon the changing of the valueproperty using the -addTarget:selector:forControlEvents: method with UIControlEventValueChanged.

Once your UIStepper is fully configured, the only concept to keep in mind when designing your application is to make sure that your user interface informs the user clearly as to which value a UIStepper changes.

Data Views

In iOS you have access to a variety of subclasses of UIView, known collectively as "data views," that allow you to easily place content in your application in very specific ways depending on the type of your application.

UIImageView

One of the most intuitive and important data views in Cocoa Touch is the UIImageView class. This view element, along with its properties and methods, is optimized to help the developer display and manage images within an application.

The core properties of a UIImageView are its image and highlightedImage properties. Both of these will be instances of the UIImage class, with the highlightedImage being displayed only if the image is selected. You can create and specify these images programmatically by using the -initWithImage:or-initWithImage:highlightedImage: designated initializers, or by simply setting the properties individually. An example is as follows:

```
self.myImageView = [[UIImageView alloc] initWithImage:[UIImage
imageNamed:@"myImage.png"]];
```

If you make use of the +imageNamed:method to create your UIImage, you will need to make sure that your actual image file is imported into your project. You can do this by dragging the file from the Finder into Xcode. When you do this, a dialog will appear, and you need to make sure that the option marked "Copy items into destination group's folder (if needed)" is checked, as in Figure 3–15.

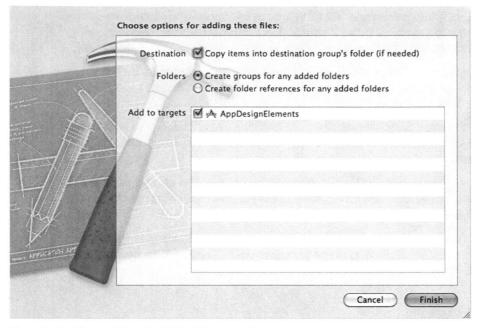

Figure 3–15. *Pop-up dialog for adding files to a project*

The UIImageView class also has built-in functionality to allow for animating multiple images by making use of the following properties:

- animationImages: This property, an NSArray of UIImage objects, specifies the actual images to be animated.

- highlightedAnimationImages: This acts just like the animationImagesproperty, but for when the UIImageView is highlighted.

- animationDuration:This value, created as an NSTimeInterval, represents the total time for all the images in animationImages to cycle through. The value, if unspecified, defaults to the number of images multiplied by 1/30 of a second.

- animationRepeatCount: Quite simply, this value specifies how many times the cycle of images will repeat. If set to 0, the default, the animation will repeat indefinitely.

Once your UIImageView's animation properties are configured, you can manage the actual animation using the -startAnimating, -stopAnimating, and isAnimatingmethods.

One of the most important properties to keep in mind when dealing with a UIImageView is the contentMode property. While this is actually inherited from UIView, it tends to become very important when dealing with images. The contentMode property essentially specifies how the view will respond to dealing with content whose aspect ratio does not fit well with the view it is placed in, such as a rectangular image being shown by a square `UIImageView`. There are a variety of options for this property, all of which are fully documented in the Apple documentation, but most of the time you will probably opt for `UIViewContentModeScaleAspectFill`. This option may end up clipping part of an image out, but it will be certain to fill the entire space of the presenting view, improving design quality. If, for any reason, you require the image to not be clipped and would prefer the empty space, you can use the `UIViewContentModeScaleAspectFit` value.

UITextView

The `UITextView` class is incredibly similar to a `UITextField` in that it allows the user to input text. However, its visual design allows for significantly greater quantities of text, as shown in Figure 3–16.

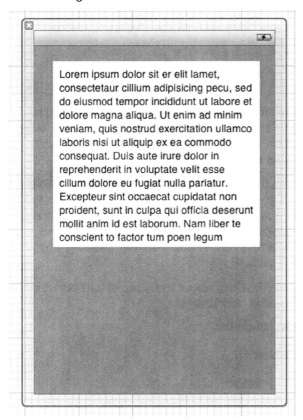

Figure 3–16. *Using a UITextView in a XIB*

Most of the `UITextView` properties are very similar to the `UITextField` properties, such as `text`, `font`, and `textColor`. Other useful properties to configure your text are `editable`, which specifies whether the text can be edited, as well as `textAlignment`. You can even specify what kind of data the text view detects, such as phone numbers or e-mail addresses, using the `dataDetectorTypes` value.

Just like the UITextField, the UITextView has a delegateproperty that receives multiple actions depending on what happens in the UITextView. This property must conform to the UITextViewDelegate protocol.

Most of the UITextViewDelegate methods are the exact same as those in the UITextFieldDelegate protocol discussed earlier. However, the UITextViewDelegate does not have any method to indicate when the return key has been pressed, making it harder to determine when the keyboard should be dismissed using the -resignFirstResponder method. Instead, you can implement the -textView:shouldChangeTextInRange:replacementText: method.

```
- (BOOL)textView:(UITextView *)textView shouldChangeTextInRange:(NSRange)range
 replacementText:(NSString *)text
{
if ([text isEqualToString:@"\n"])
    {
        [textView resignFirstResponder];
return FALSE;
    }
return TRUE;
}
```

With a UITextView, the pressing of the return key causes a text of "\n" to be added to the current text, so you can simply have this method wait for such an input, and dismiss the keyboard accordingly. In your application, you may wish to allow the user to end lines in your text view, so this implementation may not be ideal.

In terms of customization, you can easily customize the text attributes of the text field through the aforementioned properties, but you also have some level of customization over the view itself. You can access the actual input view using the inputViewproperty, as well as an inputAccessoryView. This accessory view, when non-nil, is displayed above the keyboard that appears once the UITextView is being edited, allowing you to attach a custom toolbar to your keyboard if desired.

It is also possible for any class to receive notifications about the state of a UITextView by becoming an observer to any of the following notifications:

- ▓ UITextViewTextDidBeginEditingNotification

- ▓ UITextViewTextDidChangeNotification

- ▓ UITextViewTextDidEndEditingNotification

Just as with the UITextField, one of the most important design aspects of the UITextView is to remember that at any given moment, a massive keyboard could be taking up half of your screen. As a developer, you should make sure that your UITextVieweitheris in an area that will not be blocked by the keyboard, or moves to such an area once the keyboard appears. See the previous "UITextField" section for more explanation on how to receive notifications when the keyboard appears and disappears.

UIScrollView

The `UIScrollView` class is incredibly useful for dealing with large amounts of content that you cannot fit in a single view, but belongs all in the same page. This could be a list of pictures to be displayed or simply a very large image that you want to be able to zoom and scroll with.

The content of a `UIScrollView` is defined as any subviews inside of it, so you can simply use the `-addSubview:` method to add content to your `UIScrollView`.

Absolutely any time that you use a `UIScrollView`, it is necessary to set the `contentSize` property. This specifies to the `UIScrollView` exactly how much scrolling in any direction to allow. Generally, this will be whatever the size of your content is, so if your content is a `UIImageView` with a `UIImage` of size 800x640, you will want the content size to be the same. Alternatively, if you want your `UIScrollView` not to be able to scroll in one direction, you might make that direction's aspect of your `contentSize` smaller.

You can also adjust the `contentInsetandcontentOffset` to further customize the displaying of your content. The latter of these can even be animated using the `-setContentOffset:animated:` method.

The scrolling properties of a `UIScrollView` are incredibly easy to configure both in the XIBfile and programmatically. The most important of these properties follow:

- `scrollEnabled`: Specifies whether the `UIScrollView` can scroll;you can use this property to "lock" the view.

- `directionalLockEnabled`: This property, if enabled, restricts the `UIScrollView` to scroll in only one direction at any given time, either vertical or horizontal.

- `scrollsToTop`: This enables or disables the ability of the user to tap the status bar at the top of the screen in order to scroll the `UIScrollView` to the top of its content.

- `pagingEnabled`: If this property is enabled, the scrolling gravitates to multiples of the view's bounds, rather than simply allowing constant scrolling throughout the content. This, in conjunction with a `UIPageController`, is very useful if you are using a `UIScrollView` to display multiple pages of content.

One of the most useful methods of a `UIScrollView` is `-scrollRectToVisible:animated:`, as it allows you to scroll specifically to any given area of the content based on the needs of your application.

Among many other properties, there also exist ones to manage the "bouncing" of the `UIScrollView` when the user flicks the scroll view past its bounds, such as the `bounces`, `alwaysBounceVertical`, and `alwaysBounceHorizontal` properties.

The developer also has control over the "scroll indicator," the thin bar(s) on the bottom or sides showing how far the view has scrolled. You can adjust these using the `indicatorStyle`, `scrollIndicatorInsets`, `showsHorizontalScrollIndicator`, and `showsVerticalScrollIndicator`properties. You can even manually flash the indicators using the `-flashScrollIndicators` method.

Aside from scrolling and panning, `UIScrollViews` also have a zooming ability naturally built into them. In order to implement this functionality, you must simply change the `maximumZoomScale`and/or `minimumZoomScale`properties to values other than 1.0.

The `UIScrollView` also has a `delegate` property that responds to a variety of events that occur within the `UIScrollView`. This object, which must conform to the `UIScrollViewDelegate` protocol, has multiple methods for responding to both the beginnings and endings of any scrolling, flicking, or zooming event. Refer to the Apple documentation for full details on all these methods.

UIWebView

The `UIWebView` class is a useful data presentation class for an application that "wraps" some kind of web application.

You can create a `UIWebView` in your view controller's XIBfile very easily, which also allows you to easily edit most of the properties of a `UIWebView` in the Attributes inspector. These properties, such as the `dataDetectorTypes` (similar to those used in a `UITextView`), are also accessible programmatically.

A `UIWebView` can load data from the Web in a variety of ways, depending on the type of content you need to manage. The loading of content is managed through multiple methods, including `-loadData:MIMEType:textEncodingName:baseURL:`, `-loadHTMLString:baseURL:`, and `-loadRequest:`. The simplest of these, `-loadRequest:`, takes a parameter of type `NSURLRequest`. This class is essentially a wrapped `NSURL` with extra properties specifically pertaining to accessing content online, such as a `timeoutInterval`or a `cachePolicy`. Once your content is loading, you can also make use of the `-stopLoading` or `-reload` methods as you wish.

MKMapView

The `MKMapView` is a data presentation class specifically used in conjunction with the MapKit framework to present the user with a map. For more information on this framework, including the detailed use of this view, refer toChapter5, MapKit Recipes.

UITableView

The `UITableView` is an incredibly powerful class for data presentation, based on the idea of presenting large amounts of data that is all formatted similarly. We have devoted Chapter 9, UTTableViewRecipes,to covering the general use of this class and fully explaining the nuances of developing table-based applications.

UIPickerView

A UIPickerView is similar to a UITableView, though it is not quite as complex and customizable. It allows the user to be presented with a variety of similarly formatted options, and rotate through them in order to select a specific option, as in Figure 3–17.

Figure 3–17. *The default UIPickerView*

The UIPickerView is set up similarly to the UITableView through the use of both a dataSource property and a delegate property. These properties must respectively conform to the UIPickerViewDataSource and UIPickerViewDelegate protocols, and are usually set to the UIViewController that will present the UIPickerView.

The UIPickerViewDataSource protocol requires only two methods, which define the physical configuration of the UIPickerView in terms of "rows" and "components." Components are vertical sections into which your view is split that allow you to easily choose multiple values at once. Rows contain the individual options in each component that can be chosen by the user.

You can configure the number of components, as well as the number of rows per component, through the data source methods -numberOfComponentsInPickerView:and-pickerView:numberOfRowsInComponent:.

The visual setup of a UIPickerView is handled through multiple delegate methods:

- pickerView:rowHeightForComponent:: Specifies the height of each row in a given component

- pickerView:widthForComponent:: Specifies the width of each component; your components will not automatically be fit into the UIPickerView, so make sure that the total width of your components is not more than the width of the UIPickerView.

- pickerView:titleForRow:forComponent:: Use this method to give a simple text to be displayed in each row.

- pickerView:viewForRow:forComponent:reusingView:: You can use this if you wish to display more than a simple text in a row. Try to make use of the reusingView: parameter to improve performance.

- pickerView:didSelectRow:inComponent:: This method is called every time a component stops rotating and lands on a specific row, allowing your application to update properly elsewhere.

Here is a sample configuration:

```
#pragma mark - Data Source methods
-(NSInteger)numberOfComponentsInPickerView:(UIPickerView *)pickerView
{
return 3;
}
-(NSInteger)pickerView:(UIPickerView *)pickerView
numberOfRowsInComponent:(NSInteger)component
{
return 3;
}
#pragma mark - Delegate methods
-(CGFloat)pickerView:(UIPickerView *)pickerView
rowHeightForComponent:(NSInteger)component
{
return 30;
}
-(CGFloat)pickerView:(UIPickerView *)pickerView widthForComponent:(NSInteger)component
{
return 100;
}
-(void)pickerView:(UIPickerView *)pickerView didSelectRow:(NSInteger)row
inComponent:(NSInteger)component
{
NSLog(@"Selected. Row:%i, Component:%i", row, component);
}
-(NSString *)pickerView:(UIPickerView *)pickerView titleForRow:(NSInteger)row
forComponent:(NSInteger)component
{
return [NSString stringWithFormat:@"R:%i, C:%i", row, component];
}
```

This will configure the UIPickerView shown in Figure 3–18, along with logging each selected row within each component.

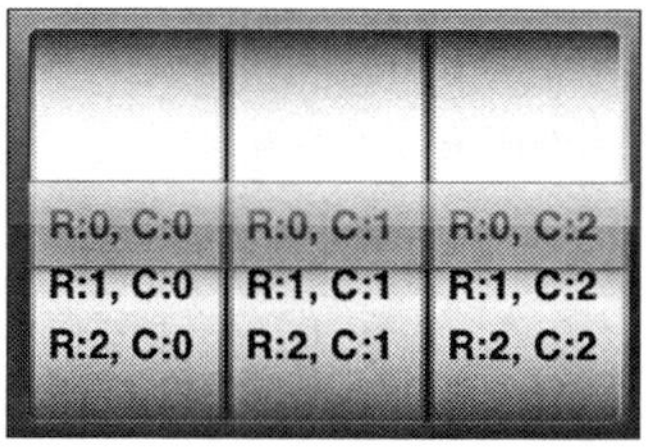

Figure 3–18. *A UIPickerView configured by rows and columns*

Once your UIPickerView is configured, you can access the selected row in each component using the -selectedRowInComponent:method.

You can also toggle the appearance of the center bar that signifies the chosen rows through the showsSelectionIndicator property.

UIDatePickerView

The `UIDatePickerView` is a specialized version of a `UIPickerView` configured to handle any selection of times, dates, or countdowns, shown in Figure 3–19. The class is not actually a subclass of `UIPickerView`, but instead has a customized `UIPickerView` as a subview.

Figure 3–19. *The specialized* `UIDatePickerView`

This class has a property called `datePickerMode`, which allows you to select from multiple values, representing types of pickers, to fit your specific situation.

- `UIDatePickerModeTime`: Selects a time
- `UIDatePickerModeDate`: Selects a date
- `UIDatePickerModeDateAndTime`: Selects both a date and time in one picker
- `UIDatePickerModeCountDownTimer`: Selects a countdown timer to be set

In order to be informed of changes to selected rows, add a method as an action to your `UIDatePickerView` to be called upon `UIControlEventValueChanged` events, just as with several of your previously discussed elements.

You can configure the different modes of a `UIDatePickerView` through such properties as `maximumDate`, `minimumDate`, `minuteInterval`, and `countDownDuration`.

If you wish to programmatically change the date displayed by a `UIDatePickerView`, you can set the `date` property, but this will not animate the change. It is recommended that you use the `-setDate:animated:` method to make such changes if the `UIPickerView` is visible.

Gesture Recognizers

In iOS you are able to improve the functionality of your application by adding "gesture recognizers" to instances or subclasses of `UIView`. "Gesture" refers to a touch-based event driven by the user, such as a tap, swipe, or pinch. These elements can then perform actions in your application, extending your normal functionality. Though it is possible to create your own subclasses of `UIGestureRecognizer`, you will focus on those already incorporated into iOS 5.0.

Whenever using a UIGestureRecognizer, it is important to remember that a large percentage of users will not know to look for the existence of the gestures that you can implement. Therefore, you should implement a UIGestureRecognizeronlyin order to expedite a task that can be performed elsewhere. Essential functions should not be built into these without explicitly informing the user.

The UIGestureRecognizer class is itself an abstract class that defines the behavior of multiple subclasses, each representing different gestures. However, no matter the subclass, a gesture recognizer is added to any UIView by use of the -addGestureRecognizer: method. To add an instance of UITapGestureRecognizer called tapGesture to your entire view controller's view, for example, you write the following:

```
[self.view addGestureRecognizer:tapGesture];
```

> **TIP:** Any subclass of UIGestureRecognizer can be added to any instance or subclass of UIView, so you can easily build custom gesture functionality into nearly any element, resulting in very flexible applications.

Some elements, such as UILabels, will not respond to any UIGestureRecognizers unless their userInteractionEnabled property is set to YES.

The UIGestureRecognizer property state allows you to evaluate the current condition of any specific subclass as its gesture is recognized. It has multiple different possible values, each representing a possible step of the gesture recognition process:

1. UIGestureRecognizerStatePossible: Indicates a gesture is possibly in the process of being performed, but its requirements have not yet been met

2. UIGestureRecognizerStateBegan: Indicates a continuous gesture has been recognized and is continuing

3. UIGestureRecognizerStateChanged: Signifies a change to an already begun continuous gesture

4. UIGestureRecognizerStateEnded: Indicates a gesture has finished

5. UIGestureRecognizerStateCancelled: A gesture recognizer has received touches to cancel a continuous gesture.

6. UIGestureRecognizerStateRecognized: Equivalent to UIGestureRecognizerStateEnded

Especially when dealing with continuous gestures, you can run into an issue where several of these states cause a UIGestureRecognizer to perform its action, resulting in a method being called repeatedly unnecessarily. By checking the state property for specific states, you can help avoid this.

Ideally, you will set up a single method to be called by any and all instances of UIGestureRecognizer subclasses, and simply differentiate them inside the method. You can make use of the +isKindOfClass method, as well as the multiple properties of each subclass, and even the view the gesture was recognized in, in order to identify which of multiple UIGestureRecognizer objects performed your action. This action will have the following handler:

```
-(void)handleGesture:(UIGestureRecognizer *)gestureRecognizer;
```

Another useful functionality that all UIGestureRecognizer subclasses inherit is the ability to determine exactly where in a view the gesture was performed through the use of the -locationInView: and -locationOfTouch:inView: methods. By using these values, you can easily adjust your application's behavior depending on the specific location of a touch within a single view. One example of this would be to draw at the point of a user's touch, allowing users to essentially draw on their screen.

All subclasses of UIGestureRecognizer inherit the delegate property, which can be set to the view controller containing the recognizer's view. This property conforms to the UIGestureRecognizerDelegate protocol, and allows the view controller extra control in responding to gestures.

Multiple subclasses of UIGestureRecognizer allow for gestures that require multiple touches to be recognized. When dealing with these, it is important to keep in mind the maximum number of touches each device can handle. As of the writing of this text, the iPhone can handle up to five touches, while the iPad can handle up to eleven.

UITapGestureRecognizer

A UITapGestureRecognizer recognizes, as you can guess, when the user taps on its assigned view.

You are able to create very specific gesture functionalities by adjusting the numberOfTapsRequired and numberOfTouchesRequired. By setting both properties to 2, for example, you can look specifically for events of when the user taps the screen twice with two fingers. Your configuration would look like so:

```
UITapGestureRecognizer *tapGesture = [[UITapGestureRecognizer alloc] initWithTarget:self
action:@selector(handleGesture:)];

tapGesture.numberOfTapsRequired = 2;
tapGesture.numberOfTouchesRequired = 2;
[self.view addGestureRecognizer:tapGesture];
```

When you implement handleGesture:, you should make sure to look for the UIGestureRecognizerStateEnded state with any UITapGestureRecognizer.

UISwipeGestureRecognizer

The UISwipeGestureRecognizer recognizes when the user swipes across a screen with one or more fingers. The swipe is a discrete gesture, so its action is called only once.

The UISwipeGestureRecognizer class has the property direction, which specifies the direction in which the swipe must occur to be recognized. Possible values are

UISwipeGestureRecognizerDirectionRight, UISwipeGestureRecognizerDirectionLeft, UISwipeGestureRecognizerDirectionUp, and UISwipeGestureRecognizerDirectionDown.

This class also has a numberOfTouchesRequired, allowing you to specify multi-touch swipe gestures in your application.

UIPanGestureRecognizer

The UIPanGestureRecognizer class recognizes "panning" gestures, which are continuous gestures. As such, you generally perform actions with them in reaction to either the UIGestureRecognizerStateChanged or UIGestureRecognizerStateEnded states.

Pan gestures can be configured with both minimum and maximum numbers of touches, allowing you to create a range of allowable touch numbers. Use the maximumNumberOfTouches and minimumNumberOfTouches properties to implement this.

With a UIPanGestureRecognizer, you can access the distance moved, as well as the velocity of a gesture, through the use of the -translationInView: and -velocityInView: methods.

In most cases of using a UIPanGestureRecognizer, it is important to reset the translation and/or velocity values of the pan gesture after acquiring and using them. If you don't, your values will accumulate, resulting in abnormally large values very quickly.

The following is a sample implementation, extracted from your -handleGesture: method, to drag and drop the view that your pan was recognized in.

```
if ([gestureRecognizer isKindOfClass:[UIPanGestureRecognizer class]])
    {
UIPanGestureRecognizer *pan = (UIPanGestureRecognizer *)gestureRecognizer;
if (pan.state == UIGestureRecognizerStateChanged || pan.state ==
UIGestureRecognizerStateEnded)
        {
CGPoint movement = [pan translationInView:pan.view];
            [pan.view setCenter:CGPointMake(pan.view.center.x + movement.x,
pan.view.center.y + movement.y)];
            [pan setTranslation:CGPointZero inView:pan.view];
        }
    }
```

If you did not reset your translation to zero after moving your view, your translations would build up rapidly, violently throwing your view off of the screen.

If you experience a Linker error when using the CGPointZero value, add the CoreGraphics.framework library to your project.

UILongPressGestureRecognizer

The UILongPressGestureRecognizer looks for "long presses," which are simply when the user holds one or more fingers in the same position for longer than a normal tap.

Just as with several of the previous gesture recognizers, you can specify a required number of taps, as well as a number of fingers/touches used using the numberOfTapsRequired and numberOfTouchesRequired properties.

This subclass of UIGestureRecognizer has extra properties to configure the nature of the "long press." The minimumPressDuration specifies how long a touch must be held for before the recognizer's state turns to UIGestureRecognizerStateBegan. The allowableMovementproperty, which takes a float, specifies how much "wiggle-room" the user has before the long-press gesture fails. This value should be made large enough that a normal person can easily hold the touch, but not so large as to allow for significant movement that could cross multiple elements.

A UILongPressGestureRecognizer will trigger its action both when it begins and when it ends, which can cause unwanted behavior. Generally, you will want to respond only to the UIGestureRecognizerStateBegan state, so that the user can easily be notified that the gesture has been recognized.

UIPinchGestureRecognizer

This subclass of UIGestureRecognizer looks for pinch gestures, which involve a user moving two touches toward or away from each other. This class is continuous, meaning it stays active as long as the pinch is held, but has constantly changing values.

You are able to access two properties from each pinch gesture:

1. scale: The scaling factor created by the pinch
2. velocity: The velocity of the given pinch gesture

Depending on your use, you will want to look for different values of state.

UIRotationGestureRecognizer

This class recognizes a fairly uncommon gesture: a rotation. This gesture is composedof a user moving two fingers in a circular motion.

Information about the gesture performed can be accessed through the rotationandvelocity properties, similar to the UIPinchGestureRecognizer.

View Controllers

When you design iOS applications, you tend to organize your view controllers in fairly consistent ways based on the flow of data in your application. Built into Cocoa Touch are multiple special subclasses of the UIViewController class that allow you to easily organize, customize, and present your data depending on your type of application. By combining these controllers, you can create complex organizational schemes for your applications to present information to the user in the most optimized manner.

UINavigationController

The UINavigationController is by far one of the most commonly used classes in terms of workflow design and view presentation. It not only helps to organize transitions from one view to another, but also provides a highly customizable toolbar across the top of each view in order to help present and manage different parts of an application. These classes can then be placed into other organizational controllers, allowing you to create a nested flow of information from one level of your application to another.

A UINavigationController starts off with a "root view controller," which is the view controller that will be visible if no others are added to it. Then, other view controllers can be either "pushed" onto a stack of controllers, or "popped" off using various methods. Views in a UINavigationController's stack are displayed from the top down, so pushing a new view controller instructs the UINavigationController to display it. Likewise, when you pop off the current view controller, it is removed from the view, revealing the next controller in the stack.

Creating a UINavigationController is as simple as creating any other class. You can use a handy designated initializer called -initWithRootViewController: to set your root view, or you can simply call the -init method (after allocating), and then use the -pushViewController:animated:method to push in your root view.

Figure 3–20 features a configured UINavigationController with multiple elements.

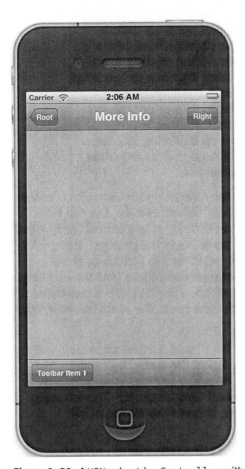

Figure 3–20. *A* UINavigationController *with left and right buttons and a toolbar*

The top edge of this view, presented in a UINavigationController, features the navigation bar. This area is meant to direct users in their navigation throughout your application through three features:

■ *Title*: The center of the navigation bar features the title of the presented view controller. This can easily be set in each -viewDidLoad method by changing the title property inherited from the UIViewController class. (e.g.,self.title = @"More Info"). You can also create a custom title view.

■ *Back Button*: The left side of the navigation bar, if the root view controller is not currently shown, automatically contains an arrowed button, and by default contains the title of the previously shown view controller, so as to help the user navigate back.

■   *Right Bar Item(s)*: The right side of the navigation bar is by default empty, but can be configured using either the `rightBarButtonItem` or `rightBarButtonItems` properties (the latter for adding multiple items). On an iPhone, you most likely will not have more than one or two small buttons here, but an iPad has space for a larger quantity. Usually buttons in this location provide options to manipulate or operate on information shown in the current view controller, such as a `UITableView`'s edit button or a button to open up a printing interface. The aforementioned properties are accessed through the navigation item, i.e., `self.navigationItem.rightBarButtonItem`.

The bottom edge of the view in Figure 3–20contains the navigation toolbar, which comes built into the `UINavigationController`. This toolbar is by default hidden, but can be easily shown by setting the `toolbarHidden` property on `UINavigationController` to `NO`, or by using the `-setToolbarHidden:animated:` method (to animate the change). Be careful when doing this, however, as the state of the toolbar, whether it is hidden or shown, remains the same across the pushing and popping of view controllers until the property is set again. This means you may have to make use of the `-viewWillAppear:animated:` and `-viewWillDisappear:animated:` methods in each view controller to show or hide the toolbar as appropriate.

The contents of the `UIToolbar` are easily set, not by the `UINavigationController`, but instead by the `UIViewController` that is currently on top of the stack. By calling `-setToolbarItems:` with each view controller in your `-viewDidLoad` methods, you can easily implement a differently configured toolbar in each view controller. The following example, taken from a view controller's `-viewDidLoad`, shows how an individual controller's toolbar can be easily built.

```
[self setToolbarItems:[NSArray arrayWithObject:[[UIBarButtonItem alloc]
initWithTitle:@"Toolbar Button "style:UIBarButtonItemStyleBordered target:nil
action:NULL]] animated:NO];
```

By simply changing the `target` and `action` to an actual value and selector, you will easily be able to implement functionality in your toolbar's buttons.

The `UINavigationController` also has a delegate property, which conforms to the `UINavigationControllerDelegate` protocol. Utilize this to gain extra control over actions performed right before and after view controllers are pushed or popped from the stack.

UITabBarController

Another special view controller, almost as ubiquitously used as the `UINavigationController`, is the `UITabBarController`. This class is specially designed to handle applications that contain multiple sections or "tabs," each with their own flow of information. The Twitter application has an excellent example of this implementation. Each tab can include other controllers, including `UINavigationController` objects, allowing for more complex networks of view controllers. The `UITabBarController`, however, should not be placed inside of any other controllers, as it is unsupported by the iOS API.

Each view controller in a UITabBarController has a tab, which by default is populated with the view controller's title, and no image. Creating a new instance of the UITabBarItem and setting it as the view controller's tabBarItem will override this, allowing you to add images and slightly customize your tabs.

The -viewDidLoad method for each view controller is not actually called until the specific tab containing that view controller is selected, which means that any configuration done in this method, such as setting a title, does not occur right away, leaving you with unlabeled tabs until they are selected. Setting the view controller's title when it is declared can simply solve this, though adding the title configuration into the view controller's designated initializer will work as well.

Figure 3–21 features a screenshot of a simple UITabBarController with three tabs, each with configured titles and system-based images, as well as the sample code used to create it.

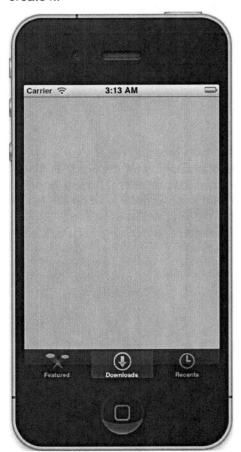

Figure 3–21. *A UITabBarController configured with three tabs*

This uses the following configuration code, taken from an -application:didFinishLaunchingWithOptions: method, assuming that two

UIViewController subclasses, MainViewController and SecondViewController, have been created and imported to the application delegate file.

```
self.viewController = [[MainViewController alloc] initWithNibName:@"MainViewController"
bundle:nil];
self.viewController.title = @"First";
self.viewController.tabBarItem = [[UITabBarItem alloc]
initWithTabBarSystemItem:UITabBarSystemItemFeatured tag:0];

__strong SecondViewController *second = [[SecondViewController alloc] init];
second.title = @"Second";
second.tabBarItem = [[UITabBarItem alloc]
initWithTabBarSystemItem:UITabBarSystemItemDownloads tag:1];

__strong SecondViewController *third = [[SecondViewController alloc] init];
third.title = @"third";
third.tabBarItem = [[UITabBarItem alloc]
initWithTabBarSystemItem:UITabBarSystemItemRecents tag:2];

__strong UITabBarController *tabcon = [[UITabBarController alloc] init];
[tabcon setViewControllers:[NSArray arrayWithObjects:self.viewController, second, third,
nil]];

self.window.rootViewController = tabcon;
```

UISplitViewController

The UISplitViewController is another element built to help organize other view controllers. This class, however, is available only when developing for the iPad, as it requires a large amount of space to utilize. It features two UIViewControllers, a "master pane" and a "detail pane." The master pane is displayed in a narrower view on the left side of the screen, with the remainder taken up by the detail pane, as in Figure 3–22. Generally this setup is used to select an item from the master pane and give details on that item in the detail pane.

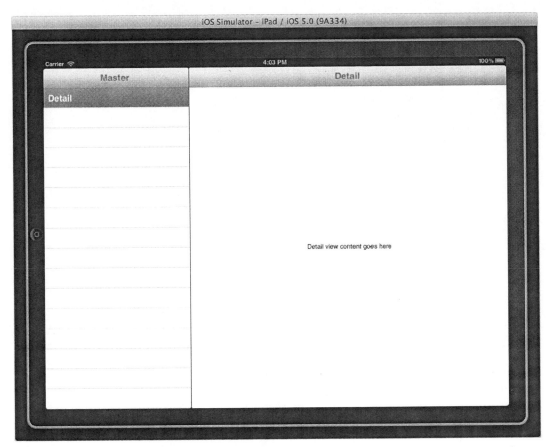

Figure 3-22. *The iPad-specific* `UISplitViewController`

Figure 3–22 shows a pre-configured `UISplitViewController`-based application created from the Master-Detail Application template. If you wish to build your application using this controller, this template can easily help you get started. This option can be found in the first menu presented upon creating a new project, shown in Figure 3–23. Like the Empty Application template, it also provides an option to include the Core Data framework and automatic setup.

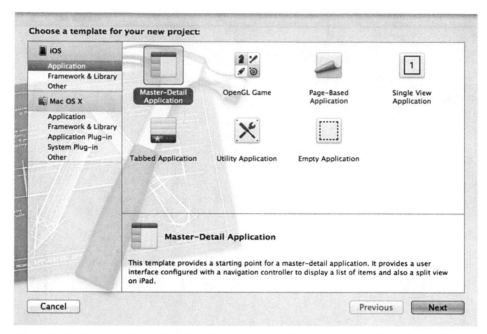

Figure 3–23. *Using the Master-Detail Application template to create a pre-configured* `UISplitViewController`

The `UISplitViewController` class has two properties, `viewControllers` and `delegate`. The former of these is an `NSArray` that must contain exactly two controllers: first the master pane controller, then the detail pane controller.

By default, if the iPad is portrait-oriented, the master pane is not shown. You can adjust this through the `UISplitViewControllerDelegate` protocol method -`splitViewController:shouldHideViewController:inOrientation:`.Generally the `delegate` property of a `UISplitViewController` is set to the view controller for your detail pane, as it contains the relevant information of your application.

When using a `UISplitViewController`, be careful to ensure that all parts of your view are clear in their related actions and controllers. Avoid placing toolbars in both panes, as they might appear connected. Make sure also that any selection made in your master pane visibly persists, so that the user can always tell which item was selected to display the current view.

UIPopoverController

The `UIPopoverController` class is an element specific only to the iPad. It is used to present information over top of your current view, usually to present options to users as to how they want to proceed. `UIPopoverControllers` are very convenient to implement as their location can easily be specified to any location, improving the visual flow of your application.

Figure 3–24 is from Chapter 13 (Data Transmission Recipes), Recipe 13–2,dealing with mailing and printing material, in which you presented a `UIPopoverController` from a `UIBarButtonItem` to select a saved image to display.

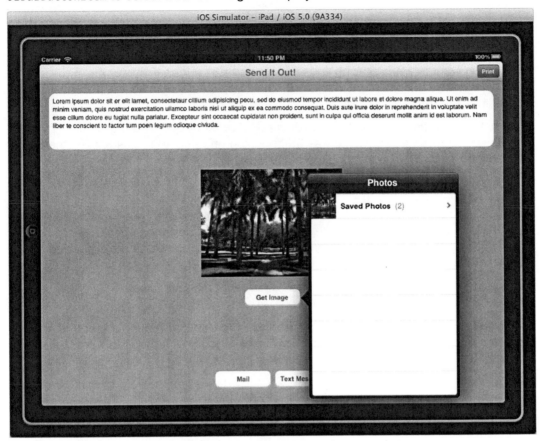

Figure 3–24. *Your example from Chapter 13 (Data TransmissionRecipes) of a* `UIPopoverController`

A `UIPopoverController` is easily configured to contain a content view using the designated initializer `-initWithContentViewController:`, and the content size can be configured using `-setPopoverContentSize:animated:`.If you wish to change the content view of a `UIPopoverController` while it is currently visible, you can make use of the -`setContentViewController:animated:` method.

The `UIPopoverController` class has a `delegate` protocol with methods -`popoverControllerShouldDismissPopover:`and-`popoverControllerDidDismissPopover:`. These can easily be used to make sure any user data is saved before a pop-over is dismissed.

When presenting a pop-over, you can make use of either the -`presentPopoverFromRect:inView:permittedArrowDirections:animated:` method, or the -`presentPopoverFromBarButtonItem:permittedArrowDirections:animated:` method. The former is generally used for presenting from any element in your main view, while the latter is used when presenting a pop-over from any item in a toolbar. Using these methods in their correct situation will drastically improve the visual organization quality of your application.

When designing iPad applications making use of a UIPopoverController, always keep in mind the overall visual quality of the view. Make sure your pop-over does not cover the entire screen, and that its arrow points to the element that caused it to appear.

Usually you want to avoid placing any kind of "dismiss" button inside of a UIPopoverController's content view, as the user can simply dismiss the pop-over by tapping outside of the pop-over.

If you have the option of displaying multiple pop-over controllers from a single view, try to write your application in such a way that opening one pop-over closes any others that are open, so as to avoid obscuring the entire view.

UIPageViewController

The UIPageViewController is a controller new to iOS 5.0, designed specifically to help organize applications that deal with multiple "pages" of content that are organized on the same level of information.

An instance of UIPageViewController has its content views set using -setViewControllers:direction:animated:completion:.

The spineLocation property is used to customize the visual animation method of your page turning. You can imagine your application as a book, with the spineLocation referring to the pivot point of your page turning.

This class also has two properties, a delegateanddataSource, thathelp to configure the page view controller. The dataSource, which conforms to the UIPageViewControllerDataSource protocol, allows you to specially configure your view controller's order through the -pageViewController:viewControllerBeforeViewController:and-pageViewController:viewControllerAfterViewController: methods. The delegateproperty deals more with the visual setup of the controller, with the UIPageViewControllerDelegate protocol method -pageViewController:spineLocationForInterfaceOrientation:.

Modal Controllers

Amodalview controller is any view controller that is presented "modally," meaning it is shown either on top of or in place of its presenting controller. These can be anything from a normal UIViewController subclass to a specific view element. The general use of any modal view controller is to either provide or request specific information from the user, so you generally will not want to modally present a controller that implements the main functionality of your application.

Modal view controllers are presented by other view controllers using the `-presentModalViewController:animated:` method. Changing the `modalTransitionStyle` property, inherited from `UIViewController`, can set the style of animation. This property takes the following possible values, whose names give excellent description as to their style:

- `UIModalTransitionStyleCoverVertical`
- `UIModalTransitionStyleFlipHorizontal`
- `UIModalTransitionStyleCrossDissolve`
- `UIModalTransitionStylePartialCurl`

The differences between these options tend to be fairly cosmetic, especially when implementing modal presentation on an iPhone, although the `UIModalTransitionStylePartialCurl`style will, instead of covering the entire view, reveal only the lower area in the modal view controller. This is good for providing small amounts of information, such as your developer's information, without having to populate the entire view.

If you make use of the `UIModalTransitionStylePartialCurl`transition style, avoid placing any `UITextField` or `UITextView` elements in the modal controller, as the keyboard will end up covering the entire modal controller, keeping your users from seeing what they are entering.

When developing on the iPhone, modal view controllers will always require the entire screen. However, on the iPad, you are able to customize the appearance of the controller in your view. The `modalPresentationStyle` property defines how your view controller is presented on an iPad, taking the following possible values:

- `UIModalPresentationFullScreen`: Presents the modal controller over the entire device screen

- `UIModalPresentationPageSheet`:Displays the controller with the width set as the device's portrait width, leaving the presenting controller visible on either side; the background is then dimmed to bring focus to the presented controller.

- `UIModalPresentationFormSheet`: Centers the modal controller on the iPad screen, at a smaller display size than the presenting controller; if the keyboard is visible, the view is shifted up to remain visible, and all uncovered areas are dimmed.

- `UIModalPresentationCurrentContext`: The view is presented exactly as its presenting controller is. This is particularly useful when dealing with a split-pane controller or other view that does not fill the entire screen.

Whenever implementing a modal view controller, you need to be able to dismiss it programmatically. Dismissal can be implemented by calling the `-dismissModalViewControllerAnimated:`method from either the modal controller or the presenting controller. If you wish to dismiss your view from the presenting controller, you will need to define a delegate method for your modal controller to call when it is ready to be dismissed. This method can also be used to pass information gathered from your modal controller back into its parent controller.

Temporary User Interface Elements

Many applications deal with instances where user input is required at various points in an application, but only at that certain point. For these situations, incorporating an element directly into a view as a permanent element becomes wasteful of the precious space that you have to use. Instead, you can make use of certain elements that are shown when input or output is required, and then are dismissed afterward.

UIAlertView

A `UIAlertView` is an incredibly simple yet effective class. Most of the time it is used to present information, though it can be configured to allow text input.

A `UIAlertView` has a property `alertViewStyle`, which specifies the type of alert presented, with possible values:

- `UIAlertViewStyleDefault`
- `UIAlertViewStyleSecureTextInput`
- `UIAlertViewStylePlainTextInput`
- `UIAlertViewStyleLoginAndPasswordInput`

The default style refers to a simple alert presenting information, while the remaining three all allow text input. Their names give a straightforward idea of their specific uses.

The simplest way to configure a Default-styled `UIAlertView` is through its designated initializer,`-initWithTitle:message:delegate:cancelButtonTitle:otherButtonTitles:`. The next example demonstrates the purpose of the configuration properties.

The following code will configure the `UIAlertView` shown in Figure 3–25.

```
UIAlertView *alert = [[UIAlertView alloc] initWithTitle:@"Title" message:@"This is our
message" delegate:self cancelButtonTitle:@"Ok" otherButtonTitles:@"Other Button", nil];
```

Figure 3–25. *A `UIAlertView` presented*

Once your `UIAlertView` is fully configured, it can be presented quite simply by calling the `-show` method.

```
[alert show];
```

The UIAlertView also has a delegateproperty, as you set in the initializer, which you have set to your view controller in this example. This property conforms to the UIAlertViewDelegate protocol. It contains multiple methods called upon the presenting, cancelling, or dismissing of a UIAlertView. More importantly, though, is its -alertView:clickedButtonAtIndex: method, which allows your application to specifically react to each different button pressed.

If you wish to manually dismiss a UIAlertView, possibly by some outside event or after a certain amount of time, you can call the -dismissWithClickedButtonIndex:animated: method.

In general, the UIAlertView is used to present or request information in response to specific events, such as changes in outside conditions that affect your application, or loss in availability of some service.

UIActionSheet

The UIActionSheet class is often used in cases of presenting a user with multiple options to choose from so that an application knows how to proceed. It consists of a variety of large labeled buttons, which can have certain colors depending on the nature of their effect on the application, as in Figure 3–26.

Figure 3–26. *A simple* UIActionSheet *configured with multiple buttons*

The UIActionSheet has a property actionSheetStyle. Unlike the similar property in UIAlertView, this simply determines the cosmetic style of the action sheet, with possible values:

- UIActionSheetStyleAutomatic
- UIActionSheetStyleDefault
- UIActionSheetStyleBlackTranslucent
- UIActionSheetStyleBlackOpaque

The automatic style will simply mimic, if specified, the visual style of the bottom bar. Otherwise, it will revert to the UIActionSheetStyleDefault value.

The simplest way to set up a UIActionSheet is through its designated initializer, initWithTitle:delegate:cancelButtonTitle:destructiveButtonTitle:otherButtonTitles:. The following line, for example, will reproduce the UIActionSheet displayed in Figure 3–26.

```
UIActionSheet *actionSheet = [[UIActionSheet alloc] initWithTitle:@"Title" delegate:self
cancelButtonTitle:@"Cancel" destructiveButtonTitle:@"Delete" otherButtonTitles:@"Other
Button 1", @"Other Button 2", nil];
```

As you can see, the Cancel button tends to be a darker color to indicate its result, as it is most often used to implement cancellation of some behavior. The Destructive button, however, is a bright red color in order to indicate that it usually implements some kind of method that will permanently delete user data.

When presenting a UIActionSheet, you must take into account the device being used. Due to the smaller screen of the iPhone compared to the iPad, a UIActionSheet will only ever be presented from the bottom of the view. On the iPad, however, multiple methods can be used to present the action sheet from any specified point, bar button item, toolbar, tab bar, or view.

The device being used also brings in certain considerations aboutbutton use. On the iPhone, tapping outside of a UIActionSheet does nothing, so a Cancel button is absolutely necessary. On the iPad, however, a user can usually dismiss the action sheet by tapping outside of the actual sheet. Unless the action sheet is being presented inside of a UIPopoverController, then a Cancel button is fairly unnecessary, and can be confusing.

Just as with the UIAlertView, you can manually dismiss a UIActionSheet using -dismissWithClickedButtonIndex:animated:.

Finally, your UIActionSheet'sdelegate property, which conforms to the UIActionSheetDelegate protocol, allows you to react to the presenting, cancellation, and dismissing of your action sheet, as well as the selection of each button. By implementing the -actionSheet:clickedButtonAtIndex: method, you can implement specific functionality in accordance with the selection of each option.

Summary

By this point, you should have an excellent understanding of the various elements of iOSdesign and development. We have reviewed the most commonly used design objects, and their general guidelines, as well as their most common implementations and little nuances of their use. Once you have a key understanding of the many options a developer has in creating anapplication, designing and creating useful, well-designed, and visually appealing products become simply second nature.

Chapter 4

Location Recipes

The Core Location framework provides a new way to provide information to applications that is relevant to where the device is geographically located. With the features of this framework, your application can accurately tell where a device is located and even what direction it is facing. There is a variety of applications that have successfully seized opportunities to utilize location-aware information, such as Facebook and Foursquare. iOS 5 continues to improve on the possibilities available and provides new features to convert human-readable locations into geographical locations.

There are three main capabilities that we will deal with in this chapter: location services, GPS, and the magnetometer. Location services are the bare essential functionality that allows your application to access the location of the user. On top of this, by using assisted GPS, you can greatly improve your location accuracy (often at the price of battery life). The magnetometer is included on certain newer devices, which allows an application access to both the heading and bearing of a device.

Supported Devices

The first thing you need to consider when you are planning to incorporate location-based services into your application is what devices will support those services. Not all Apple devices are created equal, or rather not all of them include the capability to support location services. Specifically, none of the iPod Touches includes a GPS, and they can provide the device's location only based on a WiFi connection (if available and connected). Refer to Table 4–1 to see the supported location capabilities of current Apple devices.

Table 4–1. *Location-Supported Devices*

	iPhone	iPhone	iPhone	iPhone	iPod	iPod	iPod	iPod	iPad	iPad	iPad 2	iPad 2
Assisted GPS	-	X	X	X	-	-	-	-	-	X	X	X
Magnetometer	-	-	X	X	-	-	-	-	-	X	X	X

Requiring Location Services

If your application is completely dependent on location services, you may want to prevent it from being loaded on a device that does not support location services. You can require GPS, magnetometer, or location services in general. Place these requirements only if these capabilities are absolutely critical to the functionality of your application. To configure these requirements, click the project in the navigator pane, and select your project target in the editor window.

If you wish to add these requirements to an existing project, select the Info tab and add a row to the Custom iOS Target Properties listing. You can add a row by clicking the small "+" icon to the right of the key name, or to the right of the name of any existing rows. The key you want to add is "Required device capabilities" or `UIRequiredDeviceCapabilities`. There is no difference between these two names, as the latter will automatically be replaced by the former. This key contains an array of values that reference device capabilities that are required for a device to run your application. Expand the key, and add the required capabilities as items in the key, as highlighted in Figure 4–1.

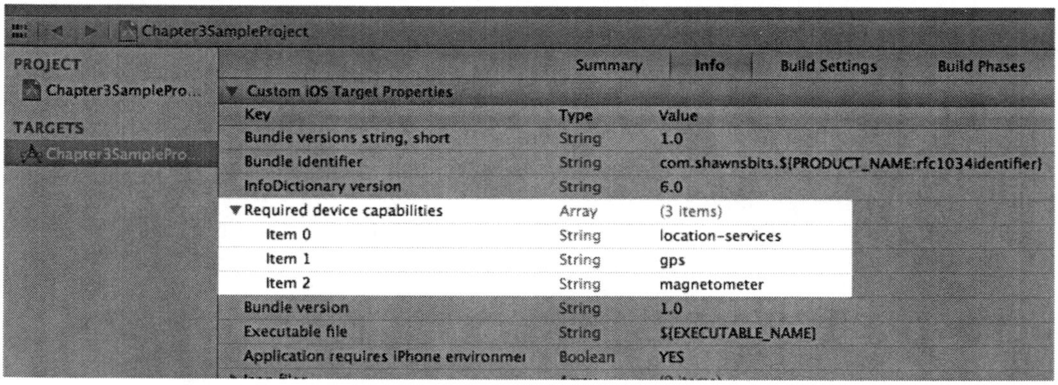

Figure 4–1. *Specifying required device capabilities for an application*

If you require just location services (i.e., knowing only the general location of a user without heading or GPS accuracy), adding the location services item alone is enough. If, however, your application requires GPS accuracy, then you may want to add the GPS requirement. If you include the GPS item, you should also include the location services item. And finally, if your device needs to know the heading of the device, you can include the magnetometer as a required capability.

How Do I Know Where I Am?

There are two primary methods for finding the location of a device: standard location service and significant location change service. Which one you use will depend on how accurate you need that information to be and how often you need to be notified that a device's location has changed.

The standard location service provides more accurate location information and will invoke the GPS if the accuracy requested requires it. This greater accuracy comes at a cost in terms of a longer time to get an accurate location and an increased drain of the battery. If you are going to use the standard location service, you should use it with precision and only when necessary. We'll discuss some best practices and techniques for using this service later in this chapter.

The significant location change service provides some flexibility and is recommended for most applications that don't need highly accurate location information. For instance, if you need to know only the town or city that someone is in, the significant location change service is perfectly acceptable. You will get a fast response without using a lot of battery power because it uses the cellular signal to determine the device's location. Another additional benefit of the significant location change service is its ability to run in the background on the device. Your app does not have to be running in the foreground to receive location updates from this service.

These two services work in very similar ways. They require a CLLocationManager object to be instantiated that sets up the location services and specifies how it is to be used. The CLLocationManager object will also have a delegate defined. This delegate should respond to at least two methods:

- locationManager:didUpdateToLocation:fromLocation:
- locationManager:didFailWithError:

The implementation of these methods for each service will be discussed in the recipes that follow.

Recipe 4–1: Getting Device Location Information

To get the most accurate location information about a device, you are going to use the standard location service. Let's start by creating a new single view application called Chapter4SampleProject to implement this functionality. If your version of Xcode allows you to specify a class prefix, enter **Chapter4SampleProject** again.

The first thing you need to do when adding location services to an application is add the Core Location framework library to the application. The location of frameworks has changed slightly from Xcode 3 to Xcode 4. You will now find them when you select the project in the navigator pane and select your project's target. Switch over to the Build Phases tab, and expand the Link Binary With Libraries area to see the included frameworks, resembling Figure 4–2. Clicking the + button will allow you to add the Core Location framework to your project, as shown in Figure 4–3.

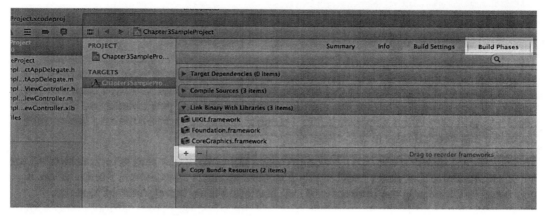

Figure 4–2. *Clicking the + button to add a framework*

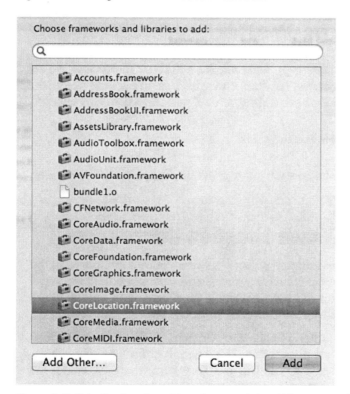

Figure 4–3. *Selecting* `CoreLocation.framework` *to add it to your project*

Now you're going to set up your XIB to display the location information. Click the `Chapter4SampleProject.xib` file in the navigator pane, and Interface Builder will be loaded. You're going to drag a `UILabel` and `UISwitch` object onto the XIB. The `UILabel` will be used to display the location information, and the `UISwitch` will be used to turn location services on and off. You're going to set the initial state of the `UISwitch` to Off in the Attributes Inspector tab of the utilities pane. Your XIB now resembles Figure 4–4.

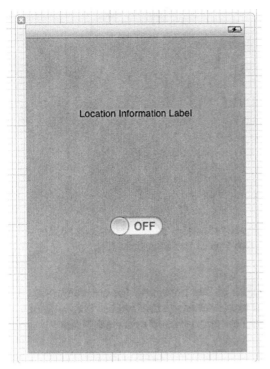

Figure 4–4. *User interface for displaying simple location information*

Now create some outlet properties and actions. Turn on the Assistant Editor, and select the UIView in the XIB. ^-click-drag from the UILabel to the interface file (.h) to create an outlet. In the pop-up that is displayed, name the UILabel "labelLocation", as demonstrated in Figure 4–5.

Figure 4–5. *Connect your UILabel to an outlet*

Repeat the same process with the UISwitch, but this time change the Connection type to Action and name the action "toggleLocationServices", following Figure 4–6.

Figure 4–6. *Creating an action to be performed by the switch*

Import the Core Location framework into the Chapter4SampleProjectViewController interface file (.h) by putting the following line at the top of the interface file:

```
#import <CoreLocation/CoreLocation.h>
```

You should also define a CLLocationManager object at this time, and for convenience, you will set the view controller to also be the CLLocationManagerDelegate. This object will act as your "hub" of action for dealing with all location-based services. Your interface file should now look like this:

```
//   Chapter4SampleProjectViewController.h

#import <UIKit/UIKit.h>
#import <CoreLocation/CoreLocation.h>

@interface Chapter4SampleProjectViewController : UIViewController
<CLLocationManagerDelegate> {
    UILabel *labelLocation;
    CLLocationManager *_locationManager;
}

@property (strong, nonatomic) IBOutlet UILabel *labelLocation;

- (IBAction)toggleLocationServices:(id)sender;
@end
```

Now that the interface has been defined, you can move to the implementation file (.m) and start implementing these methods and objects. The first thing you're going to tackle is the toggleLocationServices:sender: action. When the user touches this control, you'll want to check if location services are available to you. If they are not available, you will present an alert view stating that location services must be enabled to continue.

```
if(![CLLocationManager locationServicesEnabled]){
        UIAlertView *alertLocation = [[UIAlertView alloc] initWithTitle:@"Location
Error" message:@"Location services must be enabled for this feature to work"
delegate:nil cancelButtonTitle:@"OK" otherButtonTitles:nil];
        [alertLocation show];
        return;
    }
```

If the location service is available, you will need to check the status of the control. If it has been set to "on", you'll want to check if your CLLocationManager object has been instantiated. If it hasn't, you will want to instantiate it and set its properties and delegate. For the standard location service, you should always set the desiredAccuracy and distanceFilter properties of the CLLocationManager object.

The desiredAccuracy property tells the Core Location framework how accurate (in meters) you want your location information to be. The accuracy, however, is not guaranteed, and the device will try to use the resources available to it to get information as close to your desired accuracy as possible. Apple recommends being as conservative as possible with this setting. If you don't need to know the street address of the current device, use a higher accuracy setting. There are a number of constants available to use for your convenience:

```
kCLLocationAccuracyBestForNavigation
kCLLocationAccuracyBest
kCLLocationAccuracyNearestTenMeters
kCLLocationAccuracyHundredMeters
kCLLocationAccuracyKilometer
kCLLocationAccuracyThreeKilometers
```

As you can see, those constants that specify distances are restricted to the metric system. If you are not quite familiar with these distance units, a meter is slightly longer than a yard, and a kilometer is just over half (6/10) of a mile.

The distanceFilter property is how far a device has to move (again in meters) before you want to be notified (via your delegate) of its new position. The only constant provided for this property is kCLDistanceFilterNone, which will report all changes in location to your delegate.

One other property that you should always set when using location services is the purpose property. When the user is prompted to allow your application access to his or her location, the string in the purpose property is displayed, telling the user what you plan to do with his or her device's location information.

Once you've set the properties and the delegate, you can start the location services by calling the startUpdatingLocation method on your CLLocationManager.

Stopping the location services is a matter of calling stopUpdatingLocation on the CLLocationManager object. You will want to do this if they flip the UISwitch to off. After adding code to start and stop your CLLocationManager, your action method should look like this:

```
- (IBAction)toggleLocationServices:(id)sender {
    //Display an UIAlertView if locationServices are not enabled and return
    if(![CLLocationManager locationServicesEnabled]){
        UIAlertView *alertLocation = [[UIAlertView alloc] initWithTitle:@"Location
Error" message:@"Location services must be enabled for this feature to work"
delegate:nil cancelButtonTitle:@"OK" otherButtonTitles:nil];
        [alertLocation show];
        return;
    }

    //Future Proof: Make sure it's a UISwitch calling this action
```

```
    if([sender isKindOfClass:[UISwitch class]]){
        UISwitch *locationSwitch=(UISwitch *)sender;
        //Check if switch is "on"
        if(locationSwitch.on){
            //Check if _locationManager has been instantiated yet
            if(_locationManager==nil){
                //Instantiate _locationManager
                _locationManager = [[CLLocationManager alloc] init];
                _locationManager.desiredAccuracy=kCLLocationAccuracyBest;
                _locationManager.distanceFilter=1;
_locationManager.purpose=@"We will only use your location information to display your
present location.  We will not send it or record it.";
_locationManager.delegate=self;
            }
            //Start updating location
            [_locationManager startUpdatingLocation];
        }else{
            //Check if _locationManager has been instantiated yet
            if(_locationManager!=nil){
                //Stop updating location
                [_locationManager stopUpdatingLocation];
            }
        }
    }
}
```

The delegate methods need to be set up next. These methods are called when a location update is received or when there is an error getting the location. You will work with the error delegate method first. The most common source of an error is when the user is prompted to allow location services for your app and the user declines to allow your app access to his or her location. If this happens, you will stop requesting the location updates by calling the stopUpdatingLocation method:

```
-(void)locationManager:(CLLocationManager *)manager didFailWithError:(NSError *)error{
    if(error.code == kCLErrorDenied){
[manager stopUpdatingLocation];
    }
}
```

The delegate method that handles location updates is a little more involved. The method, - locationManager:didUpdateToLocation:fromLocation:, delivers three objects: the CLLocationManager that made the location update request, the newLocation, and the oldLocation. The two location objects are of class CLLocation. This object contains a lot of valuable information, including the location coordinate, accuracy information, and the timestamp of the location update. You will implement this method like so:

```
-(void)locationManager:(CLLocationManager *)manager didUpdateToLocation:(CLLocation
*)newLocation fromLocation:(CLLocation *)oldLocation{
    //Check to make sure this is a recent location event
    NSDate *eventDate=newLocation.timestamp;
    NSTimeInterval eventInterval=[eventDate timeIntervalSinceNow];
    if(abs(eventInterval)<30.0){
        //Check to make sure the event is accurate
        if(newLocation.horizontalAccuracy>=0 && newLocation.horizontalAccuracy<20){
            self.labelLocation.text=newLocation.description;
```

```
        }
    }
}
```

Before your app processes a CLLocation object, you want to check that the timestamp of the location object is recent. Core Location has a habit of presenting the last known location as the first call to the delegate method before it has a lock on the new location. There is no need to process a location object that represents the device's location at some point in history when you need to know where it is now. To do this, you can use code similar to the following to process only location events that have occurred within 20 seconds of the current time:

```
//Check to make sure this is a recent location event
NSDate *eventDate=newLocation.timestamp;
NSTimeInterval eventInterval=[eventDate timeIntervalSinceNow];
if(abs(eventInterval)<30.0){
    //...process event
}
```

The other property you need to check before you process an event is its accuracy. Again, there is no need to process an event if it is not within the accuracy bounds that you are expecting. It might be better to wait for the device to obtain a more accurate reading than to present bad information to the user. The CLLocation object contains two accuracy properties: horizontalAccuracy and verticalAccuracy.

The horizontalAccuracy property represents the radius of the circle, in meters, that the location could be located within. You can see this circle in the built-in Maps application when you are showing your location. A negative value indicates that the coordinate is invalid.

The verticalAccuracy property is how far, plus or minus in meters, the altitude of the device could be off. Again, a negative value indicates an invalid altitude reading. If the device does not have a GPS, the verticalAccuracy property will always be negative because a GPS is needed to determine the device's altitude.

Here is some sample code to handle horizontalAccuracy:

```
if(newLocation.horizontalAccuracy>=0 && newLocation.horizontalAccuracy<20){
    //...process event
}
```

One more property that I want to discuss is the description property. The description property returns the location information of a CLLocation object in an NSString format. It is a very easy method for seeing what location information is being returned by the device. I don't recommend showing this string to the end user directly, as it contains a great deal of information, and thus is not well formatted for display to the user, but it could be useful for debugging and verifying that location information is being updated and is correct/accurate. For this project, you have set your labelLocation text to the newLocation.description value, resulting in the previous completed delegate method.

With Xcode 4.2, you can now simulate location information in the iOS simulator. Prior to this fantastic feature, you would load up your application onto your test device and then go running outside to test out the location features. Most of the time you would miss something and have to do this over and over again. However, it certainly was a great way to get developers out of their chairs and into the sunlight.

Launch the Chapter4SampleProject on the iOS simulator. When you touch the UISwitch to "On", you will be prompted to allow this application access to your device's location. You will notice in Figure 4–7 that the string you set in the purpose property of your CLLocationManager is displayed. Click OK to continue.

Figure 4–7. *Your application requesting location permissions*

After clicking OK, you will notice that your labelLocation is not updating even though the UISwitch is on, as in Figure 4–8.

Figure 4–8. *Simulated application without any location data*

This is because you haven't started any location simulations yet. In the iOS simulator, go to the menu Debug ➤ Location ➤ Freeway Drive, and the labelLocation should start to update with information about the pre-recorded drive that Apple has provided. Figure 4–9 shows a sample of information delivered by the simulated drive.

Figure 4–9. *Displaying simulated location information*

Recipe 4–2: Significant Location Changes

The significant location change service provides two significant benefits: it is fast and it can run in the background. A lot of the code used between the two location services is the same, and the setup is virtually identical, but I will point out the differences. Let's start a new single view project named Chapter4SignificantLocationTracker, with an identically named class prefix if your version of Xcode allows.

Start by adding the Core Location framework to the project. If you need a reminder of how to add this framework, go back to the previous section to see the steps.

To enable background location services, you need to add a key to the Info.plist. Select the project in the navigator pane, and select your project's target. Switch over to the Info tab, and add a row to the Custom iOS Target Properties listing. The key you want to add is "Required background modes" or UIBackgroundModes. Now add the "App registers for location updates" to Item 0. Your result should resemble Figure 4–10.

Key	Type	Value
▼ Custom iOS Target Properties		
Key	Type	Value
Bundle versions string, short	String	1.0
Bundle identifier	String	com.shawnsbits.${PRODUCT_NAME:r
InfoDictionary version	String	6.0
Bundle version	String	1.0
Executable file	String	${EXECUTABLE_NAME}
Application requires iPhone environmer	Boolean	YES
▶ Icon files	Array	(0 items)
▶ Supported interface orientations	Array	(3 items)
Bundle display name	String	${PRODUCT_NAME}
Bundle OS Type code	String	APPL
Bundle creator OS Type code	String	????
▼ Required background modes	Array	(1 item)
Item 0	String	App registers for location updates
Localization native development region	String	en
Bundle name	String	${PRODUCT_NAME}
▶ Document Types (0)		
▶ Exported UTIs (0)		

Figure 4–10. *Specifying location changes as a required background mode*

You are going to set up the .xib file exactly as you did in the previous section, as shown by Figure 4–11.

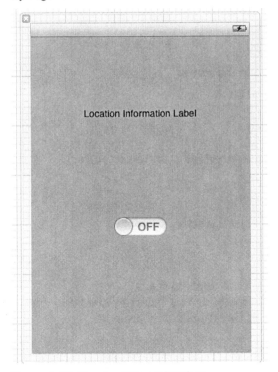

Figure 4–11. *Your familiar user interface*

Connect the location label to an outlet named `labelLocation`, and connect the `UISwitch` to an action named `toggleLocationServices`, as shown in Figures 4–12 and 4–13.

Figure 4–12. *Connecting your newest UILabel to an outlet*

Figure 4–13. *Creating your toggling action*

Your interface file (.h) is going to be set up exactly the same:

```
// Chapter4SignificantLocationTrackerViewController.h

#import <UIKit/UIKit.h>
#import <CoreLocation/CoreLocation.h>

@interface Chapter4SignificantLocationTrackerViewController : UIViewController
<CLLocationManagerDelegate>{
    CLLocationManager *_locationManager;
    UILabel *labelLocation;
}
@property (strong, nonatomic) IBOutlet UILabel *labelLocation;
- (IBAction)toggleLocationServices:(id)sender;

@end
```

Now switch to your implementation file (.m) and scroll down to the `-(IBAction)toggleLocationServices:(id)sender` method. You'll start by checking that location services are enabled and presenting a UIAlertView if they are not:

```
//Check if location services are enabled
if(![CLLocationManager locationServicesEnabled]){
    UIAlertView *alertLocation = [[UIAlertView alloc] initWithTitle:@"Location
Services Needed" message:@"Location services are needed to make this app functional"
delegate:nil cancelButtonTitle:@"OK" otherButtonTitles: nil];
```

```
        [alertLocation show];
        return;
    }
```

The rest of the code will be very similar to what you have done before, with a few exceptions. The first is that you do not need to specify the desiredAccuracy and distanceFilter properties. You should still specify the purpose property so users will know what you are going to do with their location.

```
if([sender isKindOfClass:[UISwitch class]]){
    UISwitch *locationSwitch=(UISwitch *)sender;
    if(locationSwitch.on){
        //Check if _locationManager has been instantiated
        if(_locationManager==nil){
            //Instantiate _locationManager
            _locationManager = [[CLLocationManager alloc] init];
            _locationManager.purpose=@"We will only use your location locally.  We
will not record it or send it to anyone";
            _locationManager.delegate=self;
        }
….
```

The other significant change is that you will call the startMonitoringSignificantLocationChanges method on the location manager when you are ready to start receiving location changes. So now your action looks like this:

```
- (IBAction)toggleLocationServices:(id)sender {
    //Check if location services are enabled
    if(![CLLocationManager locationServicesEnabled]){
        UIAlertView *alertLocation = [[UIAlertView alloc] initWithTitle:@"Location
Services Needed" message:@"Location services are needed to make this app functional"
delegate:nil cancelButtonTitle:@"OK" otherButtonTitles: nil];
        [alertLocation show];
        return;
    }

    //Future proof, make sure sender is UISwitch
    if([sender isKindOfClass:[UISwitch class]]){
        UISwitch *locationSwitch=(UISwitch *)sender;
        if(locationSwitch.on){
            //Check if _locationManager has been instantiated
            if(_locationManager==nil){
                //Instantiate _locationManager
                _locationManager = [[CLLocationManager alloc] init];
                _locationManager.purpose=@"We will only use your location locally.  We
will not record it or send it to anyone";
                _locationManager.delegate=self;
            }
            //Start updating location changes
            [_locationManager startMonitoringSignificantLocationChanges];
        }else{
            if(_locationManager!=nil){
                //Stop monitoring for location changes
                [_locationManager stopMonitoringSignificantLocationChanges];
            }
        }
    }
}
```

}

Now you have to set up the delegate methods. The simplest to define is the `-(void)locationManager:(CLLocationManager *)manager didFailWithError:(NSError *)error` method:

```
-(void)locationManager:(CLLocationManager *)manager didFailWithError:(NSError *)error{
    if(error.code==kCLErrorDenied){
        [manager stopMonitoringSignificantLocationChanges];
    }
}
```

For the `-(void)locationManager:(CLLocationManager *)manager didUpdateToLocation:(CLLocation *)newLocation fromLocation:(CLLocation *)oldLocation` method, you will do something a little different. In addition to updating the location label, you will also generate a local notification so that you can see when a location is updated while your app is not running.

You are going to start by performing checks to make sure the `newLocation` timestamp is recent and that it is valid (by checking that the `horizontalAccuracy` is positive):

```
NSDate *eventDate=newLocation.timestamp;
NSTimeInterval eventInterval = [eventDate timeIntervalSinceNow];
if(abs(eventInterval)<30.0){
    if(newLocation.horizontalAccuracy>=0){
        ...
```

If the app is running, you will not see the `UILocalNotification` unless you implement the delegate method `application:didReceiveLocalNotification:` in the app delegate. Instead of doing that now, you are just going to update the location label with the new location description while the app is open with `self.labelLocation.text = newLocation.description;`.

To create the `UILocalNotification`, you'll use the following recipe:

```
        UILocalNotification *locationNotification = [[UILocalNotification alloc]
init];
        locationNotification.alertBody=[NSString stringWithFormat:@"New Location:
%.3f, %.3f", newLocation.coordinate.latitude, newLocation.coordinate.longitude];
        locationNotification.alertAction=@"Ok";
        locationNotification.soundName = UILocalNotificationDefaultSoundName;
        //Increment the applicationIconBadgeNumber
        locationNotification.applicationIconBadgeNumber=[[UIApplication
sharedApplication] applicationIconBadgeNumber]+1;
        [[UIApplication sharedApplication]
presentLocalNotificationNow:locationNotification];
```

The complete code of your delegate method is as follows:

```
-(void)locationManager:(CLLocationManager *)manager didUpdateToLocation:(CLLocation *)newLocation fromLocation:(CLLocation *)oldLocation{
    NSDate *eventDate=newLocation.timestamp;
    NSTimeInterval eventInterval = [eventDate timeIntervalSinceNow];
    NSLog(@"Event Interval: %f", eventInterval);
    NSLog(@"Accuracy: %f", newLocation.horizontalAccuracy);
    if(abs(eventInterval)<30.0){
        if(newLocation.horizontalAccuracy>=0){
```

```
        self.labelLocation.text = newLocation.description;
        UILocalNotification *locationNotification = [[UILocalNotification alloc]
init];
        locationNotification.alertBody=[NSString stringWithFormat:@"New Location:
%.3f, %.3f", newLocation.coordinate.latitude, newLocation.coordinate.longitude];
        locationNotification.alertAction=@"Ok";
        locationNotification.soundName = UILocalNotificationDefaultSoundName;
        //Increment the applicationIconBadgeNumber
        locationNotification.applicationIconBadgeNumber=[[UIApplication
sharedApplication] applicationIconBadgeNumber]+1;
        [[UIApplication sharedApplication]
presentLocalNotificationNow:locationNotification];
    }
  }
}
```

Upon this new app, you will be able to receive local notifications for each significant location change, even while the application is not in the foreground. These changes will then be reflected in a notification badge on the app's icon, as well as a normal device notification.

Recipe 4–3: Determining Magnetic Bearing

Modern iPhones and iPad 2s now contain hardware, the magnetometer, which can be used to determine which direction the device is being held. The measurement is based on the device's position in relation to the magnetic north pole of the earth. The magnetic poles are not the same as the geographic poles of the earth. Magnetic north is located in Northern Canada and moves slowly by approximately 55–60km per year toward the west as the earth's core changes.

Implementing heading tracking is very similar to implementing any of the location tracking services we have discussed so far. You will include the Core Location framework in your project, create a CLLocationManager object, and define its delegate and delegate methods.

By default, it is assumed that the device heading is measured with the device held in portrait mode with the top of the device away from the user. You can change this setting by setting the headingOrientation property on the CLLocationManager object. The options for this property are as follows:

CLDeviceOrientationPortrait (default)
CLDeviceOrientationPortraitUpsideDown
CLDeviceOrientationLandscapeLeft
CLDeviceOrientationLandscapeRight

Let us start by creating a new single view application project named Chapter4HeadingTracking. If your version of Xcode allows for specifying a class prefix, supply "Chapter4HeadingTracking" again. You start by including the Core Location framework in your project by selecting the project in the navigator pane and selecting the project's target. Add the Core Location framework into the project just as you did at the beginning of the chapter.

Next you can set up the XIB to display your heading. Click the
Chapter4HeadingTrackingViewController.xib file in the navigator pane, and Interface
Builder will be loaded. Like with the previous recipes, you are going to drag a UILabel
and UISwitch object onto the XIB. The UILabel will be used to display the heading
information, and the UISwitch will be used to turn heading tracking services on and off.
You're going to set the initial state of the UISwitch to Off in the Attributes inspector
pane. Your XIB now looks like Figure 4–14.

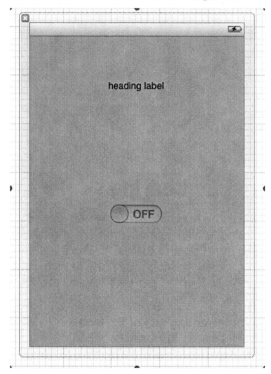

Figure 4–14. *Your still-familiar user interface setup*

With the .xib file laid out, let's create some outlet properties and actions. Turn on the
Assistant Editor and select the UIView in the XIB. ^-click-drag from the UILabel to the
interface file (.h) to create an outlet. In the pop-up that is displayed, name the UILabel
"labelHeading". These steps should resemble Figures 4–15 and 4–16.

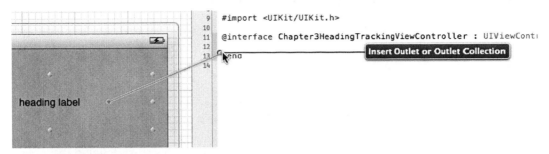

Figure 4–15. *Connecting a* `UILabel` *outlet*

Figure 4–16. *Configuring the label's outlet*

Repeat the same process with the `UISwitch`, but this time change the Connection type to Action and name the action "switchHeadingServices", as shown in Figure 4–17.

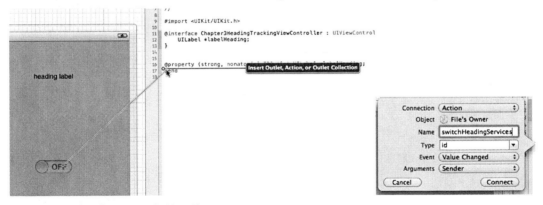

Figure 4–17. *Creating your switch's action*

In your interface file (.h) for `Chapter4HeadingTrackingViewController`, import the Core Location framework and set the view controller to comply with the `CLLocationManagerDelegate` protocol. Then define a `CLLocationManager` instance variable. The interface file should now resemble the following:

```
//  Chapter4HeadingTrackingViewController.h

#import <UIKit/UIKit.h>
#import <CoreLocation/CoreLocation.h>
```

```
@interface Chapter4HeadingTrackingViewController : UIViewController
<CLLocationManagerDelegate>{
    CLLocationManager *_locationManager;
    UILabel *labelHeading;
}

@property (strong, nonatomic) IBOutlet UILabel *labelHeading;
- (IBAction)switchHeadingServices:(id)sender;
@end
```

Switch to the implementation file (.m), and scroll to the bottom to start defining the switchHeadingService method. As with location services, you will start by checking that heading services are available by checking the return of [CLLocationManager headingAvailable]. Then you will verify that the sender is UISwitch:

```
if([CLLocationManager headingAvailable]){
        if([sender isKindOfClass:[UISwitch class]]){
            UISwitch *headingSwitch=(UISwitch *)sender;
        ...
```

If the headingSwitch is "on", you will check to make sure the instance variable _locationManager is instantiated and instantiate it if it has not been. When creating an instance of CLLocationManager that is going to track heading changes, you should specify the headingFilter property. This property specifies how far (in degrees) that your heading has to change before your delegate method is called. Then, as with the other location tracking services, you will specify the purpose property to tell the user what you intend to use the location information for and finally the delegate of the CLLocationManager. Once the instance variable has been instantiated, you can call startUpdatingHeading to start the heading tracking services, and you will also update your label so you can see the progress you are making:

```
if(headingSwitch.on){
                if(_locationManager==nil){
                    _locationManager=[[CLLocationManager alloc] init];
                    _locationManager.headingFilter=5;
                    _locationManager.purpose=@"We will use your location to tell you
where you are headed";
                    _locationManager.delegate=self;
                }
                [_locationManager startUpdatingHeading];
                self.labelHeading.text=@"Starting heading tracking...";
}else{
        ....
```

Next you will turn off heading tracking services if the switch has been moved to the off position, so the completed method looks like this:

```
- (IBAction)switchHeadingServices:(id)sender {
    if([CLLocationManager headingAvailable]){
        if([sender isKindOfClass:[UISwitch class]]){
            UISwitch *headingSwitch=(UISwitch *)sender;
            if(headingSwitch.on){
                if(_locationManager==nil){
                    _locationManager=[[CLLocationManager alloc] init];
                    _locationManager.headingFilter=5;
```

```
                          _locationManager.purpose=@"We will use your location to tell you
    where you are headed";
                          _locationManager.delegate=self;
                     }
                     [_locationManager startUpdatingHeading];
                     self.labelHeading.text=@"Starting heading tracking...";
                }else{
                     self.labelHeading.text=@"Turned heading tracking off";
                     if(_locationManager!=nil){
                          [_locationManager stopUpdatingHeading];
                     }
                }
            }
        }else{
            self.labelHeading.text=@"Heading services unavailable";
        }
}
```

The delegate methods need to be defined next. With heading tracking services, there are three delegate methods that need to be defined:

- locationManager:didFailWithError:
- locationManager:didUpdateHeading:
- locationManagerShouldDisplayHeadingCalibration:

The first method, didFailWithError, is the same delegate method you have implemented with the location tracking services discussed previously. You want to turn off heading tracking services if there is an error (most likely caused because the user is not granting you access to his or her location services):

```
-(void)locationManager:(CLLocationManager *)manager didFailWithError:(NSError *)error{
    if(error.code==kCLErrorDenied){
        [manager stopUpdatingHeading];
        self.labelHeading.text=@"ERROR: Heading tracking is denied";
    }
}
```

The next method, didUpdateHeading, handles when the change in heading of the device has exceeded your headingFilter property. In your instance, you are going to check the timestamp to make sure it is a recent reading, and then you are going to make sure the headingAccuracy property is positive. The headingAccuracy property will be negative if the heading is invalid. Finally, you will update the labelHeading with the magneticHeading reading.

```
-(void)locationManager:(CLLocationManager *)manager didUpdateHeading:(CLHeading
*)newHeading{
    NSDate *headingDate=newHeading.timestamp;
    NSTimeInterval headingInterval=[headingDate timeIntervalSinceNow];
    if(abs(headingInterval)<30){
        if(newHeading.headingAccuracy<0)
            return;

        self.labelHeading.text=[NSString stringWithFormat:@"Your new heading is: %.1f°",
newHeading.magneticHeading];
    }
}
```

NOTE: Use ⌥+⇧+8 (Option+Shift+8) to insert the degree (°) symbol.

The last delegate method you need to implement is
`locationManagerShouldDisplayHeadingCalibration`. This method determines whether
the heading calibration screen should be presented. This is the scene that prompts a
user to move his or her device in a figure-eight pattern so that it can calibrate the
magnetometer. I haven't run into an instance where I would not want to display this
scene yet, so I always return YES:

```
-(BOOL)locationManagerShouldDisplayHeadingCalibration:(CLLocationManager *)manager{
    return YES;
}
```

Figure 4–18 shows what the calibration screen looks like if the device is unable to easily
calibrate. When testing this application, you may not actually see this screen, but it is
important to have it enabled as a precaution.

Figure 4–18. *Heading calibration screen*

This is an application that will not work in the simulator. You will have to load it onto an
actual device to test it.

Recipe 4–4: Specifying True Bearing

You have figured out how to get the magnetic north heading, but what about true north?
The difference between magnetic north and true north is called declination. Declination
can vary greatly depending on where you are on the planet, but if you know where you
are, you can calculate declination. And with an iPhone or iPad 2, if the device knows

where it is located, the device will do the calculation for you and provide it in the trueHeading property of a CLHeading object.

To clarify, if you combine location-tracking services with heading tracking services, you can find out a device's orientation in reference to true north. All you need to do is also call the startUpdatingLocation method on your CLLocationManager to get the true north heading.

You can start a new project or expand on the project from the previous recipe. Select the Chapter4HeadingTrackingViewController.xib file, and add a second label for the true heading, as in Figure 4–19.

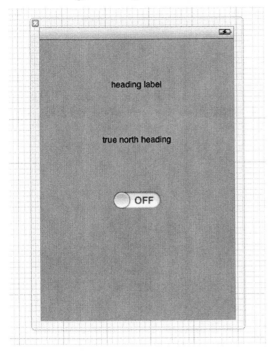

Figure 4–19. *New user interface with an added label*

Connect this new label to an outlet named "labelTrueHeading" by showing the Assistant Editor pane and doing a ^–click-drag from the label to the interface file (.h), as in Figure 4–20.

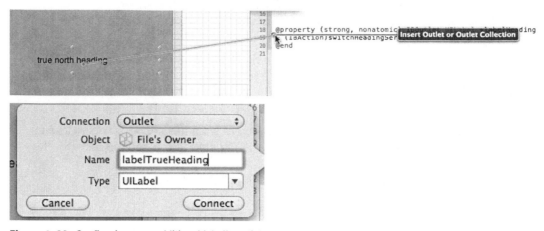

Figure 4–20. *Configuring your additional label's outlet*

Your interface file (.h) should now look like the following block. If your version of Xcode does not create the UILabel instance variables in addition to the properties, do not worry, as these are optional.

```
// Chapter4HeadingTrackingViewController.h
// Chapter4HeadingTracking

#import <UIKit/UIKit.h>
#import <CoreLocation/CoreLocation.h>

@interface Chapter4HeadingTrackingViewController : UIViewController
<CLLocationManagerDelegate>{
    CLLocationManager *_locationManager;
    UILabel *labelHeading;
    UILabel *labelTrueHeading;
}


@property (strong, nonatomic) IBOutlet UILabel *labelHeading;
@property (strong, nonatomic) IBOutlet UILabel *labelTrueHeading;
- (IBAction)switchHeadingServices:(id)sender;
@end
```

There are only some minor changes that need to be made to your code. First, you need to call startUpdatingLocation and stopUpdatingLocation in your switchHeadingServices method:

```
if(headingSwitch.on){
        if(_locationManager==nil){
                _locationManager=[[CLLocationManager alloc] init];
                _locationManager.headingFilter=5;
                _locationManager.purpose=@"We will use your location to tell you where
you are headed";
                _locationManager.delegate=self;
        }
        [_locationManager startUpdatingHeading];
        [_locationManager startUpdatingLocation];
        self.labelHeading.text=@"Starting heading tracking...";
```

```
}else{
        self.labelHeading.text=@"Turned heading tracking off";
        if(_locationManager!=nil){
                [_locationManager stopUpdatingHeading];
                [_locationManager stopUpdatingLocation];
        }
}
```

Now, in your didUpdateHeading method, you will add a new statement to check the trueHeading value. If the trueHeading is negative, it is invalid, so you want to use the trueHeading property only if it is greater than or equal to 0:

```
if(newHeading.headingAccuracy<0)
        return;

    if(newHeading.trueHeading>=0){
        self.labelTrueHeading.text=[NSString stringWithFormat:@"Your true heading
is: %.1f°", newHeading.trueHeading];
    }

    self.labelHeading.text=[NSString stringWithFormat:@"Your magnetic heading is:
%.1f°", newHeading.magneticHeading];
```

Your custom methods in your implementation file (.m) look like the following:

```
//
//  Chapter4HeadingTrackingViewController.m

#import "Chapter4HeadingTrackingViewController.h"

@implementation Chapter4HeadingTrackingViewController
@synthesize labelHeading;
@synthesize labelTrueHeading;
- (IBAction)switchHeadingServices:(id)sender {
    if([CLLocationManager headingAvailable]){
        if([sender isKindOfClass:[UISwitch class]]){
            UISwitch *headingSwitch=(UISwitch *)sender;
            if(headingSwitch.on){
                if(_locationManager==nil){
                    _locationManager=[[CLLocationManager alloc] init];
                    _locationManager.headingFilter=5;
                    _locationManager.purpose=@"We will use your location to tell you
where you are headed";
                    _locationManager.delegate=self;
                }
                [_locationManager startUpdatingHeading];
                [_locationManager startUpdatingLocation];
                self.labelHeading.text=@"Starting heading tracking...";
            }else{
                self.labelHeading.text=@"Turned heading tracking off";
                if(_locationManager!=nil){
                    [_locationManager stopUpdatingHeading];
                    [_locationManager stopUpdatingLocation];
                }
            }
        }
    }else{
        self.labelHeading.text=@"Heading services unavailable";
```

```
        }
    }

-(void)locationManager:(CLLocationManager *)manager didFailWithError:(NSError *)error{
    if(error.code==kCLErrorDenied){
        [manager stopUpdatingHeading];
        self.labelHeading.text=@"ERROR: Heading tracking is denied";
    }
}

-(void)locationManager:(CLLocationManager *)manager didUpdateHeading:(CLHeading
*)newHeading{
    NSDate *headingDate=newHeading.timestamp;
    NSTimeInterval headingInterval=[headingDate timeIntervalSinceNow];
    if(abs(headingInterval)<30){
        if(newHeading.headingAccuracy<0)
            return;

        if(newHeading.trueHeading>=0){
            self.labelTrueHeading.text=[NSString stringWithFormat:@"Your true heading
is: %.1f°", newHeading.trueHeading];
        }

        self.labelHeading.text=[NSString stringWithFormat:@"Your magnetic heading is:
%.1f°", newHeading.magneticHeading];
    }
}

-(BOOL)locationManagerShouldDisplayHeadingCalibration:(CLLocationManager *)manager{
    return YES;
}
```

Upon testing this application, you will be able to get a simple readout of your device's headings, both based on magnetic heading and true heading. Like the other recipes in this chapter that make use of the magnetometer, this functionality will work only on a physical device, and not the simulator.

Recipe 4–5: Region Monitoring

Core Location provides a method for monitoring when a device enters or exits a circular region. This could be used by an application to trigger an alert when a device enters the vicinity of a certain location, like triggering an alert to pick up milk when you get near the grocery store. You could also use it to send a notification to your family when you leave work to let them know that you are on your way home. There are many possibilities available if you let your imagination do a little wandering.

A Thing or Two About Regions

Regions are defined by a center coordinate and a radius measured in meters (again, a meter is just over three feet or a yard). The monitoring method triggers an event only when you cross a region boundary. It will not trigger an event if the device exists in the region when the monitoring starts. Events are triggered only when a device enters or exits a region.

Once you create a `CLLocationManager` object, you can register multiple regions for monitoring using the `startMonitoringForRegion:desiredAccuracy:` method. The regions that you register for monitoring are persistent across multiple launches of your application. If your application is not running when a boundary event occurs, your application is automatically relaunched in the background so that it can process the event. All of the regions you set up previously will be available in the `monitoredRegions` property of the `CLLocationManager` object.

Regions are shared system-wide, and there is a limited number of regions that can be monitored at a given time. You should always limit the number of defined regions that you are currently monitoring so as not to consume the system resources. You should remove regions for monitoring that are not near the device's current location. For instance, there is no need to monitor for regions in Maryland, if the device is on the West Coast. The error `kCLErrorRegionMonitoringFailure` will be presented to the `locationManager:monitoringDidFailForRegion:withError:` delegate method if space is unavailable when you try to register a new region for monitoring.

Welcome to Baltimore!

In this project, you are going to create a region for the city of Baltimore, MD and welcome visitors to the city when they enter it. You will start by creating a new single view application named "Chapter4RegionMonitoring". If your version of Xcode allows for the setting of a class prefix, use the same name of "Chapter4RegionMonitoring". The first thing to do is include the Core Location framework in your project by selecting the project in the navigator pane and then selecting the project's target. Go to the Build Phases tab, and expand the Link Binary With Libraries area to see the included frameworks, and add the framework as you have done in the previous sections.

With the library added, you can create the `.xib` file. Select the `Chapter4RegionMonitoringViewController.xib` in the navigator pane to open up Interface Builder. Add a `UILabel` and a `UISwitch`. Set the `UISwitch` initial state to "Off". It should resemble Figure 4–21.

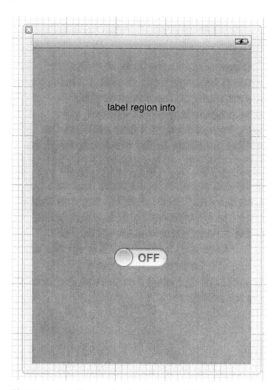

Figure 4–21. *Your quite familiar user interface*

Using the Assistant Editor, connect the outlets and actions by doing a ^-click-drag from the .xib file to the interface file (.h). Create a UILabel outlet named "labelRegionInfo" and an IBAction for the UISwitch named "regionMonitoringToggle", following Figures 4–22, 4–23, 4–24, and 4–25.

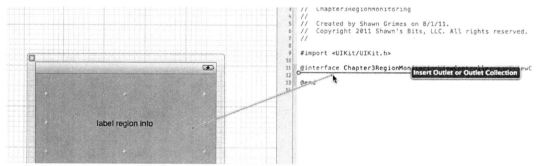

Figure 4–22. *Connecting a UILabel to an outlet*

Figure 4–23. *Configuring* `UILabel` *outlet*

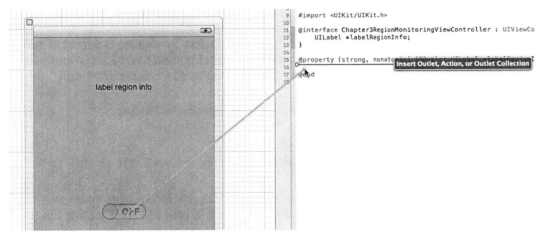

Figure 4–24. *Connecting a* `UISwitch`*'s action*

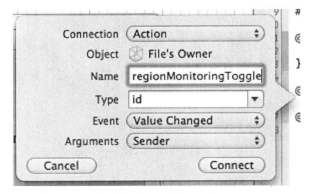

Figure 4–25. *Configuring the toggling action*

You need to import the Core Location framework into your interface file (.h) and create a `CLLocationManager` instance variable. Then declare your view controller as complying with the `CLLocationManagerDelegate` protocol. Your interface file (.h) for the view controller now looks like this:

```
// Chapter4RegionMonitoringViewController.h
```

```
#import <UIKit/UIKit.h>
#import <CoreLocation/CoreLocation.h>

@interface Chapter4RegionMonitoringViewController : UIViewController
<CLLocationManagerDelegate>{
    CLLocationManager *_locationManager;
    UILabel *labelRegionInfo;
}

@property (strong, nonatomic) IBOutlet UILabel *labelRegionInfo;
- (IBAction)regionMonitoringToggle:(id)sender;

@end
```

Switching to the implementation file (.m), you can implement your region tracking methods. The first thing you will make sure of is that region monitoring is available and enabled. Scroll to the bottom of `Chapter4RegionMonitoringViewController.m` and add the following to the - `(IBAction)regionMonitoringToggle:(id)sender` method:

```
//Check if region monitoring is available
if([CLLocationManager regionMonitoringAvailable] && [CLLocationManager
regionMonitoringEnabled]){
        ....
}else{
        self.labelRegionInfo.text=@"Region monitoring is not available on this device";
}
```

In the same method, you will want to instantiate your `CLLocationManager` instance variable if it is not already created and make sure that it is your `UISwitch` calling the method:

```
    //Check if region monitoring is available
    if([CLLocationManager regionMonitoringAvailable] && [CLLocationManager
regionMonitoringEnabled]){
        //Make sure sender is UISwitch
        if([sender isKindOfClass:[UISwitch class]]){
            UISwitch *regionSwitch=(UISwitch *) sender;
            //If UISwitch is turned On
            if(regionSwitch.on){
                if(_locationManager==nil){
                    _locationManager=[[CLLocationManager alloc] init];
                    _locationManager.purpose=@"To welcome you to Baltimore";
                    _locationManager.delegate=self;
                }
        ...
```

You need to define the center coordinate of the region you want to monitor and the radius of the region. Be careful when specifying the radius because if it is too large, the monitoring will fail. You can check to make sure your radius is within the radius bounds by comparing it to the `maximumRegionMonitoringDistance` property of the `CLLocationManager` object. Once you have the center coordinate and radius, you create the `CLRegion` object and provide it with an identifier for future reference:

```
CLLocationCoordinate2D baltimoreCoordinate=CLLocationCoordinate2DMake(39.2963, -76.613);
int regionRadius=3000;
if(regionRadius>_locationManager.maximumRegionMonitoringDistance){
regionRadius=_locationManager.maximumRegionMonitoringDistance;
```

```
}
CLRegion *baltimoreRegion=[[CLRegion alloc]
initCircularRegionWithCenter:baltimoreCoordinate
        radius:regionRadius
        identifier:@"baltimoreRegion"];
```

Once the region has been created, you can start monitoring for boundary events of that region by telling your `CLLocationManager` instance object about the region and setting the accuracy at which you want to monitor for the event:

```
[_locationManager startMonitoringForRegion:baltimoreRegion
        desiredAccuracy:kCLLocationAccuracyHundredMeters];
```

One last thing you want to do is turn off region monitoring if the user slides the `UISwitch` to the "Off" position. To do this, you will access the `monitoredRegions` property of your `CLLocationManager` instance variable and turn off region monitoring for all of the currently monitored regions. You could also choose to selectively turn off specific regions by utilizing the `identifier` property of the `CLRegion`.

```
}else{
                //If UISwitch is turned Off
                if(_locationManager!=nil){
                    for (CLRegion *monitoredRegion in [_locationManager
monitoredRegions]) {
                        [_locationManager stopMonitoringForRegion:monitoredRegion];
                        self.labelRegionInfo.text=[NSString stringWithFormat:@"Turned
off region monitoring fore : %@", monitoredRegion.identifier];
                        }
                }
}
```

The delegate methods need to be defined as well. There are two delegate methods for handling boundary events and one for handling errors:

`locationManager:didEnterRegion:`
`locationManager:didExitRegion:`
`locationManager:monitoringDidFailForRegion:withError:`

There are two main error codes that are related to region monitoring. One is `kCLErrorRegionMonitoringDenied`, and it is used when the user of the device has specifically denied access to region monitoring. The other is `kCLErrorRegionMonitoringFailure`, and it is used when monitoring for a specific region has failed, usually because the system has no more region resources available to the application.

```
-(void)locationManager:(CLLocationManager *)manager monitoringDidFailForRegion:(CLRegion
*)region withError:(NSError *)error{
    switch (error.code) {
        case kCLErrorRegionMonitoringDenied:
        {
            self.labelRegionInfo.text=@"Region monitoring is denied on this device";
            break;
        }
        case kCLErrorRegionMonitoringFailure:
        {
```

```
                    self.labelRegionInfo.text=[NSString stringWithFormat:@"Region monitoring
failed for region: %@", region.identifier];
            break;
        }
        default:
        {
            self.labelRegionInfo.text=[NSString stringWithFormat:@"An unhandled error
occured: %@", error.description];
            break;
        }
    }
}
```

Did enter and did exit can perform any function that you want, and since the application could be in the background when the boundary event occurs, you will use local notifications in addition to updating the label to let the user know the event occurred:

```
-(void)locationManager:(CLLocationManager *)manager didEnterRegion:(CLRegion *)region{
    self.labelRegionInfo.text = @"Welcome to Baltimore!";
    UILocalNotification *locationNotification = [[UILocalNotification alloc] init];
    locationNotification.alertBody=@"Welcome to Baltimore!";
    locationNotification.alertAction=@"Ok";
    locationNotification.soundName = UILocalNotificationDefaultSoundName;
    [[UIApplication sharedApplication]
presentLocalNotificationNow:locationNotification];
}
-(void)locationManager:(CLLocationManager *)manager didExitRegion:(CLRegion *)region{
    self.labelRegionInfo.text = @"Thanks for visiting Baltimore! Come back soon!";
    UILocalNotification *locationNotification = [[UILocalNotification alloc] init];
    locationNotification.alertBody=@"Thanks for visiting Baltimore! Come back soon!";
    locationNotification.alertAction=@"Ok";
    locationNotification.soundName = UILocalNotificationDefaultSoundName;
    [[UIApplication sharedApplication]
presentLocalNotificationNow:locationNotification];

}
```

In order to test this functionality using the iOS simulator, you must be able to feed custom coordinates in to be simulated. Like the freeway simulation in previous recipes, you can enter custom coordinates by navigating to Debug ➤ Location ➤ Custom Location…, from which you can enter your own coordinates to test with.

Recipe 4–6: Reverse and Forward Geocoding

Location coordinates are useful to applications, but they are not very friendly to human beings. When is the last time you wrote your address using latitude and longitude coordinates? It's just not human-friendly. Human locations are expressed in names that reference countries, states, cities, etc. So when a device's user asks, "Where am I?", the user doesn't want to know the GPS coordinates—the user wants to know what town or city he or she is in.

Fortunately, Apple has provided a method for converting location coordinates into a human-readable format. The method is called reverse geocoding, and the Core Location framework in iOS 5 provides it. In versions of iOS prior to 5, the Map Kit framework provided this feature.

Here are some best practices to be aware of when using reverse geocoding:

- You should send only one geocoding request at a time.

- If the user performs an action that will result in the same location being geocoded, the results should be reused rather than requesting the same location multiple times.

- You should not send more than one geocoding request per minute. You should check to see if the user has moved a significant distance before calling another geocoding request.

- Do not perform a geocoding request if the user will not see the results (such as if your application is running in the background).

- A device must have network access to perform a geocoding request.

Geocoding is performed using the `CLGeocoder` class. You instantiate a `CLGeocoder` object and then pass it a coordinate and a block of code to perform once it has performed the geocoding. This is a little different than the other location recipes discussed thus far that used delegate methods.

Let's create a new single view application that will tell us where we are called "Chapter4Geocoder". If you can specify a class prefix, use the same name of "Chapter4Geocoder". Add the Core Location framework to the application by selecting the project in the navigator pane and selecting the target. Now click the Build Settings tab, expand the area labeled Link Binary With Libraries, and add the Core Location framework as you did in previous recipes.

Select the `Chapter4GeocoderViewController.xib` file to load Interface Builder, and add a `UILabel` and rounded `UIButton` to the XIB, resembling Figure 4–26.

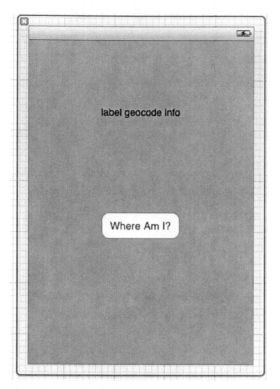

Figure 4–26. *Geocoding user interface*

Using the Assistant Editor, ⌃-click-drag the UILabel to the interface file (.h) to create an outlet named "labelGeocodeInfo". Repeat the process with the UIButton to an action named "actionWhereAmI". These steps are demonstrated by Figures 4–27, 4–28, and 4–29.

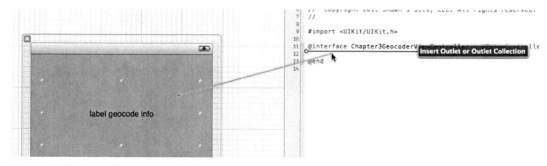

Figure 4–27. *Connecting your UILabel's outlet*

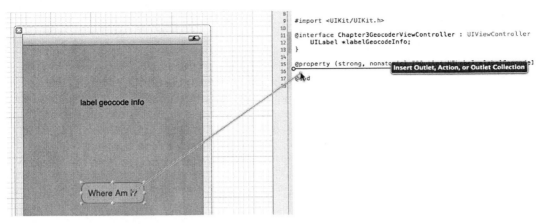

Figure 4–28. *Connecting a UISwitch's action*

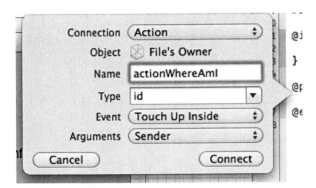

Figure 4–29. *Configuring an action's creation*

Import the Core Location library into the Chapter4GeocoderViewController interface file (.h), and define the view controller as complying with the CLLocationManagerDelegate protocol. This is used only to get the device's current location; it is not necessary for geocoding.

You will also create an instance variable of class CLLocationManager to get the current location of the device and an instance of CLGeocoder to perform the geocoding. When completed, the interface file should resemble this:

```
// Chapter4GeocoderViewController.h

#import <UIKit/UIKit.h>
#import <CoreLocation/CoreLocation.h>

@interface Chapter4GeocoderViewController : UIViewController
<CLLocationManagerDelegate>{
    CLLocationManager *_locationManager;
    CLGeocoder *_geoCoder;
    UILabel *labelGeocodeInfo;
}

@property (strong, nonatomic) IBOutlet UILabel *labelGeocodeInfo;
```

```
- (IBAction)actionWhereAmI:(id)sender;
@end
```

Switch to the Chapter4GeocoderViewController implementation file (.m), and scroll to the bottom to implement the method actionWhereAmI. Since this has been covered in previous recipes in this chapter, I'm not going to go into detail about this, but I will cover some highlights. You want to follow the best practices of geocoding and not geocode a location that is too near to one you have already geocoded or that is too recent, so you're going to set your distanceFilter property on your CLLocationManager object to 500 meters. You are also going to set your desired accuracy to the constant kCLLocationAccuracyHundredMeters so that you get a faster response from the location tracking services and limit the drain on the battery.

```
- (IBAction)actionWhereAmI:(id)sender {
    if([CLLocationManager locationServicesEnabled]){
        if([sender isKindOfClass:[UIButton class]]){
            if(_locationManager==nil){
                _locationManager=[[CLLocationManager alloc] init];
                _locationManager.purpose=@"To tell you where you are";
                _locationManager.delegate=self;
                _locationManager.distanceFilter=500;
                _locationManager.desiredAccuracy=kCLLocationAccuracyHundredMeters;
            }
            [_locationManager startUpdatingLocation];
            self.labelGeocodeInfo.text=@"Getting location...";
        }
    }else{
        self.labelGeocodeInfo.text=@"Location services are unavailable";
    }
}
```

Now you will add your delegate methods for the CLLocationManager object. The first is the didFailWithError method:

```
-(void)locationManager:(CLLocationManager *)manager didFailWithError:(NSError *)error{
    if(error.code==kCLErrorDenied){
        self.labelGeocodeInfo.text=@"Location information denied";
    }
}
```

Next is the didUpdateToLocation delegate method to be defined. You will start with the standard checks to make sure the newLocation timestamp property is recent and that it is accurate:

```
-(void)locationManager:(CLLocationManager *)manager didUpdateToLocation:(CLLocation
*)newLocation fromLocation:(CLLocation *)oldLocation{
    NSDate *locationDate=newLocation.timestamp;
    NSTimeInterval locationInterval=[locationDate timeIntervalSinceNow];
    if(abs(locationInterval)<30){
        if(newLocation.horizontalAccuracy<0)
            return;
    ...
```

You will check if the _geoCoder instance variable has been instantiated, and if not, you will create it. Then you will also make sure that you stop any existing geocoding services before performing a new one:

```
//Instantiate _geoCoder if it has not been already
if(_geoCoder==nil)
_geoCoder=[[CLGeocoder alloc] init];

//Only one geocoding instance per action
//so stop any previous geocoding actions before starting this one
if([_geoCoder isGeocoding])
[_geoCoder cancelGeocode];
```

Finally, you will start your reverse geocoding process and define the completion handler. The completion handler receives two objects, an NSArray of CLPlacemarks named placemarks and an NSError. If the array contains one or more objects, then the reverse geocode was successful. If not, then you can check the error code for details. The resulting didUpdateToLocation method is as follows:

```
-(void)locationManager:(CLLocationManager *)manager didUpdateToLocation:(CLLocation
*)newLocation fromLocation:(CLLocation *)oldLocation{
    NSDate *locationDate=newLocation.timestamp;
    NSTimeInterval locationInterval=[locationDate timeIntervalSinceNow];
    if(abs(locationInterval)<30){
        if(newLocation.horizontalAccuracy<0)
            return;

        //Instantiate _geoCoder if it has not been already
        if(_geoCoder==nil)
            _geoCoder=[[CLGeocoder alloc] init];

        //Only one geocoding instance per action
        //so stop any previous geocoding actions before starting this one
        if([_geoCoder isGeocoding])
            [_geoCoder cancelGeocode];


        [_geoCoder reverseGeocodeLocation:newLocation
                    completionHandler:^(NSArray* placemarks, NSError* error){
                        if([placemarks count]>0){
                            CLPlacemark *foundPlacemark=[placemarks objectAtIndex:0];
                            self.labelGeocodeInfo.text=[NSString stringWithFormat:@"You
are in: %@", foundPlacemark.description];
                        }else if(error.code==kCLErrorGeocodeCanceled){
                            NSLog(@"Geocoding cancelled");
                        }else if(error.code==kCLErrorGeocodeFoundNoResult){
                            self.labelGeocodeInfo.text=@"No geocode result found";
                        }else if(error.code==kCLErrorGeocodeFoundPartialResult){
                            self.labelGeocodeInfo.text=@"Partial geocode result";
                        }else{
                            self.labelGeocodeInfo.text=[NSString
stringWithFormat:@"Unknown error: %@", error.description];
                        }
                    }];

        //Stop updating location until they click the button again
        [manager stopUpdatingLocation];
    }
}
```

Upon testing this application, you should be able to receive the location, including street name, city, country, and other valuable information of the given device. This can of course be tested on a physical device, or in the simulator using the same location-simulating functions you have used previously.

Getting Coordinates from Place Names

iOS 5 has introduced forward geocoding as well. This means that you can pass a CLGeocoder object an address and receive the coordinates for that address as a result. The CLGeocoder processes address strings as a parameter, and the more information you can provide about an address, the more accurate the resulting forward geocode will be. If the geocode process results in multiple coordinates being identified as possible matches, these coordinates will be returned in the NSArray placemarks of the completionHandler. A sample implementation of this could be as follows:

```
CLGeocoder *_geoCoder=[[CLGeocoder alloc] init];
[_geoCoder geocodeAddressString:@"2400 Boston Street, Baltimore, MD, USA"
        completionHandler:^(NSArray* placemarks, NSError* error){
                for (CLPlacemark* aPlacemark in placemarks)
                {
                        // Process the placemark.
                }
}];
```

Summary

The Core Location framework is a powerful framework that can be utilized by any number of application features. As demonstrated in this chapter, you can determine where a device is located, which direction a device is facing, and when a device enters or exits a specific region. Beyond those powerful features, you can also perform lookups on geographical coordinates to determine human-readable location information to be presented to your end user as well as provide complementary services to perform the reverse.

Apple has walked a fine line of making powerful features available to developers while also respecting a user's privacy and the battery drain on a device. As developers, we should work to deliver exciting features and functionality in our applications while maintaining the same level of respect for our users. The use of the purpose property on a CLLocationManager object and judicious use of location services are steps in the right direction.

Chapter **5**

Map Kit Recipes

The Map Kit framework is an incredibly powerful and useful toolkit that adds immense functionality to the location services that iOS devices offer. The framework's key focus is the ability to place a user-interactive map in an application, with countless other features expanding functionality, allowing for a nearly entirely customizable mapping interface. iOS 5 has continued to improve the capabilities of Map Kit, improving developer capability and making map-based applications increasingly dynamic and useful.

For all projects in this chapter, as in all other chapters, make sure that ARC (Automatic Reference Counting) is enabled.

Recipe 5–1: Showing a Map with the Device's Location

The core foundation of any Map Kit application is the actual displaying of the world map. In this section, you will go over how to create a Map Kit application, display a map, and allow the map to show the user's location.

You will start by creating a new project using the Single View Application template, as shown by Figure 5–1.

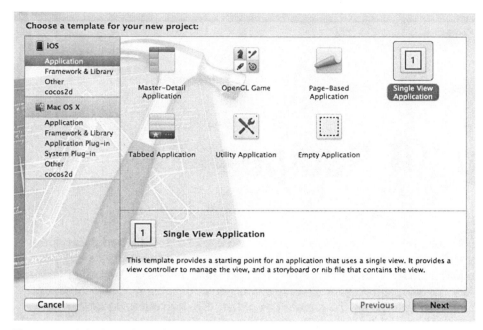

Figure 5–1. *Selecting a single view application*

Figure 5–2 shows the configuration settings you will use for this project. Your version of Xcode may also include a box for Use Automatic Reference Counting. Make sure this box is always checked. You can name the project Chapter5Recipe1.

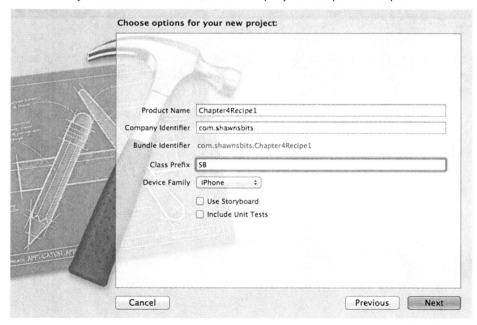

Figure 5–2. *Configuring your project*

To begin, you will need to add the Map Kit framework and the Core Location framework to the project. In the navigator pane, select the Chapter5Recipe1 project file, and then make sure the Chapter5Recipe1 target is selected in the Editor view (if not already selected). Click the Build Phases tab, and expand the Link Binary With Libraries section. Click the + button to add the frameworks to the labels, as highlighted in Figure 5–3, and use the resulting pop-up resembling Figure 5–4 to add the required frameworks.

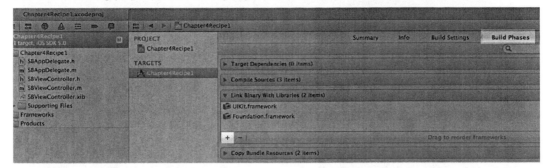

Figure 5–3. *Clicking the + button to add a framework*

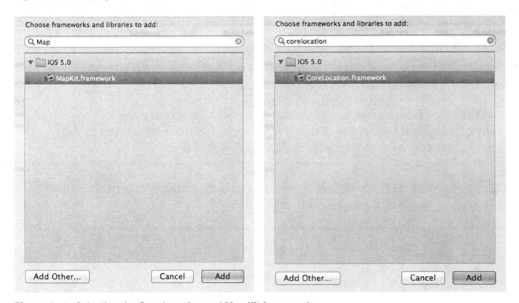

Figure 5–4. *Selecting the Core Location and Map Kit frameworks*

Now that the frameworks have been added, you can start to build your interface. Select the view controller's .xib file from the navigation pane, and drag a MKMapView from the objects browser to the workspace so that it fills the view.

Next, add a UILabel on top of the MKMapView that will be used to display the device's latitude and longitude. Figure 5–5 shows an example of what your user interface will resemble.

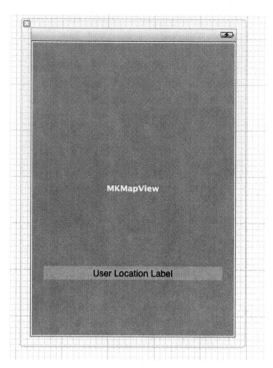

Figure 5–5. .*xib file with* MKMapView *and* UILabel

Using the Assistant Editor, drag a connection from the MKMapView to the SBViewController interface file (.h) with a ^-click-drag from the MKMapView to the SBViewController file, as demonstrated in Figures 5–6 and 5–7.

> **NOTE:** If the interface file is not shown in the second pane of the Assistant Editor, make sure you click your view controller in the workspace.

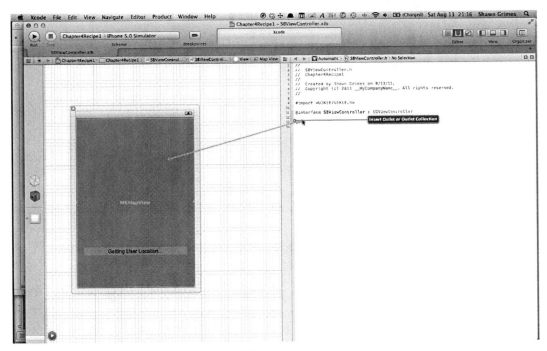

Figure 5–6. *Connecting the* `MKMapView` *to an outlet*

Name the `MKMapView` outlet "mapViewUserMap".

Figure 5–7. *Configuring the map view outlet*

Repeat the same steps with the `UILabel`, and name the outlet "labelUserLocation".

Your user interface is fully set up, so you can simply focus on the interface file (.h) now. Select the `SBViewController.h` file in the navigation pane. There are two additions you need to make to this class interface before moving to the implementation file. The first is to add the `MapKit/MapKit.h` framework library to the class with an import statement, and the second is to define the class as complying with the `MKMapViewDelegate` protocol. Apple recommends that when you use a `MapView`, you should assign it a delegate object. The completed interface file (.h) looks like this:

```
// SBViewController.h
// Chapter5Recipe1
```

```
#import <UIKit/UIKit.h>
#import <MapKit/MapKit.h>

@interface SBViewController : UIViewController <MKMapViewDelegate> {
    MKMapView *mapViewUserMap;
    UILabel *labelUserLocation;
}

@property (strong, nonatomic) IBOutlet MKMapView *mapViewUserMap;
@property (strong, nonatomic) IBOutlet UILabel *labelUserLocation;

@end
```

Switch to the implementation file, SBViewController.m, and let's start by setting up the MKMapView in the viewDidLoad method. Whenever you use an MKMapView object, you should set its delegate and its region.

The region is the portion of the map that is currently being displayed. The region consists of a center coordinate and a distance in latitude and longitude to show surrounding the center coordinate. If you are like most people, you don't think of distances in latitudinal and longitudinal degrees, so you can use the method MKCoordinateRegionMakeWithDistance to create a region using a center coordinate and meters surrounding the coordinate. If you are unfamiliar with the metric system, a meter is just a tiny bit longer than a yard.

In this recipe, I chose to start with the map initially panned to show my hometown of Baltimore, MD. I define a coordinate for this location and then define a region that contains the area 10km x 10km around this center coordinate.

```
//Set MKMapView delegate
self.mapViewUserMap.delegate=self;

//Set MKMapView starting region
CLLocationCoordinate2D coordinateBaltimore = CLLocationCoordinate2DMake(39.303, -
76.612);
self.mapViewUserMap.region=
    MKCoordinateRegionMakeWithDistance(coordinateBaltimore,
                                       10000,
                                       10000);
```

Two optional properties worth mentioning are .zoomEnabled and .scrollEnabled. These two properties control the interactions a user can have with the map. They can prevent a user from zooming or panning a map, respectively.

```
//Optional Controls
//    self.mapViewUserMap.zoomEnabled=NO;
//    self.mapViewUserMap.scrollEnabled=NO;
```

Finally, you will define the map as showing the user's location. This is easily done with the .showUserLocation property. Setting this property to YES will start the Core Location tracking methods and prompt the user to authorize location tracking for this application.

> **NOTE:** Just because showUserLocation is set to YES, the user's location is not automatically visible on the map. To determine if the location is visible in the current region of the map, use the property userLocationVisible.

After you have told the map that you want to show the user location, you can also tell the map to track the user location by setting the .userTrackingMode property or using the method setUserTrackingMode:animated:. This property accepts three possible values:

- MKUserTrackingModeNone: Does not track the user's location; the map can be moved to a region that does not contain the user's location.

- MKUserTrackingModeFollow: Map will be panned to keep the user's location at the center. The top of the map will be North. If the user pans the map manually, tracking will stop.

- MKUserTrackingModeFollowWithHeading: Map will be panned to keep the user's location at the center, and the map will be rotated so that the user's heading is at the top of the map. If the user pans the map manually, tracking will stop.

Initially, you are going to set userTrackingMode to MKUserTrackingModeFollow, but later I will show how to give users the ability to control the tracking mode themselves. The following if statement will confirm that location services have already been enabled on the device.

```
//Control User Location on Map
if ([CLLocationManager locationServicesEnabled])
{
    mapViewUserMap.showsUserLocation = YES;
    [mapViewUserMap setUserTrackingMode:MKUserTrackingModeFollow animated:YES];
}
```

In whole, your viewDidLoad method looks like the following:

```
- (void)viewDidLoad
{
    [super viewDidLoad];

    //Set MKMapView delegate
    self.mapViewUserMap.delegate=self;

    //Set MKMapView starting region
    CLLocationCoordinate2D coordinateBaltimore = CLLocationCoordinate2DMake(39.303, -
76.612);
    self.mapViewUserMap.region=
        MKCoordinateRegionMakeWithDistance(coordinateBaltimore,
                                           10000,
                                           10000);

    //Optional Controls
//    self.mapViewUserMap.zoomEnabled=NO;
```

```
//    self.mapViewUserMap.scrollEnabled=NO;

    //Control User Location on Map
    if ([CLLocationManager locationServicesEnabled])
    {
        mapViewUserMap.showsUserLocation = YES;
        [mapViewUserMap setUserTrackingMode:MKUserTrackingModeFollow animated:YES];
    }
}
```

The next important thing is the `viewDidUnload` method. Whenever you set a delegate for an object, you should set the delegate = nil before you release the object in order to avoid any memory issues. So you'll need to add a line in your `viewDidUnload` to set the delegate to nil on `self.mapViewUserMap`:

```
- (void)viewDidUnload
{
    self.mapViewUserMap.delegate=nil;
    [self setMapViewUserMap:nil];
    [self setLabelUserLocation:nil];
    [super viewDidUnload];
}
```

The last thing you will do is set up one of the `mapView` delegate methods to update the label with the user's current location. You will use the `-mapView:didUpdateUserLocation:` delegate method. Your implementation of the method will look like this:

```
-(void)mapView:(MKMapView *)mapView didUpdateUserLocation:(MKUserLocation
*)userLocation{
    self.labelUserLocation.text=
        [NSString
            stringWithFormat:@"Current Location: %.5f°, %.5f°",
                userLocation.coordinate.latitude,
                userLocation.coordinate.longitude];
}
```

You have enough of a start that you can now run your app on the simulator. You can run the app by using the keyboard shortcut ⌘R. When the app launches on the simulator, the user will be prompted to allow the app access to his or her location. Figure 5–8 shows your application displaying this exact prompt.

Figure 5–8. *App's prompt to access location*

If you click OK and you are looking at the city of Baltimore on your device (and there is no sign of your location on the map), then you may need to start the location debug services. On the simulator, go to the menu option **Debug ➤ Location ➤ Freeway Drive**, and this will start the location simulation services on the simulator. The map should pan to the new location (a drive recorded in California) and update the location label.

One of the problems users will experience with this recipe is if they try to manually pan the map, the user location tracking stops. Apple has provided a new UIBarButtonItem class named MKUserTrackingBarButtonItem. This button can be added to any UIToolBar or UINavigationbar and will toggle the user tracking modes on the specified map view.

You initialize the MKUserTrackingBarButtonItem by passing it the MKMapView that you want it to control with the initWithMapView: method.

To set this up, you'll add a UIToolbar to your .xib file in Interface Builder and create an outlet for it named "toolbarMapTools". You can delete the default BarButtonItem it adds to the toolbar or your viewDidLoad method will override it. If you delete it from the .xib file, your user interface will now resemble Figure 5–9.

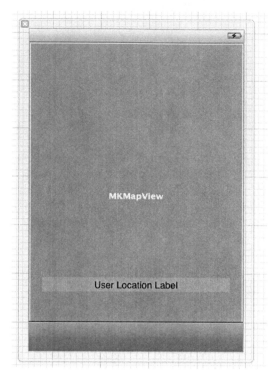

Figure 5–9. *Adding a toolbar to the bottom of the* .xib

Now you will add your MKUserTrackingBarButtonItem in code. Switch to the view controller implementation file, SBViewController.m, and scroll to the viewDidLoad method. Add the following code at the bottom of viewDidLoad:

```
//Create BarButtonItem for controller user location tracking
MKUserTrackingBarButtonItem *trackingBarButton =
    [[MKUserTrackingBarButtonItem alloc] initWithMapView:self.mapViewUserMap];

//Add UserTrackingBarButtonItem to UIToolbar
[self.toolbarMapTools
    setItems:[NSArray arrayWithObject:trackingBarButton]
    animated:YES];
```

With this new add-on, users can manually pan the map and then get back to tracking their location with the push of this new bar button. Figure 5–10 demonstrates the user-tracking functionality you have implemented.

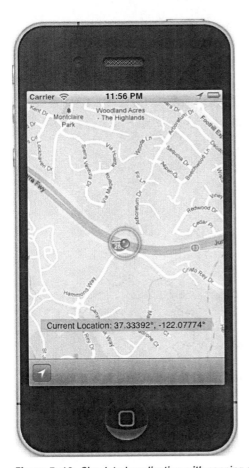

Figure 5–10. *Simulated application with panning and user tracking*

> **NOTE:** MKUserLocationFollowWithHeading is not functional in the iOS Simulator.

Recipe 5–2: Marking Locations with Pins

Often, one of the most useful things about having a map is to see not only where the user is, but also where whatever the user is looking for is as well. To do this, you add annotations to your map. This recipe will build on top of the previous recipe.

First, you need to define your annotations by creating a subclass of NSObject. To do this, go to File ➤ New ➤ New File, and under the Cocoa Touch category, choose "Objective-C class," as in Figure 5–11.

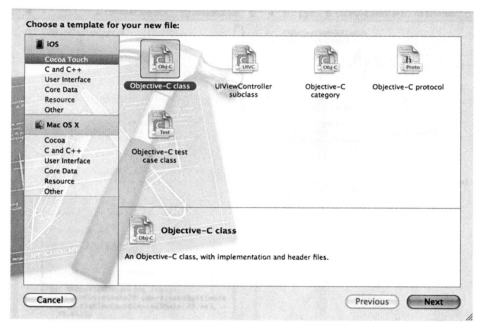

Figure 5–11. *Creating an Objective-C class to act as an annotation*

Name your class something clear like "MyAnnotation", and make sure it is a subclass of NSObject, as shown in Figure 5–12.

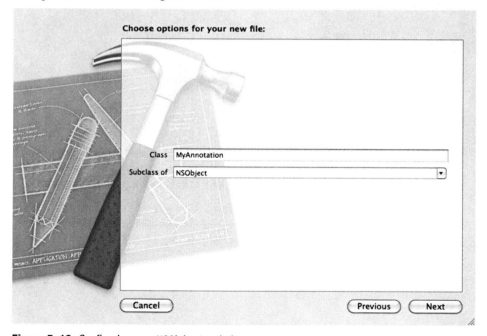

Figure 5–12. *Configuring your NSObject subclass*

Click Next and then Create to add the class to your project.

The next thing to do is set up your MyAnnotation to conform to the MKAnnotation protocol. This will require an import statement for <MapKit/MapKit.h> in your header file, as well as a required coordinate property. You will also be implementing the optional title and subtitle properties, and creating an initWithCoordinate method. The code to do this is as follows:

```
#import <Foundation/Foundation.h>
#import <MapKit/MapKit.h>

@interface MyAnnotation : NSObject <MKAnnotation>
{
    NSString *title;
    NSString *subtitle;
}

@property (nonatomic) CLLocationCoordinate2D coordinate;
@property (nonatomic, copy) NSString *title;
@property (nonatomic, copy) NSString *subtitle;

-(id) initWithCoordinate:(CLLocationCoordinate2D) aCoordinate;

@end
```

Make sure to synthesize these three properties in your MyAnnotation.m implementation file. This file will read like so:

```
#import "MyAnnotation.h"

@implementation MyAnnotation

@synthesize coordinate, title, subtitle;

-(id) initWithCoordinate:(CLLocationCoordinate2D) aCoordinate
{
    self=[super init];
     if (self){
        coordinate = aCoordinate;
    }
    return self;
}

@end
```

Now you need to define how your MKMapView deals with annotations back in your view controller's implementation file. To do this, you will implement the following -mapView:viewForAnnotation: method. This method is quite similar to that used to make views for TableView cells. Be sure to import your MyAnnotation.h file into your view controller, or this will not compile.

```
- (MKAnnotationView *)mapView:(MKMapView *)mapView
viewForAnnotation:(id<MKAnnotation>)annotation
{
    if ([annotation isKindOfClass:[MyAnnotation class]]) //Ensures the User's location
is not affected.
    {
```

```
        static NSString *annotationIdentifier=@"annotationIdentifier";
        //Try to get an unused annotation, similar to uitableviewcells
        MKAnnotationView *annotationView=[self.mapViewUserMap
dequeueReusableAnnotationViewWithIdentifier:annotationIdentifier];
        annotationView.annotation = annotation;
        //If one isn't available, create a new one
        if(!annotationView)
        {
            annotationView=[[MKPinAnnotationView alloc] initWithAnnotation:annotation
reuseIdentifier:annotationIdentifier];
        }

        //Optional properties to change
        annotationView.canShowCallout = YES;
        annotationView.rightCalloutAccessoryView = [UIButton
buttonWithType:UIButtonTypeDetailDisclosure]; //Creates button on right of callout
        return annotationView;
    }
    return nil;
}
```

Your two optional properties, canShowCallout and rightCalloutAccessoryView, are very useful for making interactive maps. The first causes a small callout to pop up if a pin is pressed, and the second changes the appearance of the right side of the callout. By default, the text in the callout will be the title and subtitle of the annotation, meaning that if you intend to show callouts, your annotations should have at least a title.

Finally, the last thing to do is to create your annotations with their information and add them to the map. You create a mutable array to store your annotations, and then add the array of annotations to your mapView, as follows. This code goes in your viewDidLoad method.

```
//Create and add Annotations
    NSMutableArray *annotations = [[NSMutableArray alloc] initWithCapacity:2];
    MyAnnotation *ann1 = [[MyAnnotation alloc]
initWithCoordinate:CLLocationCoordinate2DMake(25.802, -80.132)];
    ann1.title = @"Miami";
    ann1.subtitle = @"Annotation1";
    MyAnnotation *ann2 = [[MyAnnotation alloc]
initWithCoordinate:CLLocationCoordinate2DMake(39.733, -105.018)];
    ann2.title = @"Denver";
    ann2.subtitle = @"Annotation2";
    [annotations addObject:ann1];
    [annotations addObject:ann2];

    [self.mapViewUserMap addAnnotations:annotations];
```

I chose to make your pins drop in Miami and Denver, but any coordinates will work just as well. If you run this app now, you should see your normal map, but with a couple of pins stuck in, as in Figure 5–13. You will probably need to zoom out in order to see them; this can be done in the simulator by holding ⌥, to simulate a pinch, and dragging.

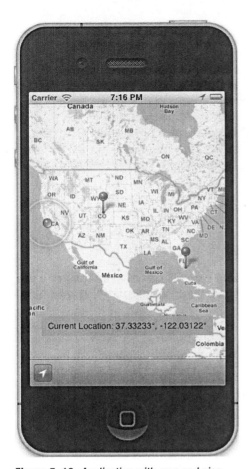

Figure 5–13. *Application with map and pins*

Oftentimes it may be useful to have an application in which a map's annotations are moveable by dragging them across the map. Implementing this functionality is incredibly simple, and can be done by adding a single line to your -viewForAnnotation: delegate method:

```
annotationView.draggable = YES;
```

As long as you have synthesized your annotation's coordinate property, your pins (or any other AnnotationView you decide to use) will be draggable.

Recipe 5–3: Creating Custom Annotations

While the majority of the time the default MKPinAnnotationView objects are incredibly useful, you may at some point decide you want a different image instead of the pin to represent an annotation on your map. This could be anything from an image of your friend representing his or her hometown, to your logo representing your company's location. In order to create a custom annotation view, you will be subclassing the

MKAnnotationView class. You will also be customizing your callouts to display more than simply a title and subtitle.

First, you must create your project the same way as earlier in this chapter, naming it "customAnnotationViews", and add your Map Kit and Core Location frameworks. You will then add your Map Kit to your view controller, making sure to use your #import statements for both <MapKit/MapKit.h> and <CoreLocation/CoreLocation.h>, and setting your view controller to conform to the MKMapViewDelegate protocol (refer to the beginning of this chapter on how to perform these tasks). You must also not forget to set your MapView's delegate to your view controller, by modifying your -viewDidLoad method like so:

```
- (void)viewDidLoad
{
    [super viewDidLoad];
    self.mapViewUserMap.delegate = self;
}
```

Before going any further, you will import the image that you will be using instead of a pin into your project. For this, I have chosen a small image called "avatar.png", shown here in Figure 5–14.

Figure 5–14. *Custom annotation image*

Obviously this image is too large to use on a map, so you will be scaling it down later.

The best way to import the file is to simply drag the file from the Finder into your navigation pane. I prefer to put such files under the Supporting Files group. In the dialog that appears, make sure the box marked "Copy items into destination group's folder (if needed)" is checked. Figure 5–15 should resemble the window in which this option appears, with the specific box at the top.

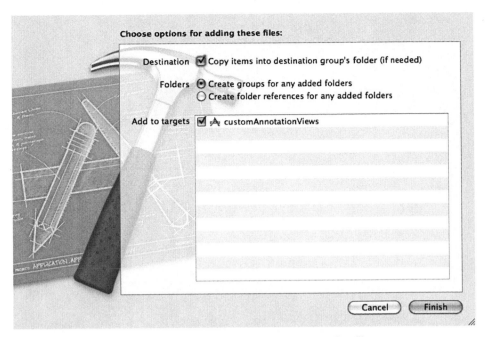

Figure 5–15. *Making sure the "Copy items" box is checked when adding files*

Next, you will create your annotation class. Select File ➤ New ➤ New File…, and under "Cocoa Touch" select "Objective-C class". On the next screen, you will name your class "MyAnnotation", and make sure it is a subclass of NSObject. Figure 5–16 shows this configuration.

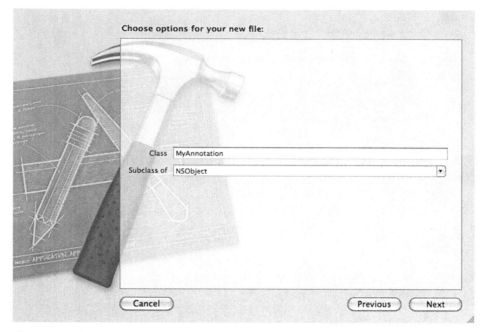

Figure 5–16. *Subclassing NSObject to create annotations*

After clicking Next and then Create, you will begin to edit this class.

The first thing you need to do is import your frameworks with the following lines:

```
#import <CoreLocation/CoreLocation.h>
#import <MapKit/MapKit.h>
```

Next, you will make sure that your class conforms to the MKAnnotation protocol. To do this, you add <MKAnnotation> to the header of your class, and you will declare three properties: coordinate, title, and subtitle. You will also declare a designated initialization method in order to create your annotations with coordinates. Your header file will look like so after all these changes:

```
#import <Foundation/Foundation.h>
#import <CoreLocation/CoreLocation.h>
#import <MapKit/MapKit.h>

@interface MyAnnotation : NSObject <MKAnnotation>

@property (nonatomic) CLLocationCoordinate2D coordinate;
@property (nonatomic, copy) NSString *title;
@property (nonatomic, copy) NSString *subtitle;

-(id)initWithCoordinate:(CLLocationCoordinate2D)coord;
@end
```

Now you simply need to build your implementation file. Since you are not doing anything horribly complex with these annotations, simply their views, your MyAnnotation.m file will look like so:

```
#import "MyAnnotation.h"

@implementation MyAnnotation

@synthesize coordinate, title, subtitle;
-(id)initWithCoordinate:(CLLocationCoordinate2D)coord
{
    self = [super init];
    if (self)
    {
        self.coordinate = coord;
    }
    return self;
}
@end
```

Now you can proceed to create your subclass of MKAnnotationView. Start off by going to File ➤ New ➤ New File…, and under "Cocoa Touch" choose "Objective-C class", just as before. On the next screen, you will name your class "CustomAnnotationView". The key here is to make sure you set the parent object correctly. Under "Subclass of", replace "NSObject" by typing **MKAnnotationView** in its place, as shown in Figure 5–17.

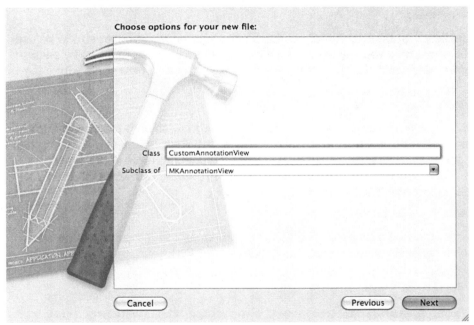

Figure 5–17. *Subclassing* MKAnnotationView

Click Next and then Create to proceed.

In the header file of your CustomAnnotationView, you will need to declare only one method to initialize your class, so that your header file looks like so:

```
#import <MapKit/MapKit.h>

@interface CustomAnnotationView : MKAnnotationView
```

```
-(id)initWithAnnotation:(id <MKAnnotation>) annotation reuseIdentifier:(NSString
*)annotationIdentifier;
@end
```

You may notice that this is the exact same name as the MKAnnotationView's designated initializer. This is done on purpose, in order to make your subclassing as simple as possible. In your implementation file, you will start this method by simply starting the view off as if it were a regular MKAnnotationView by calling the super's designated initializer:

```
-(id)initWithAnnotation:(id <MKAnnotation>) annotation reuseIdentifier:(NSString
*)annotationIdentifier
{
    self = [super initWithAnnotation:annotation reuseIdentifier:annotationIdentifier];
    return self;
}
```

Now, you can add to this initWithAnnotation:reuseIdentifier: method to customize your view. First, you will create the UIImage that you will set as your view's image to be used instead of the pin, and set it as your image.

```
UIImage *myImage = [UIImage imageNamed:@"avatar.png"];
self.image = myImage;
```

It is highly unlikely that the image that you have used is of an appropriate size to be used on a map. To offset this, you will standardize the size of these custom views by setting the frame of the view, and changing the content scaling mode to best scale your image.

```
self.frame = CGRectMake(0, 0, 40, 40);
self.contentMode = UIViewContentModeScaleAspectFill;
```

If necessary, you can also adjust the position of the image relative to the coordinates by using the centerOffset property. This is especially useful if the image you are using has a particular point, such as a pin or arrow, that you would like to have at the exact coordinates. The centerOffset property takes a CGPoint value, with the easiest way to make one being through the CGPointMake() function.

```
self.centerOffset = CGPointMake(1, 1);
```

Overall, your full method, along with a quick check to ensure that the annotation was initialized correctly, will resemble that shown here.

```
-(id)initWithAnnotation:(id <MKAnnotation>) annotation reuseIdentifier:(NSString
*)annotationIdentifier
{
    self = [super initWithAnnotation:annotation reuseIdentifier:annotationIdentifier];
    if (self)
    {
        //Create your UIImage to be used.
        UIImage *myImage = [UIImage imageNamed:@"avatar.png"];
        //Set your view's image
        self.image = myImage;
        //Standardize your AnnotationView's size.
        self.frame = CGRectMake(0, 0, 40, 40);
        //Use contentMode to ensure best scaling of image
        self.contentMode = UIViewContentModeScaleAspectFill;
        //Use centerOffset to adjust the image's position
```

```
        self.centerOffset = CGPointMake(1, 1);

    }
    return self;
}
```

> **NOTE:** All your customization points are placed in the `if (self){}` block in order to ensure that your view has been correctly initialized. This is not entirely necessary, but merely a matter of good practice. In the case that your `self` is not correctly initialized, the condition will evaluate as false, causing the method to simply return `nil`.

Now that your custom classes are all set up, you can return to your view controller in order to implement your map's delegate method. This is done almost exactly the same as with a regular implementation, but you must change the type of MKAnnotationView created from "MKPinAnnotationView" to your "CustomAnnotationView". Remember that your application will not work if you have not imported the MyAnnotation.h and CustomAnnotationView.h files.

```
- (MKAnnotationView *)mapView:(MKMapView *)mapView
viewForAnnotation:(id<MKAnnotation>)annotation
{
    if ([annotation isKindOfClass:[MyAnnotation class]])
    {
        static NSString *annotationIdentifier=@"annotationIdentifier";
        MKAnnotationView *annotationView=[self.mapViewUserMap
dequeueReusableAnnotationViewWithIdentifier:annotationIdentifier];
        annotationView.annotation = annotation;
        if(!annotationView)
        {
            annotationView=[[CustomAnnotationView alloc] initWithAnnotation:annotation
reuseIdentifier:annotationIdentifier];
        }

        annotationView.canShowCallout = YES;
        return annotationView;
    }
    return nil;
}
```

Finally, all you need to run this is some test data. In your -viewDidLoad method, you will add the following lines to create a few annotations and add them to your map. You will give them each a title and subtitle as well for testing purposes.

```
MyAnnotation *test1 = [[MyAnnotation alloc]
initWithCoordinate:CLLocationCoordinate2DMake(37.68, -97.33)];
test1.title = @"test1";
test1.subtitle = @"subtitle";
MyAnnotation *test2 = [[MyAnnotation alloc]
initWithCoordinate:CLLocationCoordinate2DMake(41.500, -81.695)];
test2.title = @"test2";
test2.subtitle = @"subtitle2";
[self.mapViewUserMap addAnnotation:test1];
[self.mapViewUserMap addAnnotation:test2];
```

> **NOTE:** Even if an MKAnnotationView's canShowCallout property is set to YES, the callout
> will not display unless the view's annotation has been given a title. The subtitle is optional.

At this point, when you run the app, you should see your two annotations appear on the
map with your image (shrunk down to a reasonable size) over Wichita, KS and
Cleveland, OH. Figure 5–18 is the simulation of this app.

Figure 5–18. *Application with map and custom annotations*

Now you will add a few extra lines of code to customize your callouts.

First, you will place an image to the left of the annotation's title and subtitle. This is done
through the use of the annotationView's property leftCalloutAccessoryView. Your
CustomAnnotationView class inherits a getter method for this from MKAnnotationView,
so we will override this to make all our custom views display a specific image. You will
do this by adding the following method to your CustomAnnotationView.m file.

```
-(UIView *)leftCalloutAccessoryView
{
```

```
    UIImageView *imageView = [[UIImageView alloc] initWithImage:[UIImage
imageNamed:@"avatar.png"]];
    imageView.frame = CGRectMake(0, 0, 20, 20);
    imageView.contentMode = UIViewContentModeScaleAspectFill;
    return imageView;
}
```

This is very similar to the way you set your image for the annotation view, but with an extra step of having to create a UIImageView to hold your avatar.png image. You resize it down again (this time even smaller) and then return it. Since UIImageView is a subclass of UIView, this works perfectly well.

Just as you can edit the leftCalloutAccessoryView, you can do the same thing on the right side of the callout. Here, you'll simply place a small disclosure button that can then be used to perform further functions.

```
-(UIView *)rightCalloutAccessoryView
{
    return [UIButton buttonWithType:UIButtonTypeDetailDisclosure];
}
```

With this addition, your annotation callouts will resemble those in Figure 5–19.

Figure 5–19. *Map with custom annotations and callouts*

At this point, your callouts are all set up visually, but there's a massive amount of potential in having those buttons inside the callouts that you haven't tapped into yet. Most map-based apps that use buttons on their callouts will usually use the button to push another view controller onto the screen. An application focused on displaying the locations of a specific business on the map might allow the user to view all the details or pictures from a specific location.

In order to increase your functionality, you will implement another one of your map's delegate methods, `-mapView:annotationView:calloutAccessoryControlTapped:`, and have it present a modal view controller. For demonstration purposes, you will have it display only your particular annotation's title and subtitle, but it is quite easy to see how this could be used much more extensively.

First, you will create your new view controller to be presented modally. Go to **File ➤ New ➤ New File…**. Under "Cocoa Touch", select "UIViewController subclass". Name the file "DetailViewController", and make sure that the box marked Targeted for iPad is unchecked (unless you are developing on the iPad), and the box marked With XIB for User Interface is checked, as in Figure 5–20.

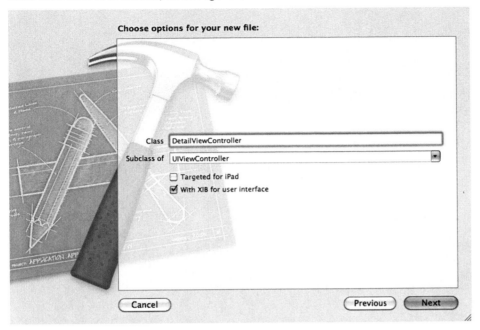

Figure 5–20. *Configuring a detail view controller*

Up next, you will go into your DetailViewController's .xib file, and add in your labels. Drag two UILabels from the object library out into the view. Change their names to "title" and "subtitle". Your user interface will look like Figure 5–21.

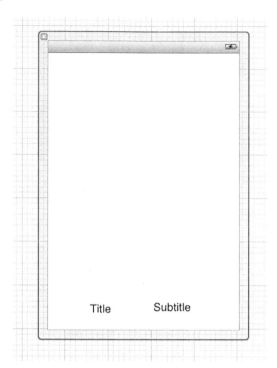

Figure 5–21. *DetailViewController .xib view*

Now, you will connect these two labels over to your DetailViewController's header file. Just as with your MKMapView, hold ^ and drag the labels over into your header file. You will name their respective properties titleLabel and subtitleLabel.

Next, in the rest of your DetailViewController, you will need a couple of NSString variables to store your title and subtitle, so you will simply declare them as instance variables. You will also need to declare a designated initializer method that takes two NSStrings that you will set your labels to. Your header file will now look like so:

```
#import <UIKit/UIKit.h>

@interface DetailViewController : UIViewController {
    UILabel *titleLabel;
    UILabel *subtitleLabel;
    NSString *myTitle;
    NSString *mySubtitle;
}

@property (strong, nonatomic) IBOutlet UILabel *titleLabel;
@property (strong, nonatomic) IBOutlet UILabel *subtitleLabel;

-(id)initWithTitle:(NSString *)title subtitle:(NSString *)subtitle;
@end
```

The implementation of your designated initializer will look like so:

```
-(id)initWithTitle:(NSString *)title subtitle:(NSString *)subtitle
```

```
{
    self = [super init];
    if (self)
    {
        myTitle = title;
        mySubtitle = subtitle;
    }
    return self;
}
```

Finally, you need to add the following two lines to your `-viewDidLoad` method in order to set your labels' text once the view is loaded.

```
self.titleLabel.text = myTitle;
self.subtitleLabel.text = mySubtitle;
```

Finally, you are ready to implement your map's delegate method back in your main view controller. In this method, you will create your `DetailViewController` and give it the necessary text, set it to do only a partial curl transition, and then present it. After you have correctly imported your header file using `#import "DetailViewController.h"`, your method implementation will look like so:

```
-(void)mapView:(MKMapView *)mapView annotationView:(MKAnnotationView *)view
calloutAccessoryControlTapped:(UIControl *)control
{
    MyAnnotation *ann = view.annotation;
    DetailViewController *dvc = [[DetailViewController alloc] initWithTitle:ann.title
subtitle:ann.subtitle];
    dvc.modalTransitionStyle = UIModalTransitionStylePartialCurl;
    [self presentViewController:dvc animated:YES completion:^{}];
}
```

> **NOTE:** It is necessary to declare the variable ann as an instance of `MyAnnotation` in order to assure the compiler that the annotation you are being given will have the properties of `.title` and `.subtitle` that you are asking for.

Once this code has been added, your application should resemble Figure 5–22 when a detail disclosure button is pressed.

Figure 5–22. *Application responding to the tapping of callouts*

Recipe 5–4: Adding Overlays to a Map

Annotations are not the only thing that can be added to a map. Here, you will go over how to add overlays to a map, which can take on a variety of shapes, from circles to polygons to lines. This recipe will build off of the first recipe in this chapter.

You will be adding two kinds of overlays to your MapView, both polygon overlays and line overlays. The process to add these is very similar to that of adding annotations, but you do not have to create a separate class for the overlays like you did with the annotations.

First, you will implement the MapView delegate method to tell your MapView how to deal with overlays. You will be setting up your method to handle both polygons and lines by using the class methods to check the type of overlay.

```
-(MKOverlayView *)mapView:(MKMapView *)mapView viewForOverlay:(id )overlay{
    if([overlay isKindOfClass:[MKPolygon class]]){
        MKPolygonView *view = [[MKPolygonView alloc] initWithOverlay:overlay];
```

```
        //Display settings
        view.lineWidth=1;
        view.strokeColor=[UIColor blueColor];
        view.fillColor=[[UIColor blueColor] colorWithAlphaComponent:0.5];
        return view;
    }
    else if ([overlay isKindOfClass:[MKPolyline class]])
    {
        MKPolylineView *view = [[MKPolylineView alloc] initWithOverlay:overlay];

        //Display settings
        view.lineWidth = 3;
        view.strokeColor = [UIColor blueColor];
        return view;
    }
    return nil;
}
```

Now you just need to create your overlays and add them to the MapView by adding the following code to -viewDidLoad.

```
//Create and Add Overlays
    NSMutableArray *overlays = [[NSMutableArray alloc] initWithCapacity:2];
    CLLocationCoordinate2D polyCoords[5]={
        CLLocationCoordinate2DMake(39.9, -76.6),
        CLLocationCoordinate2DMake(36.7, -84.0),
        CLLocationCoordinate2DMake(33.1, -89.4),
        CLLocationCoordinate2DMake(27.3, -80.8),
        CLLocationCoordinate2DMake(39.9, -76.6)
    };
    MKPolygon *Poly = [MKPolygon polygonWithCoordinates:polyCoords count:5];
    [overlays addObject:Poly];
    CLLocationCoordinate2D pathCoords[2] = {
        CLLocationCoordinate2DMake(46.8, -100.8),
        CLLocationCoordinate2DMake(43.7, -70.4)
    };
    MKPolyline *pathLine = [MKPolyline polylineWithCoordinates:pathCoords count:2];
    [overlays addObject:pathLine];
    [self.mapViewUserMap addOverlays:overlays];
```

> **CAUTION:** When making MKPolygons, your last coordinate point should be the same as your first one. If not, you will have issues getting the correct shapes.

When you run the app now, you should see the screen in Figure 5–23 when you zoom out on the map. You will also notice the polygon and line that we've set up are rather strange in shape and location, as they are simply meant to demonstrate what you can do with overlays on a MapView.

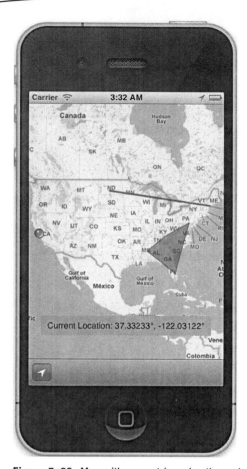

Figure 5–23. *Map with geometric and path overlays*

Overlays are incredibly useful in Map Kit apps, and can also be very easily customized. Most of the properties such as color or line width can be changed, allowing you to fully customize how your app looks and acts. Overlays can also be created from circles, as well as other user-defined shapes. Refer to the Apple documentation for details on how to use any of these other functions.

Recipe 5–5: Grouping Annotations by Location

A common issue when it comes to using annotations on a map view is the possibility of having very large numbers of annotations very close to each other, cluttering up the screen and making the application difficult to use. The solution is to group annotations together based on location and the size of the visible map. You will use a simple algorithm that compares location coordinates every time the visible region changes.

First, you need to create your project, naming it "HotspotMap", with a class prefix of "CSD", add the Map Kit and Core Location, and be sure to import them into your classes. Refer to Recipe 5–1 in this chapter for details on how to do this.

As is necessary when adding annotations to a map (see Recipe 5–2), you need to create a subclass of NSObject that conforms to the MKAnnotation protocol. Create the class by making a new file, choosing "Objective-C class", and making sure it is a subclass of NSObject. You will call your class "Hotspot", as shown in Figure 5–24.

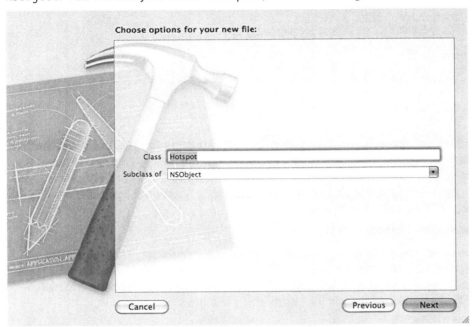

Figure 5–24. *Configuring the* Hotspot *class*

You will define your class with a few different properties. Since it is conforming to the MKAnnotation protocol, you will need a coordinate, as well as two NSStrings, a title, and a subtitle. You will also need a designated initialization method in order to create your annotations with coordinates. You will define these in your header file, like so:

```
#import <Foundation/Foundation.h>
#import <MapKit/MapKit.h>
#import <CoreLocation/CoreLocation.h>

@interface Hotspot : NSObject <MKAnnotation>

@property (nonatomic) CLLocationCoordinate2D coordinate;
@property (nonatomic, copy) NSString *title;
@property (nonatomic, copy) NSString *subtitle;
-(id)initWithCoordinate:(CLLocationCoordinate2D) c;

@end
```

> **NOTE:** Pay close attention to the import statements in this code, as well as the protocol directive `<MKAnnotation>` in the interface header. Without these, your app will not run correctly.

Now you simply need to synthesize these properties and implement your initialization method in your `.m` file, like so:

```
@synthesize coordinate, title, subtitle;
-(id)initWithCoordinate:(CLLocationCoordinate2D) c
{
    self=[super init];
    if(self){
        coordinate = c;
    }
    return self;
}
```

Next, you will move over to your view controller. The first thing to do is put your `MapView` in using Interface Builder, and link it over to your header file. In this example, I have named your `MKMapView` "mapViewUserMap". (Refer to Recipe 5–1 in this chapter on how to do this.) Also be sure to set your `MapView`'s delegate to your view controller in -viewDidLoad, with the following line of code:

```
self.mapViewUserMap.delegate = self;
```

You will also need a few helper variables throughout your program. First, you need a variable of type `CLLocationDegrees`, with which you will keep track of your current zoom level. Second, you will need a mutable array property, which you will use to hold all of your hotspots. Your header file will look something like this:

```
#import <UIKit/UIKit.h>
#import <MapKit/MapKit.h>

#import "Hotspot.h"

@interface CSDViewController : UIViewController <MKMapViewDelegate>
{
    MKMapView *mapViewUserMap;
    CLLocationDegrees zoom;
}

@property (strong, nonatomic) IBOutlet MKMapView *mapViewUserMap;
@property (strong, nonatomic) NSMutableArray *places;
@end
```

Next, in your implementation file, after synthesizing your `places` property, you'll define a few constants that will set up your starting coordinates and grouping parameters. These will also be used to help generate some random locations for demonstration purposes. Place the following statements before your import statements in the `.m` file.

```
#define centerLat   39.2953
#define centerLong -76.614
#define spanDeltaLat    4.9
#define spanDeltaLong   5.8
```

```
#define scaleLat  9.0
#define scaleLong  11.0
```

Before you get any further, you need to remember a very important aspect of dealing with NSArrays as properties, in that they do not automatically allocate or initialize themselves in their synthesized accessor method. You will need to define your own accessor method in order to lazily instantiate the array. Since you will be making 1,000 testing locations soon, you will give the array an initial capacity of 1,000, like so:

```
-(NSMutableArray *)places
{
    if (!places)
    {
        places = [[NSMutableArray alloc] initWithCapacity:1000];
    }
    return places;
}
```

Next, you will need some testing data. The following two methods will generate a good 1,000 hotspots for you to use, all within fairly close proximity to each other, so that you can see what kind of issue you are working with.

```
-(float)RandomFloatStart:(float)a end:(float)b
{
    float random = ((float) rand()) / (float) RAND_MAX;
    float diff = b - a;
    float r = random * diff;
    return a + r;
}
-(void)loadDummyPlaces
{
    srand((unsigned)time(0));

    for (int i=0; i<1000; i++)
    {
        Hotspot *place=[[Hotspot alloc]
initWithCoordinate:CLLocationCoordinate2DMake([self RandomFloatStart:37.0
end:42.0],[self RandomFloatStart:-72.0 end:-79.0])];
        place.title = [NSString stringWithFormat:@"Place %d title",i];
        place.subtitle = [NSString stringWithFormat:@"Place %d subtitle",i];
        [self.places addObject:place];
    }
}
```

Now that you have your testing data, you'll make sure your –viewDidLoad method is all set up to do what you need. It should look like so:

```
- (void)viewDidLoad
{
    [super viewDidLoad];
    self.mapViewUserMap.delegate = self;
    [self loadDummyPlaces];
    [self.mapViewUserMap addAnnotations:self.places]; //For setup purposes only. This
line will be unnecessary          when grouping is implemented.
    CLLocationCoordinate2D centerPoint = {centerLat, centerLong};
        MKCoordinateSpan coordinateSpan = MKCoordinateSpanMake(spanDeltaLat,
spanDeltaLong);
```

```
        MKCoordinateRegion coordinateRegion = MKCoordinateRegionMake(centerPoint,
coordinateSpan);

        [self.mapViewUserMap setRegion:coordinateRegion];
        [self.mapViewUserMap regionThatFits:coordinateRegion];
}
```

Before you finish up your initial setup, you'll jump down to your `-viewDidUnload` method and add in a few lines to keep your memory clean. The following two lines will help recycle memory if you ever want to use this class in a larger application later.

```
[self.places removeAllObjects];
self.places = nil;
```

Finally, you will need to implement your map's `viewForAnnotation` method so that you can correctly display your pins. This is very similar to your previous recipe, as shown here:

```
- (MKAnnotationView *)mapView:(MKMapView *)mV viewForAnnotation:(id
<MKAnnotation>)annotation{

    // if it's the user location, just return nil.
    if ([annotation isKindOfClass:[MKUserLocation class]]){
        return nil;
    }
    else{
        static NSString *StartPinIdentifier = @"PinIdentifier";
        MKPinAnnotationView *startPin = (id)[mV
dequeueReusableAnnotationViewWithIdentifier:StartPinIdentifier];
                if (startPin == nil) {
            startPin = [[MKPinAnnotationView alloc] initWithAnnotation:annotation
reuseIdentifier:StartPinIdentifier];
        }
        startPin.canShowCallout = YES;
        return startPin;
        }
}
```

At this point, if you run the application, you should see a view resembling Figure 5–25, a perfect illustration of the problem you are trying to solve. Now that you have your test data set up, you will work on implementing the solution.

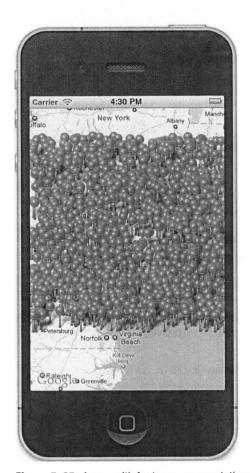

Figure 5–25. *A map with far too many annotations*

In order to properly iterate through your annotations and group them, you will be going through each hotspot and determining how it should be placed. If it is close to another pin that has already been dropped, it will be considered "found," and will be removed from the map. If not, you will add it to the list of those already in the map, and add it to the map itself as an annotation. The following method provides an efficient implementation, and should be placed in your view controller's .m file.

```
-(void)group:(NSArray *)hotspots{
    float latDelta=self.mapViewUserMap.region.span.latitudeDelta/scaleLat;
    float longDelta=self.mapViewUserMap.region.span.longitudeDelta/scaleLong;
    NSMutableArray *visibleHotspots=[[NSMutableArray alloc] initWithCapacity:0];

    for (Hotspot *current in hotspots) {
        CLLocationDegrees lat = current.coordinate.latitude;
        CLLocationDegrees longi = current.coordinate.longitude;

        bool found=FALSE;
        for (Hotspot *tempHotspot in visibleHotspots) {
```

```
                    if(fabs(tempHotspot.coordinate.latitude-lat) < latDelta &&
    fabs(tempHotspot.coordinate.longitude-longi)<longDelta ){
                [self.mapViewUserMap removeAnnotation:current];
                found=TRUE;
                break;
            }
        }
        if (!found) {
            [visibleHotspots addObject:current];
            [self.mapViewUserMap addAnnotation:current];
        }
    }
}
```

> **NOTE:** In this method, you use the `fabs` function. This is different from the `abs` function in that it is specifically used for floats. Using the `abs` function here would result in grouping only at the integer level of coordinates, and your app would not work correctly.

Next, you need to deal with your application re-grouping the points every time the visible section of the map is changed. This is fairly easy to do by implementing the following delegate method:

```
-(void)mapView:(MKMapView *)mapView regionDidChangeAnimated:(BOOL)animated{
    if (zoom!=mapView.region.span.longitudeDelta) {
        [self group:places];
        zoom=mapView.region.span.longitudeDelta;
    }
}
```

> **NOTE:** When implementing these methods, make sure that any methods that use the `-group:` method are implemented after it, otherwise the compiler will complain. Another way to solve this problem is to simply define `-(void)group(NSArray *)hotspots;` in your header file.

This method will check to see if the user has zoomed in or out, and if so, re-group the annotations accordingly. Now you just need to make one change to your `-viewDidLoad` method. You can remove the following line, as its function will be performed by your group: method.

```
[self.mapViewUserMap addAnnotations:self.places];
```

You actually should not need to call `[self group:self.places];` at the end of your `viewDidLoad` method, because when the map is first displayed, your delegate method `-mapView: regionDidChangeAnimated:` will be called, and will do the initial grouping automatically.

Upon running the app now, you should see your map populated with significantly fewer annotations, with a somewhat regular distance in between them, as in Figure 5–26. Upon zooming in or out, you can see annotations appear or disappear respectively as the map changes.

Figure 5–26. *Grouped annotations by location*

Now that you have successfully grouped your annotations, you may choose to animate your pins as they are added to drop down, so that your ungrouping transition looks smoother. This can be done with a simple "startPin.animatesDrop = YES;" in your viewForAnnotation: method, directly after the "startPin.canShowCallout = YES;" line.

While your annotations are correctly grouping at this point, you have a new issue, in that you cannot easily tell whether a single annotation is standing on its own, or if it is encapsulating multiple hotspots. In order to correct this, you will add in functionality to allow hotspots to keep track of the number of other hotspots they represent.

First, you will need to go to your Hotspot class, and add in an NSMutableArray property, "places". You will also add a few method definitions that you will use shortly to help manage this array. The following lines need to be added to "Hotspot.h".

```
@property (nonatomic, strong) NSMutableArray *places;
-(void)addPlace:(Hotspot *)hotspot;
-(int)placesCount;
```

Not only do you need to implement these methods, but you also need to change your -initWithCoordinate: method in order to ensure that your places array is correctly created. You will also have to implement your own version of your title property's getter, so that the callout title will show the number of hotspots represented. Your implementation file now looks like so:

```
#import "Hotspot.h"
@implementation Hotspot
@synthesize coordinate, title, subtitle;
@synthesize places;
-(id)initWithCoordinate:(CLLocationCoordinate2D) c
{
    self=[super init];
    if(self){
        coordinate = c;
        self.places = [[NSMutableArray alloc] initWithCapacity:0];
    }
    return self;
}
-(NSString *)title
{
    if ([self placesCount] == 1)
    {
        return title;
    }
    else
        return [NSString stringWithFormat:@"%i Places", [self.places count]];
}
-(void)addPlace:(Hotspot *)hotspot
{
    [self.places addObject:hotspot];
}
-(int)placesCount{
    return [self.places count];
}
-(void)cleanPlaces{
    [self.places removeAllObjects];
    [self.places addObject:self];
}
@end
```

The foregoing -placesCount method is not necessary; it just makes accessing the number of places represented by a single hotspot slightly easier. Your -cleanPlaces method will be used simply to reset the places array whenever you re-group your annotations. All you have to do now is make sure your -group: method correctly calls -cleanPlaces by adding the following two lines in their appropriate places, which you will see in the full method implementation that follows.

```
[hotspots makeObjectsPerformSelector:@selector(cleanPlaces)];
[tempHotspot addPlace:current];
```

Your full -group: method should now look like so:

```
-(void)group:(NSArray *)hotspots{
    float latDelta=self.mapViewUserMap.region.span.latitudeDelta/scaleLat;
    float longDelta=self.mapViewUserMap.region.span.longitudeDelta/scaleLong;
```

```
//New lines:
[hotspots makeObjectsPerformSelector:@selector(cleanPlaces)];
//End of new lines.
NSMutableArray *visibleHotspots=[[NSMutableArray alloc] initWithCapacity:0];

for (Hotspot *current in hotspots) {
    CLLocationDegrees lat = current.coordinate.latitude;
    CLLocationDegrees longi = current.coordinate.longitude;
    bool found=FALSE;
    for (Hotspot *tempHotspot in visibleHotspots) {
            if(fabs(tempHotspot.coordinate.latitude-lat) < latDelta &&
fabs(tempHotspot.coordinate.longitude-longi)<longDelta ){
                [self.mapViewUserMap removeAnnotation:current];
                found=TRUE;
                //New lines:
                [tempHotspot addPlace:current];
                //End of new lines.
                break;
            }
    }
    if (!found) {
        [visibleHotspots addObject:current];
        [self.mapViewUserMap addAnnotation:current];
    }
  }
}
```

Now you have a fairly easy way to determine whether any given hotspot is representing any other hotspots, but only by selecting that specific hotspot. It would be much better if you could easily see which hotspots are groups, and which are individuals. To do this, you will give each hotspot a pointer to its own MKPinAnnotationView. From there, you can control which color they are based on the number of places they represent.

First, you will add the following property to your hotspot file. Don't forget to @synthesize it in the .m file!

```
@property (nonatomic, strong) MKPinAnnotationView *annotationView;
```

Next you need to tell your map's delegate how to display the pins correctly, as shown in the new version of your -viewForAnnotation: method here.

```
- (MKAnnotationView *)mapView:(MKMapView *)mV viewForAnnotation:(id
<MKAnnotation>)annotation{

    // if it's the user location, just return nil.
    if ([annotation isKindOfClass:[MKUserLocation class]]){
        return nil;
    }
        else{
        static NSString *StartPinIdentifier = @"PinIdentifier";
        MKPinAnnotationView *startPin = (id)[mV
dequeueReusableAnnotationViewWithIdentifier:StartPinIdentifier];
                if (startPin == nil) {
            startPin = [[MKPinAnnotationView alloc] initWithAnnotation:annotation
reuseIdentifier:StartPinIdentifier];
        }
        startPin.canShowCallout = YES;
```

```
              startPin.animatesDrop = YES;
              //NEW CODE
              Hotspot *place = annotation;
              place.annotationView = startPin;
              if ([place placesCount] > 1)
              {
                  startPin.pinColor = MKPinAnnotationColorGreen;
              }
              else if ([place placesCount] == 1)
              {
                  startPin.pinColor = MKPinAnnotationColorRed;
              }
              //END OF NEW CODE
              return startPin;
              }
    }
```

This will make all of your annotations correctly appear as either green or red, depending on whether they are groups or individualized. However, if you zoom in on a specific green annotation, it will not correctly change color as it goes from a group to an individual. As your final step, to correct this, you will add code to our -mapView:regionDidChangeAnimated: to change the pin color based on the number of places represented, as shown here.

```
-(void)mapView:(MKMapView *)mapView regionDidChangeAnimated:(BOOL)animated{
    if (zoom!=mapView.region.span.longitudeDelta) {
        [self group:places];
        zoom=mapView.region.span.longitudeDelta;
        //NEW CODE
        NSSet *visibleAnnotations = [mapView
annotationsInMapRect:mapView.visibleMapRect];
        for (Hotspot *place in visibleAnnotations)
        {
            if ([place placesCount] > 1)
                place.annotationView.pinColor = MKPinAnnotationColorGreen;
            else
                place.annotationView.pinColor = MKPinAnnotationColorRed;
        }
        //END OF NEW CODE
    }
}
```

Now, any pins that represent groups of hotspots will be green, while individual ones will be red, as demonstrated in Figure 5–27.

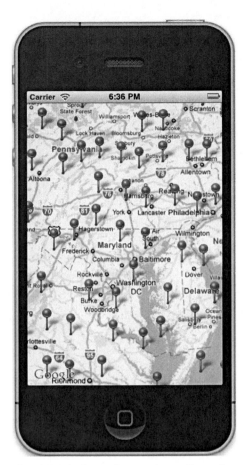

Figure 5–27. *Grouped annotations with number-specific colors*

Summary

The Map Kit framework is probably one of the most popularly used frameworks, purely for its powerful yet incredibly flexible ability to provide a fully customizable yet simplistic map interface. In this chapter, you have discussed the major capabilities of Map Kit, from locating the user, to adding annotations and overlays, to even the important issue of annotation grouping. However, you have only scratched the surface of the capabilities of Map Kit, especially in the areas of map-based problem solving. A quick look at the Map Kit documentation reveals the various other commands, methods, and properties you did not cover, which range from isolating particular sections of a map to entirely customizing how touch events are handled by the map. The effectiveness of these countless capabilities is limited only by the developer's imagination.

Chapter 6

Camera Recipes

There are a great number of mobile applications that make use of interaction with the device's camera, including such tasks as taking images, recording videos, and providing overlay, such as with augmented-reality applications. iOS developers have a great deal of control in how they can interact with any given device's hardware. In this chapter, you will go over multiple ways to access and use these functionalities, from simple, pre-defined interfaces to incredibly flexible, custom implementations.

> **NOTE:** The iOS simulator does not support camera hardware. In order to test most recipes in this chapter, they must be run on a physical device.

Recipe 6–1: Taking Pictures

iOS has an incredibly handy and simple interface built into it to utilize your device's camera through fairly standard, pre-defined settings. Through these, you can set up basic camera-focused apps, allowing users to take pictures and video from inside an app. Here, you will go over the basics of starting the camera interface in order to capture a still image.

You will again start by creating a new project using the Single View Application template, as shown in Figure 6–1.

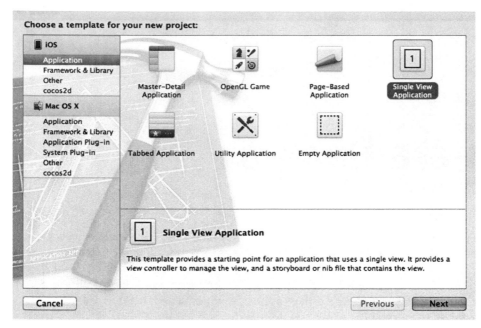

Figure 6–1. *Creating a single view application*

You will name your project "Chapter6Recipe1". Set the Class Prefix to Capture, as shown in Figure 6–2, and, if your version of Xcode includes it, make sure that Use Automatic Reference Counting is enabled.

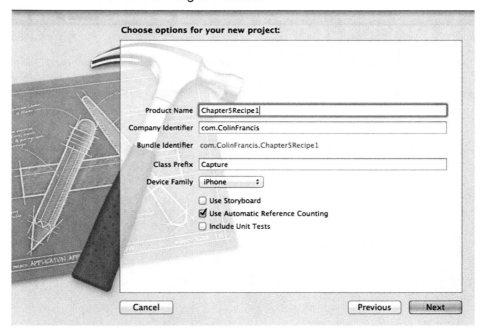

Figure 6–2. *Specifying your project settings*

Click Next and then Create to start the project.

In order to access your camera in the pre-defined way that you will be using, you do not need to import any extra frameworks into your project, so you will proceed to build your user interface.

You will be making a simple project that will allow you to pull up your camera, take a picture, and then display the most recently taken image on your screen.

First, you need to switch over to your view controller's .xib file, which, if you used all the same names as shown in Figure 6–3, will be called CaptureViewController.xib. From the object library on the right-hand side of the screen, click and drag out a UIImageView into your view, and rearrange it to fill the entire view. Next, you will drag out a UIButton into your view, which will be used to access the camera, so you will set its text to say "Change Image" by double-clicking the button's text.

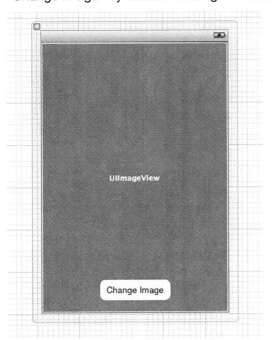

Figure 6–3. *CaptureViewController's user interface*

Next, make sure that you are in Assistant Editor mode by selecting the middle "editing" button in the top right area of your screen, as shown in Figure 6–4. This will allow you to view both your interface file and your header file at the same time and work across them synchronously.

Figure 6–4. *Selecting the Assistant Editor*

Once in the Assistant Editor mode, create an outlet for your UIImageView called "imageViewRecent". Repeat this process for your UIButton, naming it "cameraButton". Figure 6–5 shows the resulting window of these operations.

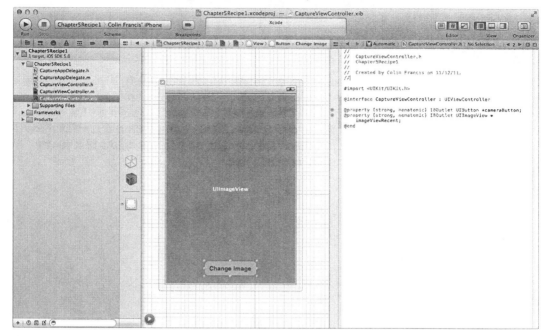

Figure 6–5. *Completed user interface with connected outlets and actions*

Before you leave this setup, you will declare an action for your button to perform when it is pressed, called -cameraButtonPressed:, by adding a method declaration to your header file, and then connecting your UIButton to it by holding ^ (Ctrl), clicking the button, dragging a blue line up to the method name in the header file, and releasing it. When you do this, the method declaration should become highlighted, and a small message box will display saying "Connect Action". Your method declaration will look like so:

```
- (IBAction)cameraButtonPressed:(id)sender;
```

Now that your interface file is put together, you can switch over to view your CaptureViewController.m file.

The first thing you will do for simple aesthetics' sake is to change the background color of your UIImageView to gray so that it is easier to distinguish from your UIButton when there is no image set as the background. To do this, place the following line of code into the -viewDidLoad method.

```
self.imageViewRecent.backgroundColor = [UIColor lightGrayColor];
```

Next, you will be handling what your app will do when your Change Image button is pressed. Since your button is already hooked up to perform your -

cameraButtonPressed: method, all you need to do is implement this method. You will be using an instance of the UIImagePickerController class to access your camera.

Whenever dealing with the camera hardware on iOS, it is essential that, as a developer, you include a function to have your app check for hardware availability. This is done through the static UIImagePickerController method +isSourceTypeAvailable:, which takes several pre-defined constants as arguments. The options for this method are as follows:

```
UIImagePickerControllerSourceTypeCamera
UIImagePickerControllerSourceTypePhotoLibrary
UIImagePickerControllerSourceTypeSavedPhotosAlbum
```

You will be using the first choice here, UIImagePickerControllerSourceTypeCamera. UIImagePickerControllerPhotoLibrary is used to access all the stored photos on the device, while UIImagePickerControllerSavedPhotosAlbum is used to access only the Camera Roll album.

For your application, you will check if the Camera source type is available, and if not, display a UIAlertView saying so, by using the following code in your -viewDidLoad method.

```
if ([UIImagePickerController
isSourceTypeAvailable:UIImagePickerControllerSourceTypeCamera] == NO)
    {
        UIAlertView *alert = [[UIAlertView alloc] initWithTitle:@"Error"
message:@"Camera Unavailable" delegate:self cancelButtonTitle:@"Cancel"
otherButtonTitles:nil, nil];
        [alert show];
        return;
    }
```

If you are running this application in the simulator, you will notice that this condition always evaluates to true, resulting in your error message, as demonstrated in Figure 6–6. As mentioned earlier, the simulator has no camera functionality, so in order to fully test this application, you will need to test it on a physical device.

Figure 6–6. *Simulation of your app, which does not support camera use*

Now you can handle the case that you actually hope for, in which the Camera is available. First, you will create an instance of UIImagePickerController, naming it imagePicker.

```
UIImagePickerController *imagePicker = [[UIImagePickerController alloc] init];
```

Next, you will set the delegate and source type of imagePicker to be your view controller and UIImagePickerControllerSourceTypeCamera, respectively.

```
imagePicker.delegate = self;
    imagePicker.sourceType = UIImagePickerControllerSourceTypeCamera;
```

Finally, you will present your UIImagePickerController modally.

```
[self presentModalViewController:imagePicker animated:YES];
```

In its entirety, your method to handle your button presses should now look like so:

```
-(IBAction)cameraButtonPressed:(id)sender
{
```

```
    if ([UIImagePickerController
isSourceTypeAvailable:UIImagePickerControllerSourceTypeCamera] == NO)
    {
        UIAlertView *alert = [[UIAlertView alloc] initWithTitle:@"Error"
message:@"Camera Unavailable" delegate:self cancelButtonTitle:@"Cancel"
otherButtonTitles:nil, nil];
        [alert show];
        return;
    }
    UIImagePickerController *imagePicker = [[UIImagePickerController alloc] init];
    imagePicker.delegate = self;
    imagePicker.sourceType = UIImagePickerControllerSourceTypeCamera;
    [self presentModalViewController:imagePicker animated:YES];
}
```

By setting up your view controller as the delegate for your UIImagePickerController, you are required to ensure that your view controller conforms to a couple of protocols, specifically the UIImagePickerController and UINavigationController protocols. You will add these to your class's header file, so that it now looks like so:

```
#import <UIKit/UIKit.h>
@interface CaptureViewController : UIViewController <UIImagePickerControllerDelegate,
UINavigationControllerDelegate>
{
    UIImageView *imageViewRecent;
    UIButton *cameraButton;
}

@property (strong, nonatomic) IBOutlet UIImageView *imageViewRecent;
@property (strong, nonatomic) IBOutlet UIButton *cameraButton;
-(IBAction)cameraButtonPressed:(id)sender;
@end
```

Now that you have set up your view controller to successfully present your UIImagePickerController, you need to handle how your view controller reacts to the completion of the UIImagePickerController's selection, when a picture has been taken and selected for use. You will do this through the use of the delegate method -imagePickerController:didFinishPickingMediaWithInfo:. This method gives the delegate an instance of NSDictionary called info, with keys referring to the selected media.

First, you create an instance of UIImage to point to the selected image.

```
UIImage *originalImage = (UIImage *) [info
objectForKey:UIImagePickerControllerOriginalImage];
```

Next you will save this image to your device's album, so that the picture is usable outside of this app. Alternatively, if you did not want your app to save several pictures as you use it for testing, you could comment out this line:

```
UIImageWriteToSavedPhotosAlbum (originalImage, nil, nil , nil);
```

Now you set your UIImageView's image to be the chosen image, and also change the content mode of the UIImageView.

```
self.imageViewRecent.image = originalImage;
self.imageViewRecent.contentMode = UIViewContentModeScaleAspectFill;
```

> **NOTE:** The UIImagePickerController class does not support landscape orientation for taking pictures. You compensate for this by changing the contentMode of your UIImageView to UIViewContentModeScaleAspectFill so that your image fills the screen. Alternatively, UIViewContentModeScaleAspectFit could also be used to fit the entire landscape image on the screen, though it will not fill the view.

Finally, you will dismiss your UIImagePickerController.

```
[self dismissModalViewControllerAnimated:YES];
```

As a whole, your delegate method's implementation will look like so:

```
- (void) imagePickerController: (UIImagePickerController *) picker
 didFinishPickingMediaWithInfo: (NSDictionary *) info
{
    UIImage *originalImage = (UIImage *) [info objectForKey:
        UIImagePickerControllerOriginalImage];
    UIImageWriteToSavedPhotosAlbum (originalImage, nil, nil , nil);
    self.imageViewRecent.image = originalImage;
    self.imageViewRecent.contentMode = UIViewContentModeScaleAspectFill;
    [self dismissModalViewControllerAnimated:YES];
}
```

You will also implement another UIImagePickerController delegate method to handle the cancellation of an image selection:

```
- (void) imagePickerControllerDidCancel: (UIImagePickerController *) picker
{
    [self dismissModalViewControllerAnimated:YES];
}
```

As an optional setting, you could also allow your camera interface to be editable, allowing the user to crop and frame the picture she or he has taken. In order to do this, you simply have to set the UIImagePickerController's allowsEditing property to "YES", and, in order to acquire this edited image, you would replace the first three lines of code in your previous -imagePickerController:didFinishPickingMediaWithInfo: method with the following lines:

```
UIImage *editedImage = (UIImage *)[info
objectForKey:UIImagePickerControllerEditedImage];
UIImageWriteToSavedPhotosAlbum (editedImage, nil, nil , nil);
self.imageViewRecent.image = editedImage;
```

Assuming that you are able to run this app on a physical device, your app should now be able to correctly access the device's camera, select a picture, and set it as a background, as shown in Figure 6–7.

Figure 6–7. *Your app with a photo set as the background*

Recipe 6–2: Recording Video

Your UIImagePickerController is actually significantly more flexible in its use than how you've been using it so far, especially since you've been using it almost exclusively for still images. Here, you'll go through how to set up your UIImagePickerController to handle both still images and video as well.

For this recipe, you will be building off of the code that you have already set up in the previous recipe, as it already includes the entire setup that you need. Your app will have the added functionality of being able to record and save videos.

First, you need to edit the properties of your UIImagePickerController to specify the allowable media types, through the use of the UIImagePickerController class method +availableMediaTypesForSourceType:, so that your -cameraButtonPressed: will now look like so:

```
-(IBAction)cameraButtonPressed:(id)sender
{
    if ([UIImagePickerController
isSourceTypeAvailable:UIImagePickerControllerSourceTypeCamera] == NO)
    {
        UIAlertView *alert = [[UIAlertView alloc] initWithTitle:@"Error"
message:@"Camera Unavailable" delegate:self cancelButtonTitle:@"Cancel"
otherButtonTitles:nil, nil];
        [alert show];
        return;
```

```
    }
    UIImagePickerController *imagePicker = [[UIImagePickerController alloc] init];
    imagePicker.delegate = self;
    imagePicker.sourceType = UIImagePickerControllerSourceTypeCamera;
    imagePicker.mediaTypes = [UIImagePickerController
availableMediaTypesForSourceType:UIImagePickerControllerSourceTypeCamera];
    [self presentModalViewController:imagePicker animated:YES];
}
```

Next, you need to instruct your application on how to handle when a user records and uses a video. You will add the following code to your UIImagePickerController's delegate method:

```
NSString *mediaType = [info objectForKey: UIImagePickerControllerMediaType];

    if (CFStringCompare ((__bridge CFStringRef) mediaType, kUTTypeMovie, 0)
        == kCFCompareEqualTo) {

        NSString *moviePath = [[info objectForKey: UIImagePickerControllerMediaURL]
path];

        if (UIVideoAtPathIsCompatibleWithSavedPhotosAlbum (moviePath))
        {
            UISaveVideoAtPathToSavedPhotosAlbum (moviePath, nil, nil, nil);
        }
    }
```

The first thing you will probably notice is that there is an error focused on kUTTypeMovie, saying that it is undefined. In order to fix this, you need to import the Mobile Core Services framework into your project, and then add the following import statement to the header of your view controller. The beginning of Recipe 6–4 contains a detailed demonstration of how to add a framework to a project if you are unfamiliar with this process.

```
#import <MobileCoreServices/MobileCoreServices.h>
```

Essentially, all you are doing here is comparing the media type of the saved file. Your main issue comes into play when you attempt to compare mediaType, an NSString, with kUTTypeMovie, which is of type CFStringRef. You accomplish this by casting your NSString down to a CFStringRef. iOS 5 has made this process slightly more complicated with the introduction of Automatic Reference Counting (ARC), because ARC deals with Objective-C object types such as NSString, but not with C types like CFStringRef. You create a bridged casting by placing "__bridge" before your CFStringRef, as shown earlier, in order to instruct ARC to no longer deal with this object.

If all has gone well, your app should now be able to record video!

Recipe 6–3: Editing Videos

While your UIImagePickerController offers an extremely convenient way to record and save video files, it does nothing to allow you to edit them. Luckily, iOS has another built-in controller called UIVideoEditorController, which you will use to allow your recorded videos to be edited.

You will build this fairly simple recipe off of your second project, in which you added video functionality to your `UIImagePickerController`.

First, you will make a second button in your view controller's interface file, giving it the title "Edit Video", and the name `editButton`. You will also hook it up to an action, `-editButtonPressed:`, as shown in Figure 6–8.

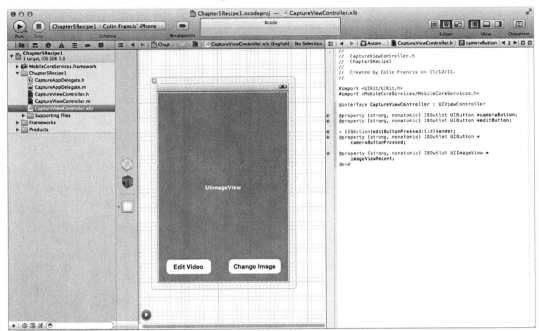

Figure 6–8. *New user interface with editing button*

Next, you define an `NSString` property to store the path to your most recently selected/edited video, as shown on the right in Figure 6–8, keeping care to @synthesize it and then setting it to "nil" in `-viewDidUnload`:

```
@property (nonatomic, strong) NSString *recentMovie;
```

You will need to add to your `UIImagePickerController`'s delegate method a statement to store your recently created video's path by adding the following line:

```
    self.recentMovie = moviePath;
```

Your delegate method now looks like so:

```
- (void) imagePickerController: (UIImagePickerController *) picker
 didFinishPickingMediaWithInfo: (NSDictionary *) info
{
    NSString *mediaType = [info objectForKey: UIImagePickerControllerMediaType];

    if (CFStringCompare ((__bridge CFStringRef) mediaType, kUTTypeMovie, 0)
        == kCFCompareEqualTo) {
```

```
        NSString *moviePath = [[info objectForKey: UIImagePickerControllerMediaURL]
path];
        self.recentMovie = moviePath;

        if (UIVideoAtPathIsCompatibleWithSavedPhotosAlbum (moviePath))
        {
            UISaveVideoAtPathToSavedPhotosAlbum (moviePath, nil, nil, nil);
        }
    }

    else
    {
    UIImage *originalImage = (UIImage *) [info objectForKey:
        UIImagePickerControllerOriginalImage];

    UIImageWriteToSavedPhotosAlbum (originalImage, nil, nil , nil);
    self.imageViewRecent.image = originalImage;
    }
    [self dismissModalViewControllerAnimated:YES];
}
```

You will implement your -editButtonPressed: action now in order to display a video to be edited if one exists, or to otherwise display an alert view telling you of your user's error.

```
-(void)editButtonPressed:(id)sender
{
    if (self.recentMovie)
    {
        UIVideoEditorController *editor = [[UIVideoEditorController alloc] init];
        editor.videoPath = self.recentMovie;
        editor.delegate = self;
        [self presentModalViewController:editor animated:YES];
    }
    else
    {
        UIAlertView *alert = [[UIAlertView alloc] initWithTitle:@"Error" message:@"No
Video Recorded Yet" delegate:self cancelButtonTitle:@"Cancel" otherButtonTitles:nil,
nil];
        [alert show];     }
}
```

Keep in mind that at this point you will need to make sure your view controller is listed as conforming to the UIVideoEditorControllerDelegate and UINavigationControllerDelegate protocols in your header file.

Finally, you only need to implement a few delegate methods for your UIVideoEditorController. First, here is a delegate method to handle a successful editing/trimming of the video:

```
-(void)videoEditorController:(UIVideoEditorController *)editor
didSaveEditedVideoToPath:(NSString *)editedVideoPath
{
    self.recentMovie = editedVideoPath;
    if (UIVideoAtPathIsCompatibleWithSavedPhotosAlbum (editedVideoPath))
    {
        UISaveVideoAtPathToSavedPhotosAlbum (editedVideoPath, nil, nil, nil);
```

```
    }
    [self dismissModalViewControllerAnimated:YES];
}
```

As you can see, your application will set the newly edited video as your next video to be edited, so that you can create increasingly trimmed clips. It will also save each edited version to your photo album as well if possible.

Lastly, you need one more delegate method to handle the cancellation of your UIVideoEditorController.

```
-(void)videoEditorControllerDidCancel:(UIVideoEditorController *)editor
{
    [self dismissModalViewControllerAnimated:YES];
}
```

Upon testing on a physical device, your application should now successfully allow you to edit your videos! Figure 6–9 shows a view of your application giving you the option to edit a recorded video.

Figure 6–9. *View seen while recording video*

Recipe 6–4: Custom Camera Overlays

There are quite a variety of applications that implement the camera interface, but also implement a custom overlay, such as for displaying constellations on the sky, or simply implementing their own custom camera controls. Here, you will learn to do a basic implementation of a custom overlay over your camera's screen, continuing from your previous recipe's project.

You need to build your custom UIView to be used as a custom overlay programmatically, meaning you will not be using a XIB interface. You will be adjusting certain specific properties of the buttons that you put in, so the first thing you need to do is import the QuartzCore interface into your project, which means adding an import statement into your header file.

```
#import <QuartzCore/QuartzCore.h>
```

You will create a method, -customView:, that will take your UIImagePicker as an argument and return your UIView.

```
-(UIView *)customView:(UIImagePickerController *)imagePicker;
{
    UIView *view = [[UIView alloc] initWithFrame:CGRectMake(0, 0, 280, 480)];
    view.backgroundColor = [UIColor clearColor];

    UIButton *flashButton = [[UIButton alloc] initWithFrame:CGRectMake(10, 10, 120,
44)];
        flashButton.backgroundColor = [UIColor colorWithRed:.5 green:.5 blue:.5 alpha:.5];
        [flashButton setTitle:@"Flash Auto" forState:UIControlStateNormal];
        [flashButton setTitleColor:[UIColor whiteColor] forState:UIControlStateNormal];
        flashButton.layer.cornerRadius = 10.0;

    UIButton *changeCameraButton = [[UIButton alloc] initWithFrame:CGRectMake(190, 10,
120, 44)];
        changeCameraButton.backgroundColor = [UIColor colorWithRed:.5 green:.5 blue:.5
alpha:.5];
        [changeCameraButton setTitle:@"Rear Camera" forState:UIControlStateNormal];
        [changeCameraButton setTitleColor:[UIColor whiteColor]
forState:UIControlStateNormal];
        changeCameraButton.layer.cornerRadius = 10.0;

    UIButton *takePictureButton = [[UIButton alloc] initWithFrame:CGRectMake(100, 432,
120, 44)];
        takePictureButton.backgroundColor = [UIColor colorWithRed:.5 green:.5 blue:.5
alpha:.5];
        [takePictureButton setTitle:@"Click!" forState:UIControlStateNormal];
        [takePictureButton setTitleColor:[UIColor whiteColor]
forState:UIControlStateNormal];
        takePictureButton.layer.cornerRadius = 10.0;

    [flashButton addTarget:self action:@selector(toggleFlash:)
forControlEvents:UIControlEventTouchUpInside];
        [changeCameraButton addTarget:self action:@selector(toggleCamera:)
forControlEvents:UIControlEventTouchUpInside];
        [takePictureButton addTarget:imagePicker action:@selector(takePicture)
forControlEvents:UIControlEventTouchUpInside];

    [view addSubview:flashButton];
    [view addSubview:changeCameraButton];
    [view addSubview:takePictureButton];

    return view;
}
```

Here, you have defined your `UIView` as well as your buttons to be put in it, given them their actions to perform, and added them into the view. You set the title of each button to be either its starting value or its purpose. You also set your `cornerRadius` so that your buttons will have rounded corners. One of the most important details here is that you set your buttons to be semi-transparent, as they will be placed over your camera's display. You do not want to cover up any of your picture, so they have to be at least partially see-through.

Now you need to simply implement your two toggling methods, `-toggleCamera:` and `-toggleFlash:`. You will need a few extra instance variables in your class to deal with these properly, including two BOOLs to keep track of your settings, as well as a pointer to a `UIImagePickerController` to pass around your camera interface. Your view controller's header file should now look like so:

```
#import <UIKit/UIKit.h>
#import <MobileCoreServices/MobileCoreServices.h>
#import <QuartzCore/QuartzCore.h> //Need this!

@interface CaptureViewController : UIViewController <UIImagePickerControllerDelegate,
UINavigationControllerDelegate>
{
    UIImageView *imageViewRecent;
    UIButton *cameraButton;
    UIImagePickerController *currentPicker;
    BOOL flashOn;
    BOOL frontCameraUsed;
}

@property (strong, nonatomic) IBOutlet UIImageView *imageViewRecent;
@property (strong, nonatomic) IBOutlet UIButton *cameraButton;

-(IBAction)cameraButtonPressed:(id)sender;
@end
```

Next, add the following line to `-cameraButtonPressed:` after `imagePicker` is created.

```
currentPicker = imagePicker;
```

Also add the following line to the camera's `-imagePickerController:didFinishPickingMediaWithInfo:` delegate method in order to "release" your `currentPicker`'s value. This can go at the very end of the method, after the view controller has been dismissed.

```
currentPicker = nil;
```

Now you can successfully define your `-toggleFlash:` and `-toggleCamera:` methods like so:

```
-(void)toggleFlash:(UIButton *)sender
{
    if (flashOn)
    {
        currentPicker.cameraFlashMode = UIImagePickerControllerCameraFlashModeOff;
        flashOn = NO;
        [sender setTitle:@"Flash Off" forState:UIControlStateNormal];
    }
```

```
        else
        {
            currentPicker.cameraFlashMode = UIImagePickerControllerCameraFlashModeOn;
            flashOn = YES;
            [sender setTitle:@"Flash On" forState:UIControlStateNormal];
        }
    }
    -(void)toggleCamera:(UIButton *)sender
    {
        if (frontCameraUsed)
        {
            currentPicker.cameraDevice = UIImagePickerControllerCameraDeviceRear;
            frontCameraUsed = NO;
            [sender setTitle:@"Rear Camera" forState:UIControlStateNormal];
        }
        else
        {
            currentPicker.cameraDevice = UIImagePickerControllerCameraDeviceFront;
            frontCameraUsed = YES;
            [sender setTitle:@"Front Camera" forState:UIControlStateNormal];
        }
    }
```

Finally, you simply need to change the visibility of the camera controls by adding two more lines to your -cameraButtonPressed: method, just before your controller is presented.

```
imagePicker.showsCameraControls = NO;
imagePicker.cameraOverlayView = [self customView:imagePicker];
```

Your camera should now have a wonderful little overlay with a couple of buttons that change how it works, as in Figure 6–10. You can see that from here, you can create your own custom overlays and easily change their functions to fit nearly any situation.

Figure 6–10. *Custom overlay view over a camera*

Recipe 6–5: AV Framework and Capture Sessions

While the UIImagePickerController and UIVideoEditorController interfaces are incredibly useful, they certainly aren't as customizable as they could be. Using the AV framework, you can create an immensely more customizable camera interface. Here, you will be creating essentially your own version of the camera, but in such a way that further customization is incredibly easy, by using a different method known as an AVCaptureSession.

First, you will create a new project, called "Chapter6Recipe5", using a class prefix of "CustomCamera".

You will need a variety of different frameworks linked to your project. Navigate to the project's main settings, select CustomCamera under Targets, and then flip over to the Build Phases tab, resembling Figure 6–11.

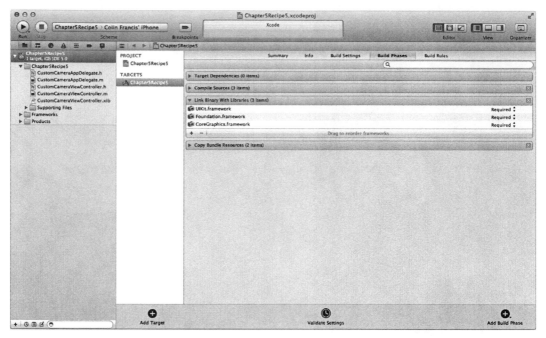

Figure 6–11. *Preparing to add frameworks to your project*

Under Link Binary With Libraries, you will use the + button to add several other frameworks. Search for and add the following frameworks:

- AV Foundation
- Core Graphics
- Core Video
- Core Media

You will actually not need to type any import statements for any of these except for the AV Foundation one. Go ahead and add the following import lines to the header file of your main view controller.

```
#import <AVFoundation/AVFoundation.h>
#import <AVFoundation/AVCaptureInput.h>
```

Next, you'll switch over to your view controller's .xib file to do a bit of quick setup. Here, all you need to do is drag a UIButton over to your view, and then connect it to your header file, naming it startButton. You need to make an action for this button to perform, so you will declare the following method header, and connect your startButton to it.

```
-(IBAction)startPressed:(id)sender;
```

Once these changes have been made, your user interface and code should resemble Figure 6–12 in the Assistant Editor.

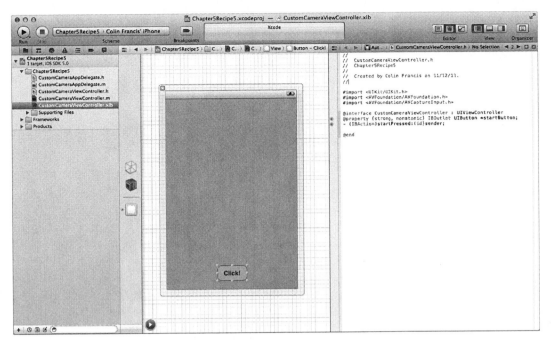

Figure 6–12. *User interface with configured outlet and action*

Next, switching away from your XIB/header file combination to view the header and implementation files, you will define a new kind of property for your view controller, like so.

```
@property (strong, nonatomic) AVCaptureSession *captureSession;
```

You must, as always, remember to "@synthesize captureSession;" and do "self.captureSession = nil" in your implementation file and -viewDidUnload respectively.

Next, you will be writing your -viewDidLoad method to prepare your view, create your AVCaptureSession, and set it up as you desire. You will add the following sets of lines to your method after the call [super viewDidLoad];.

First, you must create your AVCaptureSession, and give it a resolution preset, like so:

```
self.captureSession = [[AVCaptureSession alloc] init];
self.captureSession.sessionPreset = AVCaptureSessionPresetMedium;
```

Next, you will create an instance of AVCaptureDevice, with which you will specify your input device, which in this case will be the device's rear camera (assuming one is accessible). You specify this through the use of the AVCaptureDevice class method +defaultDeviceWithMediaType:, which can take a variety of different arguments, depending on the type of media desired, the most prominent of which are AVMediaTypeVideo and AVMediaTypeAudio.

```
AVCaptureDevice *device = [AVCaptureDevice defaultDeviceWithMediaType:AVMediaTypeVideo];
```

Next, you need to create an instance of AVCaptureDeviceInput in order to specify your chosen device as an input for your capture session. You will also include a check to make sure the input has been correctly created before adding it to your session.

```
NSError *error = nil;
    AVCaptureDeviceInput *input = [AVCaptureDeviceInput deviceInputWithDevice:device
error:&error];
    if (!input)
    {
        NSLog(@"Input Error");
    }
    else
    {
        [self.captureSession addInput:input];
    }
```

Next, you will set up an output for your capture session, like so:

```
AVCaptureVideoDataOutput *output = [[AVCaptureVideoDataOutput alloc] init];
    [self.captureSession addOutput:output];
    output.videoSettings =
    [NSDictionary dictionaryWithObject:[NSNumber
numberWithInt:kCVPixelFormatType_32BGRA]
                                    forKey:(id)kCVPixelBufferPixelFormatTypeKey];

    dispatch_queue_t queue = dispatch_queue_create("MyQueue", NULL);
    [output setSampleBufferDelegate:self queue:queue];
    dispatch_release(queue);
```

Here, you have created an AVCaptureVideoDataOutput, which is commonly used when a developer's goal is to deal with raw video input frame-by-frame, as opposed to simply saving a video as a whole. Other types of AVCaptureOutputs include the following:

▨ AVCaptureMovieFileOutput: Used for saving whole video files

▨ AVCaptureAudioDataOutput: Used for processing audio data

▨ AVCaptureStillImageOutput: Used for extracting specific still images from a session (This type of output could also be used to perform your current goal.)

You have also dispatched an extra queue to handle the processing of your frames that you will end up seeing later.

The last part of your -viewDidLoad will be the creation of an AVCaptureVideoPreviewLayer, with which you will be able to see exactly what your camera is viewing in the app. You will set your preview layer to be the layer of your main view, but with a slightly altered height, so as not to block your button from being visible.

```
AVCaptureVideoPreviewLayer *previewLayer = [AVCaptureVideoPreviewLayer
layerWithSession:self.captureSession];
    UIView *aView = self.view;
    previewLayer.frame = CGRectMake(0, 0, self.view.frame.size.width,
self.view.frame.size.height-70);
    [aView.layer addSublayer:previewLayer];
```

A Note on AVCaptureVideoPreviewLayer

The most significant part of the concept of an AVCaptureVideoPreviewLayer is not its visual output, but instead its power to be manipulated. Just like any other CALayer, it can be repositioned, rotated, and resized. At this point, you are no longer bound to using the entire screen to record video as you are with the UIImagePicker, meaning you could have your preview layer in one part of the screen and other information for the user in another. As with almost every part of iOS development, the possibilities of use are limited only by the developer's imagination.

Since you set your current view controller as the delegate for your AVCaptureVideoDataOutput, you will need to implement the AVCaptureVideoDataOutputSampleBufferDelegate protocol. Your header file should now look like so:

```
#import <UIKit/UIKit.h>
#import <AVFoundation/AVFoundation.h>
#import <AVFoundation/AVCaptureInput.h>

@interface CustomCameraViewController : UIViewController
<AVCaptureVideoDataOutputSampleBufferDelegate>{
    UIImageView *imageViewDisplay;
    UIButton *startButton;
    BOOL capture;
}

@property (strong, nonatomic) IBOutlet UIButton *startButton;
@property (strong, nonatomic) AVCaptureSession *captureSession;
-(IBAction)startPressed:(id)sender;
@end
```

Make sure to note the new addition also of the BOOL instance variable capture. You will be using this to keep track of whether your session's frames will be processed.

Next, you will implement your AVCaptureVideoDataOutputSampleBuffer's delegate method, like so:

```
- (void)captureOutput:(AVCaptureOutput *)captureOutput
didOutputSampleBuffer:(CMSampleBufferRef)sampleBuffer
      fromConnection:(AVCaptureConnection *)connection {

    if (capture)
    {
        UIImage *chosenImage = [self imageFromSampleBuffer:sampleBuffer];
        UIImageWriteToSavedPhotosAlbum (chosenImage, nil, nil , nil);
        capture = NO;
    }
}
```

As you can see, you are simply checking if your capture BOOL evaluates to a "YES", and if so, you acquire the image of the given video frame, and then save it to your device's photo album. By setting capture to "NO" immediately afterward, you limit your app to capture only one frame per button press. It should be fairly easy to see how this could be expanded to include any number of frames.

You must also define your -imageFromSampleBuffer: that you just used, as follows, making sure that it is defined above your delegate method.

```
- (UIImage *) imageFromSampleBuffer:(CMSampleBufferRef) sampleBuffer
{
    // Get a CMSampleBuffer's Core Video image buffer for the media data
    CVImageBufferRef imageBuffer = CMSampleBufferGetImageBuffer(sampleBuffer);
    // Lock the base address of the pixel buffer
    CVPixelBufferLockBaseAddress(imageBuffer, 0);

    // Get the number of bytes per row for the pixel buffer
    void *baseAddress = CVPixelBufferGetBaseAddress(imageBuffer);

    // Get the number of bytes per row for the pixel buffer
    size_t bytesPerRow = CVPixelBufferGetBytesPerRow(imageBuffer);
    // Get the pixel buffer width and height
    size_t width = CVPixelBufferGetWidth(imageBuffer);
    size_t height = CVPixelBufferGetHeight(imageBuffer);

    // Create a device-dependent RGB color space
    CGColorSpaceRef colorSpace = CGColorSpaceCreateDeviceRGB();

    // Create a bitmap graphics context with the sample buffer data
    CGContextRef context = CGBitmapContextCreate(baseAddress, width, height, 8,
                                            bytesPerRow, colorSpace,
kCGBitmapByteOrder32Little | kCGImageAlphaPremultipliedFirst);
    // Create a Quartz image from the pixel data in the bitmap graphics context
    CGImageRef quartzImage = CGBitmapContextCreateImage(context);
    // Unlock the pixel buffer
    CVPixelBufferUnlockBaseAddress(imageBuffer,0);

    // Free up the context and color space
    CGContextRelease(context);
    CGColorSpaceRelease(colorSpace);

    // Create an image object from the Quartz image
    UIImage *image = [UIImage imageWithCGImage:quartzImage];

    // Release the Quartz image
    CGImageRelease(quartzImage);

    return (image);
}
```

Now, you will implement a fairly simple capturing toggle method to handle your button presses.

```
-(void)startPressed:(id)sender
{
    if (!capture)
    {
        capture = YES;
    }
    else
```

```
    {
        capture = NO;
    }
}
```

One of the most important steps to remember is to actually "start" and "stop" your AVCaptureSession. Since you want your camera's display to be visible any time the app is open, you will start your session in your -viewWillAppear method and stop it in your -viewWillDisappear method, the two of which will now look like so:

```
- (void)viewWillAppear:(BOOL)animated
{
    [super viewWillAppear:animated];
    [self.captureSession startRunning];
}
- (void)viewWillDisappear:(BOOL)animated
{
    [super viewWillDisappear:animated];
    [self.captureSession stopRunning];
}
```

If you run this app on your device now, you will probably notice that all the saved images that you take look like they were taken in landscape mode, and then rotated to fit in portrait, obviously not filling up the entire screen anymore. You fix this by changing the video orientation of your session's output connections by changing your -viewWillAppear: method to appear like so:

```
- (void)viewWillAppear:(BOOL)animated
{
    [super viewWillAppear:animated];
    [self.captureSession startRunning];

    NSArray *array = [[self.captureSession.outputs objectAtIndex:0] connections];
    for (AVCaptureConnection *connection in array)
    {
        connection.videoOrientation = AVCaptureVideoOrientationPortrait;
    }
}
```

If you run the app now on your device, you will be able to see a preview of what your camera is recording, and whenever you press the button, the current frame will be saved to your photo library, as in Figure 6–13. While you haven't included any fancy animations to make it look like a camera, this is incredibly useful as far as a basic camera goes, especially given your new ability to fully customize its behavior in a frame-by-frame case or as a whole video (if you add a second output).

Figure 6–13. *Your app displaying a preview of the camera's view*

Recipe 6–6: Programmatically Recording Video

Now that you have covered some of the basics of using AVFoundation, you will implement a slightly more complicated project using it. This time, your application will be recording full video, rather than simply capturing specific frames. You will also add an audio input device so that your video has sound included.

First, you must make your new project, this time titled "Chapter6Recipe6", with class prefix "CustomVideo".

As usual, the first thing to do is to acquire the following necessary frameworks using the Link Binary With Libraries section in your project's Build Phases tab.

- *AV Foundation*: You will use this to deal with your camera and microphone.
- *Assets Library*: This is for saving the video that you will record to your device.

In Interface Builder, add a UIButton to the bottom center of the view controller's view, just like in the previous recipe, giving it the default label "Record". When you connect this to the header file, give the UIButton the name button. Be sure to also create an action for this button to perform called -recordPressed: (see earlier recipes on how to do this).

Just like in your previous recipe, you will be building your AVCaptureSession to manage your camera's input and the output of your video, so you will start off by adding a few variables, properties, and protocols to your view controller's header file.

■ First, you will need an instance variable of type BOOL called recording, which will simply keep track of whether your video is recording.

■ Second, you need to create two properties that will be used to store pointers to your AVCaptureSession session and your AVCaptureMovieFileOutput output, the latter of which will be your AVCaptureOutput device.

■ Third, you need to include an import statement for the AV Foundation framework in your header file.

■ Finally, you will need to tell the compiler that your view controller conforms to the AVCaptureFileOutputRecordingDelegate protocol.

With all these changes, your view controller's header file will now look like so:

```
#import <UIKit/UIKit.h>
#import <AVFoundation/AVFoundation.h>
#import <AssetsLibrary/AssetsLibrary.h>

@interface CustomVideoViewController : UIViewController
<AVCaptureFileOutputRecordingDelegate>{
    UIButton *button;
    BOOL recording;
}

@property (strong, nonatomic) IBOutlet UIButton *button;

@property (strong, nonatomic) AVCaptureSession *session;
@property (strong, nonatomic) AVCaptureMovieFileOutput *output;

-(IBAction)recordPressed:(id)sender;
@end
```

Now that your header file is all set up, you will switch over to your implementation file.

First, since you have set up two of your own properties, session and output, you absolutely have to remember to @synthesize both of them at the top of your implementation file. You should also remember to set them both equal to nil in your -viewDidUnload method.

Next, as with the previous recipe, you will start to build your -viewDidLoad method.

First, you must allocate your AVCaptureSession, like so:

```
self.session = [[AVCaptureSession alloc] init];
self.session.sessionPreset = AVCaptureSessionPresetMedium;
```

Next, you will create two instances of AVCaptureDevice, one for your rear camera, and one for your microphone, and then create AVCaptureDeviceInputs for each of them and add them to your session.

```
AVCaptureDevice *device = [AVCaptureDevice defaultDeviceWithMediaType:AVMediaTypeVideo];

NSError *error = nil;
AVCaptureDeviceInput *input = [AVCaptureDeviceInput deviceInputWithDevice:device
error:&error];

NSArray *devices = [AVCaptureDevice devicesWithMediaType:AVMediaTypeAudio];

AVCaptureDeviceInput *mic = [[AVCaptureDeviceInput alloc] initWithDevice:[devices
objectAtIndex:0] error:nil];
if (!input || !mic)
    {
        NSLog(@"Input Error");
    }
    else
    {
        [self.session addInput:input];
        [self.session addInput:mic];
    }
```

Now you create your AVCaptureOutput and add it to the session. You will make sure any connections that your output has have their video orientations set correctly.

```
self.output = [[AVCaptureMovieFileOutput alloc] init];

    NSArray *connections = self.output.connections;
    for (AVCaptureConnection *connection in connections)
    {
        if ([connection isVideoOrientationSupported])
            connection.videoOrientation = AVCaptureVideoOrientationPortrait;
    }
    if ([self.session canAddOutput:self.output])
        [self.session addOutput:self.output];
```

You will need to be able to see your camera's view, so you'll set up an instance of AVCaptureVideoPreviewLayer.

```
AVCaptureVideoPreviewLayer *previewLayer = [AVCaptureVideoPreviewLayer
layerWithSession:self.session];
UIView *aView = self.view;
previewLayer.frame = CGRectMake(0, 0, self.view.frame.size.width,
self.view.frame.size.height-70);
[aView.layer addSublayer:previewLayer];
```

Finally, you simply need to start your AVCaptureSession. You'll also set your recording instance to NO just to ensure it has the correct starting value.

```
[self.session startRunning];
    recording = NO;
```

In its entirety, your -viewDidLoad method now looks so:

```
- (void)viewDidLoad
{
    [super viewDidLoad];

    self.session = [[AVCaptureSession alloc] init];
    self.session.sessionPreset = AVCaptureSessionPresetMedium;
```

```
    AVCaptureDevice *device = [AVCaptureDevice
defaultDeviceWithMediaType:AVMediaTypeVideo];

    NSError *error = nil;
    AVCaptureDeviceInput *input = [AVCaptureDeviceInput deviceInputWithDevice:device
error:&error];

    NSArray *devices = [AVCaptureDevice devicesWithMediaType:AVMediaTypeAudio];

    AVCaptureDeviceInput *mic = [[AVCaptureDeviceInput alloc] initWithDevice:[devices
objectAtIndex:0] error:nil];

    if (!input || !mic)
    {
        NSLog(@"Input Error");
    }
    else
    {
        [self.session addInput:input];
        [self.session addInput:mic];
    }

    self.output = [[AVCaptureMovieFileOutput alloc] init];

    NSArray *connections = self.output.connections;
    for (AVCaptureConnection *connection in connections)
    {
        if ([connection isVideoOrientationSupported])
            connection.videoOrientation = AVCaptureVideoOrientationPortrait;
    }
    if ([self.session canAddOutput:self.output])
        [self.session addOutput:self.output];

    AVCaptureVideoPreviewLayer *previewLayer = [AVCaptureVideoPreviewLayer
layerWithSession:self.session];
    UIView *aView = self.view;
    previewLayer.frame = CGRectMake(0, 0, self.view.frame.size.width,
self.view.frame.size.height-70);
    [aView.layer addSublayer:previewLayer];

    [self.session startRunning];
    recording = NO;
}
```

> **TIP:** Adding sound to your videos is not a complicated process in this method! All that is required
> is to add the audio input device to your session, and the AVCaptureSession will do the rest for
> you.

You will of course need to define how your application handles when the user presses
your UIButton. This will be a fairly simple toggle function to start and stop your
AVCaptureOutput.

```
-(IBAction)recordPressed:(id)sender
{
```

```
    if (!recording)
    {
        [self.button setTitle:@"Stop" forState:UIControlStateNormal];
        recording = YES;
        NSURL *fileURL = [self tempFileURL];
        [self.output startRecordingToOutputFileURL:fileURL recordingDelegate:self];
    }
    else
    {
        [self.button setTitle:@"Record" forState:UIControlStateNormal];
        [self.output stopRecording];
        recording = NO;
    }
}
```

You probably noticed that you called the method -tempFileURL in order to set up your AVCaptureOutput early. This method, in short, returns a path for your recorded video to be temporarily saved on your device. If there is already a file saved at the location, it will delete that file. (This way, you never use more than one video's worth of disk space.)

```
- (NSURL *) tempFileURL
{
    NSString *outputPath = [[NSString alloc] initWithFormat:@"%@%@",
NSTemporaryDirectory(), @"output.mov"];
    NSURL *outputURL = [[NSURL alloc] initFileURLWithPath:outputPath];
    NSFileManager *manager = [[NSFileManager alloc] init];
    if ([manager fileExistsAtPath:outputPath])
    {
        [manager removeItemAtPath:outputPath error:nil];
    }
    return outputURL;
}
```

The last major step to set up your video is to set up your AVCaptureMovieFileOutput's delegate. It will check if there were any errors in recording the video to a file, and then save your video file into your Asset Library.

```
- (void)captureOutput:(AVCaptureFileOutput *)captureOutput
didFinishRecordingToOutputFileAtURL:(NSURL *)outputFileURL
     fromConnections:(NSArray *)connections
               error:(NSError *)error {

    BOOL recordedSuccessfully = YES;
    if ([error code] != noErr) {
        // A problem occurred: Find out if the recording was successful.
        id value = [[error userInfo]
objectForKey:AVErrorRecordingSuccessfullyFinishedKey];
        if (value) {
            recordedSuccessfully = [value boolValue];
        }
    }
    ALAssetsLibrary *library = [[ALAssetsLibrary alloc] init];

    [library writeVideoAtPathToSavedPhotosAlbum:outputFileURL
            completionBlock:^(NSURL *assetURL, NSError *error)
    {
        if (error)
```

```
    {
        NSLog(@"Error writing") ;
    }
    }];
}
```

Finally, to improve the functionality of your app's design, you will make your -viewWillAppear: and -viewWillDisappear: have a hand in your session's starting and stopping, so that you don't end up with a session running in the background or not running when you can see it.

```
- (void)viewWillAppear:(BOOL)animated
{
    [super viewWillAppear:animated];
    if (![self.session isRunning])
    {
        [self.session startRunning];
    }
}
- (void)viewWillDisappear:(BOOL)animated
{
        [super viewWillDisappear:animated];
    if ([self.session isRunning])
    {
        [self.session stopRunning];
    }
}
```

This app will look almost identical to the previous recipe's app, the main difference being the type of media saved. In the previous recipe, you were saving individual frames as images to your library, but here you will be saving recorded video with sound.

Recipe 6–7: Capturing Video Frames

For a large number of applications that utilize videos, a thumbnail image is often used to "represent" a given video. Adding on to your previous recipe, you will be adding in a capability to create a thumbnail image based on a specific point in your video. You will implement two different ways to do this, with one method based on the AVCaptureSession, and the other based on your saved video.

First, you will capture a still image from your AVCaptureSession using a different type of AVCaptureOutput, known as an AVCaptureStillImageOutput.

> **TIP:** This first method of taking images has the added ability to automatically play a shutter sound when an image is taken!

First, you will add a couple of UIImageViews to your view controller's XIB file, which will be used to display the still images that you capture. You will connect them to your header file as usual, naming them imageViewThumb and imageViewThumb2. If desired, you can set their background color to something other than the default color so that they can be distinguished from your view before your images are put in them. Figure 6–14 shows your resulting XIB file.

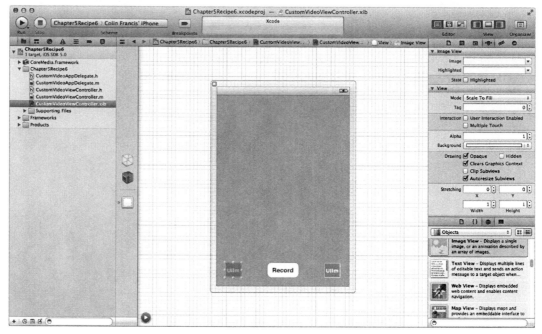

Figure 6–14. *Setting up your user interface for thumbnails*

Next you will need a property to keep track of your AVCaptureStillImageOutput, which you will declare and synthesize in your view controller as stillImageOutput, making sure to remember to set it to nil in your -viewDidUnload.

Your third step is to add this output to your AVCaptureSession in your -viewDidLoad method, which will now look like so:

```
- (void)viewDidLoad
{
    [super viewDidLoad];

    self.imageViewThumb.backgroundColor = [UIColor whiteColor];

    self.session = [[AVCaptureSession alloc] init];
    self.session.sessionPreset = AVCaptureSessionPresetMedium;

    AVCaptureDevice *device = [AVCaptureDevice
defaultDeviceWithMediaType:AVMediaTypeVideo];

    NSError *error = nil;
    AVCaptureDeviceInput *input = [AVCaptureDeviceInput deviceInputWithDevice:device
error:&error];

    NSArray *devices = [AVCaptureDevice devicesWithMediaType:AVMediaTypeAudio];
```

```
    AVCaptureDeviceInput *mic = [[AVCaptureDeviceInput alloc] initWithDevice:[devices
objectAtIndex:0] error:nil];

    if (!input || !mic)
    {
        NSLog(@"Input Error");
    }
    else
    {
        [self.session addInput:input];
        [self.session addInput:mic];
    }

    self.output = [[AVCaptureMovieFileOutput alloc] init];

    NSArray *connections = self.output.connections;
    for (AVCaptureConnection *connection in connections)
    {
        if ([connection isVideoOrientationSupported])
            connection.videoOrientation = AVCaptureVideoOrientationPortrait;
    }
    if ([self.session canAddOutput:self.output])
        [self.session addOutput:self.output];

    /////////NEW STILL IMAGE OUTPUT CODE
    self.stillImageOutput = [[AVCaptureStillImageOutput alloc] init];
    NSDictionary *outputSettings = [[NSDictionary alloc] initWithObjectsAndKeys:
                                    AVVideoCodecJPEG, AVVideoCodecKey, nil];
    [self.stillImageOutput setOutputSettings:outputSettings];

    if ([self.session canAddOutput:stillImageOutput])
    {
        [self.session addOutput:stillImageOutput];
    }
    else
    {
        NSLog(@"Unable to add still image output");
    }
    /////////END OF NEW STILL IMAGE OUTPUT CODE
    AVCaptureVideoPreviewLayer *previewLayer = [AVCaptureVideoPreviewLayer
layerWithSession:self.session];
    UIView *aView = self.view;
    previewLayer.frame = CGRectMake(0, 0, self.view.frame.size.width,
self.view.frame.size.height-70);
    [aView.layer addSublayer:previewLayer];

    [self.session startRunning];
    recording = NO;
        // Do any additional setup after loading the view, typically from a nib.
}
```

Next, you will define the method that will actually capture your image and save it to your device.

```
- (void) captureStillImage
{
    AVCaptureConnection *stillImageConnection = [self.stillImageOutput.connections
objectAtIndex:0];
```

```
        if ([stillImageConnection isVideoOrientationSupported])
            [stillImageConnection setVideoOrientation:AVCaptureVideoOrientationPortrait];

    [[self stillImageOutput]
captureStillImageAsynchronouslyFromConnection:stillImageConnection

completionHandler:^(CMSampleBufferRef imageDataSampleBuffer, NSError *error)
        {
            ALAssetsLibraryWriteImageCompletionBlock completionBlock = ^(NSURL *assetURL,
NSError *error)
            {};

        if (imageDataSampleBuffer != NULL)
        {
            NSData *imageData = [AVCaptureStillImageOutput
jpegStillImageNSDataRepresentation:imageDataSampleBuffer];
            ALAssetsLibrary *library = [[ALAssetsLibrary alloc] init];

            UIImage *image = [[UIImage alloc] initWithData:imageData];
            self.imageViewThumb.image = image;
            [library writeImageToSavedPhotosAlbum:[image CGImage]
                orientation:(ALAssetOrientation)[image imageOrientation]
                completionBlock:completionBlock];
        }
        else
            completionBlock(nil, error);

        }];
}
```

Finally, you simply need to tell your application when to perform this -
captureStillImage by placing a call to it in your recordPressed: method. I chose to
have it take the picture right at the beginning of the recording, though it could also go at
the end. Your method will now look like so:

```
-(IBAction)recordPressed:(id)sender
{
    if (!recording)
    {
        [self.button setTitle:@"Stop" forState:UIControlStateNormal];
        recording = YES;
        NSURL *fileURL = [self tempFileURL];
        [self.output startRecordingToOutputFileURL:fileURL recordingDelegate:self];

        //////CAPTURE IMAGE
        [self captureStillImage];
    }
    else
    {
        [self.button setTitle:@"Record" forState:UIControlStateNormal];
        [self.output stopRecording];
        recording = NO;
    }
}
```

At this point, your application, if run on a device, will successfully record a video as well
as take a still image at the beginning (or end if you chose) of your recording. While this is

of course very useful, it doesn't quite have that full customizability that you may desire. Next, you will implement a use of the class AVAssetImageGenerator, which can not only generate multiple images from a single video, but also create them at varied, specified times in the video.

First, you will need to link your binary with the Core Media framework. Do this as you have with all other framework links. You will not need any import statements for this framework. It will simply act as a reference for your compiler.

Next, you will add a property to your class of type AVAssetImageGenerator, making sure to synthesize and later to set it to nil correctly. Name this property imageGenerator.

You have already defined your delegate method to handle the successful saving of a video to a URL, so you will add to that your - captureOutput:didFinishRecordingToOutputFileAtURL:fromConnections:error: method, in order to access the URL and generate your images from it. Your method should now look like so, with comments identifying the newly added lines:

```
- (void)captureOutput:(AVCaptureFileOutput *)captureOutput
didFinishRecordingToOutputFileAtURL:(NSURL *)outputFileURL
      fromConnections:(NSArray *)connections
               error:(NSError *)error {

    BOOL recordedSuccessfully = YES;
    if ([error code] != noErr) {
        // A problem occurred: Find out if the recording was successful.
        id value = [[error userInfo]
objectForKey:AVErrorRecordingSuccessfullyFinishedKey];
        if (value) {
            recordedSuccessfully = [value boolValue];
        }
    }
    ALAssetsLibrary *library = [[ALAssetsLibrary alloc] init];
    [library writeVideoAtPathToSavedPhotosAlbum:outputFileURL
                        completionBlock:^(NSURL *assetURL, NSError *error)
    {
        if (error)
        {
            NSLog(@"Error writing") ;
        }

    }];

    ////////////START OF NEW STILL IMAGE CODE
    AVURLAsset *myAsset = [[AVURLAsset alloc] initWithURL:outputFileURL
options:[NSDictionary dictionaryWithObject:@"YES"
forKey:AVURLAssetPreferPreciseDurationAndTimingKey]];

    self.imageGenerator = [AVAssetImageGenerator assetImageGeneratorWithAsset:myAsset];
    self.imageGenerator.appliesPreferredTrackTransform = YES; //Makes sure images are
correctly rotated.

    Float64 durationSeconds = CMTimeGetSeconds([myAsset duration]);
    CMTime half = CMTimeMakeWithSeconds(durationSeconds/2.0, 600);
    NSArray *times = [NSArray arrayWithObjects: [NSValue valueWithCMTime:half], nil];
```

```
        [self.imageGenerator generateCGImagesAsynchronouslyForTimes:times
                        completionHandler:^(CMTime requestedTime, CGImageRef image, CMTime
actualTime,AVAssetImageGeneratorResult result, NSError *error)
        {
            NSString *requestedTimeString = (__bridge NSString *)CMTimeCopyDescription(NULL,
requestedTime);
            NSString *actualTimeString = (__bridge NSString *)CMTimeCopyDescription(NULL,
actualTime);
            NSLog(@"Requested: %@; actual %@", requestedTimeString, actualTimeString);

            if (result == AVAssetImageGeneratorSucceeded)
                {
                    self.imageViewThumb2.image = [UIImage imageWithCGImage:image];
                }

            if (result == AVAssetImageGeneratorFailed)
                {
                    NSLog(@"Failed with error: %@", [error localizedDescription]);
                }
            if (result == AVAssetImageGeneratorCancelled)
                {
                    NSLog(@"Canceled");
                }
        }];
        ///////END OF STILL IMAGE CODE
}
```

Your application can now correctly capture still images from a video in two different ways, and you should be able to see a clear view of each method on your device, as in Figure 6–15.

Figure 6–15. *Recording application with two different thumbnails*

> **NOTE:** You may notice that with the second method, the creating of the image takes significantly longer than the first. This is probably a method that would be better used at a point when the user cannot see the image in question until it has been successfully created.

Summary

As a developer, you have a great deal of choice when it comes to dealing with your device's camera. The pre-defined interfaces such as UIImagePickerController and UIVideoEditorController are incredibly useful and well designed, but Apple's implementation of the AV Foundation framework allows for infinitely more possibilities. Everything from dealing with video, audio, and still images is possible. Even a quick glance at the full documentation will reveal countless other functionalities that you have not gone over here, including everything from device capabilities (such as the video camera's LED "torch"), to the implementation of your own "Touch-To-Focus" functionality. We live in a world where images, audio, and video fly around the world in a matter of seconds, and as developers we must be able to design and create innovative solutions that fit in with our media-based community.

Chapter 7

Multimedia Recipes

In the words of Aldous Huxley, "After silence, that which comes nearest to expressing the inexpressible is music." We live in a world where we are surrounded by sound and music. From the most subtle background tune in an advertisement, to the immense blast of the electric guitar at a rock concert, sound plays an integral part in our world in all its varieties, and to ignore this fact in our development process would be detrimental to both the user experience and the developer community. Music and audio have a tremendous impact on our lives, and as developers, it is our responsibility to translate this force into our applications in order to bring the most complete and ideal experience to users, even if they don't even notice.

Throughout this chapter, a variety of recipes will make use of accessing the iPod library on the device on which the app is run. In order to fully test these, you should ensure that there are at least a few songs in your device's music library.

Recipe 7-1: Playing Audio

If you ask almost any random person what they think of when they hear the words "iPhone" and "audio," they will probably be thinking along the lines of their iPod and the thousands of songs they have downloaded. What most users tend to overlook, despite its immense importance, is the concept of background audio and sound effects. These sound clips and tunes may go completely unnoticed by the user in normal use, but in terms of app functionality and design they can tremendously improve the quality of an app. It may be the little "shutter click" when you take a picture, or the background music of a game that gets stuck in your head after you play it for too long, but regardless of whether the user notices, it can make a world of difference. The iOS "AV Foundation" framework provides an incredibly simple way to access, play, and manipulate sound files, known as the AVAudioPlayer. Here you will create a sample project that will allow you to play an audio file, as well as allow the user to manipulate the clip's playback.

First, you will create a new project, naming it "Chapter7Recipe1". Here, I have used the class prefix "Player". As with most of the previous recipes, you can use the Single View Application template to make your project. Ensure the Storyboard check box is unchecked, while the Use Automatic Reference Counting box is checked, so that your configuration resembles Figure 7–1.

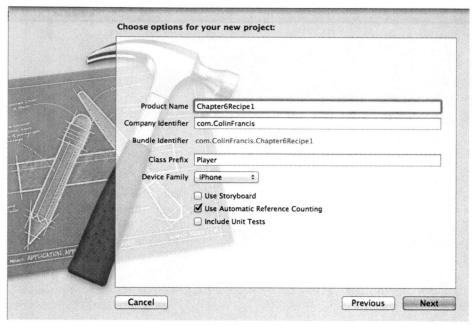

Figure 7–1. *Configuring your project's settings*

The first thing you need to do is link your project with a few frameworks that you will use to play your sound. Select your project in the navigation pane, and then navigate to **Targets ➤ SoundCheck**. Select the Build Phases tab, and drop down the section titled "Link Binary With Libraries", as shown in Figure 7–2.

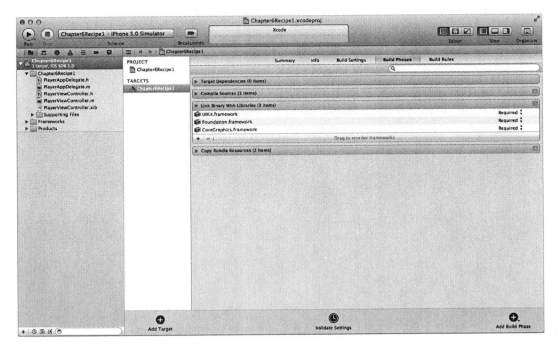

Figure 7–2. *Project before adding frameworks*

Next, click the + button, and add the following two frameworks:

1. *AV Foundation*: This includes the AVAudioPlayer class, which you will be using to play audio.

2. *Audio Toolbox*: You will use this framework to implement a button to play the "vibrate" sound on your device.

Next, switch over to your view controller's header file. You will import your frameworks' header files by adding the following import statements:

```
#import <AVFoundation/AVFoundation.h>
#import <AudioToolbox/AudioToolbox.h>
```

Now you will go build your view in the view controller's XIB file. You will be creating your view to include sliders for your audio player's pan, volume, and rate, as well as buttons that will play and pause the player, and a third button to play the device's "vibrate" system sound. You will also be monitoring your audio player's channel levels via labels at the top of the view. Set up your view so it looks like Figure 7–3.

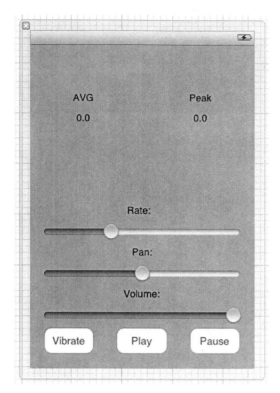

Figure 7–3. *Your view controller's XIB file with default values set*

You need your slider's values to match the possible values of the properties they control. Using the Attribute inspector, adjust the minimum and maximum values of your "rate" slider to 0.5 and 2.0 (corresponding to half speed and 2x speed), respectively, and the same values for the "pan" slider to -1 and 1 (correspond to left pan and right pan). The "volume" slider's default values should already be fine, as the volume property goes from 0 to 1.

As you have done in your past recipes, you will connect some of your view objects over to your header file by holding ^ (Ctrl) and dragging from the element over to the view controller's header file. Name the UISliders sliderRate, sliderPan, and sliderVolume as appropriate. Your UIButtons will be vibrateButton, playButton, and pauseButton. Your two level-monitoring UILabels at the top (which I have given default values so far of "0.0") will be averageLabel and peakLabel. You will define three methods (of type IBAction, not void) in your header file, one for each button, and connect your buttons to them by holding ^ and dragging from the button to the action definition. You will also define three more methods for your UISlider's to be connected to as well. Your header file should now look like so:

```
#import <UIKit/UIKit.h>
#import <AVFoundation/AVFoundation.h>
#import <AudioToolbox/AudioToolbox.h>

@interface PlayerViewController : UIViewController
```

```
@property (strong, nonatomic) IBOutlet UIButton *vibrateButton;
@property (strong, nonatomic) IBOutlet UIButton *playButton;
@property (strong, nonatomic) IBOutlet UIButton *pauseButton;
@property (strong, nonatomic) IBOutlet UISlider *sliderVolume;
@property (strong, nonatomic) IBOutlet UISlider *sliderPan;
@property (strong, nonatomic) IBOutlet UISlider *sliderRate;
@property (strong, nonatomic) IBOutlet UILabel *averageLabel;
@property (strong, nonatomic) IBOutlet UILabel *peakLabel;
-(IBAction)vibratePressed:(id)sender;
-(IBAction)playPressed:(id)sender;
-(IBAction)pausePressed:(id)sender;

-(IBAction)volumeSliderChanged:(UISlider *)sender;
-(IBAction)panSliderChanged:(UISlider *)sender;
-(IBAction)rateSliderChanged:(UISlider *)sender;

@end
```

You will also add a property to your header file to keep track of your AVAudioPlayer, written like so:

```
@property (nonatomic, strong) AVAudioPlayer *player;
```

Synthesize this new property in your implementation file, and add the following lines to your -viewDidUnload method to make sure your application is as efficient as possible in memory use.

```
self.player.delegate = nil;
[self setPlayer:nil];
```

The last step in your header file is to make your view controller conform to the AVAudioPlayerDelegate protocol.

```
@interface PlayerViewController : UIViewController <AVAudioPlayerDelegate>
```

Before you proceed, you need to select and import the sound file that your application will be playing. The file I use is called systemCheck.mp3, and the following code will reflect this file name. You will need to change any file name or file type according to the file that you choose. You should consult Apple's documentation on which file types are appropriate, but it is fairly safe to assume that most commonly used file types such as .wav or .mp3 will work.

In order to catch any errors in playing files, you can implement one of the methods in the AVAudioPlayerDelegate protocol:

```
-(void)audioPlayerDecodeErrorDidOccur:(AVAudioPlayer *)player error:(NSError *)error
{
    NSLog(@"Error playing file: %@", [error localizedDescription]);
}
```

Find your sound clip in the Finder, and then click and drag the file into your project in Xcode. My preference is to put such files in the Supporting Files group, but this is entirely optional. A dialog will appear prompting you to choose options for adding the file. The only change you may need to make is to make sure that the box next to "Copy items into destination group's folder (if needed)" is checked, as in Figure 7–4.

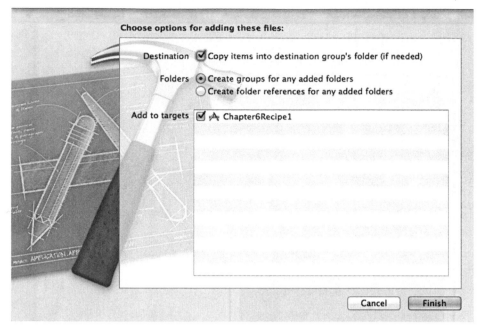

Figure 7–4. *Pop-up dialog for importing files—make sure the first box is checked.*

Now that you have your sound file, you can implement your -viewDidLoad method to set up your AVAudioPlayer.

```
- (void)viewDidLoad
{
    [super viewDidLoad];
    NSString *fileName = @"systemCheck";
    NSString *fileType = @"mp3";
    NSString *soundFilePath = [[NSBundle mainBundle] pathForResource:fileName
ofType:fileType];
    NSURL *soundFileURL = [NSURL fileURLWithPath:soundFilePath];

    NSError *error;
    self.player = [[AVAudioPlayer alloc] initWithContentsOfURL:soundFileURL
error:&error];
    self.player.enableRate = YES; //Allows us to change the playback rate.
    self.player.meteringEnabled = YES; //Allows us to monitor levels
    self.player.delegate = self;
    self.sliderVolume.value = self.player.volume;
    self.sliderRate.value = self.player.rate;
    self.sliderPan.value = self.player.pan;

    [self.player prepareToPlay]; //Preload audio to decrease lag

    NSTimer *timer = [NSTimer scheduledTimerWithTimeInterval:0.1 target:self
selector:@selector(updateLabels) userInfo:nil repeats:YES];

    [timer fire];
}
```

As you can see, you've gotten the URL for your sound file, and then created your AVAudioPlayer with it. You set up the enableRate property to allow you to change the playback rate, and set the meteringEnabled property to allow you to monitor the player's levels. You called the optional -prepareToPlay on your player in order to pre-load the sound file, hopefully making your application slightly faster. You created a timer at the end, which will perform your -updateLabels method ten times a second. This way you can have your labels updating at a nearly constant rate.

Let's put in a simple implementation of the -updateLabels method.

```
-(void)updateLabels
{
    [self.player updateMeters];
    self.averageLabel.text = [NSString stringWithFormat:@"%f", [self.player
averagePowerForChannel:0]];
    self.peakLabel.text = [NSString stringWithFormat:@"%f", [self.player
peakPowerForChannel:0]];
}
```

You need to call -updateMeters anytime that you use the -averagePowerForChannel or -peakPowerForChannel methods in order to get the most up-to-date information, as these values do not automatically refresh. Both methods take an NSUInteger argument that specifies the channel to retrieve information for. By giving it the value of 0, you specify the left channel for a stereo track, or the single channel for a mono track. Given that you are dealing with only a basic use of the functionality, channel 0 is a good default.

Next, you will implement your action methods for your UISliders, which will be performed every time the slider's value is changed.

```
-(void)volumeSliderChanged:(UISlider *)sender
{
    self.player.volume = sender.value;
}
-(void)panSliderChanged:(UISlider *)sender
{
    self.player.pan = sender.value;
}
-(void)rateSliderChanged:(UISlider *)sender
{
    self.player.rate = sender.value;
}
```

Now, you will implement your button action methods, which are also quite simple.

```
-(void)vibratePressed:(id)sender
{
    AudioServicesPlaySystemSound(kSystemSoundID_Vibrate);
}
-(void)playPressed:(id)sender
{
    [self.player play];
}
-(void)pausePressed:(id)sender
{
    [self.player pause];
}
```

The `AudioServicesPlaySystemSound()` is a function defined in the Audio Toolbox that plays pre-defined system sounds, such as the one just shown, which causes the phone to vibrate. You can also register your own sound systems with certain file types.

> **NOTE:** While most of the AV Foundation functionalities that you are currently working with will work on the simulator using your computer's microphone and speakers, the foregoing vibrate sound will not. You will need a physical device to test this functionality.

At this point, your app should be able to successfully play and pause your music, and you can adjust your playback rate, pan, and volume, and monitor your output levels.

Whenever you are dealing with an app that has sound or music involved, there is always a concern that your app may be interrupted by a phone call or text, and you should always include functionality to deal with these concerns. This is done through the `AVAudioPlayer` delegate methods. Since you have already set your view controller as your `AVAudioPlayer`'s delegate, you simply need to implement these methods to pause and play your sound clip when an interruption begins or ends, respectively.

```
-(void)audioPlayerBeginInterruption:(AVAudioPlayer *)player
{
    [self.player pause];
}
-(void)audioPlayerEndInterruption:(AVAudioPlayer *)player
{
    [self.player play];
}
```

This is an incredibly simple implementation of these delegate methods. For your app, you may choose to add in further functionality to possibly save data or any other tasks that might need to be done before an application is interrupted.

You should now be able to see the flexibility with which you can use the `AVAudioPlayer`, despite its simplistic use. By using multiple instances of `AVAudioPlayer`, you can implement complex audio designs using multiple sounds at the same time. One could possibly have a background music track running in one `AVAudioPlayer`, and have one or two others to handle event-based sound effects. The power, simplicity, and flexibility of the `AVAudioPlayer` class are what make it so popularly used among iOS developers.

Recipe 7–2: Recording Audio

Now that you have dealt with the key concept of playing audio, you can deal with the reverse: recording audio. This process is very similar in both structure and implementation to playing audio. You will use the `AVAudioRecorder` class to do your recording in conjunction with another `AVAudioPlayer` to handle the playback of your recording.

Make a new project, titling it "Chapter7Recipe2", with a class prefix "Recording", using the Single View Application template.

You will need to import the AV Foundation framework into your project again. See the previous recipe on how to do this. Unlike the previous recipe, you will not need the Audio Toolbox framework, as you will not include the device vibrate function in this project. Make sure to add the following import statement to your view controller's header file.

```
#import <AVFoundation/AVFoundation.h>
```

Next, you will set up your view in your controller's XIB file, so that it looks like Figure 7–5.

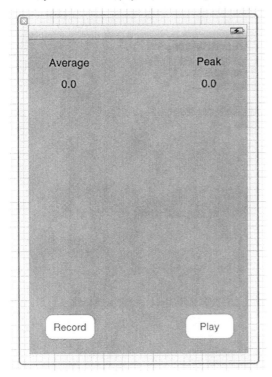

Figure 7–5. *User interface for recording and playing audio*

Next, you will connect your two buttons, as well as your two monitoring labels, over to your header file. Switch over to the Assistant Editor. By holding ^ (Ctrl) and dragging from your view elements to your header file, connect your buttons and labels to your header file. For this project, I have named the buttons recordButton, playButton, averageLevel, and peakLevel.

You will also define two action methods for your buttons to perform, named -recordPressed: and -playPressed:, and connect your buttons to them. To do this, hold ^ (Ctrl) again, and drag from each button in the XIB file to its respective action in your header file.

Before you proceed to your implementation file, you will add an instance variable, named url, of type NSURL, to your header file, to keep track of your recording's saved locations. Finally, you need to add in two more properties, one for your AVAudioPlayer, named player, and one for your AVAudioRecorder, named audioRecorder. Make sure to properly handle these by synthesizing them in your implementation file, and setting them to nil (as well as their delegates) in your -viewDidUnload method. At this point, your header file should look like so:

```objc
#import <UIKit/UIKit.h>
#import <AVFoundation/AVFoundation.h>

@interface RecordingViewController : UIViewController {
    NSURL *url;
}

@property (strong, nonatomic) IBOutlet UIButton *recordButton;
@property (strong, nonatomic) IBOutlet UIButton *playButton;
@property (strong, nonatomic) IBOutlet UILabel *averageLevel;
@property (strong, nonatomic) IBOutlet UILabel *peakLevel;

@property (strong, nonatomic) AVAudioRecorder *audioRecorder;
@property (strong, nonatomic) AVAudioPlayer *player;

-(IBAction)recordPressed:(id)sender;
-(IBAction)playPressed:(id)sender;

@end
```

Now, you will write your -viewDidLoad method, which is quite similar to that in the previous recipe.

```objc
- (void)viewDidLoad
{
    [super viewDidLoad];
    url = [self tempFileURL];
    self.audioRecorder = [[AVAudioRecorder alloc] initWithURL:url settings:nil
error:nil];
    self.audioRecorder.meteringEnabled = YES;

    NSTimer *timer = [NSTimer scheduledTimerWithTimeInterval:0.01 target:self
selector:@selector(updateLabels) userInfo:nil repeats:YES];
    [timer fire];

    [self.audioRecorder prepareToRecord];
}
```

Just as in the previous recipe, you are sending your AVAudioRecorder the -prepareToRecord action in order to help improve your application's running speed. You have again set up a timer to repeatedly update your level-monitoring labels.

The foregoing implementation uses the method -tempFileURL to retrieve your URL, which is implemented as follows. In order to avoid a compiler warning, make sure to include this method before the -viewDidLoad method, or simply place its handler of -(NSURL *)tempFileURL: in the header file.

```objc
- (NSURL *) tempFileURL
{
    NSString *outputPath = [[NSString alloc] initWithFormat:@"%@%@",
NSTemporaryDirectory(), @"recording.wav"];
    NSURL *outputURL = [[NSURL alloc] initFileURLWithPath:outputPath];
```

```
    NSFileManager *manager = [[NSFileManager alloc] init];
    if ([manager fileExistsAtPath:outputPath])
    {
        [manager removeItemAtPath:outputPath error:nil];
    }
    return outputURL;
}
```

Your -updateLabels method is again implemented like so:

```
-(void)updateLabels
{
    [self.audioRecorder updateMeters];
    self.averageLevel.text = [NSString stringWithFormat:@"%f", [self.audioRecorder
averagePowerForChannel:0]];
    self.peakLevel.text = [NSString stringWithFormat:@"%f", [self.audioRecorder
peakPowerForChannel:0]];
}
```

Finally, you just need to implement your buttons' actions.

```
-(void)recordPressed:(id)sender
{
    if ([self.audioRecorder isRecording])
    {
        [self.audioRecorder stop];
        [self.recordButton setTitle:@"Record" forState:UIControlStateNormal];
    }
    else
    {
        [self.audioRecorder record];
        [self.recordButton setTitle:@"Stop" forState:UIControlStateNormal];
    }
}
-(void)playPressed:(id)sender
{
    NSFileManager *manager = [[NSFileManager alloc] init];
    NSString *outputPath = [[NSString alloc] initWithFormat:@"%@%@",
NSTemporaryDirectory(), @"recording.wav"];
    if (![self.player isPlaying])
    {
        if ([manager fileExistsAtPath:outputPath])
        {
            self.player = [[AVAudioPlayer alloc] initWithContentsOfURL:url error:nil];
            [self.player play];
            [self.playButton setTitle:@"Pause" forState:UIControlStateNormal];
        }
    }
    else
    {
        [self.player pause];
        [self.playButton setTitle:@"Play" forState:UIControlStateNormal];
    }
}
```

> **CAUTION:** In the foregoing implementation, it is incredibly important to include the check to confirm that a file exists at the given path, in case the user presses the "play" button when no sound has been recorded yet. Initializing an AVAudioPlayer with a URL with no file in it will cause your application to throw an exception.

At this point, your application will now successfully record and play a sound. Before you can be finished, you need to implement an AVAudioPlayerDelegate method in order to handle the ending of your playback. First, you need to make sure the view controller conforms to the AVAudioPlayerDelegate protocol, so the top of your view controller's header file now looks like so:

```
@interface RecordingViewController : UIViewController <AVAudioPlayerDelegate>
```

Now you need to make your view controller your player's delegate in your -playPressed: method after it has been created with the following line.

```
self.player.delegate = self;
```

Finally, you can implement your delegate method.

```
-(void)audioPlayerDidFinishPlaying:(AVAudioPlayer *)player successfully:(BOOL)flag
{
    [self.playButton setTitle:@"Play" forState:UIControlStateNormal];
}
```

As with the previous recipe, you can implement delegate methods for both your AVAudioRecorder and your AVAudioPlayer to handle interruptions such as phone calls or text messages by pausing and re-starting your recording or playback.

Other useful methods for AVAudioRecorder that you have not implemented here include the -pause method, which pauses recording, but allows for the -play method to be called again to continue recording to the same file, and the -recordForDuration method, which allows you to specify a limitation on recording time.

As you can see, the AVAudioRecorder and AVAudioPlayer can work incredibly well in conjunction to provide a complete yet simple audio interface for the user.

Recipe 7–3: Accessing the iPod Library

So far you have been able to deal with playing and manipulating sound files that you have included in your project, but there is an easy way to access a significantly larger supply of sound files: by accessing the user's music library.

Here you will make another new project, this time called "MusicPick". First, you need to link your project with the Media Player framework, and as usual add an import statement for it to your view controller.

You will set up your view to work as a basic music player, so it looks like Figure 7–6.

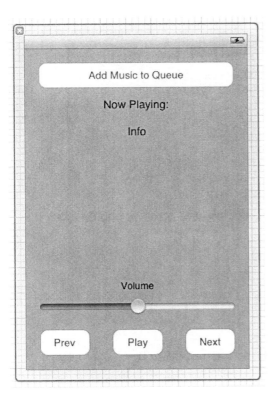

Figure 7-6. *User interface for queuing music from the iPod library*

Make sure to connect all four buttons, naming them playButton, prevButton, nextButton, and queueButton. Your slider will be sliderVolume, and your "info" UILabel will be infoLabel.

You will also define five actions for your elements, which will be -playPressed:, -prevPressed:, -nextPressed:, -queuePressed:, and -volumeChanged:. Make sure to connect each element to its respective action.

You will also define two properties in your header file, one of type MPMusicPlayerController called player, which you will use to play music, and one of type called MPMediaItemCollection called myCollection, which will help you keep track of your chosen tracks to play. Finally, you will make your view controller the delegate for a class called MPMediaPickerController, which will allow your user to select music to play, by conforming to the MPMediaPickerControllerDelegate protocol. Overall, your header file should now look like so:

```
#import <UIKit/UIKit.h>
#import <MediaPlayer/MediaPlayer.h>

@interface MainViewController : UIViewController <MPMediaPickerControllerDelegate>

@property (strong, nonatomic) IBOutlet UIButton *queueButton;
@property (strong, nonatomic) IBOutlet UIButton *prevButton;
@property (strong, nonatomic) IBOutlet UIButton *playButton;
```

```
@property (strong, nonatomic) IBOutlet UIButton *nextButton;
@property (strong, nonatomic) IBOutlet UISlider *sliderVolume;
@property (strong, nonatomic) IBOutlet UILabel *infoLabel;

@property (strong, nonatomic) MPMediaItemCollection *myCollection;
@property (strong, nonatomic) MPMusicPlayerController *player;

-(IBAction)queuePressed:(id)sender;
-(IBAction)prevPressed:(id)sender;
-(IBAction)playPressed:(id)sender;
-(IBAction)nextPressed:(id)sender;

-(IBAction)volumeChanged:(id)sender;
@end
```

Make sure to synthesize both player and myCollection, and properly handle them in -viewDidUnload as well, as usual.

Now, you can set up your -viewDidLoad method.

```
- (void)viewDidLoad
{
    [super viewDidLoad];

    self.infoLabel.text = @"...";

    self.player = [MPMusicPlayerController applicationMusicPlayer];

    [self setNotifications];

    [self.player beginGeneratingPlaybackNotifications];

    [self.player setShuffleMode:MPMusicShuffleModeOff];
    self.player.repeatMode = MPMusicRepeatModeNone;

    self.sliderVolume.value = self.player.volume;
}
```

The MPMusicPlayerController class has two important class methods that allow you to access an instance of the class. The one you used previously, +applicationMusicPlayer, returns an application-specific music player. This option can be useful for keeping your music separate from the device's actual iPod, but has the downside of being unable to play once the app enters the background. Alternatively, you can use the +iPodMusicPlayer, which allows for continuous play despite being in the background. The main thing to keep in mind in this case, however, is that your player may already have a nowPlayingItem from the actual iPod that you should be able to handle.

Whenever you use an instance of MPMusicPlayerController, it is recommended to register for notifications for whenever the playback state changes, or whenever the currently playing song changes. You will do this in your -setNotifications method, like so:

```
-(void)setNotifications
{
    NSNotificationCenter *notificationCenter = [NSNotificationCenter defaultCenter];
```

```
    [notificationCenter
     addObserver: self
     selector:    @selector (handle_NowPlayingItemChanged:)
     name:        MPMusicPlayerControllerNowPlayingItemDidChangeNotification
     object:      self.player];

    [notificationCenter
     addObserver: self
     selector:    @selector (handle_PlaybackStateChanged:)
     name:        MPMusicPlayerControllerPlaybackStateDidChangeNotification
     object:      self.player];

    [notificationCenter addObserver:self
                          selector:@selector(volumeChangedHardware:)

name:@"AVSystemController_SystemVolumeDidChangeNotification"
                          object:nil];
}
```

You have also included a third notification registration in order to make sure you know any time the user adjusts the device volume using the device's side buttons. This way, your application can be used just like a regular music player.

Each of these notifications performs a selector, which are defined as follows.

```
-(void)volumeChangedHardware:(id)sender
{
    [self.sliderVolume setValue:self.player.volume animated:YES];
}
- (void) handle_PlaybackStateChanged: (id) notification
{
    MPMusicPlaybackState playbackState = [self.player playbackState];

    if (playbackState == MPMusicPlaybackStateStopped)
    {
        [self.playButton setTitle:@"Play" forState:UIControlStateNormal];
        self.infoLabel.text = @"...";
        [self.player stop];
    }
    else if (playbackState == MPMusicPlaybackStatePaused)
    {
        [self.playButton setTitle:@"Play" forState:UIControlStateNormal];
    }
    else if (playbackState == MPMusicPlaybackStatePlaying)
    {
        [self.playButton setTitle:@"Pause" forState:UIControlStateNormal];
    }
}
- (void) handle_NowPlayingItemChanged: (id) notification
{
    MPMediaItem *currentItemPlaying = [self.player nowPlayingItem];
    if (currentItemPlaying)
    {
        NSString *info = [NSString stringWithFormat:@"%@ - %@", [currentItemPlaying
valueForProperty:MPMediaItemPropertyTitle], [currentItemPlaying
valueForProperty:MPMediaItemPropertyArtist]];
        self.infoLabel.text = info;
```

```
    }
    else
    {
        self.infoLabel.text = @"...";
    }
    if (self.player.playbackState == MPMusicPlaybackStatePlaying)
    {
        [self.playButton setTitle:@"Pause" forState:UIControlStateNormal];
    }
}
```

As you can see, when the device's volume is changed, you will simply animate your slider to adjust to the new value. When the playback state of the device is changed, you are simply adjusting your view based on the new state. Whenever the currently playing song is changed, you are updating your user interface to display basic information about whichever media item is now playing.

Next, you will define two of your MPMediaPickerController's delegate methods to handle both cancellation and successful selection of media.

```
-(void)mediaPickerDidCancel:(MPMediaPickerController *)mediaPicker
{
    [self dismissModalViewControllerAnimated:YES];
}
-(void)mediaPicker:(MPMediaPickerController *)mediaPicker
didPickMediaItems:(MPMediaItemCollection *)mediaItemCollection
{
    [self updateQueueWithMediaItemCollection:mediaItemCollection];
    [self dismissModalViewControllerAnimated:YES];
}
```

An MPMediaItemCollection is a group of media items that were selected, which you can then queue up in your MPMusicPlayerController and iterate through. You will update your player's queue by defining the -updateQueueWithMediaItemCollection: method.

```
-(void)updateQueueWithMediaItemCollection:(MPMediaItemCollection *)collection
{
    if (collection)
    {
        if (self.myCollection == nil)
        {
            self.myCollection = collection;
            [self.player setQueueWithItemCollection: self.myCollection];
            [self.player play];
        }
        else
        {
            BOOL wasPlaying = NO;
            if (self.player.playbackState == MPMusicPlaybackStatePlaying) {
                wasPlaying = YES;
            }

            MPMediaItem *nowPlayingItem       = self.player.nowPlayingItem;
            NSTimeInterval currentPlaybackTime = self.player.currentPlaybackTime;

            NSMutableArray *combinedMediaItems =
            [[self.myCollection items] mutableCopy];
```

```
            NSArray *newMediaItems = [collection items];
            [combinedMediaItems addObjectsFromArray: newMediaItems];

            [self setMyCollection:
             [MPMediaItemCollection collectionWithItems:
              (NSArray *) combinedMediaItems]];

            [self.player setQueueWithItemCollection:self.myCollection];

            self.player.nowPlayingItem      = nowPlayingItem;
            self.player.currentPlaybackTime = currentPlaybackTime;

            if (wasPlaying)
            {
                [self.player play];
            }
        }
    }
}
```

This method may seem complex, but it is actually a fairly linear progression. First, after checking to make sure that the collection is not `nil`, you check to see if there is any previous queue set up. If not, you simply set your `player`'s queue to this collection. If so, you combine the two collections, set your `player`'s queue as the result, and then restore your playback to where it previously was.

> **TIP:** If the queue is updated while an `MPMusicPlayerController` is currently playing, you will probably notice a small break in your playback as the queue is updated. This can be worked around by using a BOOL flag to update the queue only between songs.

You can fairly simply define all of your methods that are performed by your buttons and slider to perform their respective commands.

```
-(void)queuePressed:(id)sender
{
    MPMediaPickerController *picker = [[MPMediaPickerController alloc]
initWithMediaTypes:MPMediaTypeMusic];
    picker.delegate = self;
    picker.allowsPickingMultipleItems = YES;
    picker.prompt =
    NSLocalizedString (@"Add songs to play",
                        "Prompt in media item picker");
    [self presentModalViewController:picker animated:YES];
}
-(void)prevPressed:(id)sender
{
    if ([self.player currentPlaybackTime] > 5.0)
    {
        [self.player skipToBeginning];
    }
    else
    {
        [self.player skipToPreviousItem];
    }
```

```
}
-(void)volumeChanged:(id)sender
{
    if (self.player.volume != self.sliderVolume.value)
    {
        self.player.volume = self.sliderVolume.value;
    }
}
-(void)playPressed:(id)sender
{
    if ((myCollection != nil) && (self.player.playbackState !=
MPMusicPlaybackStatePlaying))
    {
        [self.player play];
        [self.playButton setTitle:@"Pause" forState:UIControlStateNormal];
    }
    else if (self.player.playbackState == MPMusicPlaybackStatePlaying)
    {
        [self.player pause];
        [self.playButton setTitle:@"Play" forState:UIControlStateNormal];
    }
}
-(void)nextPressed:(id)sender
{
        [self.player skipToNextItem];
}
```

As you can see, you have given users a five-second window in which to use the Previous button to skip to the previous song, before they must first skip back to the beginning of the current song.

Your very last step in this project is to fully implement your -viewDidUnload method to correctly handle your player's setup. Since you registered as an observer for three different kinds of notifications at the beginning of your application, you need to remove your view controller as an observer of these values. You will also be sure to -stop your MPMusicPlayerController and set its queue to nil. In its entirety, the method will look like so:

```
- (void)viewDidUnload
{
    [self.player stop];
    [self.player setQueueWithItemCollection:nil];
    [[NSNotificationCenter defaultCenter]
     removeObserver: self
     name:          MPMusicPlayerControllerNowPlayingItemDidChangeNotification
     object:        self.player];

    [[NSNotificationCenter defaultCenter]
     removeObserver: self
     name:          MPMusicPlayerControllerPlaybackStateDidChangeNotification
     object:        self.player];

    [[NSNotificationCenter defaultCenter] removeObserver:self
name:@"AVSystemController_SystemVolumeDidChangeNotification" object:nil];

    [self.player endGeneratingPlaybackNotifications];
```

```
    self.myCollection = nil;
    self.player = nil;
    [self setQueueButton:nil];
    [self setPrevButton:nil];
    [self setPlayButton:nil];
    [self setNextButton:nil];
    [self setSliderVolume:nil];
    [self setInfoLabel:nil];
    [super viewDidUnload];
}
```

One thing to note when you run this application is that until you start playing music, you will not be able to adjust your AVAudioPlayer's volume by using the external volume buttons, as these will still control the ringer volume, as opposed to the playback volume. Once you select a song to play, you will receive full control over the playback volume through these buttons.

You can probably see the pure power that this framework provides the developer. By being able to access the user's own library, you can open up a whole new level of audio customization for your application by the user, with possibilities ranging from selecting music to awake to, to specifying your own background music to a game. By giving a user the power of choice and personalization, your application's marketability and functionality increase tenfold.

Querying Media

Now that you have seen a very simple way to allow the user to select music, you can implement an even more powerful way to query, filter, and sort music from the user's media library.

Here you will simply be taking the previous recipe and adding functionality to it, specifically by allowing the user to type the name of an artist and then querying the library for music by that artist.

First, you will add a UIButton as well as a UITextField to your XIB remaining from your previous recipe, so that your view now looks like Figure 7–7.

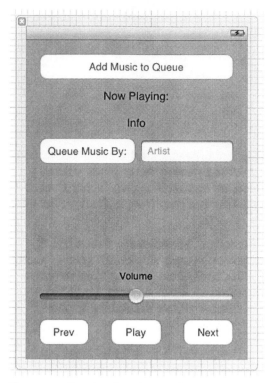

Figure 7–7. *User interface for querying music*

Make sure to correctly connect this button to an action called -queryPressed: and the text field to a property called textFieldArtist.

The first thing you will do with your new UITextField is to set its delegate to your view controller by adding the following lines to your -viewDidLoad.

```
self.textFieldArtist.delegate = self;
self.textFieldArtist.enablesReturnKeyAutomatically = YES;
```

Make sure to adjust your header file to declare that your view controller will conform to the UITextFieldDelegate protocol.

Next, you need to implement the following UITextField delegate method to have your text field correctly dismiss the keyboard upon the pressing of the return key.

```
-(BOOL)textFieldShouldReturn:(UITextField *)textField
{
    [textField resignFirstResponder];
    return NO;
}
```

You may choose to also include a call to -queryPressed: (which you will implement momentarily) from the -textFieldShouldReturn: method, so that when the return key is pressed the query is automatically performed. I opted against doing this in case the user wants to wait to perform the query after the current song has finished.

Next implement the -queryPressed: method.

```
-(void)queryPressed:(id)sender
{
    NSString *artist = self.textFieldArtist.text;
    if (artist != nil && artist != @"")
    {
        MPMediaPropertyPredicate *artistPredicate = [MPMediaPropertyPredicate
predicateWithValue:artist forProperty:MPMediaItemPropertyArtist
comparisonType:MPMediaPredicateComparisonContains];
        MPMediaQuery *query = [[MPMediaQuery alloc] init];
        [query addFilterPredicate:artistPredicate];

        NSArray *result = [query items];
        if ([result count] > 0)
        {
            [self updateQueueWithMediaItemCollection:[MPMediaItemCollection
collectionWithItems:result]];
        }
        else
            self.infoLabel.text = @"Artist Not Found.";
    }
}
```

As you can see, querying the media library is a fairly simple process, which at its bare minimum requires only an instance of the MPMediaQuery class. You can then add MPMediaPropertyPredicates to a query to make it more specific.

Using MPMediaPropertyPredicates requires a decent knowledge of the different MPMediaItemProperties, so that you can know exactly what kind of information you can acquire. Not all MPMediaItemProperties are filterable, and the filterable properties are also different if you are dealing specifically with a podcast. You should refer to the Apple documentation on MPMediaItem for a full list of properties, but following is a list of the most commonly used ones:

- MPMediaItemPropertyMediaType
- MPMediaItemPropertyTitle
- MPMediaItemPropertyAlbumTitle
- MPMediaItemPropertyArtist
- MPMediaItemPropertyArtwork

> **TIP:** Whenever you are using the MPMediaItemPropertyArtwork, you can use the -imageWithSize: method defined in MPMediaItemPropertyArtwork to create a UIImage from the artwork.

A Few Notes on MPMediaPropertyPredicates:

3. Whenever multiple filter predicates specifying different properties are added to a query, the predicates are evaluated using the AND operator, meaning that if you specify an artist name and an album name, you will receive only songs by that artist AND from that specific album.

4. Do not add two filter predicates of the same property to a query, as the resulting behavior is not defined. If you wish to query a database for multiple specific values of the same property, such as filtering for all songs by two different artists, the better method is to simply create two queries, and then combine their results afterward.

5. The `comparisonType` property of an `MPMediaPropertyPredicate` helps specify how exact you want your predicate to be. A value of `MPMediaPredicateComparisonEqualTo` returns only items with the string exactly equal to the given one, while a value of `MPMediaPredicateComparisonContains`, as shown earlier, returns items that contain the given string, proving to be usually a less specific search.

As an added functionality, `MPMediaQuerys` can also be given a "grouping property", so that they automatically group their results. You could, for example, filter a query by a specific artist, but group according to the album name. In this way, you can retrieve all the songs by a specific artist but iterate through them as if they were in albums, as demonstrated by the following code, which could be added to your `-queryPressed:` method, in which the following query object is created.

```
[query setGroupingType: MPMediaGroupingAlbum];

        NSArray *albums = [query collections];
        for (MPMediaItemCollection *album in albums)
        {
            MPMediaItem *representativeItem = [album representativeItem];
            NSString *albumName = [representativeItem valueForProperty:
MPMediaItemPropertyAlbumTitle];
            NSLog (@"%@", albumName);
        }
```

You can also set a grouping type by using class methods, such as `+albumsQuery`, for `MPMediaQuery`, which will create your query instance with a pre-set grouping property.

Recipe 7–4: Background Playing and Now Playing Info

So far you have seen multiple techniques for dealing with audio in iOS, from playing a single sound, to accessing the library, to utilizing the iPod player. Each technique tends to have its pros, cons, and specific uses depending on the goal of your application.

However, when all these functionalities are used in conjunction, the possibilities for your app become nearly limitless. Here, you will combine the use of the AVFoundation, MPMediaQuery, MPMediaPickerController, and MPNowPlayingInfoCenter (a new iOS 5.0 feature!) to create your own version, albeit a less pretty one, of the iPod user interface such that your music can continue to play even if your application is in the background.

Make a new project using the Single View Application template, naming it "Chapter7Recipe3", with class prefix "Main".

Next, you will make sure all the frameworks you need are imported. Go ahead and link the following frameworks to your project, exactly as you have in all the previous recipes in this chapter.

- AVFoundation.framework: You will use this to play your audio files.

- MediaPlayer.framework: This will allow you to access your library and media files.

- CoreMedia.framework: You won't use any classes from this framework, but you will need some of the CMTime functions to help deal with your audio player.

Add the following import statements to your view controller's header file. You do not need one for the Core Media framework in this project.

```
#import <MediaPlayer/MediaPlayer.h>
#import <AVFoundation/AVFoundation.h>
```

Your view controller is also going to end up as the delegate for several objects, so add protocol statements to your header file for the following protocols:

- UITextFieldDelegate

- AVAudioSessionDelegate

- MPMediaPickerControllerDelegate

Next you will set up your app to be able to continue playing music once it has entered the background of the device. The first thing you need to do is declare a property of type AVAudioSession, called session. Make sure to @synthesize it, and then in your -viewDidUnload set it to nil as usual.

```
@property (nonatomic, strong) AVAudioSession *session;
```

Next, add the following code to your -viewDidLoad method:

```
self.session = [AVAudioSession sharedInstance];
self.session.delegate = self;
[self.session setCategory:AVAudioSessionCategoryPlayback error:nil];
[self.session setActive:YES error:nil];
```

By specifying that your session's category is of type AVAudioSessionCategoryPlayback, you are telling your device that your application's main focus is playing music, and should therefore be allowed to continue playing audio while the application is in the background.

You need to also make sure your session is deactivated when you are done with it, so add the following line to your -viewDidUnload method.

```
[self.session setActive:NO error:nil];
```

Now that you have configured your AVAudioSession, you need to edit your application's .plist file in order to specify that your application, when in the background, must be allowed to run audio. You can usually find this file in the Supporting Files group of your project. If not, you can find the file in your project's folder, as in Figure 7–8.

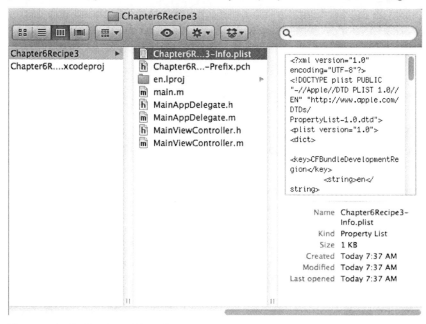

Figure 7–8. *Finding the* .plist *file*

By default, this file should open in Xcode, resembling Figure 7–9.

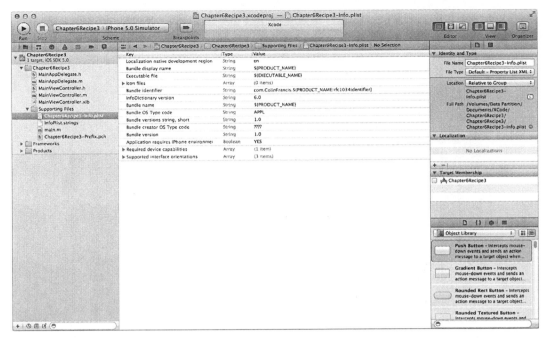

Figure 7–9. *Editing the* `.plist` *file*

Under the Editor menu, select **Add Item**. A new item should appear, looking like Figure 7–10.

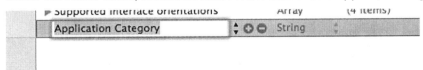

Figure 7–10. *Setting the application category*

For the Application Category item, open the drop-down menu by clicking the pair of arrows, and then select "Required Background modes".

Drop down the values list for this new item by clicking the arrow on the left. You will edit the value for "Item 0". Drop down the menu on the right side, and select "App plays audio", as in Figure 7–11. Alternatively, you could type **audio** into the value field, and once you press the return key, Xcode will change the value correctly.

Figure 7–11. *Specifying background audio capabilities*

Your application should now be ready to play audio while in the background state!

Next, you will build your user interface in your XIB file. Set up your view so that it looks like Figure 7–12.

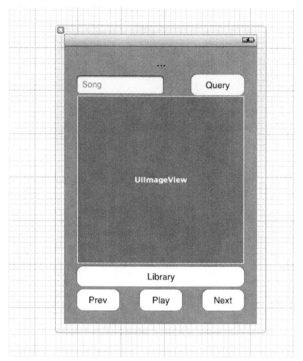

Figure 7–12. *User interface for your custom music player*

For the purposes of this project, the following variable names will be assigned to the shown view elements, so connect each element over to your header file using the name shown here:

- infoLabel: Your UILabel at the top of the view, which will display the information of the current song

- textFieldSong: Your UITextField, which you put a placeholder text of "Song" inside

- queryButton: The upper UIButton with the title "Query"

- artworkImageView: Your UIImageView, which will display album artwork for songs

- libraryButton: Large "Library" UIButton.

- playButton: Middle "Play" UIButton

- nextButton: Right-side "Next" UIButton

- prevButton: Left-side "Prev" UIButton

Define actions for the five buttons that you will use and connect each button to its respective method. Your method declarations should look like so:

```
-(IBAction)queryPressed:(id)sender;
-(IBAction)nextPressed:(id)sender;
-(IBAction)prevPressed:(id)sender;
-(IBAction)playPressed:(id)sender;
-(IBAction)libraryPressed:(id)sender;
```

Next, you will declare the additional property objects that you will need to run your application. For each of the following properties, make sure you synthesize each one and properly set it to nil at the end of your application. First, you will be using an instance of the AVQueuePlayer class to play and queue up your sound files, so you will declare one of them as a property:

```
@property (nonatomic, strong) AVQueuePlayer *player;
```

In order to manage your player, you will need two copies as NSMutableArrays of its playlist. One will have all the queued items in their original MPMediaItem class (which you can access media information for), while the other will have them all after they have been converted to instances of AVPlayerItem (which you can play through your AVQueuePlayer). You will also have a property of type NSUInteger in order to help keep track of the currently playing item. These properties will be declared like so, making sure to correctly synthesize and nil each one:

```
@property (nonatomic, strong) NSMutableArray *playlist;
@property (nonatomic, strong) NSMutableArray *myCollection;
@property (nonatomic) NSUInteger currentIndex;
```

The first thing you will do now in your implementation file is finish writing your -viewDidLoad method, so that it now looks like so:

```
- (void)viewDidLoad
{
    [super viewDidLoad];
    self.session = [AVAudioSession sharedInstance];
    self.session.delegate = self;
    [self.session setCategory:AVAudioSessionCategoryPlayback error:nil];
    [self.session setActive:YES error:nil];

    self.textFieldSong.delegate = self;
    [self.playButton setTitle:@"Play" forState:UIControlStateNormal];
}
```

The only new code here was to confirm that the title for your playButton is set correctly, and to set your view controller as the delegate for your UITextField. Implement the UITextFieldDelegate method to handle dismissing the keyboard like so:

```
-(BOOL)textFieldShouldReturn:(UITextField *)textField
{
    [textField resignFirstResponder];
    return NO;
}
```

You will also need to override the getter for your playlist in order to ensure that it correctly initializes.

```
-(NSMutableArray *)playlist
{
    if (!playlist)
    {
        playlist = [[NSMutableArray alloc] initWithCapacity:5];
    }
    return playlist;
}
```

You will also override the getter for currentIndex, so that it always returns the correct index of the currently playing item.

```
-(NSUInteger)currentIndex
{
    currentIndex = [self.playlist indexOfObject:self.player.currentItem];
    return currentIndex;
}
```

Next you will implement a method that will update your user interface every time the song changes.

```
-(void)updateNowPlaying
{
    if (self.player.currentItem != nil)
    {
        MPMediaItem *nowPlaying = [self.myCollection objectAtIndex:self.currentIndex];
//        NSLog(@"%@", [nowPlaying valueForProperty:MPMediaItemPropertyTitle]);

        self.infoLabel.text = [NSString stringWithFormat:@"%@ - %@", [nowPlaying
valueForProperty:MPMediaItemPropertyTitle], [nowPlaying
valueForProperty:MPMediaItemPropertyArtist]];

        UIImage *artwork = [[nowPlaying valueForProperty:MPMediaItemPropertyArtwork]
imageWithSize:self.artworkImageView.frame.size];
        if (artwork)
        {
            self.artworkImageView.image = artwork;
        }
        else
        {
            self.artworkImageView.image = nil;
        }
        if ([MPNowPlayingInfoCenter class])
        {
            NSString *title = [nowPlaying valueForProperty:MPMediaItemPropertyTitle];
            NSString *artist = [nowPlaying valueForProperty:MPMediaItemPropertyArtist];
            NSDictionary *currentlyPlayingTrackInfo = [NSDictionary
dictionaryWithObjects:[NSArray arrayWithObjects:title, artist, nil] forKeys:[NSArray
arrayWithObjects:MPMediaItemPropertyTitle, MPMediaItemPropertyArtist, nil]];
            [MPNowPlayingInfoCenter defaultCenter].nowPlayingInfo =
currentlyPlayingTrackInfo;
        }
    }
    else
    {
        self.infoLabel.text = @"...";
        [self.playButton setTitle:@"Play" forState:UIControlStateNormal];
        self.artworkImageView.image = nil;
```

```
        }
}
```

The method just shown, aside from updating your user interface to display the current song information, also takes advantage of a new feature in iOS 5, called the `MPNowPlayingInfoCenter`! This class allows the developer to place information on the device's lock screen, or on other devices when the application is displaying info through AirPlay. You can pass information to it by setting the `nowPlayingInfo` property of the `+defaultCenter` to a dictionary of values and properties that you created.

To make use of the foregoing `MPNowPlayingInfoCenter` implementation, you must make a few specific additions in your code. Specifically, none of this functionality will work if your application cannot handle remote control events. To do this, start by implementing the `-remoteControlReceivedWithEvent:` method that handles remote events.

```
- (void) remoteControlReceivedWithEvent: (UIEvent *) receivedEvent {
    if (receivedEvent.type == UIEventTypeRemoteControl) {

        switch (receivedEvent.subtype) {

            case UIEventSubtypeRemoteControlTogglePlayPause:
                [self playPressed:nil];
                break;

            case UIEventSubtypeRemoteControlPreviousTrack:
                [self prevPressed:nil];
                break;

            case UIEventSubtypeRemoteControlNextTrack:
                [self nextPressed:nil];
                break;

            default:
                break;
        }
    }
}
```

This aforementioned method will be called when the user taps the Pause, Previous, and Next buttons on the lock screen or the multitasking screen. All you have to do is have them call your methods to play, advance, and rewind your player, which you will implement later.

Next, in order to receive these remote control events, you must modify your -`viewDidAppear:animated:` and -`viewWillDisappear:animated:` methods.

```
- (void)viewDidAppear:(BOOL)animated
{
    [super viewDidAppear:animated];
    [[UIApplication sharedApplication] beginReceivingRemoteControlEvents];
    [self becomeFirstResponder];
}
- (void)viewWillDisappear:(BOOL)animated
{
    [[UIApplication sharedApplication] endReceivingRemoteControlEvents];
    [self resignFirstResponder];
```

```
    [super viewWillDisappear:animated];
}
```

Finally, in order for these previous two methods to work correctly and allow your view controller to become the first responder, you must override the -canBecomeFirstResponder method like so:

```
-(BOOL)canBecomeFirstResponder
{
    return YES;
}
```

If these extra steps are not followed, your application will not be able to make use of any "Now Playing" information in the lock screen or multitasking bar.

In order to assist in keeping your two NSMutableArrays in sync, you will define a method that will take an NSArray of MPMediaItems and return an NSArray of the same items, but essentially converted to the AVPlayerItem.

```
-(NSArray *)AVPlayerItemsFromArray:(NSArray *)items
{
    NSMutableArray *array = [[NSMutableArray alloc] initWithCapacity:[items count]];
    NSURL *url;
    for (MPMediaItem *current in items)
    {
        url = [current valueForProperty:MPMediaItemPropertyAssetURL];
        AVPlayerItem *playerItem = [AVPlayerItem playerItemWithURL:url];

        [[NSNotificationCenter defaultCenter]
         addObserver:self
         selector:@selector(playerItemDidReachEnd:)
         name:AVPlayerItemDidPlayToEndTimeNotification
         object:playerItem];

        if (playerItem != nil)
            [array addObject:playerItem];
    }
    return array;
}
```

In order to later be able to tell when a song has finished playing and act accordingly, you will need to add your view controller as an observer, as shown earlier. It is fairly convenient to include the -addObserver call in this method since you can so easily access all the AVPlayerItems that you will be using.

While you are dealing with your NSNotificationCenter, make sure that all the observers you just added will be properly removed. Add the following lines to your -viewDidUnload.

```
for (AVPlayerItem *playerItem in self.playlist)
    {
        [[NSNotificationCenter defaultCenter] removeObserver:self
name:AVPlayerItemDidPlayToEndTimeNotification object:playerItem];
    }
```

The implementation for the -playerItemDidReachEnd: method that you've specified to run any time a song ends is quite simple, as shown here.

```
- (void)playerItemDidReachEnd:(NSNotification *)notification
{
    [self performSelector:@selector(updateNowPlaying) withObject:nil afterDelay:0.5];
}
```

I have included the half-second delay here to ensure that the -updateNowPlaying call does not execute until the AVQueuePlayer has completely moved on to playing the next item.

Next you'll implement your two methods that will be used whenever you need to update or add to your playlist.

```
-(void)updatePlaylistWithArray:(NSArray *)collection
{
    if (([self.playlist count] == 0) || (self.player.currentItem == nil))
    {
        [self.myCollection removeAllObjects];
        self.playlist = [NSMutableArray arrayWithArray:collection];
        self.player = [[AVQueuePlayer alloc] initWithItems:self.playlist];
        [self.player play];
    }
    else
    {
        AVPlayerItem *currentItem = [self.playlist lastObject];
        for (AVPlayerItem *item in collection)
        {
            if ([self.player canInsertItem:item afterItem:currentItem])
            {
                [self.player insertItem:item afterItem:currentItem];
                currentItem = item;
            }
        }
        [self.playlist addObjectsFromArray:collection];
    }
}

-(void)updateMyCollectionWithArray:(NSArray *)mediaItems
{
    if ([self.myCollection count] == 0)
    {
        self.myCollection = [NSMutableArray arrayWithArray:mediaItems];
    }
    else
    {
        [self.myCollection addObjectsFromArray:mediaItems];
    }
}
```

Your -playPressed: and -nextPressed: methods are quite simple in their implementation since AVQueuePlayer inherits from the AVPlayer class, and has a nice little method for advancing to the next item in the queue.

```
-(void)playPressed:(id)sender
{
    if (self.playlist.count > 0)
    {
```

```
            if ([[self.playButton titleForState:UIControlStateNormal]
isEqualToString:@"Play"])
            {
                [self.player play];
                [self.playButton setTitle:@"Pause" forState:UIControlStateNormal];
            }
            else
            {
                [self.player pause];
                //Scrub back half a second to give the user a little lead-in when they
resume playing
                [self.player seekToTime:CMTimeSubtract(self.player.currentTime,
CMTimeMakeWithSeconds(0.5, 1.0)) completionHandler:^(BOOL finished)
                {
                    [self.playButton setTitle:@"Play" forState:UIControlStateNormal];
                }];
            }
        [self updateNowPlaying];
    }
}
-(void)nextPressed:(id)sender
{
    [self.player advanceToNextItem];
    if (self.player.currentItem == nil)
    {
        [self.playlist removeAllObjects];
        [self.myCollection removeAllObjects];
    }
    [self updateNowPlaying];
}
```

Unfortunately, the AVQueuePlayer does not include any easy implementation for moving backward in a queue, so your implementation of the -prevPressed: method is slightly more complex, and just involves a bit of swapping around of your AVPlayerItems.

```
-(void)prevPressed:(id)sender
{
    if (CMTimeCompare(self.player.currentTime, CMTimeMake(5.0, 1)) > 0)
    {
        [self.player seekToTime:kCMTimeZero];
    }
    else
    {
        [self.player pause];

        AVPlayerItem *current = self.player.currentItem;
        if (current != [self.playlist objectAtIndex:0])
        {
            AVPlayerItem *previous = [self.playlist objectAtIndex:[self.playlist
indexOfObject:current]-1];
            if ([self.player canInsertItem:previous afterItem:current])
            {
                [current seekToTime:kCMTimeZero];
                [previous seekToTime:kCMTimeZero];

                [self.player insertItem:previous afterItem:current];
                [self.player advanceToNextItem];
```

```
            [self.player removeItem:current];
            [self.player insertItem:current afterItem:previous];
        }
        else
        {
            NSLog(@"Error: Could not insert");
        }
    }
    else
    {
        [self.player seekToTime:kCMTimeZero];
    }

    [self.player play];
    }
    [self updateNowPlaying];
}
```

The CMTimeMake() function that you just used is a very flexible function that takes two inputs. The first represents the number of time units you want, and the second represents the timescale, where 1 represents a second, 2 represents half a second, and so on. A call of CMTimeMake(100, 10) would make 100 units of (1/10) seconds each, resulting in 10 seconds.

The function of your Query button will be to use an MPMediaQuery to retrieve any songs in the library that contain the word or phrase in your UITextField. This implementation is fairly straightforward, once you remember to update both of your NSMutableArrays afterward.

```
-(void)queryPressed:(id)sender
{
    MPMediaQuery *query = [[MPMediaQuery alloc] init];
    NSString *title = self.textFieldSong.text;
    MPMediaPropertyPredicate *songPredicate = [MPMediaPropertyPredicate
predicateWithValue:title forProperty:MPMediaItemPropertyTitle
comparisonType:MPMediaPredicateComparisonContains];
    [query addFilterPredicate:songPredicate];

    [self updatePlaylistWithArray:[self AVPlayerItemsFromArray:[query items]]];
    [self updateMyCollectionWithArray:[query items]];

    [self.playButton setTitle:@"Pause" forState:UIControlStateNormal];

    [self updateNowPlaying];
    if ([self.textFieldSong isFirstResponder])
        [self.textFieldSong resignFirstResponder];
}
```

Finally, you can set up your -libraryPressed: method, which will bring up an MPMediaPickerController, allowing you to select multiple songs for queuing.

```
-(void)libraryPressed:(id)sender
{
    MPMediaPickerController *picker = [[MPMediaPickerController alloc]
initWithMediaTypes:MPMediaTypeMusic];
    picker.delegate = self;
    picker.allowsPickingMultipleItems = YES;
```

```
    picker.prompt = @"Choose Some Music!";
    [self presentModalViewController:picker animated:YES];
}
```

You will need to implement two delegate methods to correctly handle the
MPMediaPickerController. First, here is the delegate method for a cancellation:

```
-(void)mediaPickerDidCancel:(MPMediaPickerController *)mediaPicker
{
    [self dismissModalViewControllerAnimated:YES];
}
```

Second, you have the delegate method for a successful media choice, which will look
very similar to the -queryPressed: method.

```
-(void)mediaPicker:(MPMediaPickerController *)mediaPicker
didPickMediaItems:(MPMediaItemCollection *)mediaItemCollection
{
    [self updatePlaylistWithArray:[self AVPlayerItemsFromArray:[mediaItemCollection
items]]];
    [self updateMyCollectionWithArray:[mediaItemCollection items]];
    [self.playButton setTitle:@"Pause" forState:UIControlStateNormal];
    [self updateNowPlaying];

    [self dismissModalViewControllerAnimated:YES];
}
```

You may, while testing this application, notice the slight issue of the fact that you have
not included a way to clear the queue and reset the app without playing or skipping
through to the end of the queue. This is not a problem if your queue is only a few songs
long, but if you queue any more than that, you will probably want to incorporate some
method to clear out your queue by resetting your NSMutableArrays and removing all the
items from your player's queue. For testing purposes, however, simply closing the
application by double-tapping the device's home button, holding a long press over the
application's icon, and then closing it will do.

Your music queuing player should now be fully functional! When you test the app, it
should continue to play music even after the application has entered the background of
your device! Figure 7–13 demonstrates your application playing a song, along with its
Now Playing functionality and ability to receive remote control events.

Figure 7–13. *Your application playing a song while displaying Now Playing information in the multitasking bar*

Summary

The complete multimedia experience is one that goes beyond a simple matter of whether the user can listen to music. Sound, as a product, is much more about the tiny details that make it just a little bit better, whether it's a quick fade-out when pausing, or the ability to more quickly find a song. From recording music to filtering media items to creating volume ramps, every extra detail that you, as a developer, take the care to include in your applications will eventually result in a significantly more powerful tool that your audience can enjoy. In iOS development, Apple has provided an incredibly powerful set of multimedia-based functionalities to make use of, and, as a quick search in the iTunes app store will show, the development community has gone above and beyond the call of duty in fully utilizing these in order to provide our audience, the users, with a multimedia environment beyond imagination.

Chapter 8

User Data Recipes

No two people are alike, and, in the same way, no two iOS devices are alike, as the information that one device stores is incredibly dependent on the person who uses it. We populate our devices with our lives, including our photos, calendars, notes, contacts, and music. As developers, it is incredibly important to be able to access all of this information regardless of the device, so that we may incorporate it into our applications and provide a more unique, user-specific interface. In this chapter, we will cover a variety of methods for dealing with user-based data, dealing first with the calendar, and then with the address book.

Recipe 8–1: Working with NSCalendar and NSDate

Many different applications are often used for time- and date-based calculations. This could be anything from converting calendars, to sorting to-do lists, to telling the user how much time remains before an alarm will go off. In order to use the more intricate event-based user interface, you must have a solid understanding of the simpler NSDate-focused APIs. Here, you will implement a simple application to illustrate the use of the NSDate, NSCalendar, and NSDateComponents classes by converting dates from the popular Gregorian calendar to the Hebrew calendar.

Create a new project called "Chapter8Recipe1", with the class prefix "Main," using the Single View Application template. You will not need to utilize any extra frameworks. Switch over to your view controller's XIB file. Set up your XIB file to resemble the one shown in Figure 8–1.

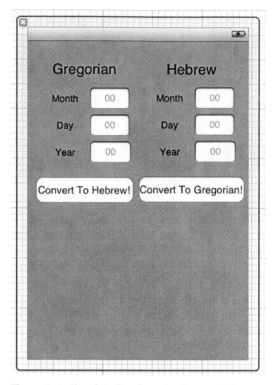

Figure 8–1. *User interface for calendar conversion*

You will need to set up properties to represent each UITextField. Once your view is set up, connect each UITextField to your header file with the following property names as appropriate.

- textFieldGMonth
- textFieldGDay
- textFieldGYear
- textFieldHMonth
- textFieldHDay
- textFieldHYear

The "G" and "H" in these property names refer to whether the given UITextField is on the Gregorian or Hebrew side of the application.

You do not need to connect the UIButtons to outlets, but make sure they are connected to respective actions -convertToHebrew: and -convertToGregorian:.

Always keep in mind that whenever you are dealing with an application that takes user input, such as the UITextFields here, there is always a possibility of a keyboard popping up and covering the bottom half of your screen. Plan your design accordingly by placing all UITextFields in the upper half of the view!

In order to better control all these UITextFields, you will need to make your view
controller the delegate for them all. First, add <UITextFieldDelegate> to your controller's
header line, so that it now looks like so:

@interface MainViewController : UIViewController <UITextFieldDelegate>

Next, you will set all the UITextField delegates to your view controller by adding the
following code to your -viewDidLoad method:

```
for (UITextField *field in self.view.subviews)
    {
        if ([field respondsToSelector:@selector(setDelegate:)])
        {
            field.delegate = self;
        }
    }
```

In this for loop, the -respondsToSelector: method call is necessary, otherwise your
application will throw an NSException. In general, this is a fairly good method to use
whenever you are dealing with the possibility of multiple types of objects in an array.

Next, define the UITextFieldDelegate method -textFieldShouldReturn: to properly
dismiss the keyboard.

```
-(BOOL)textFieldShouldReturn:(UITextField *)textField
{
    [textField resignFirstResponder];
    return NO;
}
```

The first new class that you will see here is the NSCalendar class. This is essentially used
to set a standard for the dates that you will later refer to. The NSCalendar method also
allows you to perform several useful functions dealing with a calendar, such as changing
which day a week starts on, or changing the time zone used. The NSCalendar class also
acts as a bridge between the NSDate and NSDateComponents classes that you will see
later.

You will be using two instances of the NSCalendar class in order to translate dates from
the Gregorian calendar to the Hebrew calendar. You will make these properties of your
class.

```
@property (nonatomic, strong) NSCalendar *gregorianCalendar;
@property (nonatomic, strong) NSCalendar *hebrewCalendar;
```

Go ahead and synthesize these two properties as you would any other property. You
will, however, need to implement custom implementations of the getter methods for
each of these properties.

```
-(NSCalendar *)gregorianCalendar
{
    if (!gregorianCalendar)
    {
        gregorianCalendar = [[NSCalendar alloc]
initWithCalendarIdentifier:NSGregorianCalendar];
    }
```

```
    return gregorianCalendar;
}

-(NSCalendar *)hebrewCalendar
{
    if (!hebrewCalendar)
    {
        hebrewCalendar = [[NSCalendar alloc]
initWithCalendarIdentifier:NSHebrewCalendar];
    }
    return hebrewCalendar;
}
```

These method overrides are necessary in order to make sure that your calendars are initialized with their correct calendar types. Alternatively, you could simply initialize your calendars in your -viewDidLoad method to be created when the app launches.

There are a large variety of different calendar types that are available for use, including but not limited to the following:

- NSBuddhistCalendar

- NSIslamicCalendar

- NSJapaneseCalendar

Given the immense multicultural nature of today's technological world, you may find it quite necessary to make use of some of these calendars! Consult the Apple documentation for a full list of possible calendar types.

Now that your setup is done, you can implement your conversion method, starting with the conversion from Gregorian to Hebrew.

```
-(void)convertToGregorian:(id)sender
{
    NSDateComponents *hComponents = [[NSDateComponents alloc] init];
    [hComponents setDay:[self.textFieldHDay.text integerValue]];
    [hComponents setMonth:[self.textFieldHMonth.text integerValue]];
    [hComponents setYear:[self.textFieldHYear.text integerValue]];

    NSDate *hebrewDate = [self.hebrewCalendar dateFromComponents:hComponents];

    NSUInteger unitFlags = NSDayCalendarUnit | NSMonthCalendarUnit |
NSYearCalendarUnit;

    NSDateComponents *hebrewDateComponents = [self.gregorianCalendar
components:unitFlags fromDate:hebrewDate];

    self.textFieldGDay.text = [[NSNumber numberWithInteger:hebrewDateComponents.day]
stringValue];
    self.textFieldGMonth.text = [[NSNumber numberWithInteger:hebrewDateComponents.month]
stringValue];
    self.textFieldGYear.text = [[NSNumber numberWithInteger:hebrewDateComponents.year]
stringValue];
}
```

As you can see, you are using a combination of NSDateComponents, NSDate, and NSCalendar to perform this conversion.

The NSDateComponents class is used to define the details that make up an NSDate, such as the day, month, year, time, etc. Here, only the month, day, and year are being specified.

As mentioned earlier, you use an instance of the NSCalendar to create an instance of NSDate out of the components that you have defined.

One of the more confusing parts of this method is the use of the NSUInteger unitFlags, which is formatted quite unusually. Whenever you specify creating an instance of NSDateComponents out of an NSDate, you need to specify exactly which components to include from the date. You can specify these flags, called NSCalendarUnits, through the use of the NSUInteger, as shown.

Other types of NSCalendarUnits include the following, among many others:

- NSSecondCalendarUnit
- NSWeekOfYearCalendarUnit
- NSEraCalendarUnit
- NSTimeZoneCalendarUnit

As you can see, the specificity with which you can create instances of NSDate is highly customizable, allowing you to perform unique calculations and comparisons. For a full list of NSCalendarUnit values, refer to the NSCalendar class reference in Apple's developer API.

Since the values of NSDateComponents are of type NSInteger, you must first convert them to instances of NSNumber, and then take their -stringValue before you set them into your text fields.

Once you have defined your conversion from one calendar to the other, the reverse is incredibly simple, as you just need to change which text fields and calendar you use.

```
-(void)convertToHebrew:(id)sender
{
    NSDateComponents *gComponents = [[NSDateComponents alloc] init];
    [gComponents setDay:[self.textFieldGDay.text integerValue]];
    [gComponents setMonth:[self.textFieldGMonth.text integerValue]];
    [gComponents setYear:[self.textFieldGYear.text integerValue]];

    NSDate *gregorianDate = [self.gregorianCalendar dateFromComponents:gComponents];

    NSUInteger unitFlags = NSDayCalendarUnit | NSMonthCalendarUnit |
    NSYearCalendarUnit;

    NSDateComponents *hebrewDateComponents = [self.hebrewCalendar components:unitFlags
fromDate:gregorianDate];

    self.textFieldHDay.text = [[NSNumber numberWithInteger:hebrewDateComponents.day]
stringValue];
```

```
    self.textFieldHMonth.text = [[NSNumber numberWithInteger:hebrewDateComponents.month]
stringValue];
    self.textFieldHYear.text = [[NSNumber numberWithInteger:hebrewDateComponents.year]
stringValue];
}
```

Your application should now be able to correctly convert instances of NSDate between calendars, as shown in Figure 8–2! Try experimenting with different dates or even different calendars to see what kinds of powerful date conversions you can do.

Figure 8–2. *Application successfully converting calendar dates*

Recipe 8–2: Fetching Events

Now that you have covered how to deal with basic date conversions and calculations, you can go much more into detail on dealing specifically with events and calendars, including interacting with the user's own events and schedule. The next few recipes will all compound in order to create a complete utilization of the Event Kit framework.

First, create a new project using the Single View Application template. I have called mine "Chapter8Recipe2", with class prefix "Main".

Next, you need to import the Event Kit framework into your project. You can refer to earlier recipes on exactly how to do this.

In order to use your Event Kit framework, you need to add the following line to your main view controller's header file:

```
#import <EventKit/EventKit.h>
```

For this recipe, you will simply be accessing and logging your device's already scheduled events, so you will not be dealing at all with your view controller's XIB file.

Whenever you're dealing with the Event Kit framework, the main element you will be working with most is your EKEventStore. This class will be an incredibly powerful tool in allowing you to access, delete, and save events to your calendars. You will create a property of this type in your header file like so:

```
@property (strong, nonatomic) EKEventStore *eventStore;
```

Make sure to @synthesize this property, and then set it to nil in your -viewDidUnload.

The implementation for this first recipe to log your events is incredibly simple. You will simply modify your -viewDidLoad. After initializing your eventStore property, you will create a specific version of the NSPredicate class that will allow you to query for events. Specifically, you will query for all the dates in your device's calendar within the next 48 hours. Your method will look like so:

```
- (void)viewDidLoad
{
    [super viewDidLoad];
    self.eventStore = [[EKEventStore alloc] init];
    NSDate *now = [NSDate date];
    NSDate *tomorrow = [NSDate dateWithTimeIntervalSinceNow:(2*24.0*60*60)];
    NSPredicate *predicate = [self.eventStore predicateForEventsWithStartDate:now
endDate:tomorrow calendars:nil];
    NSArray *events = [self.eventStore eventsMatchingPredicate:predicate];
    for (EKEvent *event in events)
    {
        NSLog(@"%@", event.title);
    }
}
```

The +date method is a nice little way to very easily get the current date and time represented as an NSDate. The +dateWithTimeIntervalSinceNow: method takes a float value as a parameter, representing the number of seconds you want your time interval to include. A quick calculation of 2*24*60*60 seconds gives you a two-day range for which to query.

You create your predicate using the -predicateForEventsWithStartDate:endDate:calendars: method for the EKEventStore class. By passing a value of nil to the calendars parameter of this method, you specify that you want your predicate to be applied to all calendars.

To finally get your array of `EKEvents`, you simply call the `EKEventStore` method - `eventsMatchingPredicate:` as shown in the previous snippet, and you can now iterate through your events and act accordingly.

You will need to test this application on a device in order for it to access your calendar and print valid information. Make sure that your device actually has events scheduled to serve as your test data. Since the only output you are creating here is in the log, you will also need to run this application on your device from Xcode, so as to capture the output.

Recipe 8–3: Displaying Events in a UITableView

Now that you are able to access your events, you will start by creating a better interface with which to deal with them. You will implement a grouped `UITableView` to display your events.

First, you need to add your `UITableView` into your XIB file. Go ahead and drag out a `UITableView` element from your library, and make it take up the entire view. In the Attribute inspector, make sure that the "Style" of the table view is set to "Grouped", as shown in Figure 8–3.

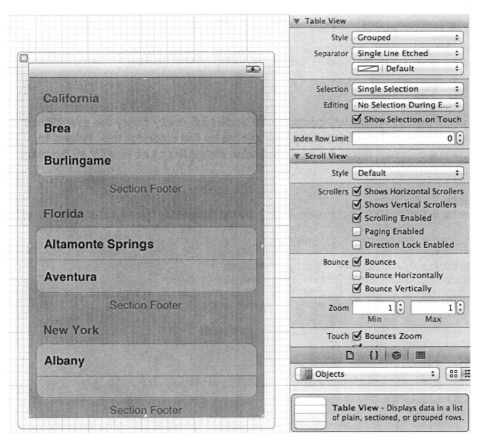

Figure 8–3. *Configuring your grouped* `UITableView`

Next, connect your `UITableView` to your view controller's header file. The property used here will be called `tableViewEvents`.

Before you switch over to your implementation file, you will define two more properties that you will use. First, an `NSArray` called `calendars` will be used to hold references to all the calendars in your `EKEventStore`. Second, an instance of `NSMutableDictionary` will be used to store all your events based on which calendar they belong to. Make sure to properly synthesize these, and also make sure they are set to `nil` in `-viewDidUnload`.

```
@property (nonatomic, strong) NSMutableDictionary *events;
@property (nonatomic, strong) NSArray *calendars;
```

The first thing you need to do is set up a newer version of your `-viewDidLoad` method in order to properly populate your array and dictionary, as well as to make sure your `UITableView` is properly set up.

```
- (void)viewDidLoad
{
    [super viewDidLoad];

    self.tableViewEvents.delegate = self;
```

```
    self.tableViewEvents.dataSource = self;

    self.eventStore = [[EKEventStore alloc] init];
    self.calendars = [self.eventStore calendars];

    [self fetchEvents];
}
```

The new -fetchEvents method will contain your code to actually query the eventStore for your events. Since you will be sorting your events by the calendar they belong to, you will perform a different query for each calendar, rather than just one for all events.

```
-(void)fetchEvents
{
    self.events = nil;
    self.events = [[NSMutableDictionary alloc] initWithCapacity:[self.calendars count]];

    for (EKCalendar *cal in self.calendars)
    {
        NSPredicate *calPredicate = [self.eventStore
predicateForEventsWithStartDate:[NSDate date] endDate:[NSDate
dateWithTimeIntervalSinceNow:(2*24.0*60*60)] calendars:[NSArray arrayWithObject:cal]];
        //Passing nil to calendars means to search all calendars.

        NSArray *eventsInThisCalendar = [self.eventStore
eventsMatchingPredicate:calPredicate];
        if (eventsInThisCalendar != nil)
        {
            [self.events setObject:eventsInThisCalendar forKey:cal.title];
        }
    }
}
```

As you can see, you will be storing your events in an NSMutableDictionary by using the titles of your calendars as keys, with their objects being arrays of events that belong to that specific calendar.

Before you continue, you need to specify that your view controller will conform to certain protocols in order for your compile to allow it to be set as the delegate and data source of your view controller. After adding the UITableViewDelegate and UITableViewDataSource protocols, your header file should now resemble the following:

```
#import <UIKit/UIKit.h>
#import <EventKit/EventKit.h>

@interface MainViewController : UIViewController <UITableViewDelegate,
UITableViewDataSource>{
    UITableView *tableViewEvents;
}


@property (nonatomic, strong) EKEventStore *eventStore;
@property (strong, nonatomic) IBOutlet UITableView *tableViewEvents;

@property (nonatomic, strong) NSMutableDictionary *events;
@property (nonatomic, strong) NSArray *calendars;
@end
```

In order to properly implement a grouped UITableView, you need to implement a method to specify exactly how many sections you will need. Since you have one section per calendar, this method is nice and easy.

```
-(NSInteger)numberOfSectionsInTableView:(UITableView *)tableView
{
    return [self.calendars count];
}
```

You can also implement a method to specify your section titles, in an equally simple manner.

```
-(NSString *)tableView:(UITableView *)tableView
titleForHeaderInSection:(NSInteger)section
{
    return [[self.calendars objectAtIndex:section] title];
}
```

You will also need to implement a method to determine the number of rows in each group, as given by the count of the array returned by your dictionary for a given section.

```
-(NSInteger)tableView:(UITableView *)tableView numberOfRowsInSection:(NSInteger)section
{
    NSString *title = [[self.calendars objectAtIndex:section] title];
    NSArray *eventsInThisCalendar = [self.events objectForKey:title];
    return [eventsInThisCalendar count];
}
```

Finally, you can build your most important method for dealing with a UITableView, which will define how your table's cells are created.

```
- (UITableViewCell *)tableView:(UITableView *)tableView
cellForRowAtIndexPath:(NSIndexPath *)indexPath {
    static NSString *CellIdentifier = @"Cell";

    UITableViewCell *cell = [tableView
dequeueReusableCellWithIdentifier:CellIdentifier];
    if (cell == nil)
    {
        cell = [[UITableViewCell alloc] initWithStyle:UITableViewCellStyleValue1
reuseIdentifier:CellIdentifier];
    }

    cell.accessoryType = UITableViewCellAccessoryDetailDisclosureButton;
    cell.textLabel.backgroundColor = [UIColor clearColor];
    cell.textLabel.font = [UIFont systemFontOfSize:19.0];

    cell.textLabel.text = [[[self.events objectForKey:[[self.calendars
objectAtIndex:indexPath.section] title]] objectAtIndex:indexPath.row] title];

    return cell;
}
```

As you can see, aside from a fairly generic setup of your cell's view, all you have done is specify the title of any given row through a short, albeit slightly convoluted, call to your array and dictionary.

Your application should now be able to give you a nice display of all the events currently in your calendar!

Recipe 8–4: Viewing, Editing, and Deleting Events

Next, you can look into how to allow your user to view, edit, and delete events through pre-defined classes in the Event Kit UI framework.

Continuing from your previous recipe, the first thing you need to do is add another framework to your project. This time, add EventKitUI.framework. Import this framework's header file into your class with an import statement.

```
#import <EventKitUI/EventKitUI.h>
```

In this recipe, you will be assigning your view controller as the delegate for a couple of other view controllers, so you will go ahead and add their protocols to your header file. Here is the total list of protocols your view controller should now contain:

- UITableViewDelegate

- UITableViewDataSource

- EKEventViewDelegate

- EKEventEditViewDelegate

First, you will implement behavior for when a user selects a specific row in your UITableView. You will use an instance of the EKEventViewController to display information on the selected event. To do this, you use the UITableView's data source method, -tableView:DidSelectRowAtIndexPath:.

```
-(void)tableView:(UITableView *)tableView didSelectRowAtIndexPath:(NSIndexPath *)indexPath
{
    EKEventViewController *eventVC = [[EKEventViewController alloc] init];
    eventVC.event = [[self.events objectForKey:[[self.calendars objectAtIndex:indexPath.section] title]] objectAtIndex:indexPath.row];
    eventVC.delegate = self;
    eventVC.allowsEditing = YES;
    UINavigationController *navcon = [[UINavigationController alloc] initWithRootViewController:eventVC];
    [self presentModalViewController:navcon animated:YES];
    [tableView deselectRowAtIndexPath:indexPath animated:YES];
}
```

You will need to implement the EKEventViewController's delegate method, - eventViewController:didCompleteWithAction:, in order to properly handle the completed use of your event's details. Here, you have a fairly simple implementation that either saves or deletes the event from your event store, depending on the action given.

```
-(void)eventViewController:(EKEventViewController *)controller didCompleteWithAction:(EKEventViewAction)action
{
    EKEvent *event = controller.event;
    if (action == EKEventViewActionDeleted)
```

```
        {
            [self.eventStore removeEvent:event span:EKSpanThisEvent error:nil];
        }
        else
        {
            [self.eventStore saveEvent:event span:EKSpanFutureEvents error:nil];
        }
        [self fetchEvents];
        [self.tableViewEvents reloadData];
        [self dismissModalViewControllerAnimated:YES];
}
```

The values you have used for the span: parameter of the saving and deleting methods are restricted to one of the two values you have used here. As you can probably tell, they specify whether your save or removal should apply only to the specific event, or to all of its recurrences as well.

Keep in mind that the fact that the user deletes an event in the EKEventViewController does not mean that it has been removed from the eventStore. You need to manually remove it, and then call your -fetchEvents method as well as your table's -reloadData method to update your UITableView.

For extra functionality, you will also make your cell's detail disclosure buttons allow the user to proceed directly to editing an event's information through the use of the EKEventEditViewController. First, you will implement a method to handle the pressing of the disclosure buttons.

```
-(void)tableView:(UITableView *)tableView
accessoryButtonTappedForRowWithIndexPath:(NSIndexPath *)indexPath
{
    EKEventEditViewController *eventEditVC = [[EKEventEditViewController alloc] init];
    eventEditVC.event = [[self.events objectForKey:[[self.calendars
objectAtIndex:indexPath.section] title]] objectAtIndex:indexPath.row];
    eventEditVC.eventStore = self.eventStore;
    eventEditVC.editViewDelegate = self;
    [self presentModalViewController:eventEditVC animated:YES];
}
```

Just like with the EKEventViewController, you need to define a delegate method for your EKEventEditViewController.

```
-(void)eventEditViewController:(EKEventEditViewController *)controller
didCompleteWithAction:(EKEventEditViewAction)action
{
    if (action == EKEventEditViewActionDeleted)
    {
        [self.eventStore removeEvent:controller.event span:EKSpanThisEvent error:nil];
    }
    else if (action == EKEventEditViewActionSaved)
    {
        [self.eventStore saveEvent:controller.event span:EKSpanThisEvent error:nil];
    }
    [self fetchEvents];
    [self.tableViewEvents reloadData];
    [self dismissModalViewControllerAnimated:YES];
}
```

Finally, you need to define one extra method in order to use an
EKEventEditViewController, which will allow you to specify one calendar to be used for
the creation of new events. In this implementation, you will simply return the default
calendar for this task that the device is already using.

```
-(EKCalendar
*)eventEditViewControllerDefaultCalendarForNewEvents:(EKEventEditViewController
*)controller
{
    return [self.eventStore defaultCalendarForNewEvents];
}
```

Just to ensure that your view always displays the most recent information, you will add
to your -viewwillAppear: method in order to consistently refresh both your current data
as well as your UITableView. The method will now appear like so:

```
- (void)viewWillAppear:(BOOL)animated
{
    [self fetchEvents];
    [self.tableViewEvents reloadData];
    [super viewWillAppear:animated];
}
```

At this point, your application can now successfully allow the user to view and edit the
details of an event in two different ways, through the use of either an
EKEventViewController (Figure 8–4) or an EKEventEditViewController (Figure 8–5).

Figure 8–4. *EKEventViewController*

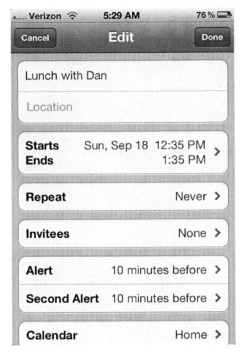

Figure 8–5. *EKEventEditViewControl*

Recipe 8–5: Creating Simple Events

While it is fairly simple to allow users to create an event by themselves, we, as developers, should always attempt to simplify the lives of the users. The less that users have to do on their own, the happier they tend to be with the final product. To this end, it is important to be able to create and edit events programmatically, such that users never even have to see an EKEventEditViewController.

Again, building off of the previous recipe, you will first go into your view controller's XIB file.

Add a UIToolbar element to the top of your view. You will have to move the top of your UITableView down by the height of the toolbar, which defaults to 44 points. Go ahead and delete the UIBarButtonItem that is inside the toolbar by default; you will implement the items inside your toolbar programmatically.

Connect your UIToolbar to your view controller's header file using the property name toolBarTop.

You will be adding a button to your toolBarTop to allow you to create a new EKEvent, so you will define in advance the header for your method to perform this task.

```
-(void)addPressed:(UIButton *)sender;
```

Next, you will edit your -viewDidLoad method to accommodate your newest features.

```
- (void)viewDidLoad
{
    [super viewDidLoad];

    //////////////////START OF NEW CODE
    UIBarButtonItem *addButton = [[UIBarButtonItem alloc]
initWithBarButtonSystemItem:UIBarButtonSystemItemAdd target:self
action:@selector(addPressed:)];
    UIBarButtonItem *fixedSpace = [[UIBarButtonItem alloc]
initWithBarButtonSystemItem:UIBarButtonSystemItemFixedSpace target:nil action:NULL];
    fixedSpace.width = 265;
    [self.toolBarTop setItems:[NSArray arrayWithObjects:fixedSpace, addButton, nil]];
    //////////////////END OF NEW CODE

    self.tableViewEvents.delegate = self;
    self.tableViewEvents.dataSource = self;

    self.eventStore = [[EKEventStore alloc] init];
    self.calendars = [self.eventStore calendars];

    [self fetchEvents];
}
```

When your addButton is pressed, you will have your application present a modal view controller in order to take an input from the user as to the name of the new event to be created. In order to do this, you need to create another view controller from scratch.

Go to File ➤ New File..., and make sure to choose the "UIViewController subclass" option, as shown in Figure 8–6.

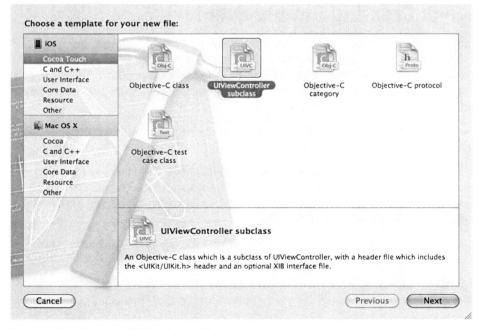

Figure 8–6. *Subclassing* UIViewController

Name your subclass "EventAddViewController", making sure that it will be created with a XIB file, as is done in Figure 8–7.

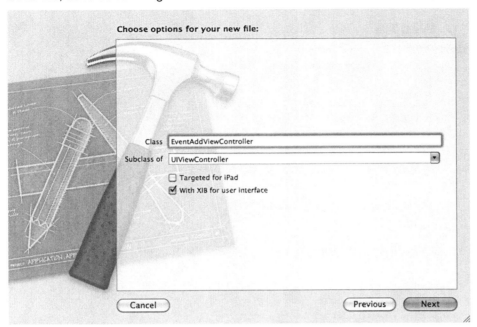

Figure 8–7. *Configuring your new view controller*

Set up your new view controller's XIB file to resemble the one in Figure 8–8.

Figure 8–8. *User interface for event creation*

Remember that here you are using a UITextField, which means at some point the bottom half of your view will be taken up by a keyboard, so you must take care not to let anything be hidden by this unnecessarily.

Connect your UITextField as well as your UIButton to your view controller's header file with the respective property names textFieldTitle and doneButton. Define also the header for an action called -donePressed:, as shown here, and connect doneButton to this action.

```
-(IBAction)donePressed:(id)sender;
```

Rather than have this class do any specific work with the Event Kit, you will simply have it return the submitted string to a delegate view controller. In order to do this, you first must declare a protocol for the delegate to conform to, by adding the following protocol declaration to the top of your header file:

```
@protocol EventAddViewControllerDelegate <NSObject>

-(void)EventAddViewController:(EventAddViewController *)controller
didSubmitTitle:(NSString *)title;

@end
```

Your compiler will complain about this circular reference of a class to itself before it has been declared, so add this extra line above the protocol declaration in order to assure the compiler that the EventAddViewController is, in fact, declared.

```
@class EventAddViewController;
```

Since, as noted previously, you are using a UITextField, you should have your new view controller conform to the UITextFieldDelegate protocol. Make this so.

Finally, declare a property of type id that conforms to your protocol for this view controller called delegate. Make sure to properly synthesize and handle this in your implementation file as always.

```
@property (strong, nonatomic) id <EventAddViewControllerDelegate> delegate;
```

In its entirety, your header file should now look like so:

```
#import <UIKit/UIKit.h>

@class EventAddViewController;

@protocol EventAddViewControllerDelegate <NSObject>
-(void)EventAddViewController:(EventAddViewController *)controller
didSubmitTitle:(NSString *)title;
@end

@interface EventAddViewController : UIViewController <UITextFieldDelegate>

@property (strong, nonatomic) IBOutlet UITextField *textFieldTitle;
@property (strong, nonatomic) IBOutlet UIButton *doneButton;
@property (strong, nonatomic) id <EventAddViewControllerDelegate> delegate;
-(IBAction)donePressed:(id)sender;

@end
```

Your implementation for this view controller will be incredibly simple, as its function will be served entirely by a delegate method.

First, you must modify your -viewDidLoad method to set your UITextField's delegate.

```
- (void)viewDidLoad
{
    [super viewDidLoad];
    self.textFieldTitle.delegate = self;
}
```

Second, you implement a very simple UITextField delegate method to handle the pressing of the "return" button.

```
-(BOOL)textFieldShouldReturn:(UITextField *)textField
{
    [textField resignFirstResponder];
    return NO;
}
```

Finally, you implement your -donePressed: method to call your view controller's delegate method.

```
-(void)donePressed:(id)sender
{
    [self.delegate EventAddViewController:self didSubmitTitle:self.textFieldTitle.text];
}
```

You can now switch back to your `MainViewController`. The first thing to remember is to add the newly created protocol to your view controller, so that, in its final stage, your header file reads like so:

```
#import <UIKit/UIKit.h>
#import <EventKit/EventKit.h>
#import <EventKitUI/EventKitUI.h>
#import "EventAddViewController.h"

@interface MainViewController : UIViewController <UITableViewDelegate,
UITableViewDataSource, EKEventViewDelegate, EKEventEditViewDelegate,
EventAddViewControllerDelegate>

@property (strong, nonatomic) IBOutlet UIToolbar *toolBarTop;

@property (nonatomic, strong) EKEventStore *eventStore;
@property (strong, nonatomic) IBOutlet UITableView *tableViewEvents;

@property (nonatomic, strong) NSMutableDictionary *events;
@property (nonatomic, strong) NSArray *calendars;
-(void)addPressed:(UIButton *)sender;
@end
```

You can now implement the -addPressed: method that you hinted at earlier to display your new view controller.

```
-(void)addPressed:(UIButton *)sender
{
    EventAddViewController *addVC = [[EventAddViewController alloc] init];
    addVC.delegate = self;
    [self presentModalViewController:addVC animated:YES];
}
```

Finally, you can create your `EventAddViewController`'s delegate method, which will take the submitted string, and create a new event with it.

```
-(void)EventAddViewController:(EventAddViewController *)controller
didSubmitTitle:(NSString *)title
{
    EKEvent *event = [EKEvent eventWithEventStore:self.eventStore];
    event.title = title;
    event.calendar = [self.eventStore defaultCalendarForNewEvents];
    event.startDate = [NSDate dateWithTimeIntervalSinceNow:60*60*24.0];
    event.endDate = [NSDate dateWithTimeInterval:60*60.0 sinceDate:event.startDate];
    [self.eventStore saveEvent:event span:EKSpanThisEvent error:nil];
    [self fetchEvents];
    [self.tableViewEvents reloadData];
    [self dismissModalViewControllerAnimated:YES];
}
```

I have chosen an incredibly simple method for creating these new events for the sake of demonstration, as you can see in the fact that you have simply made any events created in this way always be a day in advance, and last only an hour. Most likely in your application you would choose a more complex or user-input-based method for creating EKEvents.

> **NOTE:** The code we have used here may generate a "Could not load source: 6" log in Xcode. Do not worry about this, as it does not hinder your app from functioning correctly.

Recipe 8–6: Recurring Events

The Event Kit framework provides an incredibly powerful API for developers to be able to programmatically work with recurring events. Here, you will simply add to the previous recipes in order to have your application also add in a recurring event to your calendar.

In your -EventAddViewController:didSubmitTitle: method that you have created, you will simply add in extra code to create a recurring EKEvent based on the same title as the normal one. Start by adding the following code to set up the new EKEvent.

```
EKEvent *recurringEvent = [EKEvent eventWithEventStore:self.eventStore];
    recurringEvent.title = [NSString stringWithFormat:@"Recurring %@", title];
    recurringEvent.calendar = [self.eventStore defaultCalendarForNewEvents];
    recurringEvent.startDate = [NSDate dateWithTimeIntervalSinceNow:60*60*24.0];
    recurringEvent.endDate = [NSDate dateWithTimeInterval:60*60.0
sinceDate:event.startDate];
```

Next, you must create an instance of the class EKRecurrenceRule to provide to your event. This class is an incredibly flexible method with which to programmatically implement recurrent events, due to the sheer possibility of recurrence combinations. With only one method, a developer can create nearly any combination of recurrences imaginable. You will define a slightly complex one here:

```
EKRecurrenceRule *rule = [[EKRecurrenceRule alloc]
                          initRecurrenceWithFrequency:EKRecurrenceFrequencyDaily
                          interval:2
                          daysOfTheWeek:[NSArray
arrayWithObjects:[EKRecurrenceDayOfWeek dayOfWeek:2], [EKRecurrenceDayOfWeek
dayOfWeek:3], nil]
                          daysOfTheMonth:nil
                          monthsOfTheYear:nil
                          weeksOfTheYear:nil
                          daysOfTheYear:nil
                          setPositions:nil
                          end:[EKRecurrenceEnd
recurrenceEndWithOccurrenceCount:20]];
```

You would then add this rule to your event with the following line of code. The recurrenceRules property used is inherited from the EKCalendarItem class as of iOS 5.0.

```
recurringEvent.recurrenceRules = [NSArray arrayWithObject:rule];
```

The function of each parameter of this method is listed as follows. For any parameter, passing a value of `nil` indicates a lack of restriction.

- `InitRecurrenceWithFrequency`: This specifies a basic level of how often the event will repeat, whether on a daily, weekly, monthly, or annual basis.

- `Interval`: Specifies the interval of repetition based on the frequency. A recurring event with a weekly frequency and an interval of 3 will repeat every three weeks.

- `DaysOfTheWeek`: This property takes an `NSArray` of objects that must be accessed through the `EKRecurrenceDayOfWeek +dayOfWeek` method, which takes an integer parameter representing the day of the week, starting with 1 referring to Sunday. By setting this parameter, a developer can create an event to repeat every few days, but only if the event falls on specified days of the week.

- `MonthsOfTheYear`: Similar to `DaysOfTheWeek`, this parameter specifies which months to restrict a recurring event to. It is valid only for events with a yearly frequency.

- `WeeksOfTheYear`: Just like `MonthsOfTheYear`, this is restricted only to events with an annual frequency, but with specific weeks to restrict instead of months.

- `DaysOfTheYear`: Another parameter restricted to annually recurring events, this allows you to specify only certain days, counting from either the beginning or the end of the year, to filter a specific event to.

- `SetPositions`: This parameter is the ultimate filter, allowing you to entirely restrict the event you have created to only specific days of the year. In this way, an event that repeats daily could, for example, be restricted to occur only on the 28th, 102nd, and 364th days of the year for whatever reason a developer might choose.

- `End`: This parameter requires a class call to the `EKRecurrenceEnd` class, and specifies when your event will no longer repeat. The two class methods to choose between are as follows:

    - `+recurrenceEndWithEndDate`: Allows the developer to specify a date after which the event will no longer repeat

    - `+recurrenceEndWithOccurenceCount`: Restricts an event's repetition to a limited number of occurrences

Based on all this, you can see that the recurring event you have created for demonstration will repeat every two days, but only on either a Monday or a Tuesday, up to a limit of 20 occurrences.

Based on the different functionalities you have implemented, you should be able to see exactly how much possibility there is in using the Event Kit framework to interact with a user's schedule and events. Regardless of whether you wish to allow a user to interact with his or her schedule or you prefer a more programmatic, behind-the-scenes approach, the tools needed to perform your goal are easily available and incredibly simple to use, despite having immense flexibility.

Recipe 8–7: Basic Address Book Access

One of the absolutely most imperative functionalities in any modern device is the ability to store contact information, and, as such, you should take care to develop applications that can take advantage of this important data. In this recipe, you will cover three basic functionalities for accessing and dealing with a device's contacts list.

First, make a new project called "Chapter8Recipe7", with class prefix "Main", using the Single View Application template.

You will need to add in two extra frameworks to your project for this recipe: AddressBook.framework, and AddressBookUI.framework.

Next, switch over to your view controller's XIB file, and make a view that resembles the one in Figure 8–9.

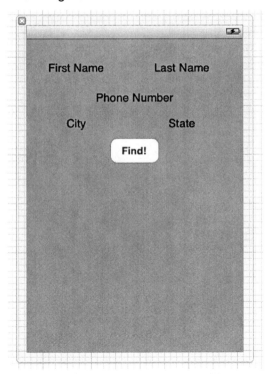

Figure 8–9. *XIB file for accessing contact info*

Connect these elements to your header file using the following property names:

- `firstLabel`
- `lastLabel`
- `phoneLabel`
- `cityLabel`
- `stateLabel`

You will not need a property for the `UIButton`, as you will not need to make any changes to it for this recipe.

Define an action in your header file for your button to perform called `-findPressed:`, like so:

```
-(IBAction)findPressed:(id)sender;
```

Now that your interface is set up, you will make sure that your header file is correctly written. First, add the following two import statements to make sure that you can use your Address Book and Address Book UI frameworks.

```
#import <AddressBook/AddressBook.h>
#import <AddressBookUI/AddressBookUI.h>
```

You will be using an instance of the class `ABPeoplePickerNavigationController`, and setting its `peoplePickerDelegate` property to your view controller, so you need to add a protocol implementation to your header file. Make your view controller conform to the `ABPeoplePickerNavigationControllerDelegate` protocol. Your header file, in its entirety, should now look like so:

```
#import <UIKit/UIKit.h>
#import <AddressBook/AddressBook.h>
#import <AddressBookUI/AddressBookUI.h>

@interface MainViewController : UIViewController
<ABPeoplePickerNavigationControllerDelegate>

@property (strong, nonatomic) IBOutlet UILabel *firstLabel;
@property (strong, nonatomic) IBOutlet UILabel *lastLabel;
@property (strong, nonatomic) IBOutlet UILabel *phoneLabel;
@property (strong, nonatomic) IBOutlet UILabel *stateLabel;
@property (strong, nonatomic) IBOutlet UILabel *cityLabel;
-(IBAction)findPressed:(id)sender;
@end
```

Switch over to your implementation file, and implement a simple `-viewDidLoad` method to reset the text on your `UILabel`s.

```
- (void)viewDidLoad
{
    [super viewDidLoad];
    self.firstLabel.text = @"...";
    self.lastLabel.text = @"...";
    self.phoneLabel.text = @"...";
    self.cityLabel.text = @"...";
```

```
    self.stateLabel.text = @"...";
}
```

You will implement the -findPressed: method you defined earlier to create an instance of ABPeoplePickerNavigationController, set its delegate, and then present it modally.

```
-(void)findPressed:(id)sender
{
    ABPeoplePickerNavigationController *picker =[[ABPeoplePickerNavigationController
alloc] init];
    picker.peoplePickerDelegate = self;
    [self presentModalViewController:picker animated:YES];
}
```

Now you just need to create your delegate methods, of which there are three you are required to implement. The first, and simplest, is for when the picker controller is canceled.

```
-(void)peoplePickerNavigationControllerDidCancel:(ABPeoplePickerNavigationController
*)peoplePicker
{
    [self dismissModalViewControllerAnimated:YES];
}
```

Next, you will define your main delegate method to handle the selection of a contact. You will go through this method implementation step-by-step to discuss each part.

First, your method header looks like so:

```
-(BOOL)peoplePickerNavigationController:(ABPeoplePickerNavigationController
*)peoplePicker shouldContinueAfterSelectingPerson:(ABRecordRef)person
```

The first odd thing you may notice about this header is that the variable person is of type ABRecordRef, which does not have a "*" after it. This essentially means that person is not a pointer, and thus will not be used to call methods. Instead, you will use pre-defined functions that utilize and access it. As you will see, many parts of the Address Book framework utilize this more "C-based" style.

Inside the method body, you will first perform your easiest accesses, which will be for the first and last names of the chosen contact.

```
self.firstLabel.text = (__bridge_transfer NSString *)ABRecordCopyValue(person,
kABPersonFirstNameProperty);
self.lastLabel.text = (__bridge_transfer NSString *)ABRecordCopyValue(person,
kABPersonLastNameProperty);
```

The ABRecordCopyValue() function will be your go-to call for any kind of accessing data in this section. It takes two parameters, the first being the ABRecordRef that you want to access, and the second being a pre-defined PropertyID that instructs the function on which piece of data to retrieve.

There are two types of values that can be dealt with by this function: single values and multi-values. For these first two calls, you are dealing only with single values, for which the ABRecordCopyValue() function returns a type of CFStringRef. You can cast this up to an NSString by adding the (__bridge_transfer NSString *) code in front of the value.

The __bridge_transfer command is new to iOS 5 with Automatic Reference Counting (ARC), and simply specifies that ARC will now handle the value being "bridged."

The next value you can access is the person's phone number, which is a multi-value. Multi-values are usually used for the properties of a person for which multiple entries can be given, such as the address, phone number, or e-mail. When you copy this, you will receive a variable of type ABMultiValueRef, which you can then use to access a specific value.

```
ABMultiValueRef multi = ABRecordCopyValue(person, kABPersonPhoneProperty);
CFStringRef phoneNumber = ABMultiValueCopyValueAtIndex(multi, 0);
self.phoneLabel.text = (__bridge_transfer NSString *)phoneNumber;
CFRelease(phoneNumber);
```

By using the call ABMultiValueCopyValueAtIndex(multi, 0);, you have specified that you want the first phone number stored for the given user. From there, you can set your label's text just as you did before.

Since you created a new CFStringRef phoneNumber to point to your value, you should release it with the CFRelease() command, as shown in the previous snippet.

The next multi-value you will deal with will be the main address of the chosen contact. When dealing with the address, an extra step is required, as an address is stored as a CFDictionary. You will retrieve this dictionary using the ABMultiValueCopyValueAtIndex() function again, and then query its values:

```
ABMultiValueRef address = ABRecordCopyValue(person, kABPersonAddressProperty);
    if (ABMultiValueGetCount(address) > 0)
    {
        CFDictionaryRef dictionary = ABMultiValueCopyValueAtIndex
        (address, 0);
        CFStringRef cityKey = kABPersonAddressCityKey;
        CFStringRef stateKey = kABPersonAddressStateKey;
        self.cityLabel.text = (__bridge_transfer NSString
*)CFDictionaryGetValue(dictionary, (void *)cityKey);
        self.stateLabel.text = (__bridge_transfer NSString
*)CFDictionaryGetValue(dictionary, (void *)stateKey);

        CFRelease(dictionary);
        CFRelease(cityKey);
        CFRelease(stateKey);
    }
    else
    {
        self.cityLabel.text = @"...";
        self.stateLabel.text = @"...";
    }
```

Finally, you can dismiss your modal view controller, as well as add your return value for this method. As a whole, your method should look like so:

```
-(BOOL)peoplePickerNavigationController:(ABPeoplePickerNavigationController
*)peoplePicker shouldContinueAfterSelectingPerson:(ABRecordRef)person
{
    self.firstLabel.text = (__bridge_transfer NSString *)ABRecordCopyValue(person,
kABPersonFirstNameProperty);
```

```
    self.lastLabel.text = (__bridge_transfer NSString *)ABRecordCopyValue(person,
kABPersonLastNameProperty);

    ABMultiValueRef multi = ABRecordCopyValue(person, kABPersonPhoneProperty);
    CFStringRef phoneNumber = ABMultiValueCopyValueAtIndex(multi, 0);
    self.phoneLabel.text = (__bridge_transfer NSString *)phoneNumber;
    CFRelease(phoneNumber);

    ABMultiValueRef address = ABRecordCopyValue(person, kABPersonAddressProperty);
    if (ABMultiValueGetCount(address) > 0)
    {
        CFDictionaryRef dictionary = ABMultiValueCopyValueAtIndex
        (address, 0);
        CFStringRef cityKey = kABPersonAddressCityKey;
        CFStringRef stateKey = kABPersonAddressStateKey;
        self.cityLabel.text = (__bridge_transfer NSString
*)CFDictionaryGetValue(dictionary, (void *)cityKey);
        self.stateLabel.text = (__bridge_transfer NSString
*)CFDictionaryGetValue(dictionary, (void *)stateKey);

        CFRelease(dictionary);
        CFRelease(cityKey);
        CFRelease(stateKey);
    }
    else
    {
        self.cityLabel.text = @"...";
        self.stateLabel.text = @"...";
    }

    [self dismissModalViewControllerAnimated:YES];
    return NO;
}
```

There is a third method you must implement in order to correctly conform to your protocol, which handles the selection of a specific contact's property. However, since this recipe is simply returning after the selection of a contact, this method will not actually be called. You will give it a simple implementation similar to your cancellation method.

```
-(BOOL)peoplePickerNavigationController:(ABPeoplePickerNavigationController
*)peoplePicker shouldContinueAfterSelectingPerson:(ABRecordRef)person
property:(ABPropertyID)property identifier:(ABMultiValueIdentifier)identifier
{
    [self dismissModalViewControllerAnimated:YES];
    return NO;
}
```

> **CAUTION:** Whenever you are copying values from an `ABRecordRef`, include a check to make sure that a value exists, like you did with the address. The previous code assumed that the first name, last name, and phone number exist, but an empty query can result in your application throwing an exception.

Your application should now be able to access the address book, select a user, and display the information for which you have queried, as demonstrated by Figures 8–10 and 8–11.

Figure 8–10. *Address book contact listing*

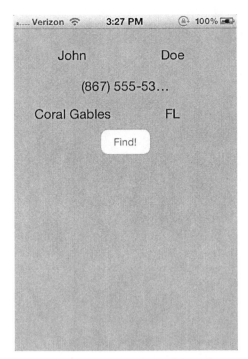

Figure 8–11. *Your application's display of contact info*

While you have not included code to access all the possible values for an `ABRecordRef`, you should be able to use any combination of the utilized functions to access whichever ones you need.

Recipe 8–8: Setting Contact Information

Just as important as being able to access values is being able to set them. To this end, you will implement two different methods for creating and setting values of a contact and adding it to your device's address book.

First, make a new project called "Chapter8Recipe8", with the class prefix "Main", using the Single View Application template.

Add in `AddressBook.framework` and `AddressBookUI.framework` to your project just as you have been doing.

You will start out with an incredibly simple user interface that allows users to create a new contact themselves, so in your view controller's XIB file, add a single `UIButton`, connected to an action called `-newContactPressed:`, as shown by Figure 8–12.

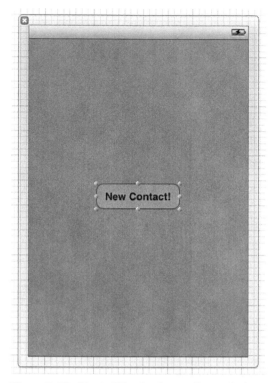

Figure 8–12. *Simple XIB setup for creating contacts*

Next, you need to import your frameworks into your header file and configure your view controller's protocol to conform to. Conform your view controller to the ABNewPersonViewControllerDelegate protocol, and then add the usual two import statements.

```
#import <AddressBook/AddressBook.h>
#import <AddressBookUI/AddressBookUI.h>
```

Now, you will create an incredibly simple implementation, for which you have to define only two methods: the action to handle the selection of your button, and the delegate method for an ABNewPersonViewController.

Your action method will look like so:

```
-(void)newContactPressed:(id)sender
{
    ABNewPersonViewController *view = [[ABNewPersonViewController alloc] init];
    view.newPersonViewDelegate = self;

    UINavigationController *newNavigationController = [[UINavigationController alloc]
initWithRootViewController:view];
    [self presentModalViewController:newNavigationController animated:YES];
}
```

Here is the delegate method:

```
-(void)newPersonViewController:(ABNewPersonViewController *)newPersonView
didCompleteWithNewPerson:(ABRecordRef)person
{
    if (person == NULL)
    {
        NSLog(@"User Cancelled Creation");
    }
    else
        NSLog(@"Successfully Created New Person");
    [self dismissModalViewControllerAnimated:YES];
}
```

Unlike most modal view controllers that you deal with, the ABNewPersonViewController has only one delegate method that handles both success and cancellation, as opposed to others that have one method for each. As you can see, you differentiate between each result by checking to see if the ABRecordRef person parameter is not NULL. Since this parameter is not a pointer, you compare it to the NULL value instead of nil.

At this point, you should be able to allow your user to create a new contact to be added to the address book, as your simulated app in Figure 8–13 shows.

Figure 8–13. *A blank* ABNewPersonViewController

While you have provided users with a great deal of flexibility as to how they want their contacts to be set up, you have also provided them with a great deal of work to do, in that they have to type in every value that they want. You will next see how to programmatically create records and set their values.

First, modify your user interface to include a series of UITextFields, each with a Placeholder text value describing their use, resembling Figure 8–14.

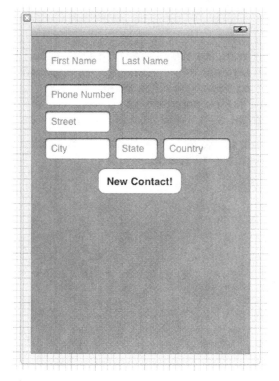

Figure 8–14. *User interface for specifying new contact info*

Connect each UITextField to your header file with the following respective property names:

- textFieldFirst
- textFieldLast
- textFieldPhone
- textFieldStreet
- textFieldCity
- textFieldState
- textFieldZip

Now, you can implement your code to create a new contact. To do this, you must obtain an ABRecordRef through the function ABPersonCreate(), and then set its values. The

overall code for this will appear like so, which can be added to your -
newContactPressed: method.

```
ABMutableMultiValueRef multi =
    ABMultiValueCreateMutable(kABMultiStringPropertyType);
    CFErrorRef anError = NULL;
    ABMultiValueIdentifier multivalueIdentifier;
    bool didAdd, didSet;

    didAdd = ABMultiValueAddValueAndLabel(multi, (__bridge
CFStringRef)self.textFieldPhone.text,
                                          kABPersonPhoneMobileLabel,
&multivalueIdentifier);
    if (!didAdd)
    {
        NSLog(@"Error Adding Phone Number");
    }

    ABRecordRef aRecord = ABPersonCreate();

    ABRecordSetValue(aRecord, kABPersonFirstNameProperty, (__bridge
CFStringRef)self.textFieldFirst.text, nil);
    ABRecordSetValue(aRecord, kABPersonLastNameProperty, (__bridge
CFStringRef)self.textFieldLast.text, nil);

    didSet = ABRecordSetValue(aRecord, kABPersonPhoneProperty, multi, &anError);
    if (!didSet)
    {
        NSLog(@"Error Setting Phone Value");
    }
    CFRelease(multi);

    ABMutableMultiValueRef address =
    ABMultiValueCreateMutable(kABDictionaryPropertyType);

    // Set up keys and values for the dictionary.
    CFStringRef keys[5];
    CFStringRef values[5];
    keys[0] = kABPersonAddressStreetKey;
    keys[1] = kABPersonAddressCityKey;
    keys[2] = kABPersonAddressStateKey;
    keys[3] = kABPersonAddressZIPKey;
    keys[4] = kABPersonAddressCountryKey;
    values[0] = (__bridge CFStringRef)self.textFieldStreet.text;
    values[1] = (__bridge CFStringRef)self.textFieldCity.text;
    values[2] = (__bridge CFStringRef)self.textFieldState.text;
    values[3] = (__bridge CFStringRef)self.textFieldZip.text;
    values[4] = CFSTR("USA");

    CFDictionaryRef aDict = CFDictionaryCreate(kCFAllocatorDefault,(void *)keys,
                                    (void *)values,5,
                                    &kCFCopyStringDictionaryKeyCallBacks,
                                    &kCFTypeDictionaryValueCallBacks);

    ABMultiValueIdentifier dictionaryIdentifier;
    bool didAddAddress;
```

```
        didAddAddress = ABMultiValueAddValueAndLabel(address, aDict, kABHomeLabel,
    &dictionaryIdentifier);
        if (!didAddAddress)
        {
            NSLog(@"Error Adding Address");
        }

        CFRelease(aDict);

        ABRecordSetValue(aRecord, kABPersonAddressProperty, address, nil);
```

By inspecting this code, you can view the different techniques for creating and setting each type of property, from single values, to multi-values, to the dictionary-based address multi-value.

As with before, you must use the __bridge command in order to move your NSString variables out of ARC.

You now have two choices as to how to implement the creation of your new person in your device. A very user-friendly method would be to then load up your ABNewPersonViewController as before, but this time give it the created ABPersonRef to populate itself with. You can do this by setting the controller's displayedPerson property, by adding the following line.

```
        view.displayedPerson = aRecord;
```

If you choose this option, your application will bring up the views shown in Figure 8–15 in order to create a new contact. Notice that the new contact's information must be approved by the user in order to complete its creation. Tap to edit any of the text fields in the contact if the Done button appears grayed out.

Figure 8–15. *On the left, your app specifying new contact information, with resulting contact created on the right*

Your second option would be to scrap the use of the ABNewPersonViewController and simply create your contact programmatically, saving the user the extra step of approving the contact. Since you already have your ABPersonRef, this is actually fairly simply done in a few lines of code, which would replace the code to set up and display an ABNewPersonViewController.

```
ABAddressBookRef addressBook = ABAddressBookCreate();
ABAddressBookAddRecord(addressBook, aRecord, nil);
ABAddressBookSave(addressBook, nil);
```

The ABAddressBookCreate() function is very simple, and simply returns an ABAddressBookRef of your device's address book. After adding the record using ABAddressBookAddRecord(), you simply have to save your changes.

No matter which option chosen, you still need to release two more variables before the end of your method, like so:

```
CFRelease(aRecord);
CFRelease(address);
```

Recipe 8–9: Viewing Contacts

Now that we have gone over accessing and setting values, a very simple next step is to discuss how to set up a view controller to see a contact's details.

In a new project called "Chapter8Recipe9", with class prefix "MainViewController", after importing the Address Book and Address Book UI frameworks and adding the appropriate #import statements for each, add a UITableView to your view controller. Connect it to your header file with the property name tableViewContacts. Make your view controller conform to the UITableViewDelegate, UITableViewDataSource, and ABPersonViewControllerDelegate protocols as well.

Create a property of type (NSArray *) called contacts to store your contact list.

Overall, your header file should look like so:

```
#import <UIKit/UIKit.h>
#import <AddressBook/AddressBook.h>
#import <AddressBookUI/AddressBookUI.h>

@interface MainViewController : UIViewController <UITableViewDelegate,
UITableViewDataSource, ABPersonViewControllerDelegate>

@property (strong, nonatomic) IBOutlet UITableView *tableViewContacts;
@property (strong, nonatomic) NSArray *contacts;
@end
```

Before we continue, you will need to set your main view controller inside of a UINavigationController. Switch over to the implementation file for your app delegate, and change your -application:DidFinishLaunchingWithOptions: method to look like so:

```
- (BOOL)application:(UIApplication *)application
didFinishLaunchingWithOptions:(NSDictionary *)launchOptions
{
    self.window = [[UIWindow alloc] initWithFrame:[[UIScreen mainScreen] bounds]];
    // Override point for customization after application launch.
    self.viewController = [[MainViewController alloc]
initWithNibName:@"MainViewController" bundle:nil];
    UINavigationController *navcon = [[UINavigationController alloc]
initWithRootViewController:self.viewController];
    self.window.rootViewController = navcon;
    [self.window makeKeyAndVisible];
    return YES;
}
```

Now, back in your view controller's implementation file, create a method to update your array of contacts like so:

```
-(void)updateContacts
{
    ABAddressBookRef addressBook = ABAddressBookCreate();
    CFArrayRef people = ABAddressBookCopyArrayOfAllPeople(addressBook);
    self.contacts = (__bridge NSArray *)people;
    CFRelease(people);
```

```
}
```

This should make your -viewDidLoad method very simple to implement.

```
- (void)viewDidLoad
{
    [super viewDidLoad];

    self.tableViewContacts.delegate = self;
    self.tableViewContacts.dataSource = self;
    self.title = @"Contacts Table";
    [self updateContacts];
}
```

You should also change your -viewWillAppear: method to refresh your table in case of any changes made outside of the application.

```
- (void)viewWillAppear:(BOOL)animated
{
    [self updateContacts];
    [self.tableViewContacts reloadData];
    [super viewWillAppear:animated];
}
```

Now you implement your UITableView data source methods. You need one to specify the number of rows you have:

```
-(NSInteger)tableView:(UITableView *)tableView numberOfRowsInSection:(NSInteger)section
{
    return [[NSNumber numberWithInt:[self.contacts count]] intValue];
}
```

You will have a fairly simple method for creating your cells, based on the accessing code that you used in previous recipes.

```
-(UITableViewCell *)tableView:(UITableView *)tableView
cellForRowAtIndexPath:(NSIndexPath *)indexPath
{
    static NSString *CellIdentifier = @"Cell";

    UITableViewCell *cell = [tableView
dequeueReusableCellWithIdentifier:CellIdentifier];
    if (cell == nil)
    {
        cell = [[UITableViewCell alloc] initWithStyle:UITableViewCellStyleValue1
reuseIdentifier:CellIdentifier];
    }

    cell.accessoryType = UITableViewCellAccessoryDisclosureIndicator;
    cell.textLabel.backgroundColor = [UIColor clearColor];
    cell.textLabel.font = [UIFont systemFontOfSize:19.0];

    ABRecordRef current = (__bridge ABRecordRef)[self.contacts
objectAtIndex:indexPath.row];

    NSString *firstName = (__bridge_transfer NSString *)ABRecordCopyValue(current,
kABPersonFirstNameProperty);
    NSString *lastName = (__bridge_transfer NSString *)ABRecordCopyValue(current,
kABPersonLastNameProperty);
```

```
    cell.textLabel.text = [NSString stringWithFormat:@"%@ %@", firstName, lastName];

    return cell;
}
```

The third data source method you need is for the selection of a cell, which will present an instance of ABPersonViewController with the selected contact's information.

```
-(void)tableView:(UITableView *)tableView didSelectRowAtIndexPath:(NSIndexPath
*)indexPath
{
    ABRecordRef chosen = (__bridge ABRecordRef)[self.contacts
objectAtIndex:indexPath.row];

    ABPersonViewController *view = [[ABPersonViewController alloc] init];
    view.personViewDelegate = self;
    view.displayedPerson = chosen;
    view.allowsEditing = NO;

    [self.navigationController pushViewController:view animated:YES];
    [tableView deselectRowAtIndexPath:indexPath animated:NO];
}
```

Finally, you just need to implement the ABPersonViewController's delegate method to handle the selection of a property. This method can simply return a BOOL that will decide whether the user will be able to call or text a phone number, or any other default property for a value, from your application.

```
-(BOOL)personViewController:(ABPersonViewController *)personViewController
shouldPerformDefaultActionForPerson:(ABRecordRef)person property:(ABPropertyID)property
identifier:(ABMultiValueIdentifier)identifier
{
    return YES;
}
```

Your application should have a very rudimentary table view displaying the names of all the contacts in your phone, assuming that you have only individuals listed in your contact list, as opposed to any groups. Figure 8–16 demonstrates the resulting view of selecting a record in your custom-made contact list. Whenever dealing with an ABRecordRef for which you are not sure whether it is an ABPersonRef or an ABGroupRef, you should always include code to check for each case and act accordingly.

Figure 8–16. *Contact info displayed after selecting a row in your table*

Summary

As you can see, there are a great variety of methods and functionalities for interacting with any specific user's personal data. From recurring events, to multiple calendars, to the vast number of contacts and phone numbers that most users have, all of this information can be used to personalize an application for each and every customer, while developing generically for all of them. In terms of user experience, being able to access, display, and edit all this information allows us as developers to create more powerful, more unique, and more useful applications, which in the end will translate to a happier customer, and a higher-quality product.

Chapter 9

UITableView Recipes

All day, every single day, we are receiving information. Whether in the form of video, radio, music, e-mails, 140-character messages, or even sights and sounds, there is always new data to acquire and process. As developers, we work to create and manage the medium between this information and the end users through data organization and display. We must be able to take the immense stream of information available and process it down to simple, concise pieces that our specific audience will be interested in. On top of this, we also have to make our data look visually appealing, while still maintaining efficiency and organization. In iOS development, one of our greatest tools in this goal is the UITableView: an incredibly flexible yet simple interface designed to be easy to use for both developers and customers. Throughout this chapter, we will focus on the step-by-step methodology for creating, implementing, and customizing these useful tools.

Recipe 9–1: Creating an Ungrouped Table

There are two kinds of UITableViews you can use in iOS: the grouped table and the ungrouped table. Your use of one or the other will depend on any given application, but you will start by focusing on an ungrouped table due to its ease of implementation.

In order to build a fully functional and customizable UITableView-based application, you will be starting from the ground up with an empty application, and ending up with a useful table to display information about various countries. Make a new project, and select the Empty Application template, as in Figure 9–1. This will give you only an application delegate, from which you can build all of your view controllers.

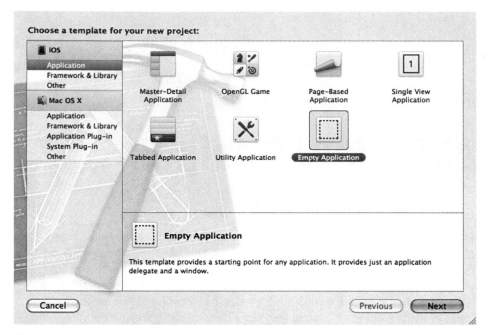

Figure 9–1. *Selecting an empty application to start from scratch*

You will be using a single project throughout this entire chapter, so, rather than naming projects by recipe name, give your project whichever name you prefer (I chose "Countries", since the application will be focused on displaying information about different countries), and create your project. I have used the class prefix "Main", which will apply only to your app delegate files since you are using an empty application.

Since you used an empty application, you will start by making your main view controller, which will contain your UITableView.

Create a new file, and select the UIViewController Subclass template.

On the next screen, enter a name for your view controller, and make sure that the class is listed as a subclass of UIViewController. Name it "MainTableViewController".

> **NOTE:** Some may find it more convenient to create a subclass of UITableViewController, as you are immediately given a UITableView as well as some of the methods required to use it. The downside of this method is that the UITableView given in the controller's XIB file is more difficult to configure and re-frame. For this reason, you are using a UIViewController subclass, and you will simply add in your UITableView, and its methods, yourself.

Since you will be focusing on the idea of a table in your application, you will start by dragging a UITableView out from the library into your view. Rather than making the table take up the entire view, you will shrink it down a bit to have a 20-point padding around it. Switch to the main view, and change the background color to a light gray so that you can differentiate it from your UITableView. This will result in the display shown in Figure 9–2.

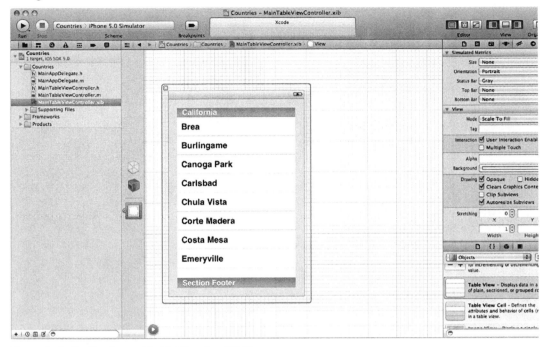

Figure 9–2. *Configuring a* UITableView *in a XIB file*

Connect your UITableView to a property in your header file using the property name tableViewCountries.

Next, switch over to your view controller's header file. You will need your view controller to conform to a couple of protocols in order to fully implement your UITableView. Add the UITableViewDelegate and UITableViewDataSource protocols, so your header now looks like so:

```
@interface MainTableViewController : UIViewController <UITableViewDelegate,
UITableViewDataSource>
```

Next, you will need a property of type NSArray to store the information that you will use to display your table's information, called countries. Make sure to properly synthesize this array, and set its pointer equal to nil in your -viewDidUnload method.

```
@property (strong, nonatomic) NSMutableArray *countries;
```

Before you continue to implement your view controller, you need to set up your model to store your data.

Create a new file as before, but choose the "Objective-C class" template. Name your class "Country", and make sure that it is a subclass of NSObject, as in Figure 9–3.

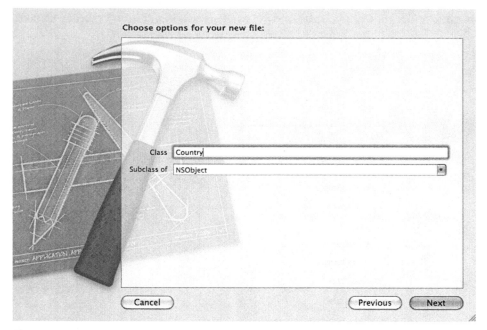

Figure 9–3. *Creating your* Country *class as a subclass of* NSObject

For your application, you will make your Country objects have four properties: three NSStrings referring to a country's name, capital city, and motto, and a UIImage that will contain the country's flag. Define these properties in your Country.h header file like so:

```
@property (nonatomic, strong) NSString *name;
@property (nonatomic, strong) NSString *capital;
@property (nonatomic, strong) NSString *motto;
@property (nonatomic, strong) UIImage *flag;
```

As with your view controllers, you need to synthesize all these properties in your implementation file. Unlike your view controllers, however, you do not need to set them equal to nil in any method, since there is no -viewdidUnload method.

```
@synthesize name, capital, motto, flag;
```

Now that your model is set up, you can return to your view controller. The compiler will need to be able to access the methods of the new Country class that you have just set up, so add the following import statement to the header of your view controller.

```
#import "Country.h"
```

Now, you can set up your data to be used in your UITableView. Before you proceed, make sure you have downloaded the image files for the flags that you will be using for the countries you add. Here, I will use those of the United States, England (as opposed to the UK), Scotland, France, and Spain. Here I have used some public domain flag images from Wikipedia, more of which are available at http://en.wikipedia.org/wiki/Gallery_of_country_flags.

> **CAUTION:** Whenever you are working with images, watch carefully for any and all copyright issues. Public domain images, such as those used here from Wikipedia, are free to use and fairly easy to find.

Once you have the files all downloaded and visible in the Finder, select and drag all of them into your project in Xcode under Supporting Files. A dialog will appear with options for adding the files to your project. Make sure that the option labeled "Copy items into destination group's folder (if needed)" is checked, as in Figure 9-4.

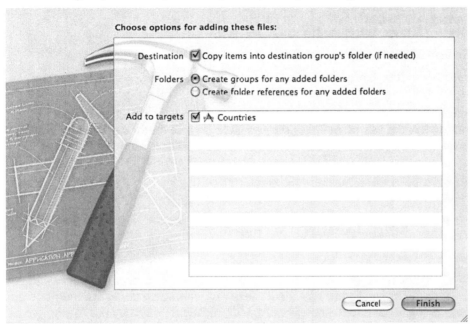

Figure 9-4. *Dialog for adding files; make sure the first box is checked.*

In your -viewDidLoad method, you will make your testing data with the five countries I mentioned earlier by adding the following code:

```
Country *usa = [[Country alloc] init];
usa.name = @"United States of America";
usa.motto = @"E Pluribus Unum";
usa.capital = @"Washington, D.C.";
usa.flag = [UIImage imageNamed:@"usa.png"];

Country *france = [[Country alloc] init];
france.name = @"French Republic";
france.motto = @"Liberté, Égalité, Fraternité";
france.capital = @"Paris";
france.flag = [UIImage imageNamed:@"france.png"];

Country *england = [[Country alloc] init];
england.name = @"England";
```

```
england.motto = @"Dieu et mon droit";
england.capital = @"London";
england.flag = [UIImage imageNamed:@"england.png"];

Country *scotland = [[Country alloc] init];
scotland.name = @"Scotland";
scotland.motto = @"In My Defens God Me Defend";
scotland.capital = @"Edinburgh";
scotland.flag = [UIImage imageNamed:@"scotland.png"];

Country *spain = [[Country alloc] init];
spain.name = @"Kingdom of Spain";
spain.motto = @"Plus Ultra";
spain.capital = @"Madrid";
spain.flag = [UIImage imageNamed:@"spain.png"];
```

Make sure to add all these Country objects to your array with the following line:

```
self.countries = [NSMutableArray arrayWithObjects:usa, france, england, scotland, spain, nil];
```

Now that your testing data is all set up, you will focus on the construction of your UITableView through the use of its delegate and data source methods. Start by setting these two properties to your view controller in your -viewDidLoad with the following lines.

```
self.tableViewCountries.delegate = self;
self.tableViewCountries.dataSource = self;
```

You can also set the title for the view controller, which will appear at the top your of navigation bar with a simple command.

```
self.title = @"Countries";
```

For the sake of organization, all the methods that a UITableView can call are split into two groups, the delegate methods and the data source methods. Delegate methods are used to handle any kind of visual elements of the UITableView, such as the row height of cells. Data source methods, on the other hand, deal with the information displayed in the UITableView, such as the configuration of any given cell's information.

In order to correctly create an ungrouped UITableView, there are two main methods that you must correctly implement.

First, you need to specify to your UITableView how many rows will be displayed via the -tableView:numberOfRowsInSection: method.

```
-(NSInteger)tableView:(UITableView *)tableView numberOfRowsInSection:(NSInteger)section
{
    return [self.countries count];
}
```

Since your table is ungrouped, you have only one section, so this method is nice and easy.

Second, you must create a method to specify how the UITableView's cells are configured using the -tableView:cellForRowAtIndexPath: method. Here is a generic implementation of this method that you will modify for your data.

```
- (UITableViewCell *)tableView:(UITableView *)tableView
cellForRowAtIndexPath:(NSIndexPath *)indexPath
{
    static NSString *CellIdentifier = @"Cell";

    UITableViewCell *cell = [tableView
dequeueReusableCellWithIdentifier:CellIdentifier];
    if (cell == nil)
    {
        cell = [[UITableViewCell alloc] initWithStyle:UITableViewCellStyleDefault
reuseIdentifier:CellIdentifier];
        cell.accessoryType = UITableViewCellAccessoryDisclosureIndicator;
        cell.textLabel.font = [UIFont systemFontOfSize:19.0];
        cell.detailTextLabel.font = [UIFont systemFontOfSize:12];
    }

    cell.textLabel.text=[NSString stringWithFormat:@"Cell %i", indexPath.row];

    return cell;
}
```

Whenever you are dealing with a UITableView, it is pretty much always a good idea to "reuse" cells. Since most of the time not all the cells in a UITableView will be currently in the view of the user, you are able to reuse any cells that are not currently being displayed through the use of the UITableView method - dequeueReusableCellWithIdentifier:, allowing you to save on both memory and time, since you can perform any generic setup, such as font size, background color, etc., only on the initial creation of the cell.

In the previous sample, you can see that you first attempt to de-queue a reusable cell. If none are available (i.e., if cell is nil), then you create a new cell and give it a generic setup that can be reused for all of your cells. Then, no matter whether the cell was de-queued or created, you update the text to the appropriate value.

It is even possible to set up multiple differently configured cells, and specify which one is used or reused via the CellIdentifier.

The last task you need to do to get your program running is ensure that the application delegate, at the start of your program, will present your view controller. Xcode did not do this for you already because you chose the empty template.

In your application delegate implementation, import the header file of your view controller so that the compiler doesn't complain.

```
#import "MainTableViewController.h"
```

You will need to set up properties in your application delegate's header file to store both your UINavigationController and your main view controller. Create these like so:

```
@property (nonatomic, strong) UINavigationController *navcon;
@property (nonatomic, strong) MainTableViewController *tableVC;
```

Make sure to synthesize both with the following line in your application delegate implementation file.

```
@synthesize navcon, tableVC;
```

Now you just need to create your UINavigationController to display and manage the view controller and add its view as a subview of your application's window. Overall, your -application:didFinishLaunchingWithOptions: method should look like so:

```
- (BOOL)application:(UIApplication *)application
didFinishLaunchingWithOptions:(NSDictionary *)launchOptions
{
    self.window = [[UIWindow alloc] initWithFrame:[[UIScreen mainScreen] bounds]];

    self.tableVC = [[MainTableViewController alloc] init];
    self.navcon = [[UINavigationController alloc] initWithRootViewController:tableVC];

    [self.window addSubview:navcon.view];
    [self.window makeKeyAndVisible];
    return YES;
}
```

Upon running this project in the simulator, you will see a basic view of a UITableView with some generic information, as in Figure 9–5.

Figure 9–5. *Basic application with a* UITableView

Now that your application is up, running, and displaying some kind of information, you can work on your specific implementation.

To configure your -tableView:cellForRowAtIndexPath: method to properly fit your data, the first thing you need to do is change the display style of your rows. Modify the allocation/initialization line in your method to resemble the following:

```
cell = [[UITableViewCell alloc] initWithStyle:UITableViewCellStyleSubtitle
reuseIdentifier:CellIdentifier];
```

There are four different UITableViewCell styles that you can use, each with a slightly different display:

- UITableViewCellStyleDefault: Only one label, as shown in Figure 9–5

- UITableViewCellStyleSubtitle: Just like the Default style, but with a second subtitle line underneath the main text

- UITableViewCellStyleValue1: Two text lines, with the primary line on the left side of the cell and the secondary detail text label on the right

- UITableViewCellStyleValue2: Two text lines with the focus on the detail text label

Of these four styles, only the UITableViewCellStyleDefault style has only one line of text.

Next, you can set the cell's text label to actually be the name of the country, rather than simply the count of the cell. Adjust the setting of the cell.textLabel.text property that is done last in the method to the following:

```
    cell.textLabel.text = [(Country *)[self.countries objectAtIndex:indexPath.row]
name];
```

All you had to do here was grab the respective Country object, and call the -name method on it that was synthesized.

You can set the subtitle of the text very similarly using the detailTextLabel property of the cell.

```
    cell.detailTextLabel.text = [(Country *)[self.countries objectAtIndex:indexPath.row]
capital];
```

The UITableViewCell class also has a property called imageView, which, when given an image, places the given image to the left of the title label. Implement this by adding the following line to your cell configuration:

```
    cell.imageView.image = [(Country *)[self.countries objectAtIndex:indexPath.row]
flag];
```

You'll probably notice that if you run your program now, all of your flags will appear, but with widely varying aspect ratios, making your view look less professional. Setting the frame of the cell's imageView will not fix this problem, so here is a quick solution.

First, define a method that will redraw a UIImage into a given size, like so:

```
+ (UIImage *)scale:(UIImage *)image toSize:(CGSize)size
{
    UIGraphicsBeginImageContext(size);
    [image drawInRect:CGRectMake(0, 0, size.width, size.height)];
    UIImage *scaledImage = UIGraphicsGetImageFromCurrentImageContext();
    UIGraphicsEndImageContext();
    return scaledImage;
}
```

Place this method's handler in your header file to avoid any potential compiler problems. This handler will be written like so:

```
+ (UIImage *)scale:(UIImage *)image toSize:(CGSize)size;
```

Then, you can adjust your image setting lines of code to utilize this method.

```
UIImage *flag = [(Country *)[self.countries objectAtIndex:indexPath.row] flag];
cell.imageView.image = [MainTableViewController scale:flag toSize:CGSizeMake(115, 75)];
```

After all these configurations, your newly configured - tableView:cellForRowAtIndexPath: method should resemble the following:

```
- (UITableViewCell *)tableView:(UITableView *)tableView
cellForRowAtIndexPath:(NSIndexPath *)indexPath {

    static NSString *CellIdentifier = @"Cell";

    UITableViewCell *cell = [tableView
dequeueReusableCellWithIdentifier:CellIdentifier];
    if (cell == nil)
    {
        cell = [[UITableViewCell alloc] initWithStyle:UITableViewCellStyleSubtitle
reuseIdentifier:CellIdentifier];
        cell.accessoryType = UITableViewCellAccessoryDisclosureIndicator;
        cell.textLabel.font = [UIFont systemFontOfSize:19.0];
        cell.detailTextLabel.font = [UIFont systemFontOfSize:12];
    }

    cell.textLabel.text = [(Country *)[self.countries objectAtIndex:indexPath.row]
name];
    cell.detailTextLabel.text = [(Country *)[self.countries objectAtIndex:indexPath.row]
capital];

    UIImage *flag = [(Country *)[self.countries objectAtIndex:indexPath.row] flag];
    cell.imageView.image = [MainTableViewController scale:flag toSize:CGSizeMake(115,
75)];

    return cell;
}
```

Your resulting application, if you run it, should resemble Figure 9–6, complete with country information and flag images!

Figure 9–6. *Your table populated with country information*

A Note on Rounded Corners

Whenever you look at any well-made iOS application, you will probably notice that almost every single element will have its corners rounded. This is one of those small details that most people don't notice, but can dramatically improve the visual quality of an application, and is actually fairly simple to implement with just two steps.

First, add the following import line to your view controller's header file:

```
#import <QuartzCore/QuartzCore.h>
```

Once you've done that, you can access the layer property of any class that inherits from UIView, which has a cornerRadius property that can be set. Here you'll go ahead and round the corners on your UITableView by adding the following line to your -viewDidLoad method, resulting in your app resembling Figure 9–7.

```
self.tableViewCountries.layer.cornerRadius = 8.0;
```

Figure 9–7. *Your* `UITableView` *with newly rounded corners*

So now that you have a nice little table with your five countries set up and looking good, you can work on extending beyond the basic functionality of the `UITableView`. First, you'll focus on the most straightforward ability of a `UITableView`: to act upon the selection of a specific row.

For the purpose of this recipe, you will build your application in such a way that upon the selection of a row, a separate view controller is presented that will display all the known information about the selected country.

First, create a new file, and choose the "UIViewController subclass" template as before, naming it "CountryInfoViewController".

Construct this controller's view in its XIB file to resemble the one shown in Figure 9–8 by using a combination of `UILabels`, `UITextFields`, and a `UIImageView`. I have added a slight shadow to the "Country Title" `UILabel` as shown in Figure 9–8 through the use of the Attribute inspector, which, though optional, adds quite a bit to the visual design of the layout.

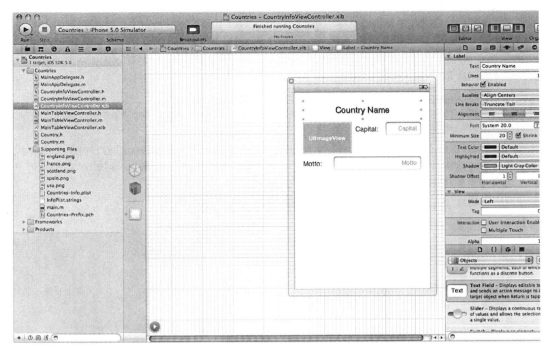

Figure 9-8. *CountryInfoViewController's XIB file and configuration*

Connect each UITextField, the UIImageView, and the top "Country Name" UILabel to your view controller with the following respective property names:

- nameLabel

- textFieldCapital

- textFieldMotto

- imageViewFlag

After switching over to your new view controller's header file, add the UITextFieldDelegate protocol to the header, since you will need to be able to manipulate the behavior of your UITextFields.

In order to make your view controller as generic as possible, you will give it a property of your Country class in order to hold the currently displayed data. This way, you will simply populate your view with the necessary data, and if desired, you could even make it possible to easily re-populate with different data without changing views. Add an import statement for the Country class.

```
#import "Country.h"
```

Create the Country property like so, and then make sure to synthesize it in the implementation file and set it to nil in -viewDidUnload.

```
@property (strong, nonatomic) Country *currentCountry;
```

You will later be implementing a delegate method for this `CountryInfoViewController` to be able to call, so create a protocol for this by adding the following class and protocol declarations before the header declaration.

```
@class CountryInfoViewController;

@protocol CountryInfoDelegate <NSObject>
-(void)countryInfoViewControllerDidFinish:(CountryInfoViewController *)countryVC;
@end
```

Now you will add a `delegate` property to your `CountryInfoViewController`, making sure that it is required to conform to the protocol you just created. Make sure to synthesize and nullify it just as with any other property.

```
@property (strong, nonatomic) id <CountryInfoDelegate> delegate;
```

In entirety, your header file should resemble the following code.

```
#import <UIKit/UIKit.h>
#import "Country.h"

@class CountryInfoViewController;
@protocol CountryInfoDelegate <NSObject>

-(void)countryInfoViewControllerDidFinish:(CountryInfoViewController *)countryVC;

@end

@interface CountryInfoViewController : UIViewController <UITextFieldDelegate>

@property (strong, nonatomic) IBOutlet UILabel *nameLabel;
@property (strong, nonatomic) IBOutlet UIImageView *imageViewFlag;
@property (strong, nonatomic) IBOutlet UITextField *textFieldCapital;
@property (strong, nonatomic) IBOutlet UITextField *textFieldMotto;

@property (strong, nonatomic) Country *currentCountry;
@property (strong, nonatomic) id <CountryInfoDelegate> delegate;

@end
```

Now, in the `CountryInfoViewController` implementation file, create a method to populate the view.

```
-(void)populateViewWithCountry:(Country *)country
{
    self.currentCountry = country;

    self.imageViewFlag.image = country.flag;
    self.nameLabel.text = country.name;
    self.textFieldCapital.text = country.capital;
    self.textFieldMotto.text = country.motto;
}
```

You will want this method to be called after your view is loaded, but right before your view is displayed, so you will implement the -`viewWillAppear:animated:` method like so:

```
-(void)viewWillAppear:(BOOL)animated
{
```

```
    [self populateViewWithCountry:self.currentCountry];
}
```

You will want to be able to dismiss the keyboard after editing your UITextFields, so implement the -textFieldShouldReturn: delegate method.

```
-(BOOL)textFieldShouldReturn:(UITextField *)textField
{
    [textField resignFirstResponder];
    return NO;
}
```

In your -viewDidLoad, configure the two UITextFields by setting their delegates to the view controller.

```
self.textFieldMotto.delegate = self;
self.textFieldCapital.delegate = self;
```

Since you are allowing the user to make changes to your data, you should include a button to "Revert" back to the original data before it has been overwritten. You will add this to the right side of your navigation bar by adding the following code to the -viewDidLoad method.

```
UIBarButtonItem *revertButton = [[UIBarButtonItem alloc] initWithTitle:@"Revert"
style:UIBarButtonItemStyleBordered target:self action:@selector(revert)];

self.navigationItem.rightBarButtonItems = [NSArray arrayWithObject:revertButton];
```

> **NOTE:** The rightBarButtonItems property of the UINavigationItem class is a new addition to iOS 5. It allows the user to set multiple objects to appear in the right side of a UINavigationBar. This was possible in previous versions of iOS, but was slightly more difficult as it required a custom-viewed UIBarButtonItem made out of UIToolbar containing the desired items.

Your entire -viewDidLoad method should look like this:

```
- (void)viewDidLoad
{
    [super viewDidLoad];

    self.textFieldMotto.delegate = self;
    self.textFieldCapital.delegate = self;

    UIBarButtonItem *revertButton = [[UIBarButtonItem alloc] initWithTitle:@"Revert"
style:UIBarButtonItemStyleBordered target:self action:@selector(revert)];
    self.navigationItem.rightBarButtonItems = [NSArray arrayWithObject:revertButton];
}
```

The selector "revert" that you specified as your revertButton's action is easily implemented:

```
-(void)revert
{
    [self populateViewWithCountry:self.currentCountry];
```

```
}
```

The last thing you need to do is implement functionality to save any changes to the given Country upon returning to your MainTableViewController. You will implement your -viewWillDisappear:animated: to do this.

```objc
-(void)viewWillDisappear:(BOOL)animated
{
    self.currentCountry.capital = self.textFieldCapital.text;
    self.currentCountry.motto = self.textFieldMotto.text;
    [self.delegate countryInfoViewControllerDidFinish:self];
}
```

Switch back over to the header file of your MainTableViewController, and add the CountryInfoDelegate protocol that you created to the header. You will need to import the class you created first.

```objc
#import "CountryInfoViewController.h"
```

To make your implementation of the CountryInfoViewController delegate method easier, you will want to create an instance variable that will refer to the index path of whichever row was selected, so that you can save processing power by refreshing only that row. After you add the variable of type NSIndexPath, called selectedIndexPath, your header file should now look like so:

```objc
#import <UIKit/UIKit.h>
#import <QuartzCore/QuartzCore.h>
#import "Country.h"
#import "CountryInfoViewController.h"

@interface MainTableViewController : UIViewController <UITableViewDelegate,
UITableViewDataSource, CountryInfoDelegate>{

    NSIndexPath *selectedIndexPath;
}

@property (strong, nonatomic) IBOutlet UITableView *tableViewCountries;
@property (strong, nonatomic) NSMutableArray *countries;

@end
```

You can now implement the CountryInfoViewController's delegate method like so:

```objc
-(void)countryInfoViewControllerDidFinish:(CountryInfoViewController *)countryVC
{
    if (selectedIndexPath)
    {
        [tableViewCountries beginUpdates];
        [self.tableViewCountries reloadRowsAtIndexPaths:[NSArray
arrayWithObject:selectedIndexPath] withRowAnimation:UITableViewRowAnimationNone];
        [tableViewCountries endUpdates];
    }
    selectedIndexPath = nil;
}
```

The -beginUpdates and -endUpdates methods, though unnecessary here, are very useful for reloading data in a UITableView, as they specify that any calls to reload data in between them should be animated. Since all of your reloading of data occurs while the UITableView is off-screen, this is not quite necessary, but it does not harm your application.

Finally, in order to actually act upon the selection of a given row in a UITableView, all you need to do is implement the UITableView's delegate method -tableView:didSelectRowAtIndexPath:.

```
-(void)tableView:(UITableView *)tableView didSelectRowAtIndexPath:(NSIndexPath
*)indexPath
{
    [tableView deselectRowAtIndexPath:indexPath animated:YES];

    selectedIndexPath = indexPath;

    Country *chosenCountry = [self.countries objectAtIndex:indexPath.row];
    CountryInfoViewController *infoVC = [[CountryInfoViewController alloc] init];
    infoVC.delegate = self;
    infoVC.currentCountry = chosenCountry;

    [self.navigationController pushViewController:infoVC animated:YES];
}
```

The UITableView class also has multiple other methods for dealing with the selection or deselection of a row, including -tableView:willSelectRowAtIndexPath: (which is called before its -tableView:didSelectRowAtIndexPath counterpart), as well as -tableView:willDeselectRowAtIndexPath: and -tableView:didDeselectRowAtIndexPath:. Through the use of these four delegate methods, you can fully customize the behavior of a UITableView to fit any application.

Upon running this project now, you will able to view and edit country information, as in Figure 9–9.

Figure 9–9. *The resulting display of your* `CountryInfoViewController`

Enhanced User Interaction

When you're dealing with applications that focus on UITableViews, you often may want to allow the user to access multiple different views from the same table. For example, the Phone application on an iPhone has a voicemail tab, which displays a UITableView containing the various voicemails left on the phone. The user can then either play the voicemail by selecting a row from the table, or, by selecting a smaller blue button on the right side of the row, view the contact information of the original caller. You can implement a similar behavior by implementing another UITableView delegate method.

First, you must change the type of "accessory" of the cells in your UITableView. This refers to the icon displayed on the far right side of any given row. In your - tableView:cellForRowAtIndexPath: method, find the following line:

```
cell.accessoryType = UITableViewCellAccessoryDisclosureIndicator;
```

Change this value to UITableViewCellAccessoryDetailDisclosureButton. This will give us the nice little blue button that can respond to touches. The four possible values for this property are as follows:

- UITableViewCellAccessoryNone: Specifies a lack of accessory

- UITableViewCellAccessoryDisclosureIndicator: Adds a gray arrow on the right side of a row, as you have been using up until now

- UITableViewCellAccessoryDetailDisclosureButton: Your most recent choice that specifies an interaction-enabled button

- UITableViewCellAccessoryCheckmark: Adds a checkmark to a given row; this is especially useful in conjunction with the -tableView:didSelectRowAtIndexPath: method in order to add and remove checkmarks from a list as you find necessary.

> **NOTE:** While these four available accessory types are pretty useful and will cover almost any generic use, it's certainly easy to think of a reason to want something entirely different over on the right side of your row. You can easily customize a UITableViewCell's accessory through the accessoryView property to be any other UIView subclass.

Now that you turned your accessory into a button, it is actually incredibly easy to implement an action to handle this interaction. You implement another UITableView delegate method, -tableView:accessoryButtonTappedForRowWithIndexPath:. For your testing purposes, you'll make this action the exact same as that of a row selection, with an extra NSLog(), though it should be very easy to see how you could implement different behavior.

```
-(void)tableView:(UITableView *)tableView
accessoryButtonTappedForRowWithIndexPath:(NSIndexPath *)indexPath
{
    [tableView deselectRowAtIndexPath:indexPath animated:YES];

    selectedIndexPath = indexPath;

    Country *chosenCountry = [self.countries objectAtIndex:indexPath.row];
    CountryInfoViewController *infoVC = [[CountryInfoViewController alloc] init];
    infoVC.delegate = self;
    infoVC.currentCountry = chosenCountry;

    NSLog(@"Accessory Button Tapped");
    [self.navigationController pushViewController:infoVC animated:YES];
}
```

When you run this app, tapping the accessory buttons should run your newest functionalities, as shown in Figure 9–10.

Figure 9–10. *Your* `UITableView` *with detail-disclosure buttons responding to events*

A Note on Cell View Customization

Just like with the accessory view, several other parts of a `UITableViewCell` are customizable by way of their views. The `UITableViewCell` class includes several properties for other views that you can edit, including the following:

- `imageView`: The `UIImageView` to the left of the `textLabel` in a cell, as shown by your flags in the previous example; if no image is given to this view, then the cell will appear as if the `UIImageView` did not exist (as opposed to a blank `UIImageView` taking up space).

- `contentView`: The main `UIView` of the `UITableViewCell`, which includes all the text; you may wish to customize this to implement a more powerful or versatile `UITableViewCell`.

- `backgroundView`: A `UIView` set to `nil` in plain-style tables (like you have used so far), and otherwise for grouped tables; this view will appear behind all other views in the table, so it is great for specifically customizing the visual display of the cell.

- selectedBackgroundView: This UIView is inserted above the backgroundView but behind all other views when a cell is selected. It can also be easily given an alpha animation (fading opacity in or out) by use of the -setSelected:animated: action.

- multipleSelectionBackgroundView: This UIView acts just like the selectedBackgroundView, but is used for when a UITableView is enabled to allow the selection of multiple rows.

- accessoryView: As discussed earlier, this allows you to create entirely different views for a row's accessory, so you could implement your own custom display and behavior beyond the pre-set values.

- editingAccessoryView: This is similar to the accessoryView property but specifically for when a UITableView is in "editing" mode, which you will see in detail soon.

While most developers stick to the pretty generic UITableView since it fits well with the iOS design theme, if you look around you can find some pretty creative implementations of custom views. All this extra customization may add a lot of development time to your project, but a high-quality, custom UITableView will certainly stand out in an application for its uniqueness.

Recipe 9–2: Editing a UITableView

If you look at almost any UITableView in an application you commonly use, such as your device's music player, you'll probably notice that you can edit the table in some way. In your Music application, you can swipe across a row in order to reveal a Delete button, which can then remove an item from a table. In your Mail application, you can press the Edit button in the upper right-hand corner to allow the selection of multiple messages for deletion, movement, and other functions. Both of these functionalities are based on the concept of "editing" a UITableView.

The first thing you can look at is the idea of putting your UITableView into "editing" mode, since for your users to be able to use your editing functionality, they need to be able to access it. You will do this by adding an Edit button to the top right-hand corner of your view. Surprisingly enough, this is very easy to do by adding the following line to your -viewDidLoad method.

```
self.navigationItem.rightBarButtonItem = self.editButtonItem;
```

This editButtonItem property is not actually a property that you need to define, as it is pre-set for every UIViewController subclass. The especially great thing about this button is that it is programmed not only to call a specific method already, but also to toggle its text between "Edit" and "Done".

The editButtonItem by default is set to call the method -setEditing:animated:, which you will create a simple implementation for:

```
-(void)setEditing:(BOOL)editing animated:(BOOL)animated
{
    [super setEditing:editing animated:animated];
    [self.tableViewCountries setEditing:editing animated:animated];
}
```

The main ideas of this method are simple, in that first you call the super method, which will handle the toggling of the button's text, and then you set the editing mode of your UITableView according to the parameters given.

At this point, your application's Edit button will trigger the editing mode of the UITableView, allowing you to reveal the Delete buttons for any given row. However, since you haven't actually implemented any behavior for these buttons, you won't actually be able to delete any rows from your table yet. To do this, you must first implement one more delegate method, - tableView:commitEditingStyle:forRowAtIndexPath:.

Here's a pretty basic implementation of this method that you'll start with:

```
-(void)tableView:(UITableView *)tableView
commitEditingStyle:(UITableViewCellEditingStyle)editingStyle
forRowAtIndexPath:(NSIndexPath *)indexPath
{
    if (editingStyle == UITableViewCellEditingStyleDelete)
    {
        Country *deletedCountry = [self.countries objectAtIndex:indexPath.row];
        [self.countries removeObject:deletedCountry];

        [tableViewCountries deleteRowsAtIndexPaths:[NSArray arrayWithObject:indexPath]
withRowAnimation:UITableViewRowAnimationAutomatic];
    }
}
```

It is *very* important in this method that you make sure to delete the actual piece of data from your model before removing the row(s) from your UITableView, just like how in the previous example you first delete the country from your array, and then remove its row. Otherwise, your application will throw an exception.

Now when you run your app, you can tap the Edit button to put your UITableView into editing mode, resembling Figure 9–11.

Figure 9–11. *Your* UITableView *in editing mode, with functionality for removing rows*

UITableView Row Animations

In the method you just added, you specified a specific animation type to be performed upon the deletion of a row, called UITableViewRowAnimationAutomatic. The parameter that accepts this value has various other pre-set values with which you can customize the visual behavior of your rows, including the following:

- UITableViewRowAnimationBottom
- UITableViewRowAnimationFade
- UITableViewRowAnimationLeft
- UITableViewRowAnimationMiddle
- UITableViewRowAnimationNone
- UITableViewRowAnimationRight
- UITableViewRowAnimationTop

The animation type that you choose won't make any significant difference in how your application performs, but it can certainly change how an application looks and feels to the end user. It's best to play around with these and see which animation looks best in your application.

At this point, your method should now be able to handle the deletion of rows from your table! Since you wrote your program to re-create your data every time the application runs, it should be pretty easy to test this out. When you are about to delete a row from a table, your table will resemble Figure 9–12.

Figure 9–12. *Deleting a row from a table*

But Wait, There's More!

Deletion is not the only kind of editing that can occur in a UITableView. While not used quite as often, iOS includes functionality to allow rows to be created and inserted with the same method with which they were deleted.

The default editing style for any row in a UITableView is
UITableViewCellEditingStyleDelete, so in order to implement row insertion, you need
to change this. For fun, you will give every other row an "insertion" editing style by
implementing the -tableView:editingStyleForRowAtIndexPath: method.

```
-(UITableViewCellEditingStyle)tableView:(UITableView *)tableView
editingStyleForRowAtIndexPath:(NSIndexPath *)indexPath
{
    if ((indexPath.row % 2) == 1)
    {
        return UITableViewCellEditingStyleInsert;
    }
    return UITableViewCellEditingStyleDelete;
}
```

Just as before, you will need to specify the behavior to be followed upon the selection of
an Insertion button. You will add a case to your -
tableView:commitEditingStyle:forRowAtIndexPath: so the method now looks like so:

```
-(void)tableView:(UITableView *)tableView
commitEditingStyle:(UITableViewCellEditingStyle)editingStyle
forRowAtIndexPath:(NSIndexPath *)indexPath
{
    if (editingStyle == UITableViewCellEditingStyleDelete)
    {
        Country *deletedCountry = [self.countries objectAtIndex:indexPath.row];
        [self.countries removeObject:deletedCountry];

        [tableViewCountries deleteRowsAtIndexPaths:[NSArray arrayWithObject:indexPath]
withRowAnimation:UITableViewRowAnimationAutomatic];
    }
    else if (editingStyle == UITableViewCellEditingStyleInsert)
    {
        Country *copiedCountry = [self.countries objectAtIndex:indexPath.row];
        Country *newCountry = [[Country alloc] init];
        newCountry.name = copiedCountry.name;
        newCountry.flag = copiedCountry.flag;
        newCountry.capital = copiedCountry.capital;
        newCountry.motto = copiedCountry.motto;

        [self.countries insertObject:newCountry atIndex:indexPath.row+1];

        [self.tableViewCountries insertRowsAtIndexPaths:[NSArray
arrayWithObject:[NSIndexPath indexPathForRow:indexPath.row+1
inSection:indexPath.section]] withRowAnimation:UITableViewRowAnimationRight];
    }
}
```

You can see that you have gone with a pretty easy implementation for insertion, in that
all you have done is inserted a copy of the row selected. It should be noted that by
changing the index values in this method, you could easily insert objects to nearly any
row in the table; it is not necessary to insert into only the following row.

As with the deletion, you must make sure that your data model is updated before your
table view is, so you add the new Country to your array before you insert the new row
into your UITableView.

Upon running your app and editing your table, you will be able to see both deletion and insertion buttons, as in Figure 9–13.

Figure 9–13. *Editing a* `UITableView` *with insertion or deletion*

There are two other `UITableView` delegate methods that can be used in combination with editing to further customize your application's behavior.

- The `-tableView:willBeginEditingRowAtIndexPath:` method allows you to get a kind of "first look" at whichever row was selected for editing, and act accordingly.

- The `-tableView:didEndEditingRowAtIndexPath:` method can be used as a completion block, in that you can specify any actions you deem necessary to be performed with a row, but only after a row's editing has finished.

Recipe 9–3: Re-ordering a UITableView

Now that we have covered deletion and insertion of rows, the next logical step in terms of functionality of a table would be to make it so that you can move your rows around. This is actually pretty simple to incorporate given how you have set up your application.

First, you have to specify exactly which of your rows are allowed to move using -tableView:canMoveRowAtIndexPath:.

```
-(BOOL)tableView:(UITableView *)tableView canMoveRowAtIndexPath:(NSIndexPath *)indexPath
{
    return YES;
}
```

I've chosen the easy way out of this by simply making them all editable, but you can easily change this depending on your application.

Now, you simply need to implement a delegate to update your data model upon the successful movement of a row.

```
-(void)tableView:(UITableView *)tableView moveRowAtIndexPath:(NSIndexPath
*)sourceIndexPath toIndexPath:(NSIndexPath *)destinationIndexPath
{
    [self.countries exchangeObjectAtIndex:sourceIndexPath.row
withObjectAtIndex:destinationIndexPath.row];
    [self.tableViewCountries reloadData];
}
```

Just as with insertion, you must make sure to correct your array to match the re-ordering, but the UITableView handles the actual swapping of rows automatically.

For extra control over the re-ordering of the table, you can implement an extra method called -tableView:targetIndexPathForMoveFromRowAtIndexPath:. This delegate method is called every time a cell is dragged over another cell as a possible movement, and its normal use is for "retargeting" a destination row. In this way, you can check the proposed destination and either confirm it or reject the proposed move and return a different destination.

Although you haven't implemented functionality to confirm or reject your proposed movements, your application will now be able to successfully move and re-order your rows in addition to your previous deletion and copying functionalities, as in Figure 9–14.

Figure 9–14. *Your table with some re-ordering of cells*

Recipe 9–4: Creating a Grouped UITableView

Now that you have nearly completely gone through all the basics of using an ungrouped UITableView, you can now adjust your application to consider a "grouped" approach. All the functionalities you implemented with an ungrouped table also apply to a grouped one, so you will not have to make a great deal of changes to implement this.

The absolute first thing you need to do in order to use a grouped table is to switch the "Style" of the UITableView from "Plain" to "Grouped". The easiest way to do this is in your view controller's XIB file by selecting your UITableView, and changing the style in the Attribute inspector, resulting in a display similar to Figure 9–15.

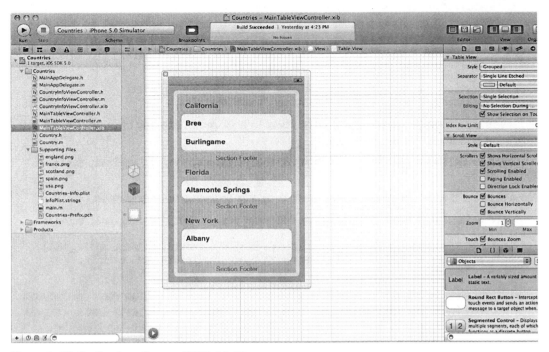

Figure 9–15. *Configuring a "grouped"* UITableView

The specific option you are looking for is in the top of your Attribute inspector under the "Style" of the "Table View", as shown here in Figure 9–16.

Figure 9–16. *Modifying the table's "Style" to create a grouped* UITableView

While this is the only thing necessary in order to change the style of your table, the problem is that up until now, your data model has been formatted for an ungrouped style. You don't even have your data grouped at all. To remedy this, you will change the organization with which your data is stored.

Rather than having one array containing all five of your countries, you will separate your countries into their groups, with each group being an NSMutableArray, and then put these arrays into a larger NSMutableArray. (Although a better practice would be to make these immutable, I have chosen a mutable version to make editing your data model from the table a more simple process.)

For your application, you will divide your five Country objects into two categories: one of countries in the United Kingdom, and one of all the others.

First, you need to create two more NSMutableArrays to be your subarrays, so add these two properties, making sure to properly handle them (synthesize!) in your implementation file. You will end up with a total of three NSMutableArray properties.

```
@property (strong, nonatomic) NSMutableArray *countries;
@property (strong, nonatomic) NSMutableArray *unitedKingdomCountries;
@property (strong, nonatomic) NSMutableArray *nonUKCountries;
```

Now you'll change your -viewDidLoad method to accommodate this change. Delete the following line from this method:

```
    self.countries = [NSMutableArray arrayWithObjects:usa, france, england, scotland,
spain, nil];
```

Now replace that line with the following to properly organize your countries.

```
    self.unitedKingdomCountries = [NSMutableArray arrayWithObjects:england, scotland,
nil];
    self.nonUKCountries = [NSMutableArray arrayWithObjects:usa, france, spain, nil];
    self.countries = [NSMutableArray arrayWithObjects:unitedKingdomCountries,
nonUKCountries, nil];
```

Now is the slightly tricky part, where you have to make sure all of your data source and delegate methods are adjusted to your new format. You have to include first a retrieval of the group's array, and then retrieve a specific country from there in each method. First, you'll change your -tableView:cellForRowAtIndexPath:. It should now look like so:

```
- (UITableViewCell *)tableView:(UITableView *)tableView
cellForRowAtIndexPath:(NSIndexPath *)indexPath {

static NSString *CellIdentifier = @"Cell";

    UITableViewCell *cell = [tableView
dequeueReusableCellWithIdentifier:CellIdentifier];
    if (cell == nil)
    {
        cell = [[UITableViewCell alloc] initWithStyle:UITableViewCellStyleSubtitle
reuseIdentifier:CellIdentifier];
        cell.accessoryType = UITableViewCellAccessoryDetailDisclosureButton;
        cell.textLabel.font = [UIFont systemFontOfSize:19.0];
        cell.detailTextLabel.font = [UIFont systemFontOfSize:12];
    }

    NSArray *group = [self.countries objectAtIndex:indexPath.section];
    Country *country = [group objectAtIndex:indexPath.row];
    cell.textLabel.text = country.name;
    cell.detailTextLabel.text = country.capital;
    UIImage *flag = country.flag;
    cell.imageView.image = [MainTableViewController scale:flag toSize:CGSizeMake(115,
75)];

    return cell;
}
```

Up next is -tableView:numberOfRowsInSection:.

```
-(NSInteger)tableView:(UITableView *)tableView numberOfRowsInSection:(NSInteger)section
{
```

```
    NSArray *group = [self.countries objectAtIndex:section];
    return [group count];
}
```

Here is -tableView:didSelectRowAtIndexPath:.

```
-(void)tableView:(UITableView *)tableView didSelectRowAtIndexPath:(NSIndexPath
*)indexPath
{
    [tableView deselectRowAtIndexPath:indexPath animated:YES];

    selectedIndexPath = indexPath;
    /////BEGIN MODIFIED CODE FOR GROUPED TABLE
    NSArray *group = [self.countries objectAtIndex:indexPath.section];
    Country *chosenCountry = [group objectAtIndex:indexPath.row];
    /////END OF MODIFIED CODE
    CountryInfoViewController *infoVC = [[CountryInfoViewController alloc] init];
    infoVC.delegate = self;
    infoVC.currentCountry = chosenCountry;

    [self.navigationController pushViewController:infoVC animated:YES];
}
```

Here is -tableView:accessoryButtonTappedForRowWithIndexPath:.

```
 -(void)tableView:(UITableView *)tableView
accessoryButtonTappedForRowWithIndexPath:(NSIndexPath *)indexPath
{
    [tableView deselectRowAtIndexPath:indexPath animated:YES];

    selectedIndexPath = indexPath;
    ////BEGIN MODIFIED CODE FOR GROUPED TABLE
    NSArray *group = [self.countries objectAtIndex:indexPath.section];
    Country *chosenCountry = [group objectAtIndex:indexPath.row];
    ////END MODIFIED CODE FOR GROUPED TABLE
    CountryInfoViewController *infoVC = [[CountryInfoViewController alloc] init];
    infoVC.delegate = self;
    infoVC.currentCountry = chosenCountry;

    NSLog(@"Accessory Button Tapped");
    [self.navigationController pushViewController:infoVC animated:YES];
}
```

For the -tableView:moveRowAtIndexPath:toIndexPath: method, you will make a quick assumption that you are moving only rows that are in the same section to make your coding easier. You will notice when you run the application later that this actually works well, as with your current implementation, the UITableView will not allow a Country to switch groups, just as is expected in this particular application. For an application where it may be reasonable to have objects change groups, you will want to be sure to include code to do so accordingly.

```
-(void)tableView:(UITableView *)tableView moveRowAtIndexPath:(NSIndexPath
*)sourceIndexPath toIndexPath:(NSIndexPath *)destinationIndexPath
{
    NSMutableArray *group = [self.countries objectAtIndex:sourceIndexPath.section];
//Assume same Section
    if (destinationIndexPath.row < [group count])
    {
```

```
        [group exchangeObjectAtIndex:sourceIndexPath.row
withObjectAtIndex:destinationIndexPath.row];
    }
    [self.tableViewCountries reloadData];
}
```

The last method you must fix is -tableView:commitEditingStyle:forRowAtIndexPath:, which will look like so:

```
-(void)tableView:(UITableView *)tableView
commitEditingStyle:(UITableViewCellEditingStyle)editingStyle
forRowAtIndexPath:(NSIndexPath *)indexPath
{
    if (editingStyle == UITableViewCellEditingStyleDelete)
    {
        //////Changed code
        NSMutableArray *group = [self.countries objectAtIndex:indexPath.section];
        Country *deletedCountry = [group objectAtIndex:indexPath.row];
        [group removeObject:deletedCountry];
        //////End of changed code

        [tableViewCountries deleteRowsAtIndexPaths:[NSArray arrayWithObject:indexPath]
withRowAnimation:UITableViewRowAnimationAutomatic];
    }
    else if (editingStyle == UITableViewCellEditingStyleInsert)
    {
        //////More changed code!
        NSMutableArray *group = [self.countries objectAtIndex:indexPath.section];
        Country *copiedCountry = [group objectAtIndex:indexPath.row];
        Country *newCountry = [[Country alloc] init];
        newCountry.name = copiedCountry.name;
        newCountry.flag = copiedCountry.flag;
        newCountry.capital = copiedCountry.capital;
        newCountry.motto = copiedCountry.motto;

        [group insertObject:newCountry atIndex:indexPath.row+1];
        //////End of changed code

        [self.tableViewCountries insertRowsAtIndexPaths:[NSArray
arrayWithObject:[NSIndexPath indexPathForRow:indexPath.row+1
inSection:indexPath.section]] withRowAnimation:UITableViewRowAnimationRight];
    }
}
```

Finally, since you did switch your UITableView over to a "grouped" style, you need to implement just two extra methods to ensure correct functionality.

First, you need to specify exactly how many sections your UITableView will have with the following method:

```
-(NSInteger)numberOfSectionsInTableView:(UITableView *)tableView
{
    return [self.countries count];
}
```

Second, you should specify "headers" for each section, which will basically be the titles for your groups. Since you already know how your data is formatted, this is pretty easy to do.

```
-(NSString *)tableView:(UITableView *)tableView
titleForHeaderInSection:(NSInteger)section
{
    if (section == 0)
    {
        return @"United Kingdom Countries";
    }
    return @"Non-United Kingdom Countries";
}
```

If your data model was more complicated, you would probably want to have the names of your groups stored somewhere with the groups themselves. Using an NSDictionary would be a particularly good way to use this by making the headers, as strings, the keys for your NSArray group objects.

The UITableViewDelegate protocol also includes a method that allows the developer to customize the text displayed in a Delete button when editing a UITableView. This method is entirely optional, and will vary in its use based on the needs of any given application.

```
-(NSString *)tableView:(UITableView *)tableView
titleForDeleteConfirmationButtonForRowAtIndexPath:(NSIndexPath *)indexPath
{
    return NSLocalizedString(@"Remove", @"Delete");
}
```

After all these changes, running your app should result in a view similar to that in Figure 9–17.

Figure 9–17. *Your application with grouped items and section headers*

As one final addition that you can make for your table, you can also add "footers" to your sections. These work just like headers, but, as you might guess, appear on the bottom of your groups. Here's a quick method to add some (slightly silly) footers to your UITableView.

```
-(NSString *)tableView:(UITableView *)tableView
titleForFooterInSection:(NSInteger)section
{
    if (section == 0)
        return @"I'm a footer!";
    return @"Me too, I guess...";
}
```

In keeping with all the other vastly customizable parts of a UITableView, these headers and footers are also incredibly easy to customize beyond a simple NSString. If you use the methods -tableView:viewForHeaderInSection: and -tableView:viewForFooterInSection:, you can programmatically create your own subview to be used as a header or footer, allowing for full control over your UITableView's display.

At this point, you now have a fully functional grouped UITableView, complete with all the same abilities as your ungrouped one! Figure 9–18 shows the final result of your setup.

Figure 9–18. *Your completed grouped UITableView with both headers and footers*

Summary

Throughout this entire chapter, you have seen how to programmatically create a UITableView, step-by-step, for two kinds of styles: "plain" and "grouped." You have also been given a glimpse at the amount of customization control the developer has over the view and display of a UITableView, though the full Apple documentation has a great deal more to say on the subject. You have even included a great deal of functionality into your UITableViews to provide them with the most powerful user interface. However, the key to UITableViews is not how they work, but the data that they present. It is up to you as a developer to find the information that users want or need, and present it to them in the most efficient, flexible way possible. A UITableView is a fantastic tool, but the purpose it serves is by far more important, and this is what will ultimately be the final product that you deliver to your customers.

Chapter 10

Data Storage Recipes

When working in iOS, one of the most important topics to understand is the concept, use, and implementation of persistence. This term refers to the idea of having information be saved and retrieved, or "persist," through the closing or restarting of an application. Just as pages from books written thousands of years ago can still be read, we are able to make use of certain key concepts in iOS to allow our information, from the simplest of values to the most complex of data structures, to stay stored in our device for indefinite periods of time. We will cover a variety of methods of persistence throughout this chapter with different advantages, disadvantages, general uses, and complexities, so that we can develop a full understanding of the best method of storage for any given situation.

Recipe 10–1: Using NSUserDefaults

When developing applications, we very often run into issues where we simply need to store simple values, such as strings, numbers, or Boolean values. While there are a variety of ways to store data, the easiest of these is NSUserDefaults, built specifically for such combinations.

The NSUserDefaults class is a simple implementation used to store basic values, such as instances of NSString, NSNumber, BOOL, etc. It can also be used to store more complex data structures, such as NSArray or NSDictionary, as long as they do not contain massive amounts of data. Any kind of image should not be stored with NSUserDefaults. In this way, it is excellent for storing any kind of preference or option for an application.

Start off by creating a new project called "Stubborn" (since you want your information to stick around).

Select the Single View Application template to create a simple application for you to configure. After entering your name and ensuring the device is set to the iPhone family, as in Figure 10–1, click through to finish creating your project.

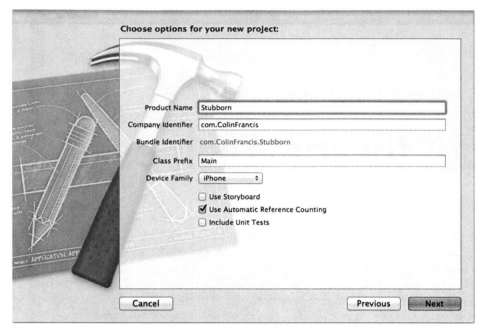

Figure 10–1. *Configuring your Stubborn project*

Now, in your newly created view controller's XIB file, you will start off by setting up your basic user interface. Drag and drop three UILabels, two UITextFields, a UISwitch, and a UIActivityIndicatorView so as to create the view shown in Figure 10–2.

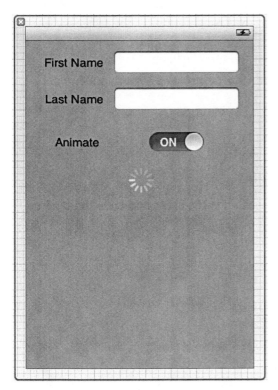

Figure 10–2. *Your view controller's XIB for storing values*

As you can probably guess, you will simply be using text fields to set the text of your labels, and using the switch to control whether the activity indicator view is animating.

Next, connect each of these elements in your XIB file to a property in your view controller's header file by holding ^ (Ctrl), and click-dragging from each element into your header file. This will automatically create your property, synthesize it, and add a statement to nullify it in the application's -viewDidUnload method. The following header file excerpt shows the property names you will use to manage each element.

```
#import <UIKit/UIKit.h>

@interface MainViewController : UIViewController

@property (strong, nonatomic) IBOutlet UILabel *firstLabel;
@property (strong, nonatomic) IBOutlet UILabel *secondLabel;
@property (strong, nonatomic) IBOutlet UILabel *animateLabel;
@property (strong, nonatomic) IBOutlet UITextField *firstNameTextField;
@property (strong, nonatomic) IBOutlet UITextField *lastNameTextField;
@property (strong, nonatomic) IBOutlet UISwitch *animateSwitch;
@property (strong, nonatomic) IBOutlet UIActivityIndicatorView *activityIndicator;

@end
```

Up next, you need to conform your view controller to the UITextFieldDelegate protocol in order to gain more control over the actions of each UITextField. The header line of your view controller's header file (the second line in the preceding code) will now look like so:

```
@interface MainViewController : UIViewController<UITextFieldDelegate>
```

Next, update your -viewDidLoad method in your view controller's interface file to set both text field delegates.

```
- (void)viewDidLoad
{
    [super viewDidLoad];
self.firstNameTextField.delegate = self;
self.lastNameTextField.delegate = self;
}
```

Now you can write a method to access the NSUserDefaults class and save the desired values of your view.

```
-(void)updateDefaults
{
//Acquire Values
NSString *first = self.firstNameTextField.text;
NSString *last = self.lastNameTextField.text;
BOOL animating = self.activityIndicator.isAnimating;

//Acquire Shared Instance
NSUserDefaults *userDefaults = [NSUserDefaults standardUserDefaults];

//Set Objects/Values to Persist
    [userDefaults setObject:first forKey:@"firstName"];
    [userDefaults setObject:last forKey:@"lastName"];
    [userDefaults setBool:animating forKey:@"animating"];

//Save Changes
    [userDefaults synchronize];
}
```

As shown in this method, it is always important to remember to call the -synchronize method when you have finished making changes to the NSUserDefaults object in order to save your data.

Along with the +standardUserDefaults method, which retrieves a shared instance of the NSUserDefaults class, this class also has a class method, +resetStandardUserDefaults, used to completely wipe all saved stored values for an application.

You can implement your UITextFieldDelegate protocol methods to now handle the entering of data to automatically save newly entered text.

```
-(BOOL)textFieldShouldReturn:(UITextField *)textField
{
    [textField resignFirstResponder];
return NO;
}

-(void)textFieldDidEndEditing:(UITextField *)textField
{
if (textField == self.firstNameTextField)
```

```
    {
self.firstLabel.text = textField.text;
    }
else if (textField == self.lastNameTextField)
    {
self.secondLabel.text = textField.text;
    }
    [self updateDefaults];
}
```

For your UISwitch, you will also create a method to handle the changing of its value.

```
-(void)switchValueChanged:(UISwitch *)sender
{
if (sender.on)
    {
        [self.activityIndicator startAnimating];
self.animateLabel.text = @"Animating";
    }
else
    {
        [self.activityIndicator stopAnimating];
self.animateLabel.text = @"Stopped";
    }
    [self updateDefaults];
}
```

In order to assign this method to be called by your UISwitch, you need to modify your -viewDidLoad again.

```
- (void)viewDidLoad
{
    [super viewDidLoad];
self.firstNameTextField.delegate = self;
self.lastNameTextField.delegate = self;

    [self.animateSwitch addTarget:self action:@selector(switchValueChanged:)
forControlEvents:UIControlEventValueChanged];
}
```

At this point, your application should be able to easily save your values entered, but you still need to include functionality to reload these values in case your application is closed. You will create a single method to access the NSUserDefaults class again, check for any stored values, and display them as appropriate.

```
-(void)setValuesFromDefaults
{
//Acquire Shared Instance
NSUserDefaults *userDefaults = [NSUserDefaults standardUserDefaults];

//Acquire Values
NSString *first = [userDefaults objectForKey:@"firstName"];
NSString *last = [userDefaults objectForKey:@"lastName"];
BOOL animating = [userDefaults boolForKey:@"animating"];

//Display Values Appropriately
if (first != nil)
    {
```

```
self.firstNameTextField.text = first;
self.firstLabel.text = first;
    }
if (last != nil)
    {
self.lastNameTextField.text = last;
self.secondLabel.text = last;
    }
if (animating)
    {
self.animateLabel.text = @"Animating";
if (self.activityIndicator.isAnimating == NO)
        {
            [self.activityIndicator startAnimating];
        }
    }
else
    {
self.animateLabel.text = @"Stopped";
if (self.activityIndicator.isAnimating == YES)
        {
            [self.activityIndicator stopAnimating];
        }
    }
    [self.animateSwitch setOn:animating animated:NO];
}
```

Finally, you just need to adjust your -viewDidLoad method again in order to load any saved preferences upon the running of the application.

```
- (void)viewDidLoad
{
    [super viewDidLoad];
self.firstNameTextField.delegate = self;
self.lastNameTextField.delegate = self;

    [self.animateSwitch addTarget:self action:@selector(switchValueChanged:)
forControlEvents:UIControlEventValueChanged];

    [self setValuesFromDefaults];
}
```

At this point, your application can successfully save your values! If you run your application on the iOS simulator or on your device, change the values, and then close and reopen it, your values should have been set as they were. Remember that to fully close an application on newer devices you must double-tap the home button, press and hold on the app icons that appear, and then press the "-" mark on the desired app. Keep in mind also to be careful closing an application in this way if running the project through Xcode, as your application may crash. In this case, you should use the Stop button in Xcode to close your app instead. Though you cannot quite tell, Figure 10–3 shows an application that has been closed and reopened multiple times with the values persisting!

Figure 10–3. *Your application persisting information*

> **NOTE:** Though you did not use a great variety of values to store with NSUserDefaults in this
> short recipe, there are in fact methods to store almost any type of lightweight value, including
> Bool, Float, Integer, Double, and URL. For any kind of more complex object, such as an
> NSString, NSArray, or NSDictionary, you use the general -setObject:forKey: method.

Recipe 10–2: Managing Files

While the NSUserDefaults class is especially useful for doing quick persistence of light
data, it is not nearly as efficient for dealing with large objects, such as videos, music, or
images. For these more complex items, you can make use of iOS's file management
system.

You will create a new application to display a table of "Hotspots," which you will be able
to edit and add to, while persisting all of your data. While these objects will be fairly

lightweight, and thus able to be stored in NSUserDefaults, you will make use of the file management system for demonstration purposes.

To start off, you will build your application's user interface without worrying about data persistence. Create a new project using the Single View Application template, following the exact same process as the previous recipe.

First, you will go through and create your Hotspot class. Create a new file, making sure to select the "Objective-C class" template using the dialog shown in Figure 10–4.

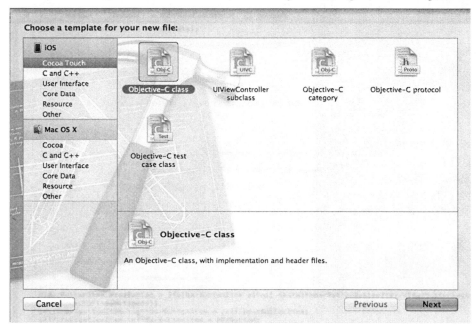

Figure 10–4. *Creating an NSObject subclass*

On the next screen, enter your file's name as "Hotspot", and make sure the subclass field is set to "NSObject". Click through to create your file.

In your Hotspot class's header file, Hotspot.h, define a series of NSString properties to represent the data for this object.

```objc
#import <Foundation/Foundation.h>

@interface Hotspot : NSObject

@property (nonatomic, strong) NSString *name;
@property (nonatomic, strong) NSString *address;
@property (nonatomic, strong) NSString *city;
@property (nonatomic, strong) NSString *state;

@end
```

In the implementation file Hotspot.m, add a single synthesize command for these four properties.

```
@synthesize name, city, state, address;
```

Next, you will create another view controller to manage the creation and editing of any Hotspot objects by the user. Create a new file, and select the "UIViewController subclass" template. Provide the class name "HotspotInfoViewController", and make sure the subclass field is set to "UIViewController", as in Figure 10–5. Make sure also that the box marked "With XIB for user interface" is also checked.

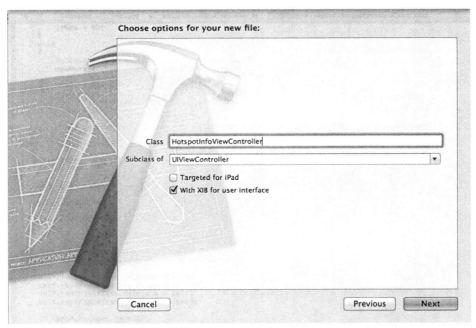

Figure 10–5. *Configuring your new view controller*

In the newly created controller's XIB file, HotspotInfoViewController.xib, create your user interface to mirror that shown in Figure 10–6.

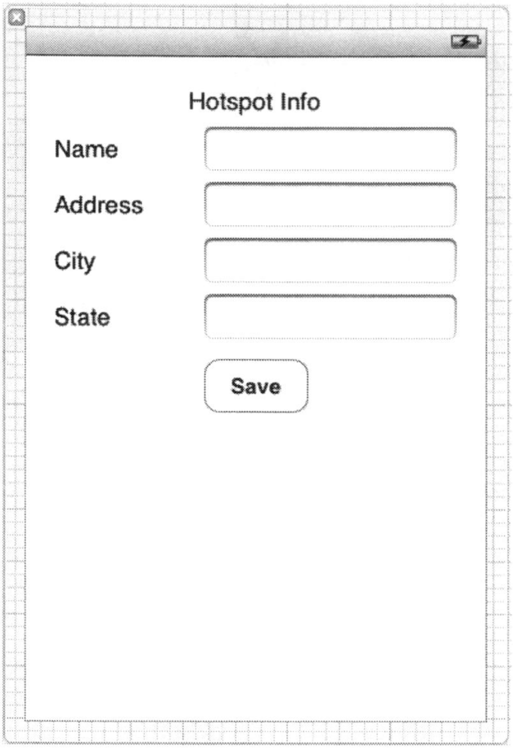

Figure 10–6. *Configuring the HotspotInfoViewController.xib file*

Connect each UITextField element to your view controller's header file using the respective property identifiers textFieldName, textFieldAddress, textFieldCity, and textFieldState. You will not need to define a property for your UIButton, but connect it to an IBAction -saveButtonPressed:. These changes should add the following property and method declarations to your header file.

```
@property (strong, nonatomic) IBOutlet UITextField *textFieldName;
@property (strong, nonatomic) IBOutlet UITextField *textFieldAddress;
@property (strong, nonatomic) IBOutlet UITextField *textFieldCity;
@property (strong, nonatomic) IBOutlet UITextField *textFieldState;
- (IBAction)saveButtonPressed:(id)sender;
```

This class will need a Hotspot property to reference the Hotspot currently being viewed. Add an import statement for the Hotspot class.

```
#import "Hotspot.h"
```

Declare the Hotspot property.

```
@property (strong, nonatomic) IBOutlet Hotspot *hotspot;
```

You will also create a delegate property to handle the completion of this class's use. Define the protocol "HotspotInfoDelegate" by adding the following code above the main "interface" section of the header file.

```
@class HotspotInfoViewController;
```

```
@protocol HotspotInfoDelegate <NSObject>
-(void)HotspotInfoViewController:(HotspotInfoViewController *)hotspotInfoVC
didReturnHotspot:(Hotspot *)hotspot isNew:(BOOL)isNew;
@end
```

You can now declare your delegate property like so:

```
@property (strong, nonatomic) id<HotspotInfoDelegate> delegate;
```

Make sure that both the `delegate` and `hotspot` properties are properly synthesized, and that both are set to `nil` in your controller's `-viewDidUnload` method.

Finally, you will make this view controller the delegate to all four of the `UITextField` elements that you added, so make sure this class conforms to the `UITextFieldDelegate` protocol by adding the `<UITextFieldDelegate>` code to your interface line.

In its entirety, your `HotspotInfoViewController.h` file should now look like so:

```
#import <UIKit/UIKit.h>
#import "Hotspot.h"

@class HotspotInfoViewController;

@protocol HotspotInfoDelegate <NSObject>
-(void)HotspotInfoViewController:(HotspotInfoViewController *)hotspotInfoVC
didReturnHotspot:(Hotspot *)hotspot isNew:(BOOL)isNew;
@end

@interface HotspotInfoViewController : UIViewController<UITextFieldDelegate>

@property (strong, nonatomic) IBOutlet UITextField *textFieldName;
@property (strong, nonatomic) IBOutlet UITextField *textFieldAddress;
@property (strong, nonatomic) IBOutlet UITextField *textFieldCity;
@property (strong, nonatomic) IBOutlet UITextField *textFieldState;
- (IBAction)saveButtonPressed:(id)sender;

@property (strong, nonatomic) Hotspot *hotspot;

@property (strong, nonatomic) id<HotspotInfoDelegate> delegate;

@end
```

In your `HotspotInfoViewController`'s implementation file, you will add a method to populate the view with a given Hotspot's information.

```
-(void)populateWithHotspot
{
self.textFieldName.text = hotspot.name;
self.textFieldAddress.text = hotspot.address;
self.textFieldCity.text = hotspot.city;
self.textFieldState.text = hotspot.state;
}
```

This method will then be called in your `-viewDidLoad` method, which will also configure your user interface.

```
- (void)viewDidLoad
{
    [super viewDidLoad];
```

```
self.textFieldName.placeholder = @"Name";
self.textFieldAddress.placeholder = @"Address";
self.textFieldCity.placeholder = @"City";
self.textFieldState.placeholder = @"State";

self.textFieldName.delegate = self;
self.textFieldAddress.delegate = self;
self.textFieldCity.delegate = self;
self.textFieldState.delegate = self;

if (self.hotspot != nil)
    {
        [self populateWithHotspot];
    }
}
```

If you did not put the code for the -populateWithHotspot method above that of your -viewDidLoad, you will need to add a method signature for the former to your header file.

Include a simple method to dismiss the keyboard when the user is done editing a UITextField

```
-(BOOL)textFieldShouldReturn:(UITextField *)textField
{
    [textField resignFirstResponder];
    return NO;
}
```

Finally, your -saveButtonPressed: will be written to either save the current Hotspot, if one was given, or create a new one. This object will then be passed back to your delegate property through the -HotspotInfoViewController:didReturnHotspot:isNew: method to be properly handled.

```
- (IBAction)saveButtonPressed:(id)sender
{
BOOL isNew;
if (self.hotspot != nil)
    {
self.hotspot.name = self.textFieldName.text;
self.hotspot.address = self.textFieldAddress.text;
self.hotspot.city = self.textFieldCity.text;
self.hotspot.state = self.textFieldState.text;[1]
        isNew = NO;
    }
else
    {
Hotspot *newHotspot = [[Hotspot alloc] init];
        newHotspot.name = self.textFieldName.text;
        newHotspot.address = self.textFieldAddress.text;
        newHotspot.city = self.textFieldCity.text;
        newHotspot.state = self.textFieldState.text;
self.hotspot = newHotspot;
        isNew = YES;
```

```
    }
    [self.delegate HotspotInfoViewController:self didReturnHotspot:self.hotspot
isNew:isNew];
}
```

Now, you can build your main view controller. In this class's XIB file, add a UITableView to fill the entire view, resembling Figure 10–7.

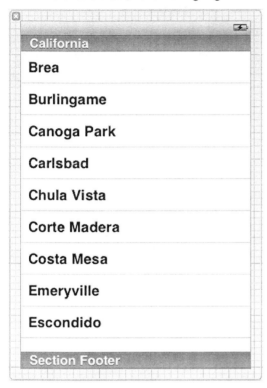

Figure 10–7. *Adding a* UITableView *to your main view controller*

Connect this UITableView to your header file using the property name tableViewHotspots.

Create an NSMutableArray property in your main view controller's header file to hold the Hotspot objects.

```
@property (strong, nonatomic) NSMutableArray *hotspots;
```

Add the following two import statements to this header file.

```
#import "HotspotInfoViewController.h"
#import "Hotspot.h"
```

Finally, make sure that this controller is told to conform to the UITableViewDelegate and UITableViewDataSource protocols, as well as the HotspotsInfoDelegate protocol that you created.

After all these changes, your header file should resemble the following:

```
#import <UIKit/UIKit.h>
#import "HotspotInfoViewController.h"
#import "Hotspot.h"

@interface MainViewController : UIViewController<UITableViewDelegate,
UITableViewDataSource, HotspotInfoDelegate>

@property (strong, nonatomic) IBOutlet UITableView *tableViewHotspots;
@property (strong, nonatomic) NSMutableArray *hotspots;

@end
```

In the implementation file for this class, after synthesizing the hotspots property, you need to declare a custom getter method to ensure that your array is properly created.

```
-(NSMutableArray *)hotspots
{
if (!hotspots)
    {
    hotspots = [[NSMutableArray alloc] initWithCapacity:10];
    }
return hotspots;
}
```

You will write your -viewDidLoad method to set the UITableView's delegate and dataSource properties, as well as configure the user interface to work inside a UINavigationController.

```
- (void)viewDidLoad
{
[super viewDidLoad];
self.title = @"Hotspots";

self.tableViewHotspots.delegate = self;
self.tableViewHotspots.dataSource = self;

UIBarButtonItem *addButton = [[UIBarButtonItem alloc]
initWithBarButtonSystemItem:UIBarButtonSystemItemAdd target:self
action:@selector(newHotspot:)];
self.navigationItem.rightBarButtonItem = self.editButtonItem;
self.navigationItem.leftBarButtonItem = addButton;
}
```

The -newHotspot: selector used will be easily implemented to present an instance of your HotspotInfoViewController, with no hotspot pre-set.

```
-(void)newHotspot:(id)sender
{
    HotspotInfoViewController *hotspotVC = [[HotspotInfoViewController alloc] init];
    hotspotVC.delegate = self;
    [self.navigationController pushViewController:hotspotVC animated:YES];
}
```

In order to respond to the completed use of a HotspotInfoViewController, you should implement the HotspotInfoDelegate method that you specified earlier.

```
-(void)HotspotInfoViewController:(HotspotInfoViewController *)hotspotInfoVC
didReturnHotspot:(Hotspot *)hotspot isNew:(BOOL)isNew
```

```
{
if (isNew)
    {
        [self.hotspots addObject:hotspot];
    }
    [self.tableViewHotspots reloadData];

    [self.navigationController popViewControllerAnimated:YES];
}
```

You will also make slight changes to the behavior of your view controller in order to handle the disappearing and re-appearing of your view by overriding the following two methods.

```
- (void)viewWillAppear:(BOOL)animated
{
    self.title = @"Hotspots";
    [super viewWillAppear:animated];
}

- (void)viewDidDisappear:(BOOL)animated
{
    self.title = @"Cancel";
    [super viewDidDisappear:animated];
}
```

Now to configure your UITableView, you must specify the number of rows to display, which will be based off of the count of your hotspots array.

```
- (NSInteger)tableView:(UITableView *)tableView numberOfRowsInSection:(NSInteger)section
{
return [self.hotspots count];
}
```

You will configure the display of your table's cells to simply display the name and address of each Hotspot object.

```
- (UITableViewCell *)tableView:(UITableView *)tableView
cellForRowAtIndexPath:(NSIndexPath*)indexPath
{
static NSString *CellIdentifier = @"Cell";

UITableViewCell *cell = [tableView dequeueReusableCellWithIdentifier:CellIdentifier];
if (cell == nil)
    {
        cell = [[UITableViewCell alloc] initWithStyle:UITableViewCellStyleSubtitle
reuseIdentifier:CellIdentifier];
        cell.accessoryType = UITableViewCellAccessoryDisclosureIndicator;
    }

Hotspot *currentHotspot = [self.hotspots objectAtIndex:indexPath.row];

    cell.textLabel.text = currentHotspot.name;
    cell.detailTextLabel.text = currentHotspot.address;

return cell;
}
```

You will implement your table such that the selection of a row presents a HotspotInfoViewController with that row's information, so that the user can easily edit any given object.

```
- (void)tableView:(UITableView *)tableView didSelectRowAtIndexPath:(NSIndexPath
*)indexPath
{
    [self.tableViewHotspots deselectRowAtIndexPath:indexPath animated:YES];

    HotspotInfoViewController *hotspotVC = [[HotspotInfoViewController alloc] init];
    hotspotVC.delegate = self;
    hotspotVC.hotspot = [self.hotspots objectAtIndex:indexPath.row];
    [self.navigationController pushViewController:hotspotVC animated:YES];
}
```

Finally, you will also make your UITableView allow for both the rearranging and deletion of objects. To allow editing and deletion, you need to implement the following two methods.

```
- (BOOL)tableView:(UITableView *)tableView canEditRowAtIndexPath:(NSIndexPath
*)indexPath
{
return YES;
}


- (void)tableView:(UITableView *)tableView
commitEditingStyle:(UITableViewCellEditingStyle)editingStyle
forRowAtIndexPath:(NSIndexPath *)indexPath
{
if (editingStyle == UITableViewCellEditingStyleDelete)
    {
        [self.hotspots removeObjectAtIndex:indexPath.row];
        [tableView deleteRowsAtIndexPaths:[NSArray arrayWithObject:indexPath]
withRowAnimation:UITableViewRowAnimationFade];
    }
}
```

You must also override the -setEditing:animated: method to properly entwine your UITableView and your Edit button.

```
-(void)setEditing:(BOOL)editing animated:(BOOL)animated
{
    [super setEditing:editing animated:animated];
    [self.tableViewHotspots setEditing:editing animated:animated];
}
```

To allow for the rearranging of cells, the following two methods will also be added.

```
- (BOOL)tableView:(UITableView *)tableView canMoveRowAtIndexPath:(NSIndexPath
*)indexPath
{
return YES;
}


- (void)tableView:(UITableView *)tableView moveRowAtIndexPath:(NSIndexPath
*)fromIndexPath toIndexPath:(NSIndexPath *)toIndexPath
{
Hotspot *movingHotspot = [self.hotspots objectAtIndex:fromIndexPath.row];
```

```
    [self.hotspots removeObject:movingHotspot];
    [self.hotspots insertObject:movingHotspot atIndex:toIndexPath.row];
    [self.tableViewHotspots reloadData];
}
```

Finally, before you test your app, you will need to modify your application delegate's implementation file to put your view controller in a UINavigationController. Adjust your -application:didFinishLaunchingWithOptions: method to resemble the following.

```
- (BOOL)application:(UIApplication *)application
didFinishLaunchingWithOptions:(NSDictionary *)launchOptions
{
    self.window = [[UIWindow alloc] initWithFrame:[[UIScreen mainScreen] bounds]];
    self.viewController = [[MainViewController alloc]
initWithNibName:@"MainViewController" bundle:nil];
    __strong UINavigationController *navcon = [[UINavigationController alloc]
initWithRootViewController:self.viewController];
    self.window.rootViewController = navcon;
    [self.window makeKeyAndVisible];
    return YES;
}
```

Your user interface is now fully set up, allowing you to create Hotspot objects to be displayed, edited, or removed from a UITableView, as shown in Figure 10–8 after some sample data has been created.

Figure 10–8. *Your app's `UITableView` with sample data*

Now, the only task left to do with this application is to be able to save your data, persisting it between uses.

In order to implement persistence in your application, you will make use of the file system, as well as the concepts of "archiving" and "unarchiving" objects.

In order to archive, or "encode" any given object, it, and all the properties stored within it, must be specifically told how to be encoded. For any pre-made iOS object, such as an `NSArray` or `NSDictionary` this is already done. However, in order to encode your Hotspot objects, you will need to add some specific instructions on how they are to be handled.

In your `Hotspot.h` class, specify that your class will conform to the `NSCoding` protocol by changing your `@interface` line to the following:

```
@interface Hotspot : NSObject<NSCoding>
```

Now, you must implement the `-encodeWithCoder:` method to specify how a Hotspot object is coded for saving.

```
- (void) encodeWithCoder:(NSCoder *)encoder
{
    [encoder encodeObject:self.name forKey:@"name"];
    [encoder encodeObject:self.address forKey:@"address"];
    [encoder encodeObject:self.city forKey:@"city"];
    [encoder encodeObject:self.state forKey:@"state"];
}
```

In the reverse process of loading data, you must implement the -initWithCoder: method to create instances of the Hotspot class using archived data. By using the same keys as in the preceding method, you can easily pull out the NSString objects that you need.

```
- (id)initWithCoder:(NSCoder *)decoder
{
self = [super init];
if (self)
    {
self.name = [decoder decodeObjectForKey:@"name"];
self.address = [decoder decodeObjectForKey:@"address"];
self.city = [decoder decodeObjectForKey:@"city"];
self.state = [decoder decodeObjectForKey:@"state"];
    }
return self;
}
```

Now, back in your main view controller, you can create a method to save your data to a specific file.

```
-(void)saveData
{
NSString *rootPath = [NSSearchPathForDirectoriesInDomains(NSDocumentDirectory,
NSUserDomainMask, YES) objectAtIndex:0];
NSString *savePath = [rootPath stringByAppendingPathComponent:@"hotspotsData"];
NSFileManager *fileManager = [NSFileManager defaultManager];
NSMutableData *saveData = [[NSMutableData alloc] init];

NSKeyedArchiver *archiver = [[NSKeyedArchiver alloc]
initForWritingWithMutableData:saveData];
    [archiver encodeObject:self.hotspots forKey:@"DataArray"];
    [archiver finishEncoding];

    [fileManager createFileAtPath:savePath contents:saveData attributes:nil];
}
```

This method consists of the following steps:

1. Acquire the root directory path in which you will save your data. You have specified the "Documents Directory", though there are other possible directories to use depending on your application's needs.

2. Append a file name "hotspotsData" onto the root path to create the data file's path.

3. Acquire a shared instance of the NSFileManager class.

4. Acquire an empty instance of NSMutableData.

5. Encode your `hotspots` NSArray with the key "DataArray" using the `NSKeyedArchiver` class. The resulting encoded data will be in the `NSMutableData` `saveData` object you acquired.

    a. Though you cannot see the actual code of it, the `-encodeObject:forKey:` call will make use of the `-encodeWithCoder:` method you defined in your `Hotspot.m` file to archive all the Hotspot objects in your array.

6. Using the `NSFileManager`, create your file at the specified path, using your encoded data. If a file already exists at this path, it will be overwritten, which works quite well for your application.

Now, to work in the reverse process, you can create a `-loadData` method like so:

```
-(void)loadData
{
NSString *rootPath = [NSSearchPathForDirectoriesInDomains(NSDocumentDirectory,
NSUserDomainMask, YES) objectAtIndex:0];
NSString *savePath = [rootPath stringByAppendingPathComponent:@"hotspotsData"];
NSFileManager *fileManager = [NSFileManager defaultManager];
if ([fileManager fileExistsAtPath:savePath])
    {
NSData *data = [fileManager contentsAtPath:savePath];
NSKeyedUnarchiver *unarchiver = [[NSKeyedUnarchiver alloc] initForReadingWithData:data];
self.hotspots = [unarchiver decodeObjectForKey:@"DataArray"];
    }
}
```

This method works almost the same as the previous one in reverse, as it acquires NSData from a specific file path, unarchives it, and then creates your NSArray back from the decoded data. Just as the `encodeObject:forKey:` method made use of your `-encodeWithCoder:`, the `decodeObjectForKey:` method will make use of the `-initWithCoder:` method for all the objects involved in your decoded object, including your NSArray and all the Hotspots it contains.

Now, you simply need to place calls to your two new methods in the correct places. Add a call to `-loadData` to your `-viewDidLoad` method.

```
[self loadData];
```

Add method signatures for both the `-saveData` and `-loadData` methods to your view controller's header file to avoid any compiler problems.

You will need to add calls to the `-saveData` method every time your array is altered, including in the following methods:

```
-(void)HotspotInfoViewController:(HotspotInfoViewController *)hotspotInfoVC
didReturnHotspot:(Hotspot *)hotspot isNew:(BOOL)isNew
{
    if (isNew)
    {
        [self.hotspots addObject:hotspot];
    }
    [self.tableViewHotspots reloadData];
```

```
    //New call to save data
    [self saveData];

    [self.navigationController popViewControllerAnimated:YES];
}
- (void)tableView:(UITableView *)tableView
commitEditingStyle:(UITableViewCellEditingStyle)editingStyle
forRowAtIndexPath:(NSIndexPath *)indexPath
{
    if (editingStyle == UITableViewCellEditingStyleDelete)
    {
        [self.hotspots removeObjectAtIndex:indexPath.row];
        [tableView deleteRowsAtIndexPaths:[NSArray arrayWithObject:indexPath]
withRowAnimation:UITableViewRowAnimationFade];
        //New call to save data
        [self saveData];
    }
}
- (void)tableView:(UITableView *)tableView moveRowAtIndexPath:(NSIndexPath
*)fromIndexPath toIndexPath:(NSIndexPath *)toIndexPath
{
    Hotspot *movingHotspot = [self.hotspots objectAtIndex:fromIndexPath.row];
    [self.hotspots removeObject:movingHotspot];
    [self.hotspots insertObject:movingHotspot atIndex:toIndexPath.row];
    [self.tableViewHotspots reloadData];
    //New call to save data
    [self saveData];
}
```

Once these calls have been added, your application will be able to automatically save any new changes to your data to an outside file, to be read upon the reopening of the application!

In your demo application, you did not implement any saving of images to file, even though this is one of the most effective and common uses of the iOS file management system. This process is even simpler than the foregoing implementation. In order to save an image, acquire the NSData object representing the image, and then use the NSFileManager method -createFileAtPath:contents:attributes to write out the data. Alternatively, you can use the NSData method -writeToFile:atomically: to perform the same task.

To acquire the data representing a UIImage, you can make use of the UIImagePNGRepresentation() or UIImageJPEGRepresentation() functions, which both return NSData. To re-build a UIImage using NSData read from a file, use the +imageWithData: or -initWithData: methods.

Core Data

So far you have dealt with the very quick implementation of NSUserDefaults for lightweight values, as well as the file management systemfor more complex or larger amounts of data. While using the file management system is incredibly powerful for storing data, it can easily become quite cumbersome when dealing with complex data models of intertwined classes. For such cases of complex data models made up of lightweight objects, the best option for persistence becomes Core Data. This framework, based around a MySQL table system, allows for easy creation, manipulation, and persistence of intricate class interactions and properties. The use of this class is quite complex, and thus is covered in great detail in the next chapter.

Recipe 10–3: Persistence with iCloud

One of the most expansive additions to iOS with the release of iOS 5.0 is the ability to create applications that have access to the new iCloud service. By using concepts similar to the file management system from the previous recipe, you are able to save, persist, and load data, not just in a local device, but also across multiple devices using the same application.

Throughout this section, all recipes will require access to an iOS development program, as well as a physical iOS device.

In order to configure an application for use with iCloud, a variety of configuration tasks must first be completed. Start by creating a new project using the Single View Application template as before. Make sure your project name is "iCloudTest", and your class prefix is "iCloudStore". While these values normally do not make much difference in your applications, it will help simplify this demonstration if your names follow those used in this recipe. Your project configuration should resemble Figure 10–9.

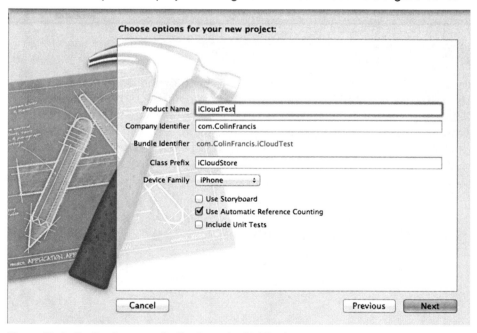

Figure 10–9. *Configuring an application to work with iCloud*

First, you must configure your project to allow for "entitlements." In your new project, navigate to the project's Target settings, and scroll down to the bottom section called "Entitlements". Click the check box labeled "Enable Entitlements", as shown in the bottom of Figure 10–10, to have Xcode automatically generate your entitlements file.

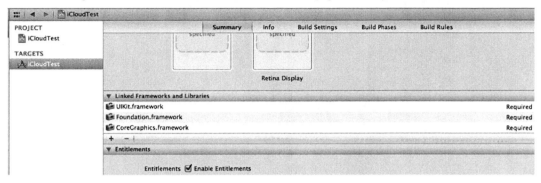

Figure 10–10. *Enabling entitlements to allow communication with iCloud*

Next, you need to generate a special "App ID" for this application. In your web browser, log into the iOS Developer's Member Center at `http://developer.apple.com/membercenter/`. Navigate to the iOS Provisioning Portal, and then move to the App IDs section. Click the button titled "New App ID".

The next screen you see will prompt you to enter a description, as well as a bundle identifier. Set the description to "iCloudTest". For the bundle identifier, you need to enter the exact same identifier that Xcode has given your app. This can be found at the top of the project's Targets settings, above the Entitlements section, as in Figure 10–11. It will most likely have a format along the lines of "com.domainName.iCloudTest". Copy the text listed under "Identifier" into the Bundle Identifier line in your browser.

Figure 10–11. *Finding the identifier for your app to configure*

In Figure 10–11, my identifier is "com.ColinFrancis.iCloudTest", so I will copy this to my browser as the bundle identifier, as in Figure 10–12.

Figure 10–12. *Copying your project's identifier into the Bundle Identifier field*

Upon creating this new App ID, you will be returned to your table of created App IDs. Find the one that you just created, and click the Configure link.

In this screen, all you need to do is check the box labeled "Enable for iCloud", shown in Figure 10–13. If a dialog appears warning you of having to manually regenerate profiles, simply click OK.

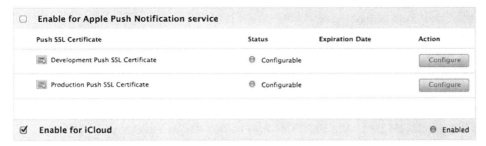

Figure 10–13. *Enabling iCloud for your certificate*

Click Done to finish configuring your App ID.

Next, move down to the Provisioning tab listed on the left-hand side of the screen underneath the App IDs tab. Click on the New Profile button to begin creating a new provisioning profile.

Name this new profile "iCloudProfile". Select your certificate that you should already have as an iOS developer. Set the App ID field to your recently made "iCloudTest" App ID, and make sure to check the boxes next to whichever devices you want to test this application on. Figure 10–14 shows my configuration screen, which yours should resemble with your own information.

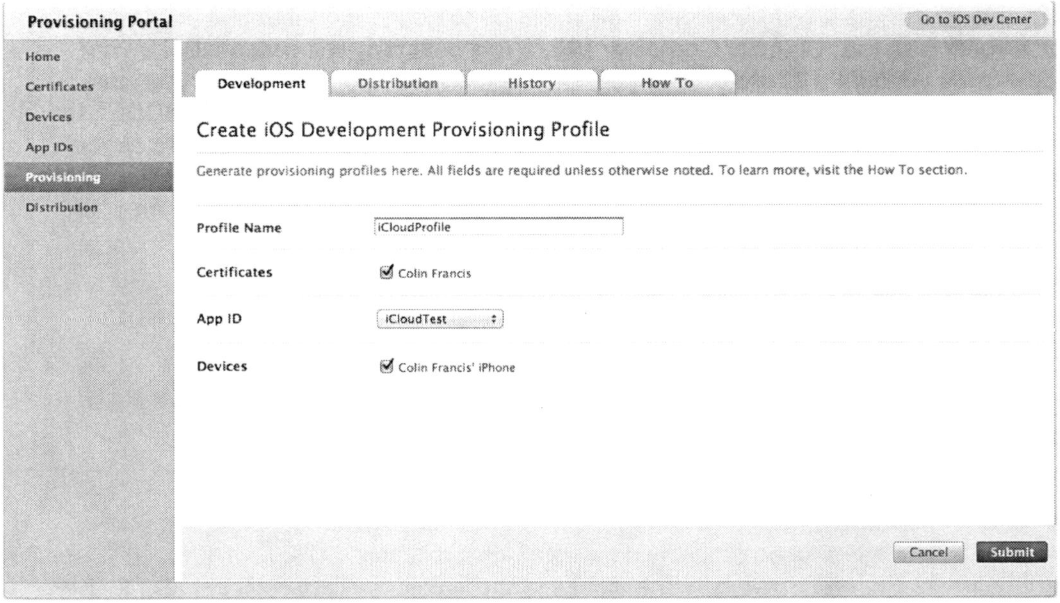

Figure 10–14. *Creating a new provisioning profile for your iCloud app*

Click Submit to return to your list of provisioning profiles. You should see your new profile listed. If its status is listed as "Pending", simply refresh the page until it says "Active".

Next, click the Download button next to your newly created profile to download it to your computer.

Once your file has finished downloading (it shouldn't take long), drag the file from the Finder to the Xcode icon in your dock to import it into Xcode. This should bring up the Organizer window as well, which will list all of your provisioning profiles.

Finally, in the Organizer, while your device is connected to your computer, drag the new profile from the displayed list to the Provisioning Profiles section under your device, shown in Figure 10–15.

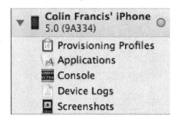

Figure 10–15. *Copying your new profile into the Provisioning Profiles section of your device*

At this point, your device is fully configured to run the project you have created.

You must perform one last step in your project in order for the application to physically be able to use the iCloud services. You will need to define a constant in your view controller with the "Ubiquity Container URL". This NSString will essentially be your developer account's ID prefixed to your bundle identifier. For example, if you have your bundle identifier "com.domainName.iCloudTest" and account ID "12345ABCDE", the URL will be "12345ABCDE.com.domainName.iCloudTest". If you are unsure of your account ID, you can find it by navigating to the Member Center again and going to the Your Account tab. If you are using an individual account, it will be listed under your name next to "Individual ID".

Throughout this project, you will use the example URL of "12345ABCDE.com.domainName.iCloudTest". Make sure that you change this according to your own account ID and domain name.

Add the following definition to the top of your iCloudStoreViewController.m file so that you can reference it later.

```
#define UBIQUITY_CONTAINER_URL @"12345ABCDE.com.domainName.iCloudTest"
```

In order for your application to work properly, you must also make sure that your entitlements file has been properly configured with this same URL. Navigate to your entitlements file, and make sure the values for both com.apple.developer.ubiquity-container-identifiers (Item 0) and com.apple.developer.ubiquity-kvstore-identifier are set to this value. Xcode should have automatically set these, but it is best to always confirm this setup. If not, set them, as shown in Figure 10–16.

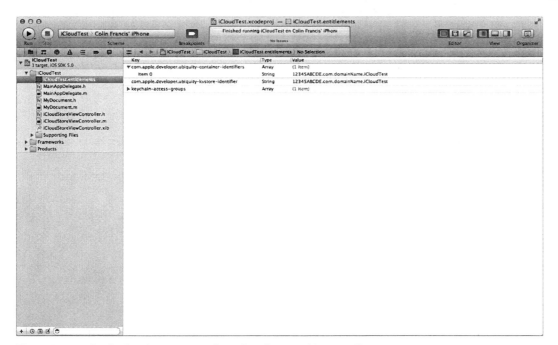

Figure 10–16. *Confirming the correct configuration of your entitlements file*

Now that your application and device are configured to work with iCloud, you can
continue to build your actual application.

In order to build a simple program to save a text document to iCloud, you need to make
use of the UIDocument abstract class. Your subclass of this will contain all the
information needed to encode your text information into a file that can be saved online.
Create a new file and select the "Objective-C class" template. The easiest way to
configure this file is to start off by naming the NSObject class as the parent class. You
will change the actual superclass shortly. Name the file "MyDocument".

Once your class has been created, modify the @interface line of the MyDocument.h file to
the following in order to specify your class as a subclass of UIDocument.

@interface MyDocument : UIDocument

You will give this class only one property, userText, of type NSString, which will store
the text to be encoded and decoded. Make sure to synthesize this property in the
implementation file. Your MyDocument.h file should look like so:

#import <Foundation/Foundation.h>

@interface MyDocument : UIDocument

@property (strong, nonatomic) NSString *userText;

@end

Now, you must, at a bare minimum, implement two classes to correctly subclass UIDocument: -contentsForType:error: and -loadFromContents:ofType:error:. These methods will essentially act as your encoding and decoding methods respectively, similar to the previous recipe.

Your first method will return an NSData object representing your userText property.

```
-(id)contentsForType:(NSString *)typeName error:(NSError *__autoreleasing *)outError
{
return [NSData dataWithBytes:[self.userText UTF8String] length:[self.userText length]];
}
```

Your second method will do the reverse, building an NSString out of raw data and setting it to your property.

```
-(BOOL) loadFromContents:(id)contents ofType:(NSString *)typeName error:(NSError
*__autoreleasing *)outError
{
if ([contents length] >0)
    {
self.userText = [[NSString alloc] initWithBytes:[contents bytes] length:[contents
length] encoding:NSUTF8StringEncoding];
    }
else
    {
self.userText = @"";
    }
return YES;
}
```

Now that your data model is configured (yes, it is that simple!), you can move on to building your user interface. Switch over to the iCloudStoreViewController.xib file and, using a UITextView and a UIButton, set up the view shown in Figure 10–17.

Figure 10–17. *A simple user interface to save text*

Make sure to leave the lower half of the view entirely blank, as the keyboard used to edit your UITextView will cover this area.

You may also wish to change some of the background colors of your main UIView and UITextView to clearly separate them. I made them different shades of gray, as shown later in Figure 10–19.

Connect the UITextView to your view controller's header file using the textViewDisplay property. Make sure to synthesize and properly handle this property as usual. Connect the UIButton to an IBAction with the handler -savePressed:.

You will also need several other properties to help perform your iCloud operations. Add an import statement for the MyDocument.h file.

```
#import "MyDocument.h"
```

Add the following three properties as well, making sure to synthesize each and nil them in -viewDidUnload as usual.

```
@property (strong, nonatomic) MyDocument *document;
@property (strong, nonatomic) NSURL *ubiquityURL;
@property (strong, nonatomic) NSMetadataQuery *metadataQuery;
```

Next, you will implement your -viewDidLoad method to create a query for iCloud to search for any saved versions of your document by using the NSFileManager and NSMetadataQuery classes.

```
- (void)viewDidLoad
{
    [super viewDidLoad];

NSFileManager *filemgr = [NSFileManager defaultManager];

self.ubiquityURL = [[filemgr URLForUbiquityContainerIdentifier:UBIQUITY_CONTAINER_URL]
URLByAppendingPathComponent:@"Documents"];

if (self.ubiquityURL != nil)
    {
if ([filemgr fileExistsAtPath:[self.ubiquityURLpath]] == NO)
            [filemgr createDirectoryAtURL:self.ubiquityURL
withIntermediateDirectories:YES
attributes:nil
error:nil];

self.ubiquityURL = [self.ubiquityURL URLByAppendingPathComponent:@"document.doc"];

self.metadataQuery = [[NSMetadataQuery alloc] init];
        [self.metadataQuery setPredicate:[NSPredicate
predicateWithFormat:@"%K like 'document.doc'",
NSMetadataItemFSNameKey]];
        [self.metadataQuery setSearchScopes:[NSArray
arrayWithObjects:NSMetadataQueryUbiquitousDocumentsScope,nil]];

        [[NSNotificationCenter defaultCenter]
addObserver:self
selector:@selector(metadataQueryDidFinishGathering:)
name: NSMetadataQueryDidFinishGatheringNotification
object:metadataQuery];
        [self.metadataQuery startQuery];
    }
}
```

This method contains the following steps to create a query for any saved data:

1. Acquire the ubiquityURL using the -URLForUbiquityContainerIdentifier: method. This call uses your identifier that you defined earlier based on your account ID and domain name. If this value is not nil, then your device and application are correctly configured to store documents in iCloud.

2. Ensure that the property directories exist at the target URL by using the -createDirectoryAtURL:withIntermediateDirectories:attributes:error: method.

3. Append the file name "document.doc" onto the full URL.

4. Create an instance of NSMetadataQuery with a predicate for your file name and a search scope for ubiquitous documents.

5. Add the view controller as an observer for the completion of the query.

6. Start the query.

After calling this method, your application will be off attempting to find any information stored on iCloud. In order to react to its results, you must implement the -metadataQueryDidFinishGathering: selector you mentioned in the previous notification registration.

```objc
- (void)metadataQueryDidFinishGathering: (NSNotification *)notification
{
NSMetadataQuery *query = [notification object];
    [query disableUpdates];

    [[NSNotificationCenter defaultCenter]
removeObserver:self
name:NSMetadataQueryDidFinishGatheringNotification
object:query];

    [query stopQuery];
NSArray *results = [[NSArray alloc] initWithArray:[query results]];

if ([results count] == 1)
    {
self.ubiquityURL = [[results lastObject] valueForAttribute:NSMetadataItemURLKey];
self.document = [[MyDocument alloc] initWithFileURL:ubiquityURL];

        [self.document openWithCompletionHandler:^(BOOL success)
        {
if (success)
            {
NSLog(@"Opened iCloud doc");
self.textViewDisplay.text = self.document.userText;
            }
else {
NSLog(@"Failed to open iCloud doc");
            }
        }];
    }
else
    {
self.document = [[MyDocument alloc] initWithFileURL:self.ubiquityURL];
        [self.document saveToURL:self.ubiquityURL forSaveOperation:
UIDocumentSaveForCreating completionHandler:^(BOOL success)
        {
if (success)
            {
NSLog(@"File created and saved to iCloud");
            }
else
            {
NSLog(@"Error, could not save file to iCloud");
            }
        }];
    }
}
```

This method completes your search for any previously stored information in iCloud by running through the following steps:

1. Retrieves the original NSMetadataQuery object in order to disable any further updates, remove the view controller as an observer, and stop the query.

2. Create an NSArray of documents found using the results property of NSMetadataQuery.

3. Acquire the last/only object in this array, and then create a UIDocument using its key-valued URL.

4. Open the document, and, upon completion, display the document's text to the user.

This method also includes code for the case in which no documents (or more than one) are found. In this case, the program attempts to save an empty file directly to iCloud, so that the file will exist in the future.

At this point, your application will be able to load any previously stored text from iCloud, so you simply need to implement a saving functionality to have any information to retrieve! The process of saving data is much simpler than retrieving it.

```
- (void)savePressed:(id)sender
{
self.document.userText = self.textViewDisplay.text;
    [self.document saveToURL:self.ubiquityURL
forSaveOperation:UIDocumentSaveForOverwriting completionHandler:^(BOOL success)
    {
if (success)
        {
NSLog(@"Written to iCloud");
        }
else
        {
NSLog(@"Error writing to iCloud");
        }
    }];
}
```

Before you continue on to test your application, you must make sure that your test device is properly configured to work with iCloud. In the Settings app on your device, navigate to the iCloud section. In order for this application to properly store data, your iCloud account must be properly configured and verified. This will require you to have verified your e-mail address and registered it as your Apple ID. The item marked "Documents & Data" should also be set to "On", as in Figure 10–18. You can, of course, easily configure this once your account is verified.

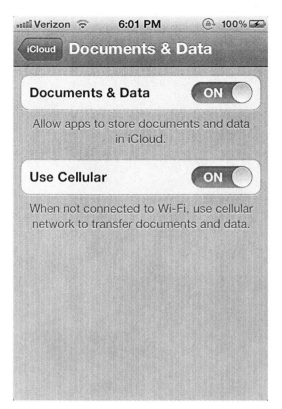

Figure 10–18. *Documents and Data must be enabled to store information in iCloud.*

Assuming your device is correctly configured, your simple application should be able to correctly store documents using the user's iCloud account, allowing you to easily persist data across multiple devices, application shutdowns, and even through system resets, as shown by Figure 10–19 with a few slightly altered background colors, as mentioned earlier.

Figure 10–19. *Your application with text saved and loaded from iCloud*

Recipe 10–4: Storing Key-Value Data in iCloud

Just as you were able to easily persist a variety of lightweight objects locally using the NSUserDefaults class at the beginning of this chapter, you are able to implement the same type of storage using the iCloud service. You will add this functionality to your application by keeping a count of the number of times that the text has been saved. While this may not seem like much, the ability to have such simple values remain synchronized in the same application across multiple devices opens up a whole world of development power.

All key-value data handling with iCloud is done through the NSUbiquitousKeyValueStore class. You will add an instance of this class as a property to your iCloudStoreViewController file, making sure to synthesize and nil it as appropriate.

```
@property (strong, nonatomic) NSUbiquitousKeyValueStore *keyStore;
```

Next, you will do a slight rearrangement of your user interface to include two UILabels, of which one will display your save count. Your view will now resemble Figure 10–20.

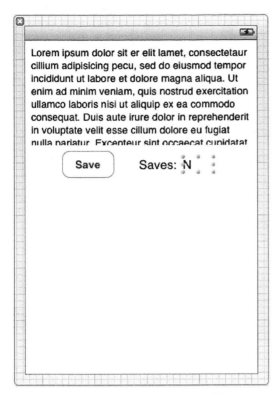

Figure 10–20. *Rearranging your XIB file with two new* UILabels

Connect the right UILabel (displaying the text "N" in Figure 10–20) to your header using the property countLabel.

```
@property (strong, nonatomic) IBOutlet UILabel *countLabel;
```

You can configure your application to immediately check for any count upon loading by adding the following code to the end of your -viewDidLoad method.

```
self.keyStore = [[NSUbiquitousKeyValueStore alloc] init];
double count = [self.keyStore doubleForKey:@"count"];
self.countLabel.text = [NSString stringWithFormat:@"%f", count];
```

The following line, added after the foregoing ones, will allow you to receive notifications upon the changing of any values in your NSUbiquitousKeyValueStore, allowing you to keep your information updated across multiple devices.

```
[[NSNotificationCenter defaultCenter] addObserver:self selector:
@selector(countChangeExternally:) name:
NSUbiquitousKeyValueStoreDidChangeExternallyNotification object:self.keyStore];
```

You can implement the -countChangeExternally: method quite simply to set your UILabel's text.

```
-(void)countChangeExternally:(id)sender
{
double count = [self.keyStore doubleForKey:@"count"];
```

```
self.countLabel.text = [NSString stringWithFormat:@"%f", count];
}
```

Finally, you need to instruct your savePressed: method to correctly update this value.
You will do this only if your text is successfully saved, so your updated method will look
like so:

```
- (void)savePressed:(id)sender
{
self.document.userText = self.textViewDisplay.text;
    [self.document saveToURL:self.ubiquityURL
forSaveOperation:UIDocumentSaveForOverwriting completionHandler:^(BOOL success)
    {
if (success)
        {
NSLog(@"Written to iCloud");
double count = [self.countLabel.text doubleValue];
        count += 1;
self.countLabel.text = [NSString stringWithFormat:@"%f", count];
        [self.keyStore setDouble:count forKey:@"count"];
        [self.keyStore synchronize];
    }
else
    {
NSLog(@"Error writing to iCloud");
    }
    }];
}
```

Your application should now be able to easily store your lightweight double value to
keep track of your save count, as shown in Figure 10–21!

Figure 10–21. *The app with both text and key-value information stored through iCloud*

Summary

Data persistence is almost always one of the most important considerations in developing an application. Developers must consider the type of data they wish to store, how much of it, how it connects, and whether their application might even stretch across multiple devices. From there, the choice must be made to decide which approach to use to storing data, whether it is the simple NSUserDefaults method, the powerful file management system, or the intricate Core Data framework (as discussed in the next chapter). In iOS 5.0, the new addition of access to the iCloud service has revolutionized the way that applications can store data, allowing persistence of data in near real time across devices running the same application. As memory, storage, and mobile applications continue to grow in size, importance, and relevance in the technological world, these topics will become even significantly more relevant. By firmly understanding the most up-to-date concepts of data persistence in iOS, you are able to always keep your users updated with the fastest, most efficient, and most powerful methods of storing data possible.

Chapter 11

Core Data Recipes

One of the most common problems that developers face is the concept of persistence, or more simply, storing data. For certainly a very high percentage of applications, it is not enough to simply store information in your variables, as everything will be lost as soon as the application is closed. While the previous chapter covered a wide variety of options for storing data between uses, none of them can quite compare to the versatility, power, and simplicity of Core Data.

There are a great many resources, including entire books (I highly recommend *Pro Core Data for iOS*, by Michael Privat and Robert Warner) that focus simply on the topic of Core Data. It would be ridiculous to assume that you could cover every part of such a multi-faceted concept in one chapter. For this reason, you will, instead of building your Core Data interface from the ground up, use pre-built Xcode templates in order to provide the easiest demonstration of the Core Data concepts. This way, you, as a developer, can more easily acquire a grasp of Core Data applications, and later focus on more targeted, complex points of the subject through other, more dedicated sources.

What Is Core Data?

Core Data is persistence. Not only is Core Data persistence, but also it is by far one of the best methods for implementing persistence in iOS.

Put simply, Core Data, in conjunction with Xcode, allows a developer to perform three main tasks:

1. Create a data model

2. Persist information

3. Access data

First, it is important to understand exactly what a data model is. This term applies essentially to whatever structure any given application's data is built around. This could be anything as simple as an NSString or an NSArray in a simple application, all the way up to a complex, interconnected system of object types, each with their own properties, methods, and pointers to other objects.

Next, you should have a basic understanding of the various types of objects and classes that are involved in Core Data when you need to create, save, and retrieve information, and how you use them.

1. NSManagedObjectModel: This is an unusual class, because you don't quite ever deal with it directly when you are writing code if you use a template. This is how iOS refers to your data model, which you will create later. When you create your project for the first recipe shortly, you will see an instance of this type in your application delegate, and you will see it used in some pre-generated methods, but aside from that, you will have no reason to deal with this class programmatically.

2. NSPersistentStoreCoordinator: This class is one that you very rarely will need to deal with. It works mostly in the background of an application to "coordinate" between your application and the underlying database or "Persistent Store", but you will not need to send any actions to it. The most important part of this class that you need to know about is the "type" of persistent store that is being used. There are three types of persistent stores:

   a. NSSQLiteStoreType

   b. NSBinaryStoreType

   c. NSInMemoryStoreType

   The default value is the first, NSSQLiteStoreType, specifying that you are using a persistent store built around the SQLite foundation. You will continue to use this type for your applications.

   Depending on your application, you may also find the NSInMemoryStoreType useful, even though it does not actually persist data between application uses. This may be more suited to an application that caches information from a remote source, and thus needs a data model built around Core Data, but does not actually need to store the information, as it can be retrieved again from the remote source.

3. NSManagedObjectContext: This class, unlike the previous two, is one that you will be dealing with quite often. In the simplest terms, this class acts as a sort of "workspace" for your information. Any time you need to retrieve or store information, you will need a pointer to this class to perform the action. For this reason, a very common practice in Core Data–based applications is to "pass around" a pointer to this class between each part of the application by giving each view controller an NSManagedObjectContext property.

4. NSFetchedResultsController: This is the primary class for actually "fetching" results through the NSManagedObjectContext. It is not only very powerful, but also very easy to use, especially in conjunction with a UITableView. You will see plenty of examples of using this class throughout this chapter.

You will utilize a variety of other classes specific to Core Data throughout this chapter, but these are more easily explained once you have gone through the creation of your data model.

Recipe 11–1: Creating a Data Model

For this entire chapter, you will create a new project called "MusicSchool". Make sure to select the Empty Application template, as in Figure 11–1.

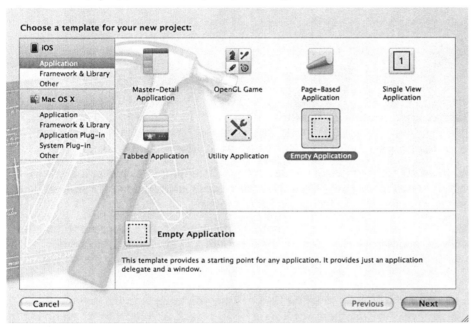

Figure 11–1. *Creating an empty application to start from scratch*

On the next screen, when you enter the project name of "MusicSchool", be sure to select the box labeled "Use Core Data". This is the easiest way to get a nice template for using Core Data, which will simplify your life greatly, pre-generating a great deal of necessary code. Set the class prefix to "Main", and make sure the Use Automatic Reference Counting box is checked as well, as shown in Figure 11–2. The Company Identifier should be changed to your own name or company name.

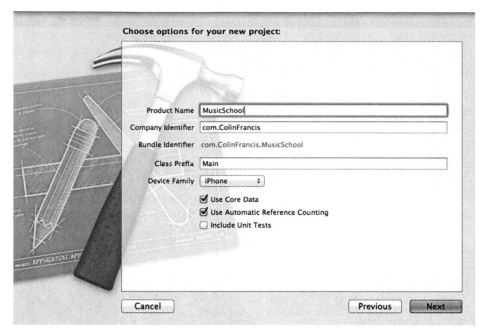

Figure 11–2. *Configuring your project to use Core Data*

Click Create on the next screen to finish the creation of your project as usual.

Now that you have set up your project to use a Core Data template, you actually have a lot of the work involved in using the Core Data framework already done for you, so you are able to move directly on to building your data model.

As you've probably guessed already, your data model will be built to represent the idea of a music school, specifically focusing on the teachers and students. Before you proceed to do anything in Xcode, you need to plan out exactly how your model will work.

When working with a data model, the first kind of item you have to make is an "entity." An entity is essentially the Core Data equivalent of an object, and represents an object in the exact same way.

In the same way that objects (or NSObjects in Objective-C) have properties, entities have "attributes." These are the simpler pieces of data associated with any given entity, such as a name, age, or birthday, that do not require a pointer to any other entity.

Whenever you want one entity to have a pointer to another, you use a "relationship." A relationship can be either "to-one" or "to-many," referring to whether an entity has a pointer to one instance of another entity or multiple ones. When dealing with the "to-many" relationship, you will notice that the entity will have a pointer to a set of multiple other entities. Entities can easily have relationships that point to themselves, which might be the case of a Person entity having a relationship to another Person, in the form of a spouse. You can also set up "inverse relationships," which act as paths back and forth between entities. For example, a Teacher entity might have a "to-many" relationship to a Student entity called "students", and the Student's relationship to the Teacher, called "teachers", will be the inverse of this. With this, you can access any Teacher's list of Students and their respective list of Teachers quite easily.

So for your data model, you will have three entities with their respective attributes and relationships like so:

1. Teacher

    a. Attributes: Name, age, primary language, and number of years teaching

    b. Relationships: Students (to-many) and Instruments (to-many)

2. Student

    a. Attributes: Name, age, primary language, and skill level

    b. Relationships: Teacher (to-one) and Instrument (to-one)

3. Instrument

    c. Attributes: Name and family

    d. Relationships: Students (to-many) and Teachers (to-many)

While all these relationships going back and forth between your objects may seem a bit convoluted, this will actually allow you to create a very well-defined data model from which you can query nearly any piece of information you need from another. For example, you might be able to easily find all the teachers who play the piano, and then access their respective names.

Now that you have your data model planned out, you can build this in Xcode. Switch over to view your data model file, which will probably be called `MusicSchool.xcdatamodeld` if you used the "MusicSchool" project name. Your view should resemble Figure 11–3.

Figure 11–3. *Your empty data model*

If your window instead resembles Figure 11–4, you should change to the first Editor style of the two options in the lower-right of the Xcode window. For this recipe, you will use only the first Editor style to actually configure your data model.

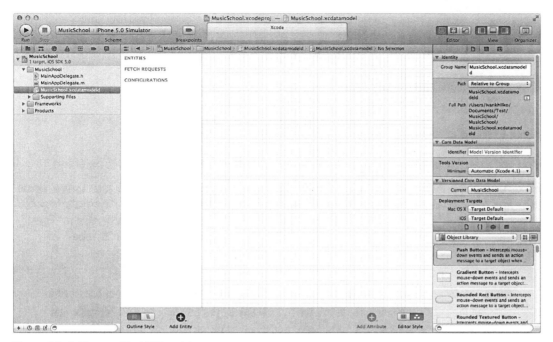

Figure 11–4. *The graphical Editor style*

You can easily change the Editor style for configuring a data model through the selection in the lower right-hand corner of your screen. Select the left option of the two, which will be the first of the two previous figures, so that the selector looks like Figure 11–5.

Figure 11–5. *Make sure to select the first Editor style for these recipes.*

Next, you will add your three entities. You can do this from either the Editor menu, or by using the Add Entity button in the lower-central area of your view, which resembles Figure 11–6.

Figure 11–6. *Use this button to create new entities.*

You will immediately be able to change the name of the entity, so rename it to "Teacher" and hit return.

Repeat this twice more to create the "Student" and "Instrument" entities. It is easier to create all your entities first, rather than trying to configure each after you create it, as you need them to build your relationships. Afterward, if you select the Teacher entity, your entities list should resemble Figure 11–7.

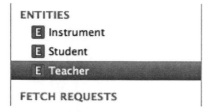

Figure 11–7. *Rename your entities to match your data plan.*

You will start by configuring your Teacher entity, so make sure this one is selected.

Next, under the Attributes area for the Teacher entity, click the + button four times, once for each of your attributes. Name each attribute according to your plan ("name", "age", "language", and "years" will do fine). For each attribute, you must also choose a "Type". Use the "String" type for the "name" and "language" attributes, and the "Integer 16" type for the others, as in Figure 11–8.

NOTE: The different types of integer (i.e., Integer 16, 32, 64), refer to the number of bits used to store each value. These numbers restrict the highest values you can use, as a 16-bit value can store only values up to 65,535. A 32-bit value can store values up to 4,294,967,295, and a 64-bit can hold massive values on the scale of 10^{18}. Since your numbers are fairly low, you can simply use the "Integer 16" type.

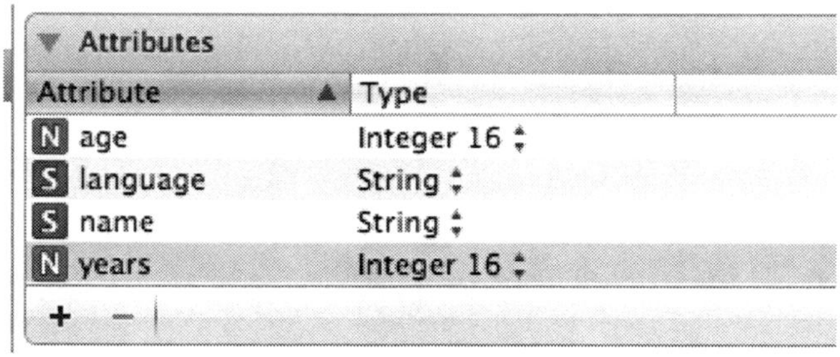

▼ Attributes	
Attribute ▲	**Type**
N age	Integer 16 ⬍
S language	String ⬍
S name	String ⬍
N years	Integer 16 ⬍
+ −	

Figure 11–8. *Configuring the Teacher entity's attributes*

Now under the Relationships area, add two relationships using the + button. Name them "students" and "instruments", and make sure their destination values are set accordingly, as in Figure 11–9. ("Student" for the students relationship, and so on.) Until you create more relationships in other entities, you cannot set up your "Inverse" relationships yet.

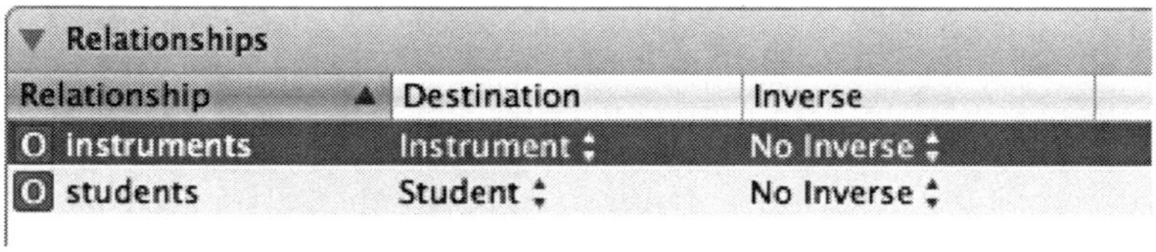

▼ Relationships		
Relationship ▲	**Destination**	**Inverse**
O instruments	Instrument ⬍	No Inverse ⬍
O students	Student ⬍	No Inverse ⬍

Figure 11–9. *Configuring the Teacher entity's relationships*

Pull up the Data Model inspector just as you would pull up the Attributes inspector for any view element in a XIB file. After selecting one of the created relationships, check the box in the inspector labeled "To-Many Relationship", as in Figure 11–10. Make sure to do this for both of the Teacher relationships, since they both are "to-many" according to your plan.

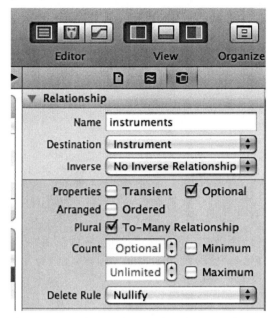

Figure 11–10. *Configuring relationships to be "To-Many"*

While you will most likely not need to worry about most of the other values in this inspector (at least for your purposes), one of the values of higher import is the Delete Rule drop-down menu, as shown in Figure 11–10. This value specifies exactly how this relationship is handled when an instance of the given entity is deleted from the NSManagedObjectContext. It has four possible values:

1. *No Action*: This is probably the most dangerous value, as it simply allows related objects to continue to attempt to access the deleted object, which could easily lead to accessing problems without proper care.

2. *Nullify*: The default value, this specifies that the relationship will be nullified upon deletion, and will thus return a nil value.

3. *Cascade*: This value can be slightly dangerous to use, as it specifies that if one object is deleted, all of the objects it is related to via this Delete Rule will also be deleted, so as to avoid having nil values. If you're not careful with this, you can delete unexpectedly large amounts of data, though it can also be very good for keeping your data clean. You may use this, for example, in the case of a "folder" with multiple objects. When a folder is deleted, you would want to delete all the contained objects as well.

4. *Deny*: This will prevent the object from being deleted as long as the relationship does not point to `nil`.

You will keep the Delete Rule on "Nullify" for your recipe.

Now, after selecting the Student entity that you will now configure, add your four attributes ("age", "language, "name", and "skill"), with their appropriate types, as in Figure 11–11 ("String" for all but the age, which will be "Integer 16" again).

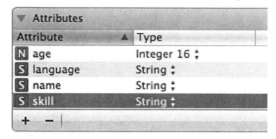

Figure 11–11. *Configuring the Student entity's attributes*

Create another two relationships, "instrument" and "teacher", with their respective destinations. You can now also set the "Inverse" relationship of the teacher relationship to the value of "students", as shown in Figure 11–12. The students relationship in your Teacher entity will automatically now be given the teacher relationship you just made as its inverse as well.

> **NOTE:** Inverse relationships are not always required, though they tend to make the organization and flow of your application a little bit better, allowing you to more easily access any piece of data you need from any other piece of data.

If you look back at your original plan for your data model, you will see that the two relationships for the Student are not meant to be "to-many," so you don't have to make this change.

Relationships		
Relationship ▲	Destination	Inverse
instrument	Instrument ⬍	No Inverse ⬍
teacher	Teacher ⬍	students ⬍

Figure 11–12. *Configuring the Student entity's relationships*

Now, you shall configure your third entity, the Instrument. It will have two attributes of type "String", called "name" and "family", as in Figure 11–13.

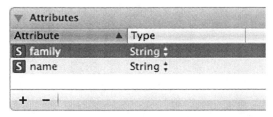

Figure 11–13. *Configuring the Instrument entity's attributes*

You will create your two relationships as "teachers" and "students" with their respective destinations. You should be able to set inverse relationships for both of these, as is done in Figure 11–14.

▼ Relationships		
Relationship ▲	Destination	Inverse
Ⓜ students	Student ⇕	instrument ⇕
Ⓜ teachers	Teacher ⇕	instruments ⇕
+ −		

Figure 11–14. *Configuring the Instrument entity's relationships*

Finally, make sure to specify that both of these relationships *are* "to-many" in the Data Model inspector, just as before.

This is actually all you need to do to create your data model! If you switch over to the second Editor style, you can even see a neat little graphic of your interconnect entities, their attributes, and their relationships, where a single arrow represents a "to-one" relationship, and a double arrow represents a "to-many" relationship. The blocks may initially appear all stacked on top of each other, but if you drag them apart, your display should resemble Figure 11–15.

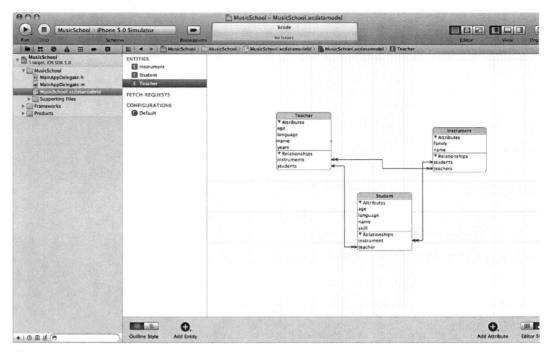

Figure 11–15. *The resulting graphical view of your finished data model*

Recipe 11–2: Working with NSManagedObjects

Now that you have your data model set up, you can start to build your application's actual user interface.

You will build your application in such a way that you can view three different tabs, each with a UITableView displaying all of an entity in your data, with each tab displaying a different entity. Rather than build three different view controllers with nearly the exact same setup, you will simply build one, then customize the information displayed.

Create a new UIViewController subclass file called "MainTableViewControlle in your project. In your XIB file, add a UITableView to your view, and connect it to the view controller's header file with the property name tableViewMain. Refer to Chapter 8 for specific instructions on how to do this.

You can go ahead and make this UITableView fill the whole view, and leave it as a "Plain" style, as in Figure 11–16.

Figure 11–16. *Setting up your* UITableView

Go ahead and set your delegate and data source for your table in the -viewDidLoad method with the following two lines:

```
self.tableViewMain.delegate = self;
self.tableViewMain.dataSource = self;
```

You will of course have to add the UITableViewDelegate and UITableViewDataSource protocols to your view controller's header file.

Add the following line to your -viewDidLoad method as well to create an Add button in your navigation bar. You will implement the action for it to perform later.

```
self.navigationItem.rightBarButtonItem = [[UIBarButtonItem alloc]
initWithBarButtonSystemItem:UIBarButtonSystemItemAdd target:self action:@selector(add)];
```

You will need to add a few more properties to your view controller to keep track of your Core Data objects. Add the following three properties, making sure to properly synthesize and handle them.

```
@property (nonatomic, strong) NSEntityDescription *entityDescription;
@property (nonatomic, strong) NSFetchedResultsController *fetchedResultsController;
@property (nonatomic, strong) NSManagedObjectContext *managedObjectContext;
```

An instance of the NSEntityDescription class is, in rather redundant terms, a description of an entity. In its simplest use, you simply give it a name. Then, when you query your database via the NSManagedObjectContext with this NSEntityDescription, it specifically fetches instances of the specified entity.

Your entityDescription property will allow you to easily keep track of whether a view controller is fetching data for Teachers, Students, or Instruments. The fetchedResultsController will keep track of your fetched data, and the managedObjectContext property allows you to make any necessary requests for data.

Next, you need to implement the required delegate and data source methods for your UITableView. First, the method to specify the number of rows:

```
-(NSInteger)tableView:(UITableView *)tableView numberOfRowsInSection:(NSInteger)section
{
    return [[self.fetchedResultsController fetchedObjects] count];
}
```

As shown, the NSFetchedResultsController class contains a method -fetchedObjects, which returns an NSArray of the objects that were queried for.

Here is your method to configure your UITableView's cells:

```
-(UITableViewCell *)tableView:(UITableView *)tableView
cellForRowAtIndexPath:(NSIndexPath *)indexPath
{
    static NSString *CellIdentifier = @"Cell";

    UITableViewCell *cell = [tableView
dequeueReusableCellWithIdentifier:CellIdentifier];
    if (cell == nil)
    {
        cell = [[UITableViewCell alloc] initWithStyle:UITableViewCellStyleSubtitle
reuseIdentifier:CellIdentifier];
        cell.accessoryType = UITableViewCellAccessoryDetailDisclosureButton;
        cell.textLabel.font = [UIFont systemFontOfSize:19.0];
        cell.detailTextLabel.font = [UIFont systemFontOfSize:12];
    }

    NSManagedObject *object = [self.fetchedResultsController
objectAtIndexPath:indexPath];
    cell.textLabel.text = [object valueForKey:@"name"];

    if ([object.entity.name isEqualToString:@"Instrument"])
    {
        cell.detailTextLabel.text = [object valueForKey:@"family"];
    }
    else
    {
        cell.detailTextLabel.text = [[object valueForKey:@"age"] stringValue];
    }
        return cell;
}
```

As you can see, you are able to access attributes of your entities by using the NSManagedObject class to point to an instance of an entity, then using the -valueForKey: method to query specific attributes. You will later see an even easier, more natural way to do this, but it is important to understand the concepts of NSManagedObject as a class that can represent any entity.

You may also notice that you don't have to access the row value of the indexPath to give to your NSFetchedResultsController. This is one of the niceties of using Core Data, in that the results of a fetch request are very easy to implement into a UITableView.

Now that your UITableView is set up, you simply need to make sure that your view controller actually gets the information that it needs to display. You will set up a separate method for this like so:

```
-(void)fetchResults
{
    NSFetchRequest *fetchRequest = [NSFetchRequest
fetchRequestWithEntityName:self.entityDescription.name];
    NSString *cacheName = [self.entityDescription.name
stringByAppendingString:@"Cache"];

    NSSortDescriptor *sortDescriptor = [NSSortDescriptor sortDescriptorWithKey:@"name"
ascending:YES];
    [fetchRequest setSortDescriptors:[NSArray arrayWithObject:sortDescriptor]];

    self.fetchedResultsController = [[NSFetchedResultsController alloc]
initWithFetchRequest:fetchRequest managedObjectContext:self.managedObjectContext
sectionNameKeyPath:nil cacheName:cacheName];
    BOOL success;
    NSError *error;
    success = [self.fetchedResultsController performFetch:&error];
    if (!success)
    {
        NSLog(@"%@", [error localizedDescription]);
    }
}
```

If you need to, add the handler of this method to your header file to avoid any compiler warnings (i.e., if you implement this method after your -viewDidLoad).

Considering the importance of the previous method, it's important to understand the exact steps required in order to perform the "fetch" for data.

1. The first thing you need for a fetch is an instance of the NSFetchRequest class. Here, you have used a designated initializer to specify an NSEntityDescription, though you can also add it later using the -setEntity: method.

2. While not required, you have set up a "cache name" to be used with your fetch request, with a different cache for each entity. This allows you to slightly improve the speed of your application if you are making frequent fetch requests, as a local cache is first checked to see if the request has already been performed.

3. Every instance of NSFetchRequest is required to have at least one NSSortDescriptor associated with it. Here, you have specified a very simple alphabetic sort of the name property for each of your entities. Once all your NSSortDescriptors have been created, they must be attached to the NSFetchRequest using the -setSortDescriptors: method.

4. Once your NSFetchRequest is fully configured, you can fully initialize your NSFetchedResultsController using your NSFetchRequest and your NSManagedObjectContext. The last two parameters are both optional, though you have specified a cacheName for optimization. You can set both of these to nil if you wish to ignore them.

5. Finally, you must use the performFetch: method to actually complete your fetch request and retrieve your stored data. With this method, you can pass a pointer to an NSError, as shown previously, to keep track of and log any errors that occur with a fetch.

Finally, you will add a quick line to call this method in the -viewDidLoad method.

```
[self fetchResults];
```

In entirety, your -viewDidLoad method should look like so:

```
- (void)viewDidLoad
{
    [super viewDidLoad];

    self.tableViewMain.delegate = self;
    self.tableViewMain.dataSource = self;

    self.navigationItem.rightBarButtonItem = [[UIBarButtonItem alloc]
initWithBarButtonSystemItem:UIBarButtonSystemItemAdd target:self action:@selector(add)];

    [self fetchResults];
}
```

Now that you have finished configuring your view controller, you need to go back to your application delegate and set up your basic navigation system to use it.

First, in your application delegate header file, add an import statement for your view controller's header file to appease the compiler.

```
#import "MainTableViewController.h"
```

Now you will declare all of your view controllers as properties of your application delegate. You will also set up each view controller in a UINavigationController, and all three of these inside a UITabBarController, just to get a nice flow of information. Add all the following properties to your application delegate, making sure to synthesize them as always.

```
@property (strong, nonatomic) MainTableViewController *teacherTable;
@property (strong, nonatomic) MainTableViewController *studentTable;
@property (strong, nonatomic) MainTableViewController *instrumentTable;
```

```objc
@property (strong, nonatomic) UINavigationController *teacherNavcon;
@property (strong, nonatomic) UINavigationController *studentNavcon;
@property (strong, nonatomic) UINavigationController *instrumentNavcon;

@property (strong, nonatomic) UITabBarController *tabBarController;
```

Now you need to change up your -application:didFinishLaunchingWithOptions: method in the Application Delegate class to correctly configure all of your view controllers. Overall, it will look like so:

```objc
- (BOOL)application:(UIApplication *)application
didFinishLaunchingWithOptions:(NSDictionary *)launchOptions
{
    self.window = [[UIWindow alloc] initWithFrame:[[UIScreen mainScreen] bounds]];
    self.window.backgroundColor = [UIColor whiteColor];

    self.teacherTable = [[MainTableViewController alloc] init];
    self.teacherTable.entityDescription = [NSEntityDescription entityForName:@"Teacher"
inManagedObjectContext:self.managedObjectContext];
    self.teacherTable.managedObjectContext = self.managedObjectContext;
    self.teacherTable.title = @"Teachers";

    self.studentTable = [[MainTableViewController alloc] init];
    self.studentTable.entityDescription = [NSEntityDescription entityForName:@"Student"
inManagedObjectContext:self.managedObjectContext];
    self.studentTable.managedObjectContext = self.managedObjectContext;
    self.studentTable.title = @"Students";

    self.instrumentTable = [[MainTableViewController alloc] init];
    self.instrumentTable.entityDescription = [NSEntityDescription
entityForName:@"Instrument" inManagedObjectContext:self.managedObjectContext];
    self.instrumentTable.managedObjectContext = self.managedObjectContext;
    self.instrumentTable.title = @"Instruments";

    self.teacherNavcon = [[UINavigationController alloc]
initWithRootViewController:self.teacherTable];
    self.studentNavcon = [[UINavigationController alloc]
initWithRootViewController:self.studentTable];
    self.instrumentNavcon = [[UINavigationController alloc]
initWithRootViewController:self.instrumentTable];

    self.tabBarController = [[UITabBarController alloc] init];
    [self.tabBarController setViewControllers:[NSArray
arrayWithObjects:self.teacherNavcon, self.studentNavcon, self.instrumentNavcon, nil]];

    [self.window addSubview:self.tabBarController.view];
    [self.window makeKeyAndVisible];
    return YES;
}
```

The configuration for each of your MainTableViewControllers was fairly simple, with all you had to do being to set up an NSEntityDescription, give it a pointer to your NSManagedObjectContext, and then give it a title to display in your UITabBarController.

At this point, if you run your application, all you'll see is a few empty tables (just as in Figure 11–17), and with good reason. You don't have any data yet! Unfortunately, you haven't built your -add method yet, so don't go pressing that + button until you do, since you will crash your application.

Figure 11–17. *Your three empty* `UITableViews`

For your preliminary recipe, you can start by simply programmatically creating a new object in each view controller to be displayed. Add the following code to your `MainViewController`'s -viewDidLoad method, making sure it is before the call to -fetchResults.

```
NSManagedObject *add = [[NSManagedObject alloc] initWithEntity:self.entityDescription
insertIntoManagedObjectContext:self.managedObjectContext];
    if (![self.entityDescription.name isEqualToString:@"Instrument"])
    {
        [add setValue:@"Jim" forKey:@"name"];
        [add setValue:[NSNumber numberWithInt:42] forKey:@"age"];
    }
    else
    {
        [add setValue:@"Trumpet" forKey:@"name"];
        [add setValue:@"Brass" forKey:@"family"];
    }
```

Now when you run the app, some temporary data will be displayed, as shown by Figure 11–18.

Figure 11–18. *Your semi-populated* UITableView

While you have created a new instance of each of your entities in your NSManagedObjectContext, you'll probably notice that these objects are not persisting every time you run this application, as you are not seeing an increasing list with every run. This is because you did not save the changes you made to the NSManagedObjectContext. You can do this by adding the following after the previous additions, but still before the call to -fetchRequest.

```
NSError *error;
    BOOL success = [self.managedObjectContext save:&error];
    if (!success)
    {
        NSLog(@"%@", [error localizedDescription]);
    }
```

You'll notice that this is very similar to the -performFetch: method that you used in -fetchResults, in that you send it a pointer to an instance of NSError in order to log any issues. As with before, this is totally optional, and you could pass nil as this parameter, but for best practices it is safer to include the logging.

If you run your application a few times, changing the name, you can accumulate a few different pieces of data to display. Figure 11–19 shows your application after having been run a few times to collect some data.

Figure 11–19. *Your app preserving and creating new data*

To make your program run a bit better, you can go ahead and implement that -add method, so that you can create new data from inside the app. Typically, you would want to create separate view controllers to allow the user to input the information for a new object, but for your purposes, the key concept is simply to be able to add objects.

```
-(void)add
{
    NSManagedObject *add = [[NSManagedObject alloc]
initWithEntity:self.entityDescription
insertIntoManagedObjectContext:self.managedObjectContext];
    if (![self.entityDescription.name isEqualToString:@"Instrument"])
    {
```

```
        [add setValue:@"Peter" forKey:@"name"];
        [add setValue:[NSNumber numberWithInt:35] forKey:@"age"];
    }
    else
    {
        [add setValue:@"Guitar" forKey:@"name"];
        [add setValue:@"Strings" forKey:@"family"];
    }

    NSError *error;
    BOOL success = [self.managedObjectContext save:&error];
    if (!success)
    {
        NSLog(@"%@", [error localizedDescription]);
    }

    [self fetchResults];

    [self.tableViewMain reloadData];
}
```

In the previous method, you must make sure to call the -fetchResults method once you are done creating the new object, but before you reload your UITableView's data, in order to make sure that your NSFetchedResultsController contains the most recent changes.

Just as Core Data makes a UITableView very easy to populate, it is also very easy to implement deletion of items from a UITableView in conjunction with the Core Data classes. You can implement your UITableView's -tableView:commitEditingStyle:forRowAtIndexPath: like so:

```
-(void)tableView:(UITableView *)tableView
commitEditingStyle:(UITableViewCellEditingStyle)editingStyle
forRowAtIndexPath:(NSIndexPath *)indexPath
{
    if (editingStyle == UITableViewCellEditingStyleDelete)
    {
        NSManagedObject *deleted = [self.fetchedResultsController
objectAtIndexPath:indexPath];
        [self.managedObjectContext deleteObject:deleted];
        NSError *error;
        BOOL success = [self.managedObjectContext save:&error];
        if (!success)
        {
            NSLog(@"%@", [error localizedDescription]);
        }
        [self fetchResults];
        [self.tableViewMain deleteRowsAtIndexPaths:[NSArray arrayWithObject:indexPath]
withRowAnimation:UITableViewRowAnimationRight];
    }
}
```

While it is certainly possible to allow deletion only by having the user swipe over a row, it is generally a good idea to also provide an Edit button, in case the user is unfamiliar with the swiping functionality. To do this, you first need to make a simple adjustment to your -viewDidLoad method to create the button, which will now resemble the following:

```
- (void)viewDidLoad
{
    [super viewDidLoad];

    self.tableViewMain.delegate = self;
    self.tableViewMain.dataSource = self;

    /////Adjusted code to add Edit button
    UIBarButtonItem *addButton = [[UIBarButtonItem alloc]
initWithBarButtonSystemItem:UIBarButtonSystemItemAdd target:self action:@selector(add)];
    UIBarButtonItem *editButton = self.editButtonItem;
    self.navigationItem.rightBarButtonItems = [NSArray arrayWithObjects:addButton,
editButton, nil];
    /////End of adjusted code

    [self fetchResults];
}
```

Now you just need a quick implementation of the -setEditing:animated: method to get your nice little animations correct.

```
-(void)setEditing:(BOOL)editing animated:(BOOL)animated
{
    [super setEditing:editing animated:animated];
    [self.tableViewMain setEditing:editing animated:animated];
}
```

Upon running your app now, you'll notice you can not only add, but also delete information from your table, just as is done in Figure 11–20.

Figure 11-20. *Your app, adding and deleting data*

Recipe 11–3: Subclassing NSManagedObject

Now that you have your basic UITableView set up to display the information you can store with Core Data, it's time to improve a bit on your program design. The first thing you can do is an incredible time saver that will make programming with Core Data significantly easier. You will be subclassing the NSManagedObject class for each of the entities that you created. Unlike most subclassing, however, this is incredibly easy to set up.

First, switch back to view your MusicSchool.xcdatamodeld file in which you created your entities.

The next step can be done individually, but you will create your three subclasses all at once. Select each entity from the view by holding the "command" key and clicking each one, so that all three become highlighted. You will also notice that all of their combined attributes and relationships will be visible as well, as shown in Figure 11–21.

The NSManagedObject subclassing technique that you will be using creates a subclass based on which entity or entities are selected, so it is important to make sure that all the entities you want subclasses for are selected.

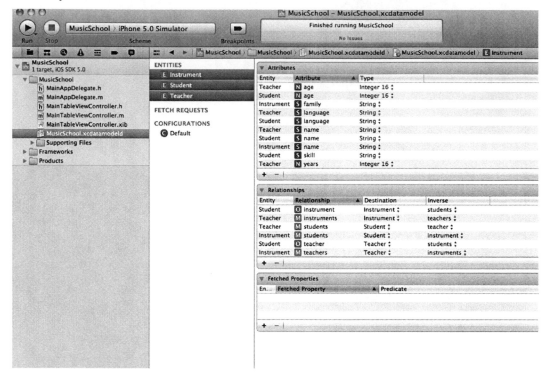

Figure 11–21. *Selecting all three entities to be turned into* NSManagedObject *subclasses*

Next, under the File menu, select **New ➤ New File…** to bring up the New File dialog. Navigate to the Core Data section under iOS, and select the "NSManagedObject subclass" option, as shown in Figure 11–22.

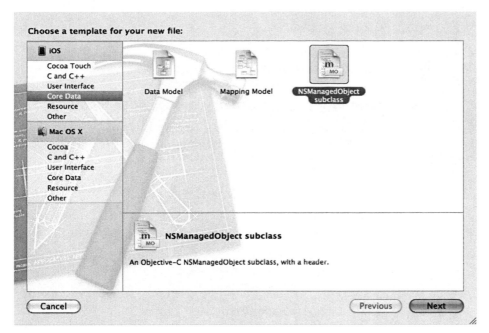

Figure 11–22. *Selecting the "NSManagedObject subclass" template to automatically generate classes for your entities*

Click through, and hit Create to have Xcode create your three NSManagedObject subclasses.

By subclassing the NSManagedObject class, you have effectively turned your entities into classes that you can use and manipulate normally, especially when it comes to accessing their attributes. Now, rather than having to use the -setValue:forKey: and -valueForKey: methods, you can simply use the setter and getter methods, or, more simply, the properties created with the same names as your attributes. This also allows you to more easily specify exactly which entity any given instance of NSManagedObject is associated with, so that your compiler can assist you in accessing properties and methods for that entity.

To demonstrate these abilities, you can rewrite your -tableView:cellForRowAtIndexPath: method to first cast your NSManagedObject down to its appropriate subclass, and then populate your cell's content using the subclass properties.

First, make sure to import the newly created header files into your view controller.

```
#import "Instrument.h"
#import "Student.h"
#import "Teacher.h"
```

Once this is taken care of, you can implement your simplified method.

```
-(UITableViewCell *)tableView:(UITableView *)tableView
cellForRowAtIndexPath:(NSIndexPath *)indexPath
```

```objc
{
    static NSString *CellIdentifier = @"Cell";

    UITableViewCell *cell = [tableView
dequeueReusableCellWithIdentifier:CellIdentifier];
    if (cell == nil)
    {
        cell = [[UITableViewCell alloc] initWithStyle:UITableViewCellStyleSubtitle
reuseIdentifier:CellIdentifier];
        cell.accessoryType = UITableViewCellAccessoryDetailDisclosureButton;
        cell.textLabel.font = [UIFont systemFontOfSize:19.0];
        cell.detailTextLabel.font = [UIFont systemFontOfSize:12];
    }

    NSManagedObject *object = [self.fetchedResultsController
objectAtIndexPath:indexPath];

    if ([object.entity.name isEqualToString:@"Instrument"])
    {
        Instrument *instrument = (Instrument *)object;
        cell.textLabel.text = instrument.name;
        cell.detailTextLabel.text = instrument.family;
    }
    else if ([object.entity.name isEqualToString:@"Student"])
    {
        Student *student = (Student *)object;
        cell.textLabel.text = student.name;
        cell.detailTextLabel.text = [student.age stringValue];
    }
    else
    {
        Teacher *teacher = (Teacher *)object;
        cell.textLabel.text = teacher.name;
        cell.detailTextLabel.text = [teacher.age stringValue];
    }

    return cell;
}
```

You can also simplify your -add method that creates your test data like so.

```objc
-(void)add
{
    NSManagedObject *add = [[NSManagedObject alloc]
initWithEntity:self.entityDescription
insertIntoManagedObjectContext:self.managedObjectContext];
    if ([self.entityDescription.name isEqualToString:@"Teacher"])
    {
        Teacher *teacher = (Teacher *)add;
        teacher.name = @"Peter";
        teacher.age = [NSNumber numberWithInt:36];
    }
    else if ([self.entityDescription.name isEqualToString:@"Instrument"])
    {
        Instrument *instrument = (Instrument *)add;
        instrument.name = @"Guitar";
        instrument.family = @"Strings";
    }
```

```
    else
    {
        Student *student = (Student *)add;
        student.name = @"Andrew";
        student.age = [NSNumber numberWithInt:18];
    }

    NSError *error;
    BOOL success = [self.managedObjectContext save:&error];
    if (!success)
    {
        NSLog(@"%@", [error localizedDescription]);
    }

    [self fetchResults];

    [self.tableViewMain reloadData];
}
```

Again, this doesn't really affect how your application runs, but it makes your life a great deal easier in terms of coding and debugging.

By using this subclassing technique, you will probably find yourself having fewer issues with runtime errors when using Core Data, as your compiler will now be able to confirm that you are accessing the correct properties for any given subclass.

Just as you are able to access and edit the attributes of your subclassed NSManagedObjects, you can do the same with the relationships that your entities share. You will change your program such that if a Teacher is selected, a list of Instruments entered appears, and when one of these Instruments is selected, that Instrument is added to the set of instruments for that Teacher. You may also notice that because you have your relationships set up with inverses to each other, a relationship set one way will also be set in the reverse. In your case, when you add the Instrument into the instruments set of a Teacher, that Teacher will also be added into the teachers set of the Instrument.

For demonstration purposes, you will implement this behavior only between Teachers and Instruments, but it should be easy to see how you would fully implement similar behavior between all three entities, allowing the user to connect any Teacher with his or her Students and Instruments.

First, you will declare an instance variable in your MainTableViewController's header file of type Teacher, to help keep track of the selected Teacher.

```
__strong Teacher *selectedTeacher;
```

Next, you will need to declare a new property called delegate of the same type as the class, which you will use to connect your multiple view controllers. Make sure to synthesize and nil this property as appropriate.

```
@property (nonatomic, strong) MainTableViewController *delegate;
```

Declare also the header for a method for your delegate property to perform, like so:

```
-(void)MainTableViewController:(MainTableViewController *)mainTableVC
didSelectInstrument:(Instrument *)instrument;
```

Your header file (MainTableViewController.h) should now resemble the following:

```
#import <UIKit/UIKit.h>
#import "Instrument.h"
#import "Student.h"
#import "Teacher.h"

@interface MainTableViewController : UIViewController <UITableViewDelegate,
UITableViewDataSource>{

    __strong Teacher *selectedTeacher;
}

@property (strong, nonatomic) IBOutlet UITableView *tableViewMain;

@property (nonatomic, strong) NSEntityDescription *entityDescription;
@property (nonatomic, strong) NSFetchedResultsController *fetchedResultsController;
@property (nonatomic, strong) NSManagedObjectContext *managedObjectContext;

@property (nonatomic, strong) MainTableViewController *delegate;

-(void)MainTableViewController:(MainTableViewController *)mainTableVC
didSelectInstrument:(Instrument *)instrument;

@end
```

Next, you will use the delegate property in conjunction with your UITableView's row selection method to build your new, albeit selective, functionality.

```
-(void)tableView:(UITableView *)tableView didSelectRowAtIndexPath:(NSIndexPath
*)indexPath
{
    [self.tableViewMain deselectRowAtIndexPath:indexPath animated:YES];
    if ([self.entityDescription.name isEqualToString:@"Teacher"])
    {
        selectedTeacher = [self.fetchedResultsController objectAtIndexPath:indexPath];
        MainTableViewController *selectInstrument = [[MainTableViewController alloc]
init];
        selectInstrument.entityDescription = [NSEntityDescription
entityForName:@"Instrument" inManagedObjectContext:self.managedObjectContext];
        selectInstrument.managedObjectContext = self.managedObjectContext;
        selectInstrument.delegate = self;
        [self.navigationController pushViewController:selectInstrument animated:YES];
    }
    else if ([self.entityDescription.name isEqualToString:@"Instrument"] &&
(self.delegate != nil))
    {
        [self.delegate MainTableViewController:self
didSelectInstrument:[self.fetchedResultsController objectAtIndexPath:indexPath]];
        [self.navigationController popViewControllerAnimated:YES];
    }
}
```

You can now implement the delegate method you recently declared to add the chosen Instrument to the selectedTeacher, and then save the changes to the NSManagedObjectContext.

```
-(void)MainTableViewController:(MainTableViewController *)mainTableVC
didSelectInstrument:(NSManagedObject *)instrument
{
    [selectedTeacher addInstrumentsObject:instrument];
    NSError *saveError;
    BOOL success = [self.managedObjectContext save:&saveError];
    if (!success)
    {
        NSLog(@"%@", [saveError localizedFailureReason]);
    }
}
```

Since you didn't flesh out a full system for the user to create custom data, you will need to adjust your -add method a few times, running your application each time, to create some different data in order to fully test this functionality.

Recipe 11–4: Filtering Your Fetch Requests

When you're using your instances of NSFetchRequest to get information from your NSManagedObjectContext, you are in no way limited to only requesting all of a specific entity. Through the use of the NSPredicate class, you can easily refine your results to nearly any subset depending on your application.

For your application, you will implement your filtering behavior to be applied upon the tapping of the Accessory button in your UITableViews, with different actions depending on the type of NSManagedObject tapped.

- If the Accessory button is tapped in your Teachers table, you will display another UITableView of all the instruments that the selected Teacher is associated with.

- Tapping the accessory button in your Students table will display a table of all other students of the same age as the one selected.

- In your Instruments table, you will filter your data to display all other Instruments with the same family as the selected one.

All of these behaviors will be implemented by setting an NSPredicate to your NSFetchRequest with the specified predicate.

First, you will add a property to your MainTableViewController to keep track of this NSPredicate so that it can be easily created and used to perform fetch requests.

```
@property (nonatomic, strong) NSPredicate *predicate;
```

You can implement your UITableView's delegate method like so:

```
-(void)tableView:(UITableView *)tableView
accessoryButtonTappedForRowWithIndexPath:(NSIndexPath *)indexPath
```

```
{
    if (![self.title isEqualToString:@"Filtered"])
    {
        MainTableViewController *filtered = [[MainTableViewController alloc] init];
        filtered.title = @"Filtered";
        filtered.managedObjectContext = self.managedObjectContext;

        if ([self.entityDescription.name isEqualToString:@"Teacher"])
        {
            filtered.entityDescription = [NSEntityDescription
entityForName:@"Instrument" inManagedObjectContext:self.managedObjectContext];
            NSSet *instruments = [(Teacher *)[self.fetchedResultsController
objectAtIndexPath:indexPath] instruments];
            filtered.predicate = [NSPredicate predicateWithFormat:@"self IN %@",
instruments];
        }
        else if ([self.entityDescription.name isEqualToString:@"Student"])
        {
            filtered.entityDescription = self.entityDescription;
            filtered.predicate = [NSPredicate predicateWithFormat:@"age=%i", [[(Student
*)[self.fetchedResultsController objectAtIndexPath: indexPath] age] intValue]];
        }
        else
        {
            filtered.entityDescription = self.entityDescription;
            filtered.predicate = [NSPredicate predicateWithFormat:@"family=%@",
[(Instrument *)[self.fetchedResultsController objectAtIndexPath:indexPath]family]];
        }

        [self.navigationController pushViewController:filtered animated:YES];
    }
}
```

As you can see, you have used a couple of different styles of predicates in your implementation. You have a simple comparing predicate comparing the family property with a value, and then you have a predicate to check for an object contained in a set for the Teacher.

Whenever you need to specify a certain value in a predicate, you can use "%@", and then pass the value afterward, as shown in the previous code block. In case you are unfamiliar with these kinds of values, called "format specifiers," some of the more common ones include the following:

- %@: This can be used to represent either a NSString value, or simply a reference to an object, as you used previously.

- %i: This represents an integer.

- %f: This represents a float.

- %d: This represents a double value.

These specifiers, which originated in the C programming language for printing formatted strings, are most often used in conjunction with either the NSLog() command or when displaying information for the user. For example, you may have a piece of code for testing to log a simple counter, which would look like so:

```
for (int n=0; n < 100; n++)
    {
        NSLog(@"%i", n);
    }
```

Whenever you are referring to the object being evaluated with a predicate, you use the keyword "self", as shown in the first NSPredicate.

There is a great deal of documentation on creating NSPredicates with different formats and methods, which allow the developer a great deal of power in creating filters for their results. Refer to the Apple documentation for more information on creating more complex predicates.

Just before you are quite finished with this setup, you also need to modify your -fetchResults method to take the NSPredicate into account. The new method will look like so:

```
-(void)fetchResults
{
    NSFetchRequest *fetchRequest = [NSFetchRequest
fetchRequestWithEntityName:self.entityDescription.name];
    NSString *cacheName = [self.entityDescription.name
stringByAppendingString:@"Cache"];

    ////////////New Predicate code
    if (self.predicate != nil)
    {
        [fetchRequest setPredicate:self.predicate];
    }
    ////////////End of new code

    NSSortDescriptor *sortDescriptor = [NSSortDescriptor sortDescriptorWithKey:@"name"
ascending:YES];
    [fetchRequest setSortDescriptors:[NSArray arrayWithObject:sortDescriptor]];

    self.fetchedResultsController = [[NSFetchedResultsController alloc]
initWithFetchRequest:fetchRequest managedObjectContext:self.managedObjectContext
sectionNameKeyPath:nil cacheName:cacheName];

    BOOL success;
    NSError *error;
    success = [self.fetchedResultsController performFetch:&error];
    if (!success)
    {
        NSLog(@"%@", [error localizedDescription]);
    }
}
```

At this point, if you run your application, you can see some examples of the filtered results, such as the filtering of Instruments by family in Figure 11–23.

Figure 11–23. *Your app displaying filtered results*

Recipe 11–5: Versioning

For almost any application, you will most likely need to make changes to your Core Data model at one point or another. Xcode gives you a very nice, easy way to do this in such a way that you can keep all your old models easily in case you have any issues, through a process called "versioning."

The first step you will take is to create a new version of your data model, which you can base off of the one you already have. First, select your MusicSchool.xcdatamodeld file in your navigator pane on the left.

In the Editor menu, select **Add Model Version…**. A simple dialog will appear, allowing you to specify the name of the new version model, as well as which model to base the new one off of. Since you have only the one model so far, it will be your only choice. Name the new model "MusicSchool2", as in Figure 11–24.

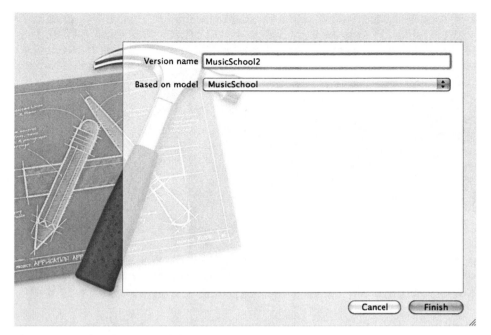

Figure 11–24. *Creating a new version*

Click Finish, and your new model will be created.

Now, you can make some changes to your data model. For the purposes of your application, you will be making only fairly simple changes so that your migration, which you will deal with shortly, is a simple process. In order to keep with a lightweight migration, you should stick to only the following possible changes:

- Adding or removing entities, attributes, or relationships

- Renaming properties or entities

- Changing whether an attribute is optional

For your new data model, you will simply add two attributes: first, an NSString called size to your Instrument entity, and another NSString called range, also to the Instrument entity. The resulting attributes table will resemble Figure 11–25.

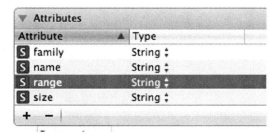

Figure 11–25. *Adding new attributes to your Instrument entity*

Next, you need to specify this newest model version to be the one that your application actually uses. First, select the top level of your `.xcdatamodel` files, which will be listed as having the file type "xcdatamodeld", and have the drop-down menu of your two actual data model files, as in Figure 11–26. (This one specifies which of the two is actually being selected.)

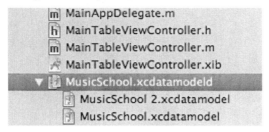

Figure 11–26. *Viewing your project's data models; the currently used one is listed as the main file.*

Next, you need to bring up the File inspector. You can do this either by navigating from the View menu to **Utilities ➤ Show File Inspector**, or by bringing up the Utilities pane on the right side of the screen, and then selecting the first tab, as shown in Figure 11–27.

> **CAUTION:** Xcode does not currently allow you to delete data model files from your project. Be careful when creating new versions, as you will not be able to easily remove them once they are created. In Figure 11–27, you can see a buildup of multiple data model files that are not needed or used.

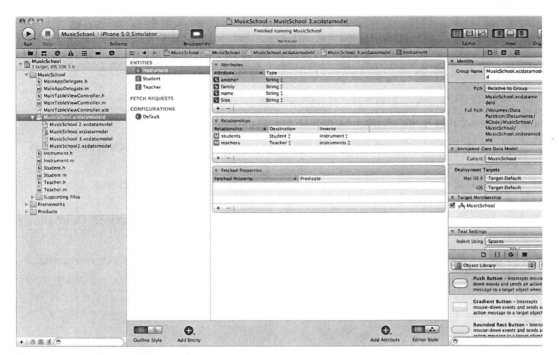

Figure 11–27. *Using the File inspector to set the current version*

Under the Versioned Core Data Model section, you need to change the current model to your new "MusicSchool2", specifically shown in Figure 11–28.

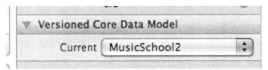

Figure 11–28. *Selecting a different current version*

At this point, you will notice that a small green check mark has been placed next to the new model version, signifying that it is now the current version, as in Figure 11–29.

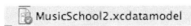

Figure 11–29. *Your new model file set as the current version*

If you try to run this application immediately, depending on how complex your changes were, your application might possibly crash upon running with a very strange reason of "The model used to open the store is incompatible with the one used to create the store". This essentially means that you are trying to migrate data from an old model to a new one, and it does not know what to do. Luckily, for those lightweight migrations, this is easy to fix.

Navigate over to your application delegate implementation file, and find the -persistentStoreCoordinator method. Look for the following line:

```
if (![__persistentStoreCoordinator addPersistentStoreWithType:NSSQLiteStoreType
configuration:nil URL:storeURL options:nil error:&error])
```

You will specify an instance of NSDictionary to pass as the options parameter of this method. Add the following code before the previous if statement.

```
NSDictionary *options = [NSDictionary dictionaryWithObjectsAndKeys:[NSNumber
numberWithBool:YES], NSMigratePersistentStoresAutomaticallyOption, [NSNumber
numberWithBool:YES], NSInferMappingModelAutomaticallyOption, nil];
```

Make sure to set this dictionary as the actual parameter so that the if statement reads like so now:

```
if (![__persistentStoreCoordinator addPersistentStoreWithType:NSSQLiteStoreType
configuration:nil URL:storeURL options:options error:&error])
```

Any lightweight migrations will now automatically take place, making your job immensely easier.

If your app runs perfectly fine without this change, then you do not need to worry about this step, but know that you may have to at some point.

An Irritating Error

Sometimes when dealing with versioning, you may run into a problem where an error is thrown by the method that states that the store could not be found. An easy, albeit frustrating solution to this is to delete your persistent store using the following command in the event of an error by adding this line inside the previously referenced if statement.

```
[[NSFileManager defaultManager] removeItemAtURL:storeURL error:nil];
```

Your if statement would then resemble the following code in this case. Keep in mind that you do not at all need or want to add this code unless you encounter this specific problem.

```
if (![__persistentStoreCoordinator addPersistentStoreWithType:NSSQLiteStoreType
configuration:nil URL:storeURL options:options error:&error])
    {
        NSLog(@"Unresolved error %@, %@", error, [error userInfo]);
        [[NSFileManager defaultManager] removeItemAtURL:storeURL error:nil];

        abort();
    }
```

After running this application once, your persistent store will be reset, so you should be able to remove this line from the method once your application is working correctly again. This way, your app does not go and reset your data without your explicit expectation.

While this should fix the problem, you will unfortunately lose all of your saved data, so it is generally best to avoid this drastic measure.

At this point, your application will work again, and you can add code to take advantage of your newer model version. However, since you have not updated your NSManagedObject subclasses, you will not be able to access any of your new attributes without using the -valueForKey: method. Since you made changes only to the Instrument entity, you will refresh only your Instrument subclass.

First, delete the Instrument subclass files. You can choose to fully delete the files, rather than simply their references, since you will not need this version of it anymore, and you can always re-create it from the data model again if you have to revert. The dialog with which to do this will resemble Figure 11–30.

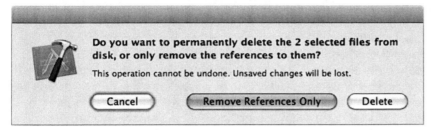

Figure 11–30. *Deleting your Instrument subclass files; use the Delete option, as you will re-create them.*

Now you can go through the exact same steps as before to create your subclass.

In your data model file, select the Instrument entity, then navigate to **File ➤ New ➤ New File....**

Under Core Data for iOS, choose the "NSManagedObject subclass" template (as in Figure 11–31), and then click through to create your new subclass.

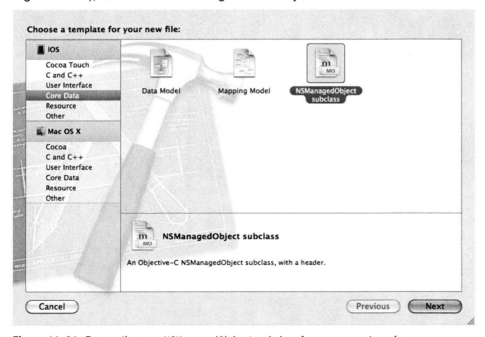

Figure 11–31. *Re-creating your NSManagedObject subclass for your newest version*

You'll now see that your `Instrument` class contains all the necessary properties and methods to handle the added attributes in your new, versioned data model!

Summary

Throughout this chapter, we have covered the basics of Core Data, one of the most integral parts of iOS development, due to its power and simplicity of use when it comes to data modeling, persistence, and access. However, we have by no means detailed every facet in the Core Data framework, or even touched on every general subject related to it. You can easily find entire books devoted to the subject of Core Data, and you probably should, in order to get a more complete view of exactly how much ability you have in controlling how your data is stored. The overview here has demonstrated a basic use of the framework and explained the key concepts needed to get started working with Core Data, so that you can implement simple persistence in your applications without worrying about the more esoteric complexities.

Chapter 12

Core Motion Recipes

The last two chapters spent an incredible amount of time on dealing with information stored and persisted inside a device's memory. Now, we will deal with an entirely opposite topic: data from the outside world—not in the sense of data given by the user, but instead, data collected by the device about the universe in which it exists at any given second. By retrieving information about the outside world, a developer can specifically build applications focused on enhancing the user's experience based on his or herphysical situation. This could be anything from simply detecting the orientation of the device to incorporating rotation into a racing game's steering system, to using an accelerometer to measure the acceleration of a roller coaster. Through the use of the Core Motion framework, we are able to accesswith great ease a variety of hardware built into our iOS device in order to acquire such unique information, from magnetic fields, to accelerations, both by gravity and otherwise, to rotation rates, about the specific situation of our device.

For all but the first recipe in this chapter, you will need a physical device with which to test functionality, since youwill be dealing with information generated by the physical presence of a device.

Recipe 12–1: Registering Shake Events

Before we dive into the Core Motion framework, we can first deal with a related topic: the shaking of a device. A large number of applications utilize this functionality in a variety of ways, with results ranging from the shuffling of songs to the refreshing of information. While this implementation does not necessarily rely on the Core Motion framework, its key concept of being able to detect physical changes to your device makes it an important functionality to understand.

You will create a very simple application to detect and log the shaking of the device. From there, you will start to build an app that can read and display motion information.

Start off by creating a new project called "Measurements", which you will use throughout this chapter. For your simple application, you will use the Single View

Application template, as in Figure 12–1, so that you can be saved some work on putting your application delegate together.

Once you select the template, enter the project name, make sure that your class prefix is set to "Main" and that only the box marked "Use Automatic Reference Counting" is checked, and then click through to create your project.

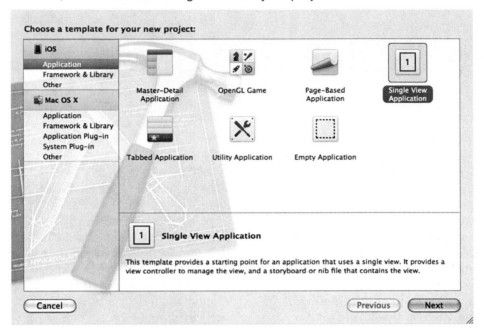

Figure 12–1. *Creating a single view application*

The first task involved in configuring the shaking functionality is that you need to instruct your application to post a notification any time the device is shaken (not stirred). To do this, you will need to subclass the UIWindow class. Create a new file using the "Objective-C class" template under the iOS Cocoa Touch section, as in Figure 12–2.

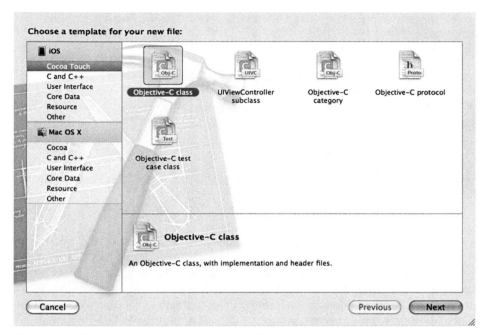

Figure 12–2. *Subclassing* `UIWindow` *by making an Objective-C class*

Go ahead and name the class "MainWindow", and make sure that you enter "UIWindow" in the "Subclass of" field, just as in Figure 12–3.

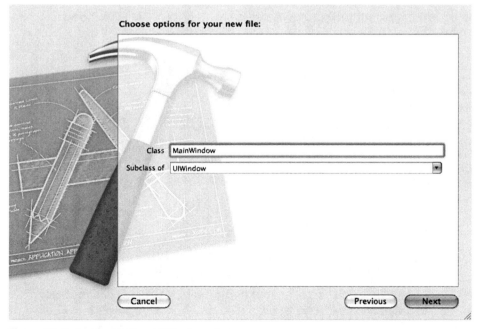

Figure 12–3. *Configuring your* `UIWindow` *subclass*

Click through to create this subclass, and then switch over to its implementation file, called `MainWindow.m`.

In this class, you will be overriding the `-motionEnded:withEvent:` method in order to properly handle the shaking of your device. Any time the device is shaken, this method will automatically be called. You will write it to post a notification, which you can then track in other classes.

```
-(void)motionEnded:(UIEventSubtype)motion withEvent:(UIEvent *)event
{
if (motion == UIEventSubtypeMotionShake)
    {
        [[NSNotificationCenter defaultCenter] postNotificationName:@"NOTIFICATION_SHAKE"
object:event];
    }
}
```

If you are not quite familiar with the concept of the `NSNotificationCenter` and posting notifications, you will quickly see that they are quite simple. Any given class can post notifications to the `NSNotificationCenter`. Any class that is "observing" the center for any notifications with the same "Name" will be notified, and can thus act accordingly. This is a fantastic way to move information between classes based on real-time events, and often deal with outside changes in userinput, such as adjustments to a device's volume or using remote controls with a music application.

Next you need to specify that your new subclass of `UIWindow` is the one that your application should use. If you switch over to your application delegate, you will notice it already has a `UIWindow` property with which it displays all of your views.

First, add an import statement to your app delegate header file to include the `MainWindow` class.

```
#import "MainWindow.h"
```

Now in the app delegate implementation file, modify your `-application:DidFinishLaunchingWithOptions:` method to read like so:

```
- (BOOL)application:(UIApplication *)application
didFinishLaunchingWithOptions:(NSDictionary *)launchOptions
{
//////////The only changed line!
self.window = [[MainWindow alloc] initWithFrame:[[UIScreen mainScreen] bounds]];
//////////Change only the previous line.

self.viewController = [[MainViewController alloc] initWithNibName:@"MainViewController"
bundle:nil];
self.window.rootViewController = self.viewController;
    [self.window makeKeyAndVisible];
return YES;
}
```

By modifying the class with which you allocated and initialized your window property from "UIWindow" to "MainWindow", you threw a nice bit of polymorphism into your code, in that the `window` property is of type `UIWindow`, but specifically behaves like a

MainWindow. Since MainWindow is a subclass of UIWindow, this won't give you any problems, and saves you from having to change the property type as well.

Now, you can switch over to your main view controller, where you need to register for your "NOTIFICATION_SHAKE" notifications by modifying your -viewDidLoad method.

```
- (void)viewDidLoad
{
    [super viewDidLoad];

    [[NSNotificationCenter defaultCenter] addObserver:self
selector:@selector(shakeDetected:) name:@"NOTIFICATION_SHAKE" object:nil];

}
```

Since you passed the shakeDetected: selector as the designated action for these notifications in the previous method, you need to implement this in order to avoid any runtime exceptions. For now, your implementation will be very simple, but you will add onto it later.

```
-(void)shakeDetected:(NSNotification *)paramNotification
{
NSLog(@"Just be careful not to drop it!");
}
```

While it may seem a little odd, you do not actually need a physical device to test out this functionality. The iOS simulator includes a function to simulate a shaking motion on the device, so that you can see if your application responds correctly.

When viewing your simulator, navigate in the Hardware menu to the "Shake Gesture" (Ctrl+⌘Z) selection, as shown in Figure 12–4.

Figure 12–4. *Simulating a shake gesture*

You won't see any kind of shaking animation in the simulator, but it should respond appropriately to make your simple little log. Figure 12–5 demonstrates the output of your application after "shaking" the simulator a couple of times.

Figure 12–5. *Resulting output from "shaking"your simulator*

If you connect your iOS device to Xcode and run through that, you'll get the same result once you give your device a bit of a shake!

Recipe 12–2: Accessing Raw Core Motion Data

Now that your application is set up with some basic shaking detection, you can start to build the Core Motion framework in, which will allow you access to accelerometer, gyroscope, and magnetometer information.

First, select your project, and then navigate to the Build Phases tab. Under Link Binary With Libraries, click the + button, and select the item labeled "CoreMotion.framework", as in Figure 12–6.

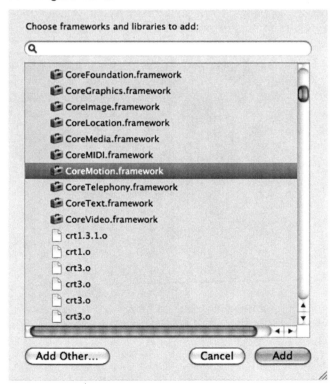

Figure 12–6. *Adding the CoreMotion framework*

Now back in your main view controller's header file, add the following import statement so that you can access the Core Motion API.

```
#import <CoreMotion/CoreMotion.h>
```

The Core Motion framework relies extremely heavily on a single class called `CMMotionManager`. This class acts as a hub through which you access all the hardware that any given device is able to access. You will create an instance of this class in your view controller as a property in order to constantly keep track of it.

```
@property (nonatomic, strong) CMMotionManager *motionManager;
```

In your view controller, make sure to synthesize this property, and then set it to nil in your -viewDidUnload, as is standard.

Unfortunately, simply synthesizing a `CMMotionManager` object is not enough to ensure its initialization (like an `NSArray`), so you will create a modified getter method to make up for this. Luckily, there's no complicated configuration needed to do this.

```
-(CMMotionManager *)motionManager
{
if (motionManager == nil)
    {
motionManager = [[CMMotionManager alloc] init];
    }
return motionManager;
}
```

Next up, you'll start by setting up your user interface.You will start off by measuring the output of three different instruments: the accelerometer, the gyroscope, and the magnetometer. You will go more into detail on the purposes of these instruments soon, but for now you must know that each of these will provide three different values for you to view. As such, you will set up your view as shown in Figure 12–7.

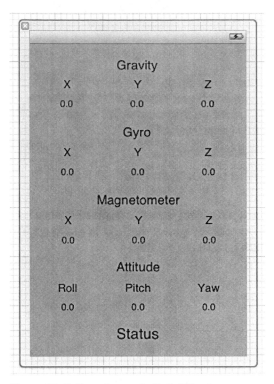

Figure 12–7. *Your view controller's XIB setup*

Make sure to connect the required UILabels to your view controller as properties so that you can change their text! You can leave all the device name labels as well as the "X", "Y", and "Z" labels alone, so you will connect only the UILabels thatwill show values (they read as "0.0" right now), as well as the bottom Status label. You will use the following property names in your code, organized by line:

- xAccLabel, yAccLabel, zAccLabel
- xGyroLabel, yGyroLabel, zGyroLabel
- xMagLabel, yMagLabel, zMagLabel
- statusLabel

You will also define a method in your header file to toggle whether you are currently retrieving hardware updates, so add the following method declaration.

-(void)toggleUpdates;

When you're done, your user interface should be fully set up for your initial application, and your view controller's header file, in its entirety, should look like so:

```
#import <UIKit/UIKit.h>
#import <CoreMotion/CoreMotion.h>

@interface MainViewController : UIViewController
```

```
@property (nonatomic, strong) CMMotionManager *motionManager;
@property (strong, nonatomic) IBOutlet UILabel *xAccLabel;
@property (strong, nonatomic) IBOutlet UILabel *yAccLabel;
@property (strong, nonatomic) IBOutlet UILabel *zAccLabel;

@property (strong, nonatomic) IBOutlet UILabel *xGyroLabel;
@property (strong, nonatomic) IBOutlet UILabel *yGyroLabel;
@property (strong, nonatomic) IBOutlet UILabel *zGyroLabel;

@property (strong, nonatomic) IBOutlet UILabel *xMagLabel;
@property (strong, nonatomic) IBOutlet UILabel *yMagLabel;
@property (strong, nonatomic) IBOutlet UILabel *zMagLabel;

@property (strong, nonatomic) IBOutlet UILabel *statusLabel;

-(void)toggleUpdates;
@end
```

Core Motion in Detail

In Core Motion, you are able to access three different pieces of hardware on a device, assuming that the device is new enough to be equipped with said hardware.

1. *Accelerometer*: This piece of hardware measures acceleration (caused by gravity or user acceleration) of a device in order to provide insight into the current orientation of the device, as well as any accelerations of the device by the user in a specific direction. This is particularly useful for detecting whether the device is at an angle (and possibly rotating a view as a result).

   Data from the accelerometer is presented in the form of a CMAccelerometerData object. This object has just one property, acceleration, which has x, y, and z values, representing the orientation or acceleration along any given axis.

2. *Gyroscope*: The gyroscope measures rotation rate of the device along multiple axes.

   Information from the gyroscope is enclosed in an instance of CMGyroData. This class has the property rotationRate, with x, y, and z values, which represent the rotation rate around a specific axis

3. *Magnetometer*: This device provides data regarding the magnetic field passing through the device, usually based on the Earth's magnetic field, as well as any other magnetic fields nearby. Remember to be careful when testing this feature, as placing any kind of powerful magnet near your device could possibly cause harm to it.

   When receiving information from the magnetometer, you access the CMMagnetometerData class, which has a single property, magneticField, which has x, y, and z values to represent the magnetic field through the device along each axis.

For all three devices, all axes are the same. If you are holding your device facing you with the bottom facing the ground, the xaxis cuts horizontally through your device, the yaxis runs from top to bottom, and the zaxis runs through the center of the device toward you.

You will start off by implementing your view controller to display the raw data for each of these pieces of hardware.

Whenever you are dealing with any internal hardware, it is the developer's responsibility to include some way of confirming that the hardware being accessed is actually available on any given device running the application. For this reason, any time you access the Core Motion hardware, you will always make use of the following methods:

- `-isAccelerometerAvailable`

- `-isGyroAvailable`

- `-isMagnetometerAvailable`

All three of these methods simply return a BOOL value, with YES indicating that the hardware is indeed accessible.

You will also make use of three other methods that check if any given hardware is currently already active to correctly toggle your updates.

- `-isAccelerometerActive`

- `-isGyroActive`

- `-isMagnetometerActive`

Whenever you want to retrieve updates from a specific piece of hardware, you must set an "update interval," to specify how often you will receive updates, as shown in the following example:

```
[self.motionManager setAccelerometerUpdateInterval:1.0/2.0]; //Update twice per second
```

There are two different methods by which you can receive updates from a particular hardware component. First, you can simply tell the `CMMotionManager` to start receiving updates from a device using -startAccelerometerUpdates, -startGyroUpdates, and -startMagnetometerUpdates, and then query the info using the `accelerometerData`, `gyroData`, and `magnetometerData` properties. This way is useful if you are not planning to make use of your updates every single time they refresh.

The second method focuses more for the user who wants to always utilize the newest data as it becomes available, as you are implementing here. You can make use of three different methods that not only start updates, but also specify a handler block of code to be performed upon updating, as well as a queue in which to perform the handler. These are listed as follows:

- `-startAccelerometerUpdatesToQueue:withHandler:`

- -startGyroUpdatesToQueue:withHandler:

- -startMagnetometerUpdatesToQueue:withHandler:

For your simple uses, you will use the main queue to perform your handlers.

Combining all these methods discussed, you can build a simple section of code that, if run, will start updating with data from the accelerometer. This code will be used to build the method -toggleUpdates

```
if ([self.motionManager isAccelerometerAvailable] && ![self.motionManager
isAccelerometerActive])
    {
        [self.motionManager setAccelerometerUpdateInterval:1.0/2.0]; //Update twice per
second
        [self.motionManager startAccelerometerUpdatesToQueue:[NSOperationQueue
mainQueue] withHandler:^(CMAccelerometerData *accelerometerData, NSError *error)
        {
self.xAccLabel.text = [NSString stringWithFormat:@"%f",
accelerometerData.acceleration.x];
self.yAccLabel.text = [NSString stringWithFormat:@"%f",
accelerometerData.acceleration.y];
self.zAccLabel.text = [NSString stringWithFormat:@"%f",
accelerometerData.acceleration.z];
        }];
    }
```

As discussed earlier, you first check to make sure the hardware is both available and inactive. Next you set your update interval, and then start asking for updates. The simple handler you have specified will update your view's information to include the raw data that you have received.

Since you are in fact building a method to toggle these updates on and off, you can add a following condition to turn off your updates.

```
else if ([self.motionManager isAccelerometerActive])
    {
        [self.motionManager stopAccelerometerUpdates];
self.xAccLabel.text = @"...";
self.yAccLabel.text = @"...";
self.zAccLabel.text = @"...";
    }
```

The other two instruments operate on the exact same principles. Overall, your -toggleUpdates method will be written like so:

```
-(void)toggleUpdates
{
if ([self.motionManager isAccelerometerAvailable] &&
![self.motionManagerisAccelerometerActive])
    {
        [self.motionManager setAccelerometerUpdateInterval:1.0/2.0]; //Update twice per
second
        [self.motionManager startAccelerometerUpdatesToQueue:[NSOperationQueue
mainQueue] withHandler:^(CMAccelerometerData *accelerometerData, NSError *error)
        {
self.xAccLabel.text = [NSString stringWithFormat:@"%f",
accelerometerData.acceleration.x];
```

```objc
self.yAccLabel.text = [NSString stringWithFormat:@"%f",
accelerometerData.acceleration.y];
self.zAccLabel.text = [NSString stringWithFormat:@"%f",
accelerometerData.acceleration.z];
        }];
    }
else if ([self.motionManager isAccelerometerActive])
    {
        [self.motionManager stopAccelerometerUpdates];
self.xAccLabel.text = @"...";
self.yAccLabel.text = @"...";
self.zAccLabel.text = @"...";
    }

if ([self.motionManager isGyroAvailable] && ![self.motionManager isGyroActive])
    {
        [self.motionManage rsetGyroUpdateInterval:1.0/2.0];
        [self.motionManager startGyroUpdatesToQueue:[NSOperationQueue mainQueue]
withHandler:^(CMGyroData *gyroData, NSError *error)
        {
self.xGyroLabel.text = [NSString stringWithFormat:@"%f", gyroData.rotationRate.x];
self.yGyroLabel.text = [NSString stringWithFormat:@"%f", gyroData.rotationRate.y];
self.zGyroLabel.text = [NSString stringWithFormat:@"%f", gyroData.rotationRate.z];
        }];
    }
else if ([self.motionManager isGyroActive])
    {
        [self.motionManager stopGyroUpdates];
self.xGyroLabel.text = @"...";
self.yGyroLabel.text = @"...";
self.zGyroLabel.text = @"...";
    }

if ([self.motionManager isMagnetometerAvailable] && ![self.motionManager
isMagnetometerActive])
    {
        [self.motionManager setMagnetometerUpdateInterval:1.0/2.0];
        [self.motionManager startMagnetometerUpdatesToQueue:[NSOperationQueue mainQueue]
withHandler:^(CMMagnetometerData *magData, NSError *error)
        {
self.xMagLabel.text = [NSString stringWithFormat:@"%f", magData.magneticField.x];
self.yMagLabel.text = [NSString stringWithFormat:@"%f", magData.magneticField.y];
self.zMagLabel.text = [NSString stringWithFormat:@"%f", magData.magneticField.z];
        }];
    }
else if ([self.motionManager isMagnetometerActive])
    {
        [self.motionManager stopMagnetometerUpdates];
self.xMagLabel.text = @"...";
self.yMagLabel.text = @"...";
self.zMagLabel.text = @"...";
    }
}
```

For a little bit of fun, you'll go ahead and make it so that your toggling is based on the shaking of the device, so you will modify your -shakeDetected: method.

```objc
-(void)shakeDetected:(NSNotification *)paramNotification
```

```
{
if ([self.statusLabel.text isEqualToString:@"Updating"])
    {
self.statusLabel.text = @"Stopped";
        [self toggleUpdates];
    }
else
    {
self.statusLabel.text = @"Updating";
        [self toggleUpdates];
    }
}
```

Whenever you deal with the CMMotionManager, you should always make sure that all of your updates are stopped at the end of your application, so you'll set up your -viewDidUnload:method like so:

```
- (void)viewDidUnload
{
if ([self.motionManager isAccelerometerAvailable] && [self.motionManager
isAccelerometerActive])
    {
        [self.motionManager stopAccelerometerUpdates];
    }
if ([self.motionManager isGyroAvailable] && [self.motionManager isGyroActive])
    {
        [self.motionManager stopGyroUpdates];
    }
if ([self.motionManager isMagnetometerAvailable] && [self.motionManager
isMagnetometerActive])
    {
        [self.motionManager stopMagnetometerUpdates];
    }

self.motionManager = nil;
    [self setXAccLabel:nil];
    [self setYAccLabel:nil];
    [self setZAccLabel:nil];
    [self setXGyroLabel:nil];
    [self setYGyroLabel:nil];
    [self setZGyroLabel:nil];
    [self setStatusLabel:nil];
    [self setXMagLabel:nil];
    [self setYMagLabel:nil];
    [self setZMagLabel:nil];
    [superview DidUnload];
}
```

You should also make sure that your application stops updating whenever it enters the background, so switch over to your application delegate and implement-applicationDidEnterBackground:.

```
- (void)applicationDidEnterBackground:(UIApplication *)application
{
if ([self.viewController.motionManager isAccelerometerAvailable] &&
[self.viewController.motionManager isAccelerometerActive])
    {
```

```
        [self.viewController.motionManager stopAccelerometerUpdates];
    }
if ([self.viewController.motionManager isGyroAvailable] &&
[self.viewController.motionManager isGyroActive])
    {
        [self.viewController.motionManager stopGyroUpdates];
    }
if ([self.viewController.motionManager isMagnetometerAvailable] &&
[self.viewController.motionManager isMagnetometerActive])
    {
        [self.viewController.motionManager stopMagnetometerUpdates];
    }
}
```

If you run the application now, a quick shake will start updating all your values, resulting in a view similar to that in Figure 12–8.

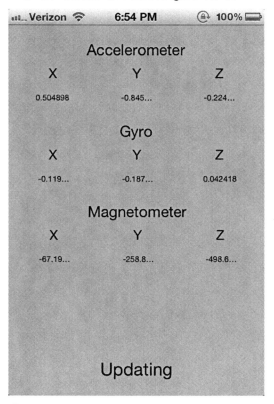

Figure 12–8. *Your application receiving raw device information*

The main problem that you will probably notice with this setup is that your data doesn't really make much sense. It is raw, biased data that isn't exactly very easy to use. Up next, you'll change your implementation around to get better using a fourth group of values you can access from CMMotionManager: CMDeviceMotion.

Just like the accelerometer, gyroscope, and magnetometer, you can access CMDeviceMotion by starting and stopping updates using very similar methods: -

startDeviceMotionUpdates and -startDeviceMotionUpdatesToQueue:withHandler:. However, you also have two extra methods on top of these that allow you to specify a "reference frame,"-startDeviceMotionUpdatesUsingReferenceFrame: and -startDeviceMotionUpdatesUsingReferenceFrame:toQueue:WithHandler:. We will go over the idea of the reference frame shortly.

When retrieving data using an instance of CMDeviceMotion (through the deviceMotion property in your CMMotionManager), you can access five different properties.

1. attitude:This property is an instance of the CMAttitude class, which gives you an incredibly detailed insight into the device's orientation at a given time as compared to a reference frame. In this class, you can access properties such as roll, pitch, and yaw. These values, measured in radians, allow you an incredibly accurate measurement of your device's orientation.

2. rotationRate:This value, measured in radians per second, is just like the previous rotationRate, but gives a more accurate reading by reducing device bias that causes a still device to have nonzero rotation values.

3. gravity:Represents the acceleration caused solely by gravity on the device

4. userAcceleration:Represents the physical acceleration imparted on a device by the user outside of gravitational acceleration

5. magneticField:This value is similar to the one you used before; however, it removes any device bias, resulting in a significantly more accurate reading than you had before.

> **NOTE:** If you are unfamiliar with them, radians are a different way of measuring rotation from the more commonly used degrees. They are based around the value pi (3.14…). A radian value of pi or roughly 3.14 is equivalent to a 180-degree rotation, so any radian value can be converted to degrees by dividing by pi, and then multiplying by 180.

You will go through your code and update it to use data only from the deviceMotion property.

Since you now have two different acceleration-based properties you can access, you'll go specifically with the gravity property. I've changed the top UILabel intheview from "Accelerometer" to "Gravity", but this is, of course, optional.

Now, your -toggleUpdates method will look like so:

```
-(void)toggleUpdates
{
if ([self.motionManager isDeviceMotionAvailable] && ![self.motionManager isDeviceMotionActive])
    {
        [self.motionManager setDeviceMotionUpdateInterval:1.0/2.0];
        [self.motionManager startDeviceMotionUpdatesToQueue:[NSOperationQueue mainQueue]
withHandler:^(CMDeviceMotion *motion, NSError *error)
```

```
          {
self.xAccLabel.text = [NSString stringWithFormat:@"%f", motion.gravity.x];
self.yAccLabel.text = [NSString stringWithFormat:@"%f", motion.gravity.y];
self.zAccLabel.text = [NSString stringWithFormat:@"%f", motion.gravity.z];

self.xGyroLabel.text = [NSString stringWithFormat:@"%f", motion.rotationRate.x];
self.yGyroLabel.text = [NSString stringWithFormat:@"%f", motion.rotationRate.y];
self.zGyroLabel.text = [NSString stringWithFormat:@"%f", motion.rotationRate.z];

self.xMagLabel.text = [NSString stringWithFormat:@"%f", motion.magneticField.field.x];
self.yMagLabel.text = [NSString stringWithFormat:@"%f", motion.magneticField.field.y];
self.zMagLabel.text = [NSString stringWithFormat:@"%f", motion.magneticField.field.z];
          }];
     }
else if ([self.motionManager isDeviceMotionActive])
     {
          [self.motionManager stopDeviceMotionUpdates];

self.xAccLabel.text = @"...";
self.yAccLabel.text = @"...";
self.zAccLabel.text = @"...";
self.xGyroLabel.text = @"...";
self.yGyroLabel.text = @"...";
self.zGyroLabel.text = @"...";
self.xMagLabel.text = @"...";
self.yMagLabel.text = @"...";
self.zMagLabel.text = @"...";
     }
}
```

You need to also change your -viewDidUnload method like so:

```
- (void)viewDidUnload
{
if ([self.motionManager isDeviceMotionAvailable] && [self.motionManager
isDeviceMotionActive])
     {
          [self.motionManager stopDeviceMotionUpdates];
     }

self.motionManager = nil;
     [self setXAccLabel:nil];
     [self setYAccLabel:nil];
     [self setZAccLabel:nil];
     [self setXGyroLabel:nil];
     [self setYGyroLabel:nil];
     [self setZGyroLabel:nil];
     [self setStatusLabel:nil];
     [self setXMagLabel:nil];
     [self setYMagLabel:nil];
     [self setZMagLabel:nil];
     [superview DidUnload];
}
```

In your application delegate, you will also update your -applicationDidEnterBackground: method.

```
- (void)applicationDidEnterBackground:(UIApplication *)application
```

```
{
if ([self.viewController.motionManager isDeviceMotionAvailable] &&
[self.viewController.motionManager isDeviceMotionActive])
    {
        [self.viewController.motionManager stopDeviceMotionUpdates];
    }
}
```

So now if you run this application, you will probably notice that most of your values are quite a bit more stable. You may also see all zeros for your magnetometer readings. Move your device in afigure-eight motion to calibrate your magnetometer until these values start updating.

Now that you have switched over to using the DeviceMotion, you will also add in fields to show your pitch, yaw, and roll from your attitude property. Update your view to resemble Figure 12–9, with your new value UILabel properties named rollLabel, pitchLabel, and yawLabel.

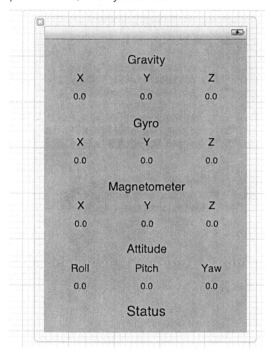

Figure 12–9. *Your new interface for displaying attitude*

Attitude Properties

For your use of the CMAttitude class, you are accessing the three simplest values you can from the class in order to determine device orientation.

1. roll: Specifies position of rotation around the yaxis

2. pitch: Specifies position of rotation around the xaxis

3. yaw: Specifies position of rotation around the zaxis

All three of these values are measured in radians, which means your displayed values will range from 0 to roughly either 3.14 or -3.14 (meaning a rotation ofpi radians, which is equal to 180 degrees).

Now you can update your -`toggleUpdates:` method again to include the new values to be displayed.

```
-(void)toggleUpdates
{
if ([self.motionManager isDeviceMotionAvailable] && ![self.motionManager
isDeviceMotionActive])
    {
        [self.motionManager setDeviceMotionUpdateInterval:1.0/2.0];
        [self.motionManager startDeviceMotionUpdatesToQueue:[NSOperationQueue mainQueue]
withHandler:^(CMDeviceMotion *motion, NSError *error)
        {
self.xAccLabel.text = [NSString stringWithFormat:@"%f", motion.gravity.x];
self.yAccLabel.text = [NSString stringWithFormat:@"%f", motion.gravity.y];
self.zAccLabel.text = [NSString stringWithFormat:@"%f", motion.gravity.z];

self.xGyroLabel.text = [NSString stringWithFormat:@"%f", motion.rotationRate.x];
self.yGyroLabel.text = [NSString stringWithFormat:@"%f", motion.rotationRate.y];
self.zGyroLabel.text = [NSString stringWithFormat:@"%f", motion.rotationRate.z];

self.xMagLabel.text = [NSString stringWithFormat:@"%f", motion.magneticField.field.x];
self.yMagLabel.text = [NSString stringWithFormat:@"%f", motion.magneticField.field.y];
self.zMagLabel.text = [NSString stringWithFormat:@"%f", motion.magneticField.field.z];

//////NEW ATTITUDE CODE
self.rollLabel.text = [NSString stringWithFormat:@"%f", motion.attitude.roll];
self.pitchLabel.text = [NSString stringWithFormat:@"%f", motion.attitude.pitch];
self.yawLabel.text = [NSString stringWithFormat:@"%f", motion.attitude.yaw];
//////END OF NEW CODE
        }];
    }
else if ([self.motionManager isDeviceMotionActive])
    {
        [self.motionManager stopDeviceMotionUpdates];

self.xAccLabel.text = @"...";
self.yAccLabel.text = @"...";
self.zAccLabel.text = @"...";
self.xGyroLabel.text = @"...";
self.yGyroLabel.text = @"...";
self.zGyroLabel.text = @"...";
self.xMagLabel.text = @"...";
self.yMagLabel.text = @"...";
self.zMagLabel.text = @"...";

//////NEW ATTITUDE CODE
self.rollLabel.text = @"...";
self.pitchLabel.text = @"...";
self.yawLabel.text = @"...";
//////END OF NEW CODE
    }
```

```
}
```

Though it's not exactly required, you will also specify a reference frame for your `attitude`, so that you have some idea of what your device is being compared to, using the `-startDeviceMotionUpdatesUsingReferenceFrame:toQueue:withHandler:`method. The reference frame parameter of this method accepts four possible values as of iOS 5.0.

- `CMAttitudeReferenceFrameXArbitraryZVertical`: Specifies a reference frame with the zaxis along the vertical and the xaxis along any arbitrary direction; more simply, the device is flat and face-up.

- `CMAttitudeReferenceFrameXArbitraryCorrectedZVertical`:This is the same as the previous value, but the magnetometer is used to provide better accuracy. This option increases CPU usage, and also requires the magnetometer to be both available and calibrated.

- `CMAttitudeReferenceFrameXMagneticNorthZVertical`: This reference frame has the zaxis vertical as before, but with the xaxis directed toward "magnetic north." This option requires the magnetometer to be available and calibrated, which means you will probably have to wave your device around a bit before you can get any readings in your application.

- `CMAttitudeReferenceFrameXTrueNorthZVertical`:This reference frame is just like the previous, but the xaxis is directed toward "true north," rather than "magnetic north." The location of the device must be available in order for the device to be able to calculate the difference between the two.

> **NOTE:** When dealing with the magnetometer, you must be sure to understand the difference between "magnetic north" and "true north."Magnetic north is the magnetic north pole of the Earth, which is where any compass will point. This point, however, is not constant due to changes in the Earth's core, moving more than 30 miles per year. True north refers to the direction toward the actual north pole of the Earth, which stays constant.

You will choose the third option, `CMAttitudeReferenceFrameXMagneticNorthZVertical`, for your application. Change your call to the `-startDeviceMotionUpdatesToQueue:withHandler:` method to the following:

```
[self.motionManager
startDeviceMotionUpdatesUsingReferenceFrame:CMAttitudeReferenceFrameXMagneticNorthZVerti
cal toQueue:[NSOperationQueue mainQueue] withHandler:^(CMDeviceMotion *motion, NSError
*error)
        {
self.xAccLabel.text = [NSString stringWithFormat:@"%f", motion.gravity.x];
self.yAccLabel.text = [NSString stringWithFormat:@"%f", motion.gravity.y];
self.zAccLabel.text = [NSString stringWithFormat:@"%f", motion.gravity.z];

self.xGyroLabel.text = [NSString stringWithFormat:@"%f", motion.rotationRate.x];
self.yGyroLabel.text = [NSString stringWithFormat:@"%f", motion.rotationRate.y];
```

```
self.zGyroLabel.text = [NSString stringWithFormat:@"%f", motion.rotationRate.z];

self.xMagLabel.text = [NSString stringWithFormat:@"%f", motion.magneticField.field.x];
self.yMagLabel.text = [NSString stringWithFormat:@"%f", motion.magneticField.field.y];
self.zMagLabel.text = [NSString stringWithFormat:@"%f", motion.magneticField.field.z];

self.rollLabel.text = [NSString stringWithFormat:@"%f", motion.attitude.roll];
self.pitchLabel.text = [NSString stringWithFormat:@"%f", motion.attitude.pitch];
self.yawLabel.text = [NSString stringWithFormat:@"%f", motion.attitude.yaw];
        }];
```

Now, when you run your application, you may start off seeing "0.0" for all your values. If you move your device around in a figure-eight motion to get your magnetometer calibrated, they should start updating soon enough. You should notice now that if you lay your device on a flat surface and then turn the device around the z axis, then at the moment that your x axis is aligned with the Earth's magnetic field, your yaw value should get very close to zero, as in Figure 12–10.

Figure 12–10. *Your application receiving calibrated device information*

Recipe 12–3: Moving a UILabel with the Accelerometer

Now that we have gone especially into detail on exactly how to access all of the data the Core Motion can provide, you can create a simple implementation to actually demonstrate its use beyond accessing values. You will simply modify your existing application, so be sure to save a new copy of your project before you continue.

You will be changing your application to utilize the gravity property that you previously accessed in order to move a UILabel around your view. To do this, you will require a very small update interval for your device motion information, so you want to minimize the actual amount of data you display. You will remove all but the statusLabel from your view, so that your user interface will look like Figure 12–11. I have changed the UILabel as well to match the instructions for your new functionality.

When you remove all the other UILabels from your view, you can leave your properties all set up in your header file from your previous recipe if you want. While it takes up a small amount of memory to still have them here, this will be fairly insignificant for your purposes.

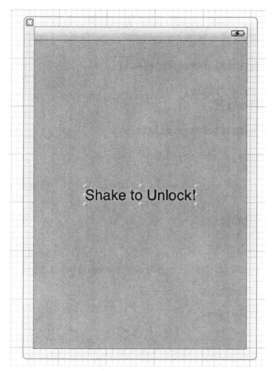

Figure 12–11. *Your re-simplified user interface for moving a* UILabel

Next, you can delete (or comment out) your line from your -toggleUpdates method that resembles the following, which sets your update interval for your CMMotionManager.

```
[self.motionManager setDeviceMotionUpdateInterval:1.0/2.0];
```

If you choose not to set an update interval, the device will default to an incredibly small value, meaning that your information will update very frequently.

You will also change your attitude's reference frame to one that does not require any calibration of the magnetometer so as to improve performance speed. Specifically, you will use the CMAttitudeReferenceFrameXArbitraryCorrectedZVertical value.

Finally, you can add in your code to retrieve the gravity values, and then adjust your UILabel's frame based on them. Overall, your –toggleUpdates method will look like so:

```
-(void)toggleUpdates
{
if ([self.motionManager isDeviceMotionAvailable] && ![self.motionManager
isDeviceMotionActive])
    {
        [self.motionManager setDeviceMotionUpdateInterval:1.0/2.0];
        [self.motionManager
startDeviceMotionUpdatesUsingReferenceFrame:CMAttitudeReferenceFrameXArbitraryCorrectedZ
Vertical toQueue:[NSOperationQueue mainQueue] withHandler:^(CMDeviceMotion *motion,
NSError *error)
        {
int scale = 5.0;
CGRect labelRect = self.statusLabel.frame;
            labelRect.origin.x += motion.gravity.x * scale;
if (!CGRectContainsRect(self.view.bounds, labelRect))
            {
                labelRect.origin.x = self.statusLabel.frame.origin.x;
            }
            labelRect.origin.y -= motion.gravity.y *scale;
if (!CGRectContainsRect(self.view.bounds, labelRect))
            {
                labelRect.origin.y = self.statusLabel.frame.origin.y;
            }
            [self.statusLabel setFrame:labelRect];
        }];
    }
else if ([self.motionManager isDeviceMotionActive])
    {
        [self.motionManager stopDeviceMotionUpdates];
    }
}
```

You can also update your -shakeDetected: method to make more sense with your text:

```
-(void)shakeDetected:(NSNotification *)paramNotification
{
if ([self.statusLabel.text isEqualToString:@"Unlocked"])
    {
self.statusLabel.text = @"Locked";
        [self toggleUpdates];
    }
else
    {
```

```
self.statusLabel.text = @"Unlocked";
      [self toggleUpdates];
   }
}
```

If your application was not linked to the CoreGraphics framework by default, you will run into a linker error, so make sure that this is done before running your app. To do this, the procedure is the same as the one you did earlier with the CoreMotion framework, but you do not need to use any actual #import statements.

Now, your newest application should give you a nice little UILabel that you can move around by tilting the device, a screenshot of which is shown in Figure 12–12.

Figure 12–12. *Your application with a UILabel moving based on the orientation of the device*

Summary

We have gone into pretty specific detail about accessing the multiple different values and information that the Core Motion framework has to offer. We were able to go from raw data to more calibrated, functional values that we were then able to translate into a mildly useful (if not slightly entertaining) application. Core Motion, however, is not a framework that can simply be an entire application in itself. You can use it to acquire values about your device, but you must then have the creativity to put them to use. From a simple application to measure the rotation speed of a person flipping, to incorporating the magnetometer into an augmented-reality application, Core Motion provides a basic framework for accessing information, which can then translate into some of the most powerful pieces of software in iOS.

Chapter 13

Data Transmission Recipes

As time has progressed and technology has developed, one of the clearest trends to be noticed is the growth in user-driven content. With the improvement of design technologies, Internet connection speeds, and network availability, the amount of data generated electronically per year has increased at a nearly unbelievable rate. The heart of this matter is based around the idea of allowing users to easily take in and re-distribute information. You can incorporate these same concepts into your development through a variety of built-in classes in order to improve the functionality and usefulness of your applications.

In this chapter, you will need only a physical device to implement texting functionality, which you will build in your first recipe. All your other functionalities will be able to be simulated.

Recipe 13–1: Composing Text Messages

Text messaging is quite easily one of the currently most incredibly popular methods of transmitting data between individuals. It's quick, easy, and powerful, and is used across nearly all age groups. In iOS you can actually incorporate text messaging into your applications in order to easily provide your users with the simple cross-application functionality that can so easily improve the overall quality of an application.

Start off by creating a new project called "SendItOut", which you will use throughout this chapter, with a class prefix "Main". Select the Single View Application template to create a simple project, as in Figure 13–1.

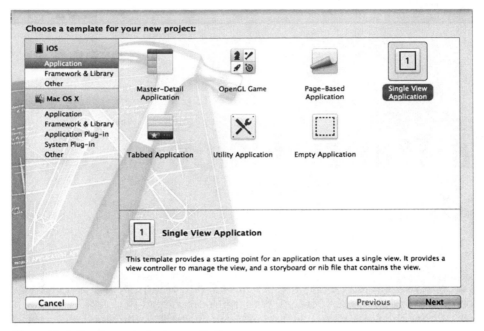

Figure 13–1. *Creating a single view application*

In order to fully demonstrate a few of the functionalities of this topic, you will specifically choose to develop your application for the iPad, rather than the iPhone. Make sure the Device Family is set accordingly in the next screen after entering the project's name. Since some of the functionalities you will test require a physical device to be fully capable, you can make this application for the iPhone as well, and simply adjust the view elements as you wish. Configure your project with the name "SendItOut", class prefix "Main", and make sure the Use Automatic Reference Counting box is checked, as in Figure 13–2.

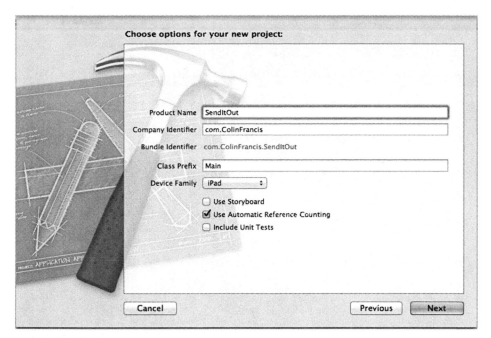

Figure 13–2. *Configuring your project settings*

After clicking through to create your project, switch over to your view controller's XIB file. In the utilities pane, set the orientation (under the Simulated Metrics section) to landscape, and make sure that the background color is set to gray.

You will start off by adding a UITextView, with the default Lorem Ipsum text, to the top half of your view, as well as a UIButton, with the label "Text Message", to the bottom. Connect these to your view controller with property names textViewInput and textButton, and connect the button to an IBAction,-textPressed:.

Before you proceed, you will go ahead and round the corners of your UITextView to improve your application's visual quality. Add the following import statement to your view controller's header file.

```
#import <QuartzCore/QuartzCore.h>
```

Next add the following line to the end of your -viewDidLoad method.

```
self.textViewInput.layer.cornerRadius = 15.0;
```

Your view should now resemble that simulated in Figure 13–3 once you rotate your simulator. This can be done through either the "Rotate Left" (⌘+left) or "Rotate Right" (⌘+right) commands found in the Hardware menu of the iOS simulator.

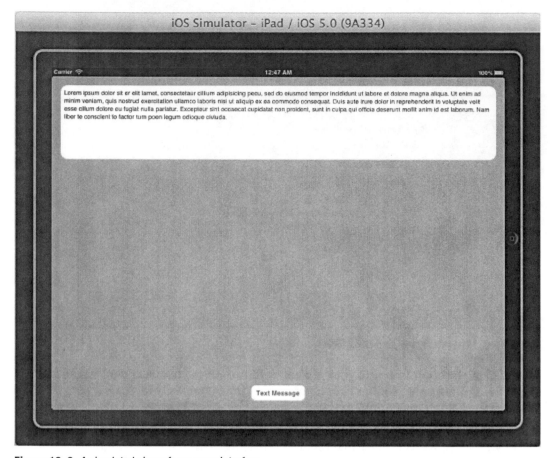

Figure 13–3. *A simulated view of your user interface*

Next, you will configure your view controller as the delegate for your UITextView. Add the following line to your -viewDidLoad method.

```
self.textViewInput.delegate = self;
```

Next, you will add the MessageUI framework to your project. Do this under the Build Phases tab of your project as usual, and add the required import statement to your view controller's header file.

```
#import <MessageUI/MessageUI.h>
```

You need to instruct your view controller to conform to certain protocols. Adjust your header file so that the UITextViewDelegate, MFMessageComposeViewControllerDelegate, and UINavigationControllerDelegate are all conformed to.

At this point, your fully set-up header file will now read like so:

```
#import <UIKit/UIKit.h>
#import <QuartzCore/QuartzCore.h>
#import <MessageUI/MessageUI.h>
```

```
@interface MainViewController : UIViewController <UITextViewDelegate,
MFMessageComposeViewControllerDelegate, UINavigationControllerDelegate>

@property (strong, nonatomic) IBOutlet UITextView *textViewInput;
@property (strong, nonatomic) IBOutlet UIButton *textButton;
-(IBAction)textPressed:(id)sender;

@end
```

Now you will implement one of your UITextView's delegate methods in order to ensure that your keyboard is properly dismissed when the user taps the Enter key.

```
- (BOOL)textView:(UITextView *)textView shouldChangeTextInRange:(NSRange)range
 replacementText:(NSString *)text
{
if ([text isEqualToString:@"\n"])
    {
        [textView resignFirstResponder];
return FALSE;
    }
return TRUE;
}
```

Now you can implement your -textPressed: method such that the text of your UITextView is transposed into a text message. You will simply set the recipient to a fake number.

```
-(void)textPressed:(id)sender
{
if ([MFMessageComposeViewController canSendText])
    {
MFMessageComposeViewController *messageVC = [[MFMessageComposeViewController alloc]
init];
        messageVC.messageComposeDelegate = self;
        messageVC.recipients = [NSArray arrayWithObject:@"3015555309"];
        messageVC.body = self.textViewInput.text;
        [self presentModalViewController:messageVC animated:YES];
    }
else
    {
NSLog(@"Error, Text Messaging Unavailable");
    }
}
```

The implementation of this method should appear fairly straightforward. After using the +canSendText method to check for texting availability, you created an instance of the MFMessageComposeViewController class, and then configured it with your fake recipient, as well as the intended text. Finally, you simply present the controller modally to allow your user to review the text message before sending it.

The MFMessageComposeViewController andits counterpart you will encounter later, the MFMailComposeViewController, are both classes that allow you to set their initial conditions and present them, but they do not allow you any control of the class once it has been shown. This is to ensure that the user has the final say in whether a message or mail sends, rather than any application sending it without informing the user.

You can implement your MFMessageComposeViewController's messageComposeDelegate method to handle the completion of the message like so:

```
-(void)messageComposeViewController:(MFMessageComposeViewController *)controller
didFinishWithResult:(MessageComposeResult)result
{
if (result == MessageComposeResultSent)
    {
self.textViewInput.text = @"Message sent.";
    }
else if (result == MessageComposeResultFailed)
    {
NSLog(@"Message Failed to Send!");
    }
    [self dismissModalViewControllerAnimated:YES];
}
```

Along with the two possible values of MessageComposeResults demonstrated in the previous code, there is a third result, MessageComposeResultCancelled, which indicates that the user cancelled the sending of the text message.

A new functionality in iOS 5.0 is the ability to receive notifications about the changing of the availability of text messaging. You can register for such notifications by adding the following line to the -viewDidLoad method:

```
[[NSNotificationCenter defaultCenter] addObserver:self
selector:@selector(availabilityChange:)
name:@"MFMessageComposeViewControllerTextMessageAvailabilityDidChangeNotification"
object:nil];
```

The selector specified here can easily be defined to simply inform you of the change. In a full application, you might likely make use of a UIAlert to notify the user of this change as well, but you will avoid this process for demonstration purposes.

```
-(void)availabilityChange:(id)sender
{
if ([MFMessageComposeViewController canSendText])
    {
NSLog(@"Text Messaging Available");
    }
else
    {
NSLog(@"Text Messaging Unavailable");
    }
}
```

Your application can now copy the body of your UITextView into a text message to be sent off to your fake recipient! If you test this, however, keep in mind that the text messaging functionality will not be available on the iOS simulator. You will have to test this on your physical device with 3G capabilities. To test this application as it is exactly, you will need a 3G-capable iPad, but you could edit the project to work for an iPhone instead.

Recipe 13–2: Composing E-mail

Just as you were able to create and configure text messages to be sent from your application, you can also use the MessageUI framework that you dealt with in the previous recipe to configure mail messages using the counterpart to the MFMessageComposeViewController class, which is known as MFMailComposeViewController.

Building upon your set-up application, you will add another button with the label "Mail". Use the property name mailButton, and assign it an action called -mailPressed:.

The setup for your -mailPressed: method is very similar to your previous -textPressed: method. You will create your composing view controller, configure it, and then present it.

```
-(void)mailPressed:(id)sender
{
if ([MFMailComposeViewController canSendMail])
    {
MFMailComposeViewController *mailVC = [[MFMailComposeViewController alloc] init];
        [mailVC setSubject:@"SendItOut"];
        [mailVC setToRecipients:[NSArray arrayWithObject:@"test@example.com"]];
        [mailVC setMessageBody:self.textViewInput.text isHTML:NO];
        mailVC.mailComposeDelegate = self;
        [self presentModalViewController:mailVC animated:YES];
    }
else
    {
NSLog(@"Error: Mail Unavailable");
    }
}
```

As you can see, the MFMailComposeViewController has a few extra properties compared to the MFMessageComposeViewController to specifically configure a more complex e-mail.

Since you set your mailComposeDelegate property to your view controller, you will need to specify that it will conform to the MFMailComposeViewControllerDelegate protocol, in addition to those already specified, so go ahead and add this to your header file.

The MFMailComposeViewControllerDelegate protocol defines only one method, which you are required to implement in order to properly handle the completed use of the view controller by the user. You will give this a simple implementation to log the result.

```
-(void)mailComposeController:(MFMailComposeViewController *)controller
didFinishWithResult:(MFMailComposeResult)result error:(NSError *)error
{
if (result == MFMailComposeResultSent)
NSLog(@"Mail Successfully Sent");
else if (result == MFMailComposeResultCancelled)
NSLog(@"Mail Cancelled");
else if (result == MFMailComposeResultFailed)
NSLog(@"Error, Mail Send Failed");
else if (result == MFMailComposeResultSaved)
NSLog(@"Mail Saved");
    [self dismissModalViewControllerAnimated:YES];
}
```

Now, your new application will be able to present a view controller for sending mail, as shown in Figure 13–4. Unlike the MFMessageViewController, however, you can actually test this functionality in the iOS simulator.

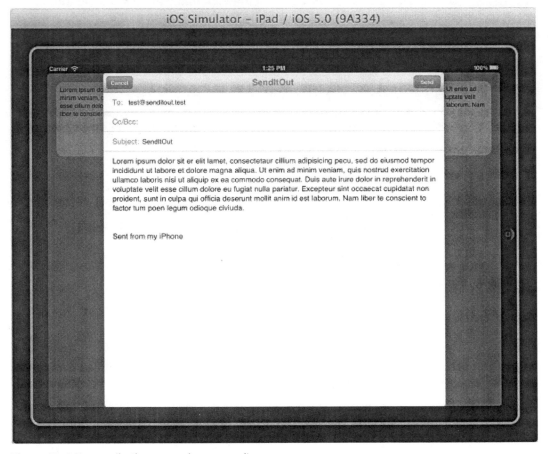

Figure 13–4. *Your application composing an e-mail*

Quite conveniently, you can easily test all the functionalities of the MFMailComposeViewController using the simulator without any fear of sending out multiple e-mails to any addresses, real or fake. The simulator will not actually send out your test messages over the Internet, so you can easily test your mailComposeDelegate method's handling of the MailComposeResults.

One additional issue that you may have to deal with when making use of the MFMailComposeViewController occurs if you allow the making of the recipients to be based on userinput. It is highly possible that a user may incorrectly format a mail address. This will not cause your application to throw an exception, though it may cause your recipient to simply be ignored by the MFMailComposeViewController. You can either format your user input to attempt to avoid this, or you can simply set up a regular expression to verify if the given address fits the required format.

Attaching Data to Mail

The MFMailComposeViewController includes functionality for you to attach data to your e-mail from your application through the use of the -addAttachmentData:mimeType:fileName: method. This method takes three parameters:

1. attachment:This instance of NSData refers to the actual data of the object that you want to send. This means for any object you want to attach, you will need to acquire the NSData for it.

2. mimeType: This property is an NSStringthat defines to the controller the data type of the attachment. These values are not local to iOS, and so are not defined in the Apple documentation. They can, however, be easily found online. Wikipedia offers a very distinct article on all the possible values athttp://en.wikipedia.org/wiki/Internet_media_type. The MIME type of a JPEG image, for example, is "image/jpeg".

3. fileName: Use this NSString property to set the preferred name for the file sent in the e-mail.

You will add functionality to your application to access the user's image library, select an image, and then use that image to attach to your e-mail.

Start off by adding a UIImageView underneath your UITextView, along with a UIButton underneath that with the label "Get Image". Your view will now resemble that simulated in Figure 13–5.

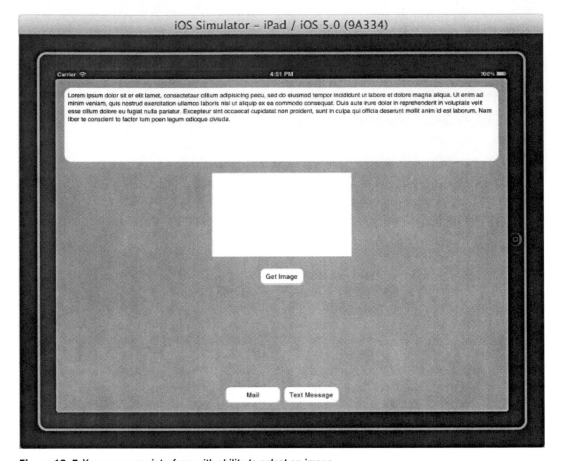

Figure 13–5. *Your new user interface with ability to select an image*

You will need properties imageViewContent andgetImageButton, along with the method -getImagePressed: for these. You will be presenting a UIPopoverController from your getImageButton, so make sure the sender type of this method is set to a UIButton* instead of id. Go ahead and make a UIImageproperty as well, called selectedImage, to store a reference to the chosen image, making sure to properly synthesize it.

Whenever you want to access the photo library of an iPad, you need to use a UIImagePickerController set inside of a UIPopoverController. You will need to create a UIPopoverController property called pop, and make sure to synthesize it as well.

Before you continue, instruct your view controller to conform to the UIImagePickerControllerDelegate and UIPopoverControllerDelegate protocols. Overall your header file should now resemble the following:

```
#import <UIKit/UIKit.h>
#import <QuartzCore/QuartzCore.h>
#import <MessageUI/MessageUI.h>
```

```
@interface MainViewController : UIViewController <UITextViewDelegate,
MFMessageComposeViewControllerDelegate, UINavigationControllerDelegate,
MFMailComposeViewControllerDelegate, UIImagePickerControllerDelegate,
UIPopoverControllerDelegate>

@property (strong, nonatomic) IBOutlet UITextView *textViewInput;
@property (strong, nonatomic) IBOutlet UIButton *textButton;
@property (strong, nonatomic) IBOutlet UIButton *mailButton;
@property (strong, nonatomic) IBOutlet UIImageView *imageViewContent;
@property (strong, nonatomic) IBOutlet UIButton *getImageButton;
@property (strong, nonatomic) UIImage *selectedImage;
@property (strong, nonatomic) UIPopoverController *pop;

-(IBAction)textPressed:(id)sender;
-(IBAction)mailPressed:(id)sender;
-(IBAction)getImagePressed:(UIButton *)sender;
///Pay close attention to the above (UIButton *) parameter type.

@end
```

If you have correctly handled all your new properties so far, your -viewDidUnload:
method should resemble the following:

```
- (void)viewDidUnload
{
    [self setPop:nil];
    [self setSelectedImage:nil];
    [self setTextViewInput:nil];
    [self setTextButton:nil];
    [self setMailButton:nil];
    [self setImageViewContent:nil];
    [self setGetImageButton:nil];
    [super viewDidUnload];
}
```

Now, you can write your -getImagePressed: method to present your popover controller
with access to the photo library.

```
-(void)getImagePressed:(UIButton *)sender
{
UIImagePickerController *picker = [[UIImagePickerController alloc] init];
if ([UIImagePickerController
isSourceTypeAvailable:UIImagePickerControllerSourceTypePhotoLibrary])
    {
        picker.sourceType = UIImagePickerControllerSourceTypePhotoLibrary;
        picker.delegate = self;

self.pop = [[UIPopoverController alloc] initWithContentViewController:picker];
pop.delegate = self;
        [pop presentPopoverFromRect:sender.frame inView:self.view
permittedArrowDirections:UIPopoverArrowDirectionAny animated:YES];
    }
}
```

Now you just need to implement your UIImagePickerControllerDelegate protocol
methods.

```
-(void)imagePickerControllerDidCancel:(UIImagePickerController *)picker
```

```
{
    [self.pop dismissPopoverAnimated:YES];
}

-(void)imagePickerController:(UIImagePickerController *)picker
didFinishPickingMediaWithInfo:(NSDictionary *)info
{
UIImage *image = [info valueForKey:@"UIImagePickerControllerOriginalImage"];
self.selectedImage = image;
self.imageViewContent.image = image;
self.imageViewContent.contentMode = UIViewContentModeScaleAspectFill;

    [self.pop dismissPopoverAnimated:YES];
}
```

At this point, your application can select an image and set it in your UIImageView. If you are testing this application in the simulator, you will need to acquire at least one image to put in your simulator's photo library. You can do this by accessing the Safari app on the simulator, finding an image online, then clicking and holding the image to save it to the library. In Figure 13–6, your app is shown with an image already selected, with the Get Image button then pressed again.

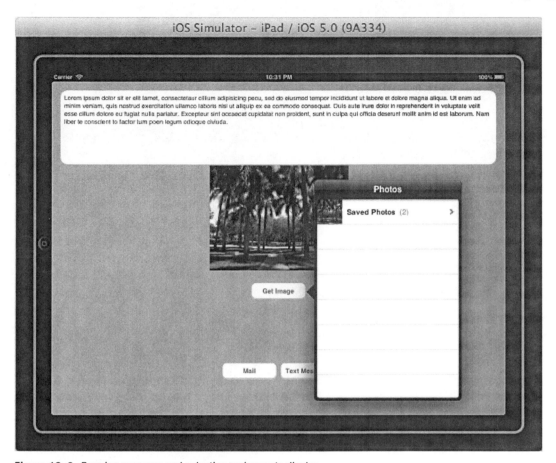

Figure 13–6. *Running your app and selecting an image to display*

Now you can continue to add the chosen image into your e-mail. You will modify your -
mailPressed: method to include attaching the image if one has been selected.

```
-(void)mailPressed:(id)sender
{
if ([MFMailComposeViewController canSendMail])
    {
MFMailComposeViewController *mailVC = [[MFMailComposeViewController alloc] init];
       [mailVC setSubject:@"SendItOut"];
       [mailVC setToRecipients:[NSArray arrayWithObject:@"test@senditout.test"]];
       [mailVC setMessageBody:self.textViewInput.text isHTML:NO];
       mailVC.mailComposeDelegate = self;

/////NEW IMAGE CODE
if (self.selectedImage != nil)
        {
NSData *imageData = UIImageJPEGRepresentation(self.selectedImage, 1.0);
          [mailVC addAttachmentData:imageData mimeType:@"image/jpeg"
fileName:@"SelectedImage"];
       }
/////END OF NEW CODE
```

```
            [self presentModalViewController:mailVC animated:YES];
    }
else
    {
NSLog(@"Error: Mail Unavailable");
    }
}
```

Finally, you can modify your `MFMailComposeViewController`'s delegate method to properly reset your application.

```
-(void)messageComposeViewController:(MFMessageComposeViewController *)controller
didFinishWithResult:(MessageComposeResult)result
{
if (result == MessageComposeResultSent)
    {
self.textViewInput.text = @"Message sent.";
self.selectedImage = nil;
self.imageViewContent.image = nil;
    }
else if (result == MessageComposeResultFailed)
    {
NSLog(@"Message Failed to Send!");
    }
    [self dismissModalViewControllerAnimated:YES];
}
```

If you test out the application in the simulator now and you attempt to send an e-mail after selecting an image, you should see the chosen image placed into your message, as in Figure 13–7.

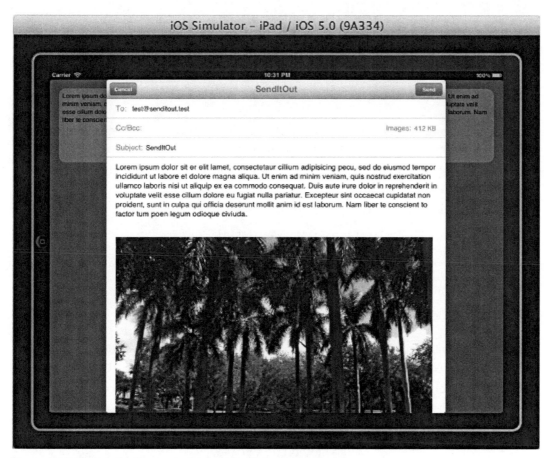

Figure 13–7. *Your application composing e-mail with an attached image*

Recipe 13–3: Printing an Image

Now that you have your application set up to be able to access both text and images, you can continue to enhance your functionality by adding the ability to print.

Before you specifically work on printing, you will reconfigure your application's user interface a bit to include your view controller inside of a UINavigationController so that you can get a nice toolbar across the top. To do this, adjust your application delegate's -application:didFinishLaunchingWithOptions method like so:

```
- (BOOL)application:(UIApplication *)application
didFinishLaunchingWithOptions:(NSDictionary *)launchOptions
{
self.window = [[UIWindow alloc] initWithFrame:[[UIScreen mainScreen] bounds]];
// Override point for customization after application launch.
self.viewController = [[MainViewController alloc] initWithNibName:@"MainViewController"
bundle:nil];

/////CHANGED CODE
```

```
__strong UINavigationController *navcon = [[UINavigationController alloc]
initWithRootViewController:self.viewController];
self.window.rootViewController = navcon;
/////END OF CHANGED CODE

    [self.window makeKeyAndVisible];
return YES;
}
```

You may also have to move up the lower buttons in your view a bit in order to make sure they aren't pushed off-screen by the navigation bar.

Add the following lines to the end of your -viewDidLoad method to configure your navigation bar.

```
self.title = @"Send It Out!";

if ([UIPrintInteractionController isPrintingAvailable])
{
UIBarButtonItem *printButton = [[UIBarButtonItem alloc]
initWithTitle:@"Print"style:UIBarButtonItemStyleBorderedtarget:self
action:@selector(printPressed:)];

self.navigationItem.rightBarButtonItem = printButton;
}
```

This condition will confirm to you that printing is possible on whichever device you run your application on before allowing the print button to be shown.

Now, you can continue on to implement your -printPressed: method in order to add your printing functionality, primarily through the use of the UIPrintInteractionController class. This class will be your "hub" of activity when it comes to configuring print jobs. You will go through and discuss the steps to setup this class individually before seeing the method as a whole.

Whenever you want to access an instance of a UIPrintInteractionController, you simply call for a reference to the shared instance through the +sharedPrintController class method.

```
UIPrintInteractionController *pic = [UIPrintInteractionController
sharedPrintController];
```

Up next, you must configure the printInfo property of your controller, which specifies the settings for the print job.

```
UIPrintInfo *printInfo = [UIPrintInfo printInfo];
printInfo.outputType = UIPrintInfoOutputPhoto;
printInfo.jobName = self.title;
printInfo.duplex = UIPrintInfoDuplexLongEdge;
```

As you can see, you have set the outputType to specify an image. The three possible values for this property are as follows:

- UIPrintInfoOutputPhoto: Used specifically for photos to be printed

- UIPrintInfoOutputGrayscale: Used when dealing only with black text so as to improve performance

▨   UIPrintInfoOutputGeneral: Used for any mix of graphics and text,
     with or without color

You did not yet set this printInfo object as the printInfo of your controller because
you will do a little bit more configuration of it shortly.

Next, you have to do an interesting specification for your
UIPrintInteractionController. I say interesting because you absolutely have to do
one, and only one, of four possible tasks:

1.   Set a single item to be printed.

2.   Set multiple items to be printed.

3.   Specify an instance of UIPrintFormatter to the controller to configure
     the layout of your page.

4.   Specify an instance of UIPrintPageRenderer, which can then have
     multiple instances of UIPrintFormatter assigned to it to gain full
     customization of your content layout over multiple pages.

You will start off with the simplest option of setting a single item to be printed. This item
must be either an image or a PDF file to use these simpler options, so you will choose to
simply print out your selectedImage.

```
UIImage *image = self.selectedImage;
pic.printingItem = image;
```

Now that you know what you want to print, you can check the orientation of the image
and configure your printInfo accordingly.

```
if (!pic.printingItem&& image.size.width> image.size.height)
    printInfo.orientation = UIPrintInfoOrientationLandscape;

pic.printInfo = printInfo;
pic.showsPageRange = YES;
```

Finally, you must simply present your UIPrintInteractionController. This class is
equipped with three different methods for presenting itself, depending on your specific
implementation.

▨   -presentFromBarButtonItem:animated:completionHandler:: If you are
     writing for an iPad, this method is designed for use when
     theapplication's Print button is placed in a toolbar, such as yours.

▨   -presentFromRect:inView:animated:completionHandler:: This method
     is also only for use with the iPad, but allows you to present the
     controller from any part of the view. Usually, the rect specified will be
     the frame of your Print button, wherever it is located.

■ -presentAnimated:completionHandler:: This method should be used whenever implementing printing on an iPhone due to the smaller screen.

With this final method call, your -printPressed:method in its entirety will look like so:

```
-(void)printPressed:(id)sender
{
if ([UIPrintInteractionController isPrintingAvailable] && (self.selectedImage != nil))
    {
UIPrintInteractionController *pic = [UIPrintInteractionController
sharedPrintController];

UIPrintInfo *printInfo = [UIPrintInfo printInfo];
        printInfo.outputType = UIPrintInfoOutputPhoto;
        printInfo.jobName = self.title;
        printInfo.duplex = UIPrintInfoDuplexLongEdge;

UIImage *image = self.selectedImage;
        pic.printingItem = image;

if (!pic.printingItem&& image.size.width> image.size.height)
            printInfo.orientation = UIPrintInfoOrientationLandscape;

        pic.printInfo = printInfo;
        pic.showsPageRange = YES;

        [pic presentFromBarButtonItem:sender animated:YES
completionHandler:^(UIPrintInteractionController *printInteractionController, BOOL
completed, NSError *error)
            {
if (!completed && (error != nil))
            {
NSLog(@"Error due to Domain: %@, Code: %@", error.domain, error.code);
            }
else
            {
NSLog(@"Printing Cancelled");
            }
        }];
    }
}
```

Now when you run your application, after selecting your image, a small controller will appear once you press the print button, from which you can select a printer and further configure your specific print job! Unfortunately, if you're testing this in your simulator or don't have any wireless printers set up, you won't see any available printers to use, as shown in Figure 13–8.

Figure 13-8. *Your app with a new Print button, unable to find any AirPrint Printers*

Luckily, when you installed the most recent version of Xcode, you were also given a fantastic application called Printer Simulator. With this program, you will be able to fully simulate print jobs from your application. It even gives you a PDF file of your simulated output, so you can see exactly how your image would have turned out without wasting any paper!

You can easily open this program by searching for it in Spotlight.

Upon running the Printer Simulator application, a variety of printer types will be automatically registered for use. It will look similar to Figure 13-9.

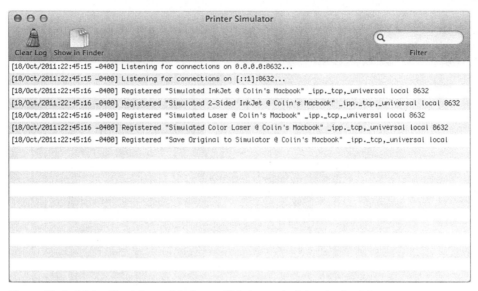

Figure 13–9. *Printer Simulator registering multiple types of printers to simulate*

Now, upon testing your application, you should see multiple different types of simulated printers with which to test your application. You can choose different types to see how your printout is affected by the style of printer, as in Figure 13–10.

Figure 13–10. *Selecting a simulated printer from your app*

Once you have selected a printer, you have the option to print multiple copies as well as change the paper type before you print. At this point, you should start seeing activity in your Printer Simulator, and shortly afterward, a PDF file will be opened with your final printout, resembling that shown in Figure 13–11.

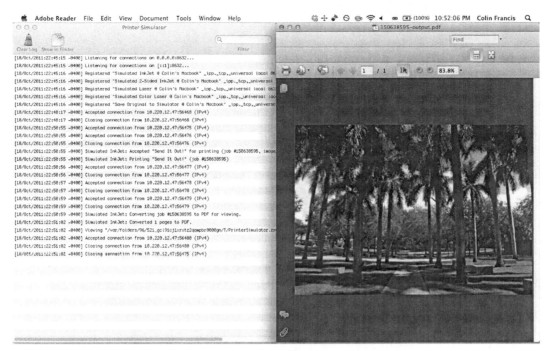

Figure 13–11. *Output of printing an image from a simulated printer*

Recipe 13–4: Printing Plain Text

Expanding on your previous recipe, you will add functionality to make use of a print formatter to allow you to print simple text.

First, you will modify your -viewDidLoad method to add an extra button to print the text in your UITextView. Change the condition statement in the method that you've already made to look like so:

```
if ([UIPrintInteractionController isPrintingAvailable])
    {
UIBarButtonItem *printButton = [[UIBarButtonItemalloc] initWithTitle:@"Print Image"
style:UIBarButtonItemStyleBordered target:self action:@selector(printPressed:)];

UIBarButtonItem *printTextButton = [[UIBarButtonItem alloc] initWithTitle:@"Print Text"
style:UIBarButtonItemStyleBordered target:self action:@selector(printTextPressed:)];

self.navigationItem.rightBarButtonItems = [NSArray arrayWithObjects:printButton,
printTextButton, nil];
    }
```

The new selector to print your text will then be implemented asfollows:

```
-(void)printTextPressed:(id)sender
{
if ([UIPrintInteractionController isPrintingAvailable])
    {
```

```
UIPrintInteractionController *pic = [UIPrintInteractionController
sharedPrintController];

UIPrintInfo *printInfo = [UIPrintInfo printInfo];
        printInfo.outputType = UIPrintInfoOutputGeneral;
        printInfo.jobName = self.title;
        printInfo.duplex = UIPrintInfoDuplexLongEdge;
        pic.printInfo = printInfo;

UISimpleTextPrintFormatter *simpleTextPF = [[UISimpleTextPrintFormatter alloc]
initWithText:self.textViewInput.text];
        simpleTextPF.startPage = 0;
        simpleTextPF.contentInsets = UIEdgeInsetsMake(72.0, 72.0, 72.0, 72.0);
        simpleTextPF.maximumContentWidth = 6*72.0;

        pic.printFormatter = simpleTextPF;

        pic.showsPageRange = YES;

        [pic presentFromBarButtonItem:sender animated:YES
completionHandler:^(UIPrintInteractionController *printInteractionController, BOOL
completed, NSError *error)
            {
if (!completed && (error != nil))
            {
NSLog(@"Error due to Domain: %@, Code: %@", error.domain, error.code);
            }
else
            {
NSLog(@"Printing Cancelled");
            }
        }];
    }
}
```

There are two main differences between this method and its predecessor:

1. The outputType property in your UIPrintInfo is modified to the
    UIPrintInfoOutputGeneral value, since you are no longer printing photos.

2. Instead of setting a UIImage to the printingItem property, you set an instance of
    UISimpleTextPrintFormatter to the printFormatter property. This object is
    initialized with the desired text, and then configured through its properties.

    a. Values of 72.0 as insets translate to 1inch, so you have given
        your output 1-inch insets, and specified a 6-inch width for your
        content.

    b. The statePageproperty will be used more at a later point, but
        allows you to specify the page in your job for your formatter to
        be applied to.

When printing simple text, it is also quite easy to apply the preceding method to printing
out HTML-formatted text. To do this, simply make use of a UIMarkupTextPrintFormatter
instead of a UISimpleTextPrintFormatter.

Just as before, by using the Printer Simulator, you can generate your test output. Since you set your text view's text as the content of your print formatter, you will simply get a document with some Lorem Ipsum text in it, as in Figure 13–12.

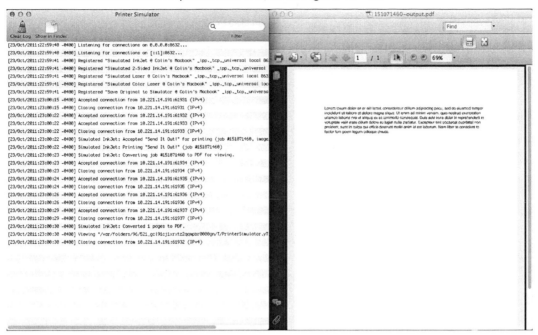

Figure 13–12. *Output of the simulated printing of a simple text page*

Recipe 13–5: Printing a View

Just as you can print text using a `UISimpleTextPrintFormatter`, you are easily able to print the contents of a view using another subclass of `UIPrintFormatter`: `UIViewPrintFormatter`.

Start by modifying your -`viewDidLoad`'s conditional setup to now appear like so:

```
if ([UIPrintInteractionController isPrintingAvailable])
    {
UIBarButtonItem *printButton = [[UIBarButtonItem alloc] initWithTitle:@"Print Image"
style:UIBarButtonItemStyleBorderedtarget:self action:@selector(printPressed:)];

UIBarButtonItem *printTextButton = [[UIBarButtonItem alloc] initWithTitle:@"Print Text"
style:UIBarButtonItemStyleBordered target:self action:@selector(printTextPressed:)];

UIBarButtonItem *printViewButton = [[UIBarButtonItem alloc] initWithTitle:@"Print View"
style:UIBarButtonItemStyleBordered target:self action:@selector(printViewPressed:)];

self.navigationItem.rightBarButtonItems = [NSArray arrayWithObjects:printButton,
printTextButton, printViewButton, nil];
    }
```

Your newest printing method,-printViewPressed:, will closely resemble your previous one, with the key change of using a UIViewPrintFormatter.

```
-(void)printViewPressed:(id)sender
{
if ([UIPrintInteractionController isPrintingAvailable])
    {
UIPrintInteractionController *pic = [UIPrintInteractionController
sharedPrintController];

UIPrintInfo *printInfo = [UIPrintInfo printInfo];
        printInfo.outputType = UIPrintInfoOutputGeneral;
        printInfo.jobName = self.title;
        printInfo.duplex = UIPrintInfoDuplexLongEdge;
        printInfo.orientation = UIPrintInfoOrientationLandscape;
        pic.printInfo = printInfo;

UIViewPrintFormatter *viewPF = [self.textViewInput viewPrintFormatter];

        pic.printFormatter = viewPF;
        pic.showsPageRange = YES;

        [pic presentFromBarButtonItem:sender animated:YES
completionHandler:^(UIPrintInteractionController *printInteractionController, BOOL
completed, NSError *error)
        {
if (!completed && (error != nil))
        {
NSLog(@"Error due to Domain: %@, Code: %@", error.domain, error.code);
        }
else
        {
NSLog(@"Printing Cancelled");
        }
        }];
    }
}
```

Unfortunately, the UIViewPrintFormatter is, at the moment, currently configured only to provide printing views of three system views: UITextView, UIWebView, and MKMapView (from the MapKit framework as discussed in Chapter 4). Since your application makes use of only one of these, you will simply have it print your UITextView's view, resulting in an output like that in Figure 13–13.

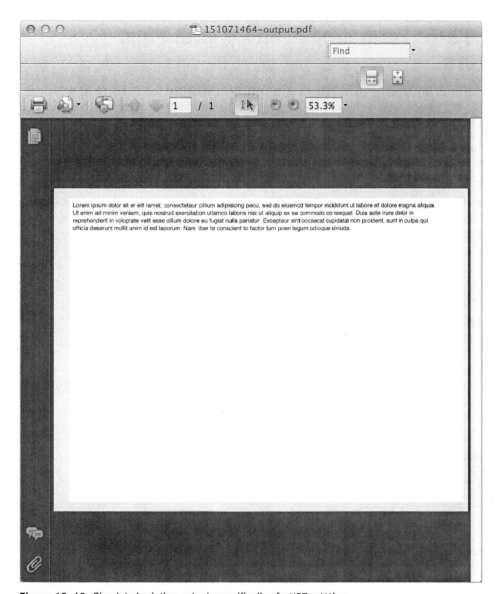

Figure 13–13. *Simulated printing output, specifically of a* `UITextView`

Despite the `UIViewPrintFormatter`'s limitations, it can be an incredibly easy to way easily print out the contents of any text, map, or web page.

Recipe 13–6: Formatted Printing with Page Renderers

A page renderer is essentially what allows you to fully customize the content of any print job. It allows you to not only format multiple pages with different print formatters, but also draw custom content in the header, body, and footer of any page.

In order to use a page renderer, you must create a custom subclass of the UIPrintPageRenderer class, from which you can override methods to customize the content of your printing job.

Create a new file, using the Objective-C class template. When you enter your file name of "SendItOutPageRenderer", make sure that the file will be a subclass of UIPrintPageRenderer, as in Figure 13–14.

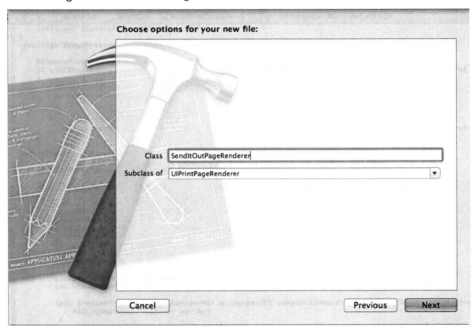

Figure 13–14. *Creating a UIPrintPageRenderer subclass*

Click through to create your new file.

Next, define two NSString properties, title and author, to be printed in the header of your renderer.

```
#import <UIKit/UIKit.h>

@interface SendItOutPageRenderer : UIPrintPageRenderer

@property (nonatomic, strong) NSString *title;
@property (nonatomic, strong) NSString *author;

@end
```

In order to customize the layout of your specific page renderer, you can override methods inherited from the UIPrintPageRenderer class. The way that this class is set up is that the -drawPageAtIndex:inRect: method then calls four other methods:

- -drawHeaderForPageAtIndex:inRect:: Used to specify header content; if the headerHeight property of the renderer is zero, this method will not be called.

- -drawContentForPageAtIndex:inRect:: Draws custom content within the page's content rectangle

- -drawFooterForPageAtIndex:inRect:: Specifies footer content; this method will also not be called if the renderer's footerHeight property is zero.

- -drawPrintFormatter:forPageAtIndex::Uses a combination of print formatters and custom content to overlay or fill in a view

You are able to override any of these five methods (including -drawPageAtIndex:inRect:) in order to customize your printing content. In your case, you will override the header, footer, and print-formatter methods.

You will have your header print out the document's author on the left, and the title on the right. Your method will then look like so:

```
- (void)drawHeaderForPageAtIndex:(NSInteger)pageIndex  inRect:(CGRect)headerRect
{
if (pageIndex != 0)
    {
UIFont *font = [UIFont fontWithName:@"Helvetica"size:12.0];
CGSize titleSize = [self.title sizeWithFont:font];

CGFloat drawXTitle = CGRectGetMaxX(headerRect) - titleSize.width;
CGFloat drawXAuthor = CGRectGetMinX(headerRect);
CGFloat drawY = CGRectGetMinY(headerRect);
CGPoint drawPointAuthor = CGPointMake(drawXAuthor, drawY);
CGPoint drawPointTitle = CGPointMake(drawXTitle, drawY);

        [self.title drawAtPoint:drawPointTitle withFont:font];
        [self.author drawAtPoint:drawPointAuthor withFont:font];
    }
}
```

Your footer-implementation method will look similar, and will print out a centered page number. Since the page indexes start with 0, you must remember to increment all your values by 1.

```
- (void)drawFooterForPageAtIndex:(NSInteger)pageIndex inRect:(CGRect)footerRect
{
UIFont *font = [UIFont fontWithName:@"Helvetica"size:12.0];
NSString *pageNumber = [NSString stringWithFormat:@"%d.", pageIndex+1];

CGSize pageNumSize = [pageNumber sizeWithFont:font];
CGFloat drawX = CGRectGetMaxX(footerRect)/2.0 - pageNumSize.width - 1.0;
CGFloat drawY = CGRectGetMaxY(footerRect) - pageNumSize.height;
CGPoint drawPoint = CGPointMake(drawX, drawY);
```

```
        [pageNumber drawAtPoint:drawPoint withFont:font];
}
```

Finally, to deal with interlaced print formatters, you will implement the -drawPrintFormatter:forPageAtIndex: method to overlay a simple text over your view. This could easily be used to place some kind of "Proprietary Content" label over images or documents in a more targeted application.

```
-(void)drawPrintFormatter:(UIPrintFormatter *)printFormatter
forPageAtIndex:(NSInteger)pageIndex
{
CGRect contentRect = CGRectMake(self.printableRect.origin.x,
self.printableRect.origin.y+self.headerHeight, self.printableRect.size.width,
self.printableRect.size.height-self.headerHeight-self.footerHeight);
    [printFormatter drawInRect:contentRect forPageAtIndex:pageIndex];

NSString *overlayText = @"Overlay Text";
UIFont *font = [UIFont fontWithName:@"Helvetica"size:26.0];
CGSize overlaySize = [overlayText sizeWithFont:font];

CGFloat xCenter = CGRectGetMaxX(self.printableRect)/2.0 - overlaySize.width/2.0;
CGFloat yCenter = CGRectGetMaxY(self.printableRect)/2.0 - overlaySize.height/2.0;
CGPoint overlayPoint = CGPointMake(xCenter, yCenter);

    [overlayText drawAtPoint:overlayPoint withFont:font];
}
```

In this method, it is important to note that you must draw the content of each printFormattermanually using its own -drawInRect:forPageAtIndex: method. In order to avoid covering your header or footer, you specified a drawing area restricted by the headerHeight and footerHeight.

Now, back in your main view controller, make sure to import the newly created SendItOutPageRenderer.h file.

```
#import "SendItOutPageRenderer.h"
```

Add a final extra UIBarButtonItem to present a Print Custom option to your user. Including all functions from your previous recipes, your -viewDidLoad method should now read like so:

```
- (void)viewDidLoad
{
    [super viewDidLoad];

    [[NSNotificationCenter defaultCenter] addObserver:self
selector:@selector(availabilityChange:)
name:@"MFMessageComposeViewControllerTextMessageAvailabilityDidChangeNotification"
object:nil];

self.textViewInput.layer.cornerRadius = 15.0;
self.textViewInput.delegate = self;

self.title = @"Send It Out!";

if ([UIPrintInteractionController isPrintingAvailable])
    {
```

```objectivec
UIBarButtonItem *printButton = [[UIBarButtonItem alloc] initWithTitle:@"Print Image"
style:UIBarButtonItemStyleBordered target:self action:@selector(printPressed:)];

UIBarButtonItem *printTextButton = [[UIBarButtonItem alloc] initWithTitle:@"Print Text"
style:UIBarButtonItemStyleBordered target:self action:@selector(printTextPressed:)];

UIBarButtonItem *printViewButton = [[UIBarButtonItem alloc] initWithTitle:@"Print View"
style:UIBarButtonItemStyleBordered target:self action:@selector(printViewPressed:)];

UIBarButtonItem *printCustomButton = [[UIBarButtonItem alloc] initWithTitle:@"Print
Custom" style:UIBarButtonItemStyleBordered target:self
action:@selector(printCustomPressed:)];

self.navigationItem.rightBarButtonItems = [NSArray arrayWithObjects:printButton,
printTextButton, printViewButton, printCustomButton, nil];
    }
}
```

Finally, you can implement your -printCustomPressed: action.

```objectivec
-(void)printCustomPressed:(id)sender
{
if ([UIPrintInteractionControllerisPrintingAvailable])
    {
UIPrintInteractionController *pic = [UIPrintInteractionController
sharedPrintController];

UIPrintInfo *printInfo = [UIPrintInfoprintInfo];
        printInfo.outputType = UIPrintInfoOutputGeneral;
        printInfo.jobName = self.title;
        printInfo.duplex = UIPrintInfoDuplexLongEdge;
        printInfo.orientation = UIPrintInfoOrientationPortrait;
        pic.printInfo = printInfo;

UISimpleTextPrintFormatter *simplePF = [[UISimpleTextPrintFormatter alloc]
initWithText:[self.textViewInput.text stringByAppendingString:@"THIS TEXT IS MY FIRST
PAGE"]];
UIViewPrintFormatter *viewPF = [self.textViewInputview PrintFormatter];

SendItOutPageRenderer *sendPR = [[SendItOutPageRendereralloc] init];
        sendPR.title = @"My Print Job Title";
        sendPR.author = @"Document Author";
        sendPR.headerHeight = 72.0/2;
        sendPR.footerHeight = 72.0/2;
        [sendPR addPrintFormatter:simplePF startingAtPageAtIndex:0];
        [sendPR addPrintFormatter:viewPF startingAtPageAtIndex:1];

        pic.printPageRenderer = sendPR;

        pic.showsPageRange = YES;

        [pic presentFromBarButtonItem:sender animated:YES
completionHandler:^(UIPrintInteractionController *printInteractionController, BOOL
completed, NSError *error)
            {
if (!completed && (error != nil))
                {
NSLog(@"Error due to Domain: %@, Code: %@", error.domain, error.code);
```

```
            }
    else
            {
    NSLog(@"Printing Cancelled");
            }
        }];
    }
}
```

This method includes the following extra steps from your previous recipe:

1. Create multiple print formatters to be given to different pages. Since you do not have a UIWebView or MKMapView in this application, you have simply chosen to print your UITextView's text, as well as its overall view.

2. Create an instance of your SendItOutPageRenderer class, and configure it with a title, author, headerHeight, and footerHeight. If you did not specify the last two of these, your header and footer customization methods would not be called.

3. Add your print formatters to your page renderer, and assign this renderer to your UIPrintInteractionController.

Upon testing this new functionality, your output will be a two-page text document, complete with simple headers, footers, and even a text overlay, as shown in Figure 13–15.

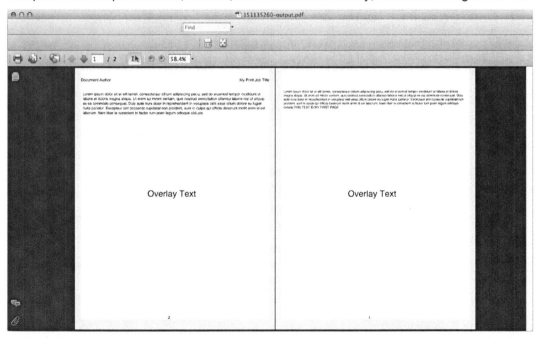

Figure 13–15. *Simulated printing output with a page renderer and multiple print formatters*

Due to the simplicity of your application, the screenshot in Figure 13–15may not look like much, but considering your application of custom headers, footers, overlay content, and page formatters, it actually gives a very good representation of the power of making use of a page renderer for printing when striving for ideal customizations.

Summary

You are responsible, when creating your applications, to always have the user in mind. Every single aspect of your application should be designed to both allow and helpthe user to accomplish a goal, and each aspect should then be optimized to expedite these goals. Functionalities to transmit data, such as sending text messages, constructing e-mails, or creating printouts, tend to be overlooked as unnecessary in this process, and most often erroneously. Developers must always be careful to think from the user's standpoint, and imagine what a user could do with any given feature. The simple possibility of printing content for later use, or being able to easily e-mail an interesting image to a friend, could easily be the dividing line between what makes a customer buy your app over someone else's. By understanding and utilizing these "extra" functionalities, you are able to drastically improve the functionality of your applications in order to better serve your endusers.

Chapter 14

Twitter Recipes

Since its incipience, the Twitter service has been rapidly expanding as a means of communication, advertising, and even organization. Its use has become widespread throughout modern technology and entertainment, allowing an unprecedented amount of masscommunication. With the release of iOS 5.0, the addition of a Twitter framework allows developers to work and program more efficiently with this incredible interface. This has opened up a whole category of app possibilities, from sending simple tweets to analyzing trending topics to suggesting articles to a user. By utilizing this framework in our applications, we are able to incorporate a variety of functionalities into our applications that allow us to communicate with the Twitter service, allowing users to contribute further to the ever-growing worldwide network of communication.

Recipe 14–1: Composing Simple Tweets

The core foundation of the Twitter service is the idea of sending "tweets". These are composed of quick bits of information, limited to 140 characters, and sometimes accompanied by an image or outside link. In the Twitter framework, you are able to access a pre-configured class that can easily send out these messages.

When making use of the Twitter framework, any functionality you build that revolves around accessing a specific Twitter account for sending or retrieving information will not actually work on your iOS simulator, as you cannot connect it to a Twitter account. Therefore, you will opt to test all of your Twitter-based recipes on a physical device.

In order to test those functionalities that require an account on your device, you need to make sure that your device is configured with at least one Twitter account. You can create an account through the Twitter website, or through the Twitter iOS app. Once you have an account, you must provide your device with your login information. This configuration can be accessed from your Settings app on your device, and will resemble Figure 14–1.

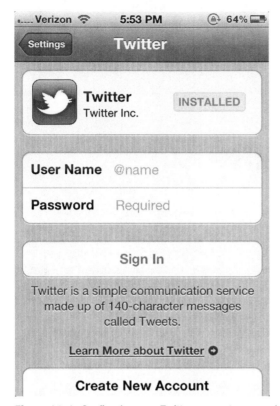

Figure 14–1. *Configuring your Twitter account on your device*

By having a Twitter account configured with your device, you will be able to fully test all the functionality that you will create.

Next, you start by creating a new project called "Tweeter" in Xcode. Select the SingleView Application template, and then click through to create your project. If you are running the newest version of Xcode, make sure also that the box marked "Automatic Reference Counting" is checked, as in Figure 14–2.

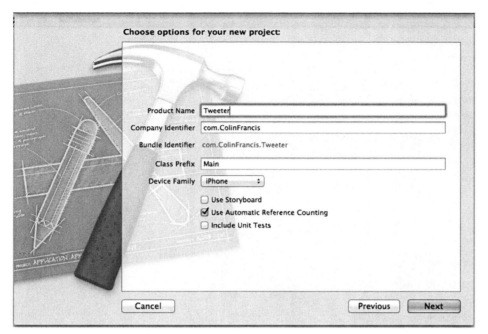

Figure 14–2. *Configuring project settings*

For all the recipes in this chapter, you need to include the Twitter framework into your project.

After selecting your project, navigate to the Build Phases tab, and in the section marked "Link Binary With Libraries, click the + button. Find the item called `Twitter.framework`, and add it, as shown in Figure 14–3.

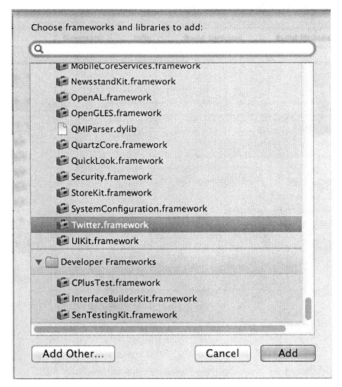

Figure 14–3. *Adding the Twitter framework*

You will also later need the Accounts framework, so repeat this process, adding the item called `Accounts.framework`.

Add import statements to your view controller's header file so that the compiler allows you to use your added frameworks.

```
#import <Twitter/Twitter.h>
#import <Accounts/Accounts.h>
```

Next you will set up your initial user interface. Add a `UIButton` to your view, and connect it to your controller using theproperty name `simpleTweetButton`. Connect it to an `IBAction` method called `-simpleTweetPressed:`, as shown in Figure 14–4.

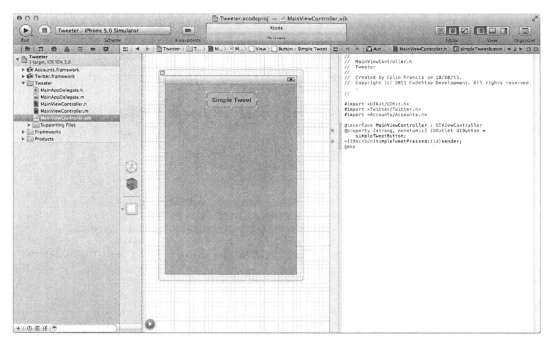

Figure 14–4. *Setting up a simple user interface*

Let's set up a convenience method to check if your application can send a tweet at any given moment. If not, you will disable and dim your UIButton.

```
-(BOOL)checkCanTweet
{
if ([TWTweetComposeViewController canSendTweet])
    {
self.simpleTweetButton.enabled = YES;
self.simpleTweetButton.alpha = 1.0;
return YES;
    }
else
    {
self.simpleTweetButton.enabled = NO;
self.simpleTweetButton.alpha = 0.6;
return NO;
    }
}
```

This method makes use of the +canSendTweet class method of TWTweetComposeViewController. You will be using this class to allow creation of simple tweets shortly.

In order to make sure your view controller correctly rechecks your functionality, you will place a call to this function in both -viewDidLoad and -viewWillAppear:animated:.

```
[self checkCanTweet];
```

It is also possible that the device your application is on could have a Twitter account configured at any moment, so you can also register for notifications to be sent upon the changing of account information. Add the following line to your -viewDidLoad method.

```
[[NSNotificationCenter defaultCenter] addObserver:self selector:@selector(checkCanTweet)
name:ACAccountStoreDidChangeNotification object:nil];
```

Now you will implement your -simpleTweetPressed: method to configure and send a simple tweet.

```
-(void)simpleTweetPressed:(id)sender
{
if ([self checkCanTweet])
    {
TWTweetComposeViewController *tweet = [[TWTweetComposeViewController alloc] init];
        [tweet setInitialText:@"Posting a simple Tweet from my app!"];
        [tweet setCompletionHandler:^(TWTweetComposeViewControllerResult result)
        {
if (result == TWTweetComposeViewControllerResultDone)
        {
NSLog(@"Tweet Successfully Sent");
        }
else
        {
NSLog(@"Tweet Cancelled");
        }
        [self dismissModalViewControllerAnimated:YES];
    }];
        [self presentModalViewController:tweet animated:YES];
    }
}
```

As shown here, you can create an initial text for your tweet, as well as set a completion handler to be called after your TWTweetComposeViewController is either cancelled or completed.

You are able to add, in addition to your initial text, images and links to be attached to your tweets by using the -addImage:and addURL: methods. Figure 14–5 demonstrates your current configuration, along with an added link.

Figure 14–5. *Your view presenting a* `TWTweetComposeViewController`

The three methods that are used to add content to your tweet, -setInitialText:,-addImage:, and -addURL:, all return BOOL values indicating whether the content was successfully added. These values will be NO if either the content does not fit in the tweet, or if the controller has already been presented.

In order to ensure that the users always have the last say in what is sent in a tweet from this controller, the developer is not allowed to set or add any content once it has been presented.

If at any point you wish to remove content from a controller before it is presented, you can make use of the -removeAllImages and -removeAllURLsmethods.

Recipe 14–2: Creating Simple TWRequests

Aside from the TWTweetComposeViewController, the only other class in the Twitter framework is the TWRequest class. This class is incredibly general, and makes use of Twitter's specific API in order to send and request information. Through its use, you can mimic the basic function of the TWTweetComposeViewController, as well as perform nearly any command you want to incorporateinyour application with the Twitter service.

It is important to remember that the Twitter API changes differently from the iOS API, so any Twitter-specific code in this section may have to be updated to the newest version.

Sending Tweets via TWRequest

You will add another `UIButton` to your view in order to implement a more complex functionality, with label "Post Tweet", property name `postTweetButton`, and action handler `-postTweetPressed:`. Place it underneath the first button, as in Figure 14–6.

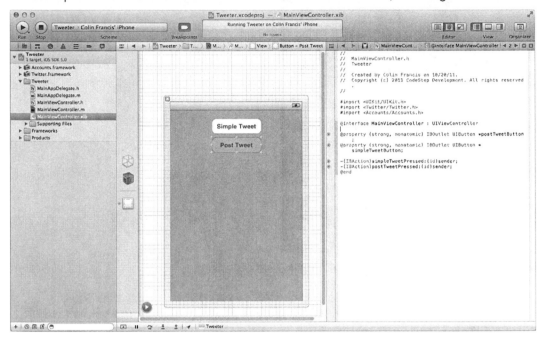

Figure 14–6. *Adding another button to your interface*

You will implement your `-postTweetPressed:`.This method will contain the following steps:

1. Access the device's account store, which has access to any accounts registered with the device.

2. Create an instance of `ACAccountType` to specify in your request for all stored Twitter accounts.

3. Request access to all accounts of the specified type. The `-requestAccessToAccountsWithType:withCompletionHandler:` method will prompt the user as to whether the application has permission to access the accounts. If permission has already been acquired by the application previously, the user will not be prompted.

4. Access an array of `ACAccount` objects from the account store referencing all registered Twitter accounts on the device.

5. Access a specific account to post with.

6. Initialize an instance of `TWRequest`. This class is given instructions as to the specific request being formed.

7. Set your chosen `ACAccount` to the `TWRequest`.

8. Perform your request and utilize your completion handler to analyze the results.

```
-(IBAction)postTweetPressed:(id)sender
{
ACAccountStore *accountStore = [[ACAccountStore alloc] init];

ACAccountType *accountType = [accountStore
accountTypeWithAccountTypeIdentifier:ACAccountTypeIdentifierTwitter];

    [accountStore requestAccessToAccountsWithType:accountType
withCompletionHandler:^(BOOL granted, NSError *error)
    {
if (granted)
    {
NSArray *accountsArray = [accountStore accountsWithAccountType:accountType];

if ([accountsArray count] >0)
        {
ACAccount *twitterAccount = [accountsArray objectAtIndex:0];

TWRequest *postRequest = [[TWRequest alloc] initWithURL:[NSURLURL
WithString:@"http://api.twitter.com/1/statuses/update.json"] parameters:[NSDictionary
dictionaryWithObject:@"Posted with a TWRequest!"forKey:@"status"]
requestMethod:TWRequestMethodPOST];

            [postRequest setAccount:twitterAccount];

            [postRequest performRequestWithHandler:^(NSData *responseData,
NSHTTPURLResponse *urlResponse, NSError *error)
            {
if ([urlResponse statusCode] == 200)
                {
NSLog(@"Tweet Posted");
                }
else
                {
NSLog(@"Error Posting Tweet");
                }
            }];
        }
    }
    }];
}
```

The key component to this method is, of course, the initialization of the `TWRequest`. Here you have made careful use of the Twitter API in order to configure your tweet post with three properties:

- ▪ *URL*: The string used to make your URL,
  `http://api.twitter.com/1/statuses/update.json`, is specially used to
  inform the Twitter service that you are initiating a status update.

- ▪ *Parameters*:Youspecify an instance of `NSDictionary` with a single key
  "status", to which you assign an `NSString` with the actual text of your
  tweet.

- ▪ *Request method*: This parameter specifies the type of request that you
  are making. Since you are posting a tweet, you use the
  `TWRequestMethodPOST` value.

The interesting thing about posting tweets using this method is that your user does not
actually get a preview of the tweet before it is sent. In fact, the only indication the user
receives in this case is the request for access to the Twitter account. It is important to
keep the user's best interests in mind when sending such posts, so as not to post
unwanted updates.

> **NOTE:** As shown in the preceding method, you can evaluate the results of a `TWRequest` by
> checking the `statusCode` of the `urlResponse`. If this value is 200, the request was
> successfully completed. Otherwise, there was some sort of error. Refer to the Twitter API at
> `https://dev.twitter.com/docs/error-codes-responses`for specific details on all the
> various error codes.

Upon testing this app, you will be able to, after requiring permission, send tweets from
your device's registered account without using the `TWTweetComposeViewController`.

Recipe 14–3: Retrieving Tweets

Now that you have covered two different methods with which you can post updates to
Twitter, you can apply the concepts used in the previous recipe, revolving around the
`TWRequest` class, in order to build an application that can acquire and display tweets.

You will build an application to display multiple different groups of tweets, so you will
use a `UITabBarController` to keep your content groups separate. Open up a new
project, and start off by selecting the Tabbed Application template, as in Figure 14–7.

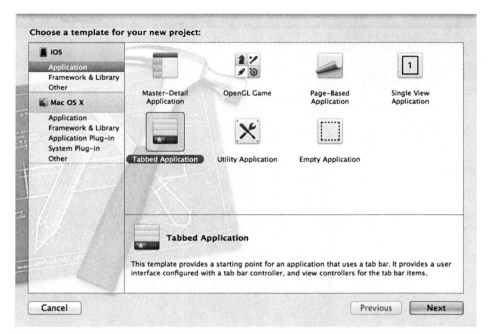

Figure 14–7. *Creating a tabbed application*

On the next screen, enter your project name. Since you will be displaying groups of tweets from a variety of sources, name your project "PulseOfTheWorld" with the class prefix of "Main". Make sure your application is configured for the iPhone device family and that Automatic Reference Counting is enabled, so that your project settings are the same as those in the previous recipe. Click through to create your project.

The template application will resemble that simulated here. Luckily for you, this layout is exactly how you will start your application off, as demonstrated in Figure 14–8, so you can display the raw data acquired from Twitter.

Figure 14–8. *Your generic tabbed application*

> **NOTE:** Since you have created a template application with two view controllers that you will format similarly, the following configuration will include changes made to both controllers simultaneously. Make sure to follow carefully and make all necessary changes to each view controller.

You will first need to configure your user interface to be programmatically editable, so first go into the XIB file for each of your two pre-made view controllers and connect both the UILabel and UITextView to properties in your header files. You will use the respective property names publicLabel and publicTextView in the first view controller, and homeLabelandhomeTextView in the second view controller.

You can change the initial text of your view elements to fit your application a bit more. Add the following lines to the -viewDidLoad of your first view controller.

```
self.publicLabel.text = @"Public Timeline";
self.publicTextView.text = @"Public Timeline data not retrieved yet.";
```

Add the equivalent lines of code to your second view controller.

```
self.homeLabel.text = @"Home Timeline";
self.homeTextView.text = @"Home Timeline data not retrieved yet.";
```

You'll also add a UIButton to each of your view controllers to actually trigger your application to retrieve data. Name each button either "Get Public Timeline" or "Get Home Timeline" as appropriate, and connect them to IBAction methods with handlers - publicPressed: and -homePressed as well as to properties publicButton and homeButton.

Before you proceed, you need to make sure to include your Twitter and Accounts frameworks in your project. Follow the same procedure discussed in the previous recipes to add them both, and make sure the correct import statements are added to both view controllers.

```
#import <Twitter/Twitter.h>
#import <Accounts/Accounts.h>
```

Back in the XIB file, you need to slightly customize your UITextViews to work correctly with your application. Make sure that for each UITextView the box marked "User Interaction Enabled" is checked, as in Figure 14–9, in order to allow the views to scroll.

Figure 14–9. *Enabling user interaction for your* UITextViews

Now make sure to set each UITextView's text alignment to the left, so that your raw data is slightly more readable. I have also increased the size of these views so as to be able to display more information at once.

At this point, your views should resemble Figure 14–10, with appropriately different text for each controller.

Figure 14–10. *Your configured user interface*

Also following is the header code for the first view controller that your program should now resemble. The second view controller's header file should be identical aside from the different property and action names.

```
#import <UIKit/UIKit.h>
#import <Twitter/Twitter.h>
#import <Accounts/Accounts.h>

@interface MainFirstViewController : UIViewController
@property (strong, nonatomic) IBOutlet UILabel *publicLabel;
@property (strong, nonatomic) IBOutlet UITextView *publicTextView;
@property (strong, nonatomic) IBOutlet UIButton *publicButton;
-(IBAction)publicPressed:(id)sender;
@end
```

Following the lines of your previous recipes, you will create a method to check for Twitter availability, and adjust your view accordingly. You need this method only in your second view controller, so it will look like so:

```
-(BOOL)checkCanTweet
{
if ([TWTweetComposeViewController canSendTweet])
    {
self.homeButton.enabled = YES;
self.homeButton.alpha = 1.0;
return YES;
    }
else
    {
```

```
self.homeButton.enabled = NO;
self.homeButton.alpha = 0.6;
return NO;
    }
}
```

Just as before, make sure to place a call to the -checkCanTweet method in both your -viewDidLoad and -viewWillAppear:animated: methods.

Now you can go ahead and work on implementing your methods to request your tweets. As you may have guessed, you will start off by retrieving data from the Public Timeline in your first view controller, and data from the Home Timeline in the second. In this case, the Home Timeline refers to the posts made by the current user, as well as any users they are following, as opposed to the Public Timeline, which simply shows public tweets. Because the Home Timeline is user-specific, you will need to make use of the Accounts framework again to access your device's registered Twitter account(s).

You will start off by implementing your -publicPressed: method in your first view controller to retrieve public tweets with the following code.

```
- (IBAction)publicPressed:(id)sender
{
TWRequest *postRequest = [[TWRequest alloc] initWithURL:[NSURL
URLWithString:@"http://api.twitter.com/1/statuses/public_timeline.json"]
parameters:nilrequestMethod:TWRequestMethodGET];

    [postRequest performRequestWithHandler:^(NSData *responseData, NSHTTPURLResponse
*urlResponse, NSError * error)
    {
        NSString *output;
if ([urlResponse statusCode] == 200)
        {
            NSError *jsonParsingError;
NSArray *publicTimeline = [NSJSONSerialization JSONObjectWithData:responseData
options:0error:&jsonParsingError];

            output = [NSString stringWithFormat:@"Public timeline:\n%@",
publicTimeline];
        }
else
        {
            output = [NSString stringWithFormat:@"HTTP response status: %i\n",
[urlResponse statusCode]];
        }
        [self.publicTextView performSelectorOnMainThread:@selector(setText:)
withObject:output waitUntilDone:NO];
    }];
}
```

This method can be broken down into several points:

1. Because the Public Timeline is available openly, you did not need to access a specific Twitter account to retrieve the data, so you went straight to configuring your TWRequest.

2. Similarly to your previous recipe, when creating your TWRequest, you used a URL specific to Twitter to access your intended service. The URL used here, http://api.twitter.com/1/statuses/public_timeline.json, is written to give you the data from the Public Timeline specifically in the JSON format (as specified by the "json" suffix).

3. Also when configuring the TWRequest, you must specify the "request method" value TWRequestMethodGET, instead of the previous TWRequestMethodPOST. The easiest way to view this is that you use the "GET" value to retrieve information, and the "POST" value to send.

4. After confirming the successful response, you have to convert your received data into a useful iOS format. Since you specified your data to use the JSON format, you can make use of the NSJSONSerialization class method +JSONObjectWithData:options:error:. This method converts your received JSON data into either an NSDictionary or NSArray, depending on the format. In this case, you receive an NSArray, whose contents you then place into the NSStringoutput.

5. Any changing of the user interface must be performed in the main thread, so you make use of the -performSelectorMainThread:withObject:waitUntilDone: method to update your user interface with the given output.

It is also important to know that you are able to further customize your TWRequest by specifying parameters, which determine what kind of results you receive. Every kind of request has its own set of available parameters, so refer to the Twitter API to find more information on specific options, which are set in an NSDictionary.

Now, in your second view controller, you can implement a similar solution to retrieve the user's Home Timeline data.

```
- (IBAction)homePressed:(id)sender
{
if ([self checkCanTweet])
    {
ACAccountStore *accountStore = [[ACAccountStore alloc] init];
ACAccountType *accountType = [accountStore
accountTypeWithAccountTypeIdentifier:ACAccountTypeIdentifierTwitter];

        [accountStore requestAccessToAccountsWithType:accountType
withCompletionHandler:^(BOOL granted, NSError *error)
        {
if (granted)
            {
NSArray *accountsArray = [accountStore accountsWithAccountType:accountType];
if ([accountsArray count] >0)
                {
ACAccount *twitterAccount = [accountsArray objectAtIndex:0];

TWRequest *postRequest = [[TWRequest alloc] initWithURL:[NSURL
URLWithString:@"http://api.twitter.com/1/statuses/home_timeline.json"] parameters:nil
requestMethod:TWRequestMethodGET];
```

```
                [postRequest setAccount:twitterAccount];

                [postRequest performRequestWithHandler:^(NSData *responseData,
NSHTTPURLResponse *urlResponse, NSError *error)
                    {
                        NSString *output;

if ([urlResponse statusCode] == 200)
                        {
                            NSError *jsonParsingError;
NSArray *homeTimeline = [NSJSONSerialization JSONObjectWithData:responseData options:0
error:&jsonParsingError];

                            output = [NSString stringWithFormat:@"Home timeline:\n%@",
homeTimeline];
                        }
else
                        {
                            output = [NSString stringWithFormat:@"HTTP response status:
%i\n", [urlResponse statusCode]];
                        }
                        [self.homeTextView
performSelectorOnMainThread:@selector(setText:) withObject:output waitUntilDone:NO];
                    }];
                }
            }
else
            {
self.homeTextView.text = @"Error, Twitter account access not granted.";
            }
        }];
    }
}
```

This method follows the same track as the previous one, with the following differences:

6. You included a quick check to -checkCanTweet in order to ensure that your device is properly configured with a Twitter account.

7. Since you are accessing a specific user's timeline, you include code to access the device's registered Twitter accounts, pick the first, and include it in the TWRequest.

8. A slightly different URL, this time http://api.twitter.com/1/statuses/home_timeline.json, is used to request a Home Timeline, as opposed to the Public Timeline.

If you run your application on a device at this point, you should be able to retrieve a good 20 tweets worth of data to your phone and view their raw data. Figure 14–11 shows the beginning of the Public Timeline data at the moment of this writing.

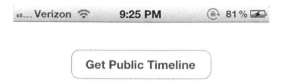

Public Timeline

```
    "in_reply_to_screen_name" = "
<null>";
    "in_reply_to_status_id" = "<null>";
    "in_reply_to_status_id_str" = "
<null>";
    "in_reply_to_user_id" = "<null>";
    "in_reply_to_user_id_str" = "<null>";
    place = "<null>";
    "retweet_count" = 0;
    retweeted = 0;
    source = "<a
href=\"http://twitter.com/#!/download/iph
```

Figure 14–11. *Sample public timeline data*

As you scroll through this massive amount of data, you can get a general sense of the format of the tweet data that you've received. You have an NSArray of a group of tweets, with each one stored as an NSDictionary. The values you see in Figure 14–11 represent the keys (on the left) and their related objects (on the right). These objects are formatted as instances ofNSString, NSNumber, NSNull, or even more complex instances of NSArray or NSDictionary. For example, to access the name of a tweet's poster, you must access a nested dictionary within your array. You first find the tweet in your array, then access the NSDictionary containing user information through the "user" key, and then retrieve the name with the "name" key. Using this information, you can begin to build a more complete application to display your tweets.

First, you will create a simple data model to encapsulate your post data into custom objects. Create a new file using the "Objective-C class" template. Name your class "Post", and make sure the subclass field is set to "NSObject", as in Figure 14–12.

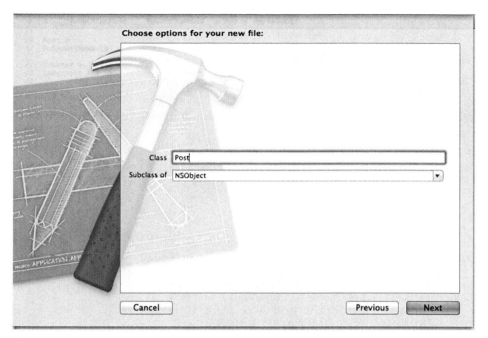

Figure 14–12. *Configuring your NSObject subclass called "Post"*

Next you can define properties for your Post object to have. You will specify properties for some of the most commonly used properties of a tweet, such as the text, user's name, and retweet count. You will also have properties to keep track of your actual NSDictionaries of data in order to simplify accessing any additional values later.

In order to create your Post objects, you will use a designated initializer that will accept the NSDictionary objects that you saw earlier as a parameter. Define these properties and method so that your Post.h file reads like so:

```
#import <Foundation/Foundation.h>

@interface Post : NSObject

@property (nonatomic, strong) NSDictionary *postData;
@property (nonatomic, strong) NSDictionary *user;
@property (nonatomic, strong) NSString *text;
@property (nonatomic, strong) NSString *screenName;
@property (nonatomic, strong) NSString *name;
@property (nonatomic, strong) NSString *userDescription;
@property (nonatomic, strong) id retweetCount; //Could be NSString (100+) or NSNumber
@property (nonatomic, strong) UIImage *userImage;
-(Post *)initWithDictionary:(NSDictionary *)dictionary;

@end
```

As commented here, you have made the property retweetCount of type "id", due to the possibility of it having two different types of values. If you looked through your earlier raw data, you might have noticed some posts with "retweet_count" values of numbers (i.e., 0, 10, etc.), and others with the string "100+". By making your property a general type, you can later check to see which value you ended up with for any given post.

You can synthesize all these properties in a single line in the Post.m file.

```
@synthesize name, text, user, postData, screenName, retweetCount, userDescription,
userImage;
```

Your initializer is fairly easy to set up, and just involves you querying your dictionaries with the various keys you will use.

```
-(Post *)initWithDictionary:(NSDictionary *)dictionary
{
self = [super init];
if (self)
    {
self.postData = dictionary;
self.user = [dictionary objectForKey:@"user"];
self.text = [dictionary objectForKey:@"text"];
self.retweetCount = [dictionary objectForKey:@"retweet_count"];
self.name = [self.user objectForKey:@"name"];
self.screenName = [self.user objectForKey:@"screen_name"];
self.userDescription = [self.user objectForKey:@"description"];
NSString *imageURLString = [self.user objectForKey:@"profile_image_url"];
NSURL *imageURL = [NSURL URLWithString:imageURLString];
NSData *imageData = [NSData dataWithContentsOfURL:imageURL];
self.userImage = [UIImage imageWithData:imageData];
    }
return self;
}
```

In this method, you may notice that you have not chosen to dispatch an alternate thread to retrieve your image data for each post. This will probably block your main thread for an extra second or two, but since you have no need to display posts before their image content is retrieved, you can work with the pause.

Now that your file is configured, you'll need to use it in your two view controllers, so add an import statement to each header file.

```
#import "Post.h"
```

Now, in each of your view controllers, you will add an NSArray property to store your retrieved posts.

```
@property (strong, nonatomic) NSMutableArray *retrievedTweets;
```

After synthesizing this property, create a custom getter to ensure that the array is correctly initialized.

```
-(NSMutableArray *)retrievedTweets
{
if (retrievedTweets == nil)
    {
retrievedTweets = [NSMutableArray arrayWithCapacity:20];
    }
return retrievedTweets;
}
```

Now, you'll do some rearranging of your user interface. Instead of simply giving a UITextView of your output, you'll organize your information into a UITableView. Remove your previously created UIButton, UILabel, and UITextView from each view controller's XIB file and replace it with a UITableView, as shown in Figure 14–13. Connect this to a property tableViewPosts in each respective view controller. I've also removed the previously used properties, though this is optional, and requires removing several lines of problematic code from your implementation file.

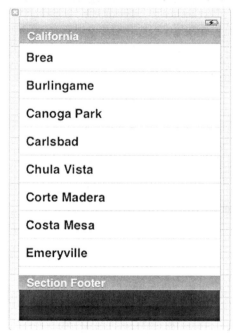

Figure 14–13. *Adding a* UITableView *to your user interface*

You'll need to go back and modify your -viewDidLoad method to set your table view's delegate and data source. Since you already have your method to retrieve data built, you can also include this.

```
- (void)viewDidLoad
{
[super viewDidLoad];
    [self publicPressed:nil];
self.tableViewPosts.delegate = self;
self.tableViewPosts.dataSource = self;
}
```

Your second view controller's -viewDidLoad method will look the same, but with a call to -homePressed:.

Make sure also to conform your view controllers to the UITableViewDelegate and UITableViewDataSource protocols.

Now your updated version of your -publicPressed: method in your first view controller will look like so:

```
- (IBAction)publicPressed:(id)sender
{
    [self.retrievedTweets removeAllObjects];

TWRequest *postRequest = [[TWRequest alloc] initWithURL:[NSURL
URLWithString:@"http://api.twitter.com/1/statuses/public_timeline.json"] parameters:nil
requestMethod:TWRequestMethodGET];

    [postRequest performRequestWithHandler:^(NSData *responseData, NSHTTPURLResponse
*urlResponse, NSError *error)
    {
if ([urlResponse statusCode] == 200)
        {
            NSError *jsonParsingError;
NSArray *publicTimeline = [NSJSONSerialization JSONObjectWithData:responseData options:0
error:&jsonParsingError];
for (NSDictionary *dict in publicTimeline)
            {
Post *current = [[Post alloc] initWithDictionary:dict];
                [self.retrievedTweets addObject:current];
            }
        }
else
        {
NSLog(@"%@", [NSString stringWithFormat:@"HTTP response status: %i\n", [urlResponse
statusCode]]);
        }
        [self.tableViewPosts reloadData];
    }];
}
```

With similar changes, the -homePressed: method will appear as shown here:

```
- (IBAction)homePressed:(id)sender
{
if ([self checkCanTweet])
    {
ACAccountStore *accountStore = [[ACAccountStore alloc] init];
ACAccountType *accountType = [accountStore
accountTypeWithAccountTypeIdentifier:ACAccountTypeIdentifierTwitter];

    [accountStore requestAccessToAccountsWithType:accountType
withCompletionHandler:^(BOOL granted, NSError *error)
    {
if (granted)
        {
NSArray *accountsArray = [accountStore accountsWithAccountType:accountType];
if ([accountsArray count] >0)
            {
                [self.retrievedTweets removeAllObjects];

ACAccount *twitterAccount = [accountsArray objectAtIndex:0];

TWRequest *postRequest = [[TWRequest alloc] initWithURL:[NSURL
URLWithString:@"http://api.twitter.com/1/statuses/home_timeline.json"] parameters:nil
requestMethod:TWRequestMethodGET];
                [postRequest setAccount:twitterAccount];
```

```
                        [postRequest performRequestWithHandler:^(NSData *responseData,
NSHTTPURLResponse *urlResponse, NSError *error)
                                {
if ([urlResponse statusCode] == 200)
                                {
                                    NSError *jsonParsingError;
NSArray *homeTimeline = [NSJSONSerialization JSONObjectWithData:responseData options:0
error:&jsonParsingError];
for (NSDictionary *dict in homeTimeline)
                                    {
Post *current = [[Post alloc] initWithDictionary:dict];
                                        [self.retrievedTweets addObject:current];
                                    }
                                }
else
                                {
NSLog(@"%@", [NSString stringWithFormat:@"HTTP response status: %i\n", [urlResponse
statusCode]]);
                                }
                    [self.tableViewPosts reloadData];
                        }];
                }
            }
else
            {
NSLog(@"Error, Twitter account access not granted.");
            }
        }];
    }
}
```

In the previous two methods, you needed to include a call to the -reloadData method in order to make sure that your tables are correctly updated once all your data has been fully retrieved. Otherwise, the tables will simply be displayed empty before you have your information.

Now, you just need to implement your delegate and datasource methods to configure your UITableViews.

```
-(NSInteger)tableView:(UITableView *)tableView numberOfRowsInSection:(NSInteger)section
{
return [self.retrievedTweets count];
}

- (UITableViewCell *)tableView:(UITableView *)tableView
cellForRowAtIndexPath:(NSIndexPath *)indexPath
{
static NSString *CellIdentifier = @"Cell";

UITableViewCell *cell = [tableView dequeueReusableCellWithIdentifier:CellIdentifier];
if (cell == nil)
    {
cell = [[UITableViewCell alloc] initWithStyle:UITableViewCellStyleSubtitle
reuseIdentifier:CellIdentifier];
        cell.accessoryType = UITableViewCellAccessoryDisclosureIndicator;
    }
```

```
Post *current = [self.retrievedTweets objectAtIndex:indexPath.row];
    cell.textLabel.text = current.text;
    cell.detailTextLabel.text = current.screenName;
    cell.imageView.image = current.userImage;

return cell;
}
```

These two methods can be copied into both view controllers with no changes.

Upon running your application now, you will be able to view two different tables of Twitter timelines, complete with text, screenname, and user image! Each table might take a few seconds to load depending on your device's connection speed.

If, when testing your application, you wish to have your tables update, you can remove the -publicPressed: or -homePressed: calls from your -viewDidLoadmethods, and move them into your -viewWillAppear:animated:methods.

Recipe 14–4: Filtering Tweets

In addition to the retrieving of tweets you have already done, you are also able to specifically filter the posts that you receive based on a variety of criteria.

Building on your previous recipe, add a new view controller to your project, calling it "MainSearchViewController".

You will build this controller's user interface to be similar to that of your first view controller, with the exception of a UISearchBar that you will use to specify your search parameters, as in Figure 14–14. Make sure that "Correction" has been turned off for this search bar so that your user is not bothered by autocorrect.

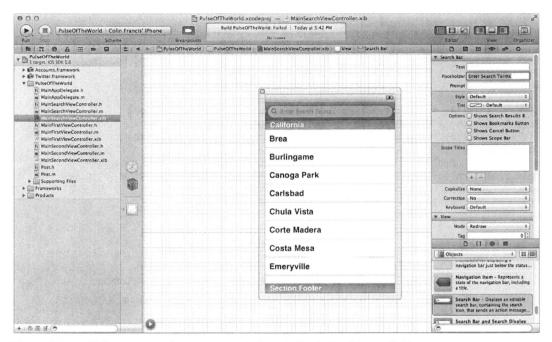

Figure 14–14. *Adding a* UISearchBar *to your* MainSearchViewController.xib *file*

Set the outlet name for the UISearchBar to be searchBarPosts.

After making sure to correctly import your frameworks and Post.h file into this new view controller and setting the proper protocols to be conformed to, you can copy your UITableView delegate/datasource methods from your first view controller. Make sure also to set up your NSMutableArray property retrievedTweets, and copy its customized getter.

In order to configure your UISearchBar, you will also need to conform your view controller to the UISearchBarDelegate protocol.

Set up your -viewDidLoad like so:

```
- (void)viewDidLoad
{
    [superview DidLoad];

self.tableViewPosts.delegate = self;
self.tableViewPosts.dataSource = self;
self.searchBarPosts.delegate = self;
}
```

In your application delegate's implementation file, import the new controller's header file.

```
#import "MainSearchViewController.h"
```

Now you need to update your -application:didFinishLaunchingWithOptions:method to include your newest view controller.

```
- (BOOL)application:(UIApplication *)application
didFinishLaunchingWithOptions:(NSDictionary *)launchOptions
{
self.window = [[UIWindow alloc] initWithFrame:[[UIScreen mainScreen] bounds]];
// Override point for customization after application launch.
UIViewController *viewController1 = [[MainFirstViewController alloc]
initWithNibName:@"MainFirstViewController" bundle:nil];
UIViewController *viewController2 = [[MainSecondViewController alloc]
initWithNibName:@"MainSecondViewController" bundle:nil];
UIViewController *viewController3 = [[MainSearchViewController alloc]
initWithNibName:@"MainSearchViewController" bundle:nil];
self.tabBarController = [[UITabBarControlleralloc] init];
self.tabBarController.viewControllers = [NSArray arrayWithObjects:viewController1,
viewController2, viewController3, nil];
self.window.rootViewController = self.tabBarController;
    [self.window makeKeyAndVisible];
return YES;
}
```

You can also add a slightly altered designated initializer back in your
MainSearchViewController.m file to correctly set your new view controller:

```
- (id)initWithNibName:(NSString *)nibNameOrNil bundle:(NSBundle *)nibBundleOrNil
{
self = [super initWithNibName:nibNameOrNil bundle:nibBundleOrNil];
if (self) {
self.title = NSLocalizedString(@"Filtered Posts", @"First");
self.tabBarItem.image = [UIImage imageNamed:@"first"];
    }
return self;
}
```

To fully configure your UISearchBar, you can create the delegate method -
shouldChangeTextInRange:replacementText:like so, assuming that your data retrieval
method in this controller will be called -searchPressed:.

```
-(BOOL)searchBar:(UISearchBar *)searchBar shouldChangeTextInRange:(NSRange)range
replacementText:(NSString *)text
{
if ([text isEqualToString:@"\n"])
    {
        [searchBar resignFirstResponder];
        [self searchPressed:searchBar.text];
return NO;
    }
return YES;
}
```

Now, you must consider the actual formatting of your request to Twitter. According to
the Twitter API, the best way to get a URL for a specific search is to enter the search
terms into the Twitter website search, and then modify the resulting URL that you are
redirected to. To give a simple example, a search for the word "test" will redirect you to
the URL http://twitter.com/#!/search/test. You then modify all but the suffix search
term of this to http://search.twitter.com/search.json?q=test. In order to process
simple search queries, you must correctly handle any spaces, hashmarks, "@" symbols,

and quotation marks. In your code, you will have to manipulate your search terms to implement this behavior.

First, you can do most of your character replacements in a single line.

```
searchText = [searchText stringByAddingPercentEscapesUsingEncoding:
NSUTF8StringEncoding];
```

This method will properly convert all the aforementioned symbols with the exception of the "@" symbol, which you can manually replace like so:

```
NSMutableString *mutableText = [[NSMutableString alloc] initWithString:searchText];
[mutableText replaceOccurrencesOfString:@"@" withString:[NSString
stringWithFormat:@"%%40"] options:NSLiteralSearch range:NSMakeRange(0, [mutableText
length])];
```

Now, you can fully assemble your URL by appending this result on top of your general search URL.

```
NSString *searchString = @"http://search.twitter.com/search.json?q-";
searchString = [searchString stringByAppendingString:mutableText];
NSURL *searchURL = [NSURL URLWithString:searchString];
```

With this functionality added into a method similar to your -publicPressed:, you end up with the overall method written as follows:

```
- (IBAction)searchPressed:(NSString *)searchText
{
    [self.retrievedTweets removeAllObjects];

    searchText = [searchText stringByAddingPercentEscapesUsingEncoding:
NSUTF8StringEncoding];

NSMutableString *mutableText = [[NSMutableString alloc] initWithString:searchText];
    [mutableText replaceOccurrencesOfString:@"@"
withString:[NSStringstringWithFormat:@"%%40"] options:NSLiteralSearch
range:NSMakeRange(0, [mutableText length])];

//    NSLog(@"Searching: %@", mutableText);

NSString *searchString = @"http://search.twitter.com/search.json?q=";
    searchString = [searchString stringByAppendingString:mutableText];
NSURL *searchURL = [NSURLURLWithString:searchString];

TWRequest *postRequest = [[TWRequest alloc] initWithURL:searchURL parameters:nil
requestMethod:TWRequestMethodGET];

    [postRequest performRequestWithHandler:^(NSData *responseData, NSHTTPURLResponse
*urlResponse, NSError *error)
    {
if ([urlResponse statusCode] == 200)
        {
            NSError *jsonParsingError;
NSDictionary *searchTimeline = [NSJSONSerialization JSONObjectWithData:responseData
options:0 error:&jsonParsingError];
NSArray *searchResults = [searchTimeline objectForKey:@"results"];
for (NSDictionary *dict in searchResults)
            {
```

```
Post *current = [[Post alloc] initWithSearchDictionary:dict];
                [self.retrievedTweets addObject:current];
            }
//            NSLog(@"Data Retrieved: HTTP response code %i", [urlResponse
statusCode]);
        }
else
        {
NSLog(@"%@", [NSString stringWithFormat:@"HTTP response status: %i\n", [urlResponse
statusCode]]);
        }
        [self.tableViewPosts reloadData];
        [self.tableViewPosts reloadInputViews];
    }];
}
```

Be careful to notice that in this case, the initial results you get after converting your JSON formatted data to an Objective-C object are not in an NSArray. This time, they are in an NSDictionary in order to provide extra information on the query. You can then access your usual NSArray by accessing the "results" key, as shown here.

When you retrieve your posts from asearch in this manner, your data is formatted with different keys than it was before. To make up for this, you will create a second designated initializer, -initWithSearchDictionary:, for your Post object, as used in the preceding method. This format does not give you quite as much information about the user in the default setting, so you will access only what you can. Make sure also to add this method's handler to your Post.h file.

```
-(Post *)initWithSearchDictionary:(NSDictionary *)dictionary
{
self = [super init];
if (self)
    {
self.postData = dictionary;
self.screenName = [dictionary objectForKey:@"from_user"];
self.text = [dictionary objectForKey:@"text"];
NSString *imageURLString = [dictionary objectForKey:@"profile_image_url"];
NSURL *imageURL = [NSURL URLWithString:imageURLString];
NSData *imageData = [NSData dataWithContentsOfURL:imageURL];
self.userImage = [UIImage imageWithData:imageData];
    }
return self;
}
```

At this point, your application should now be able to search for specific texts, hashtags, and users included in posts! You have included basic functionality to encompass the most commonly used search terms, but the Twitter API allows for far more complex queries to be made. For a full list of the variety of ways to format a search, refer to the Twitter API at https://dev.twitter.com/docs/using-search.

When you run your application now, you should be able to search for different hashtags, phrases, and usernames. Try searching for #miami and see what results you get!

> **NOTE:** If at any point you are unsure of the format of your JSON data retrieved from Twitter, you can simply take the URL used to make your request and enter it in your web browser. You will receive a text view of the exact same data you would have gotten. It can be a little difficult to read due to a lack of space formatting, but you can look for the necessary layers of content needed to build your application.

Summary

Throughout this chapter, we have gone over a great deal of sample code making use of the Twitter framework, with subjects from pre-defined user interfaces to send tweets, to custom-formatted requests to acquire specifically filtered data directly from Twitter. Our basic implementations can easily serve as the groundwork of much more complex applications. Integration with the Twitter service is not simply limited to posting and displaying tweets, and can easily enhance the functionality and power of nearly any application. Considering the popularity and consistent growth of Twitter itself, it is certain that iOS's integration can only become more profound, allowing developers simpler access to one of the modern world's most powerful web services.

Chapter 15

Image Recipes

Often times a developer is faced with an all-too common problem: Too much information to display with not enough space to show it. For this, you turn to images. Pictures and graphics allow you to convey a variety of information far beyond simple text, combining emotion, information, and style. In iOS, you have multiple different methods with which to create, utilize, manipulate, and display images. New to iOS 5.0 even is the ability to apply filters to images, allowing for drastic alteration of display with very little actual code. By understanding these inherent functionalities and techniques in iOS, you are able to more easily implement stronger, more powerful, and more informative applications.

Recipe 15–1: Drawing Simple Shapes

From the youngest age, every person is taught the most basic of images, dealing with shapes, colors, and pictures. In iOS too, you can start off with the basics of drawing simple shapes in a view. Many concepts dealt with in these first implementations will end up returning in more complex image-based recipes.

Start by creating a new project called "ShapesAndSizes". Select the Single View Application template, as in Figure 15–1, in order to build the simplest, ready-to-run pre-configured application, and make sure the device family is set to "iPhone". The box marked "Use Automatic Reference Counting" should also be checked.

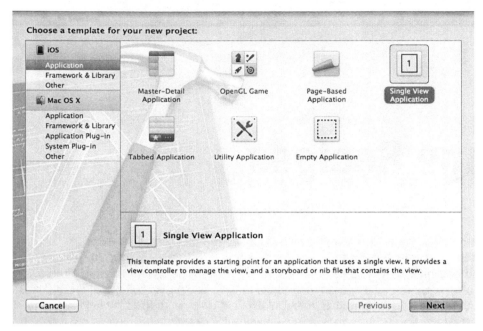

Figure 15–1. *Creating a single view application*

Next, before building your user interface, you will start by implementing your custom drawing code in a subclass of `UIView`.

Start by adding `QuartzCore.framework` and `CoreGraphics.framework` to your project by navigating to your project's Target settings. Under the Build Phases tab, in the Link Binary With Libraries section, click the + button. Find the Quartz Core and Core Graphics frameworks in the window resembling Figure 15–2, and add them both separately.

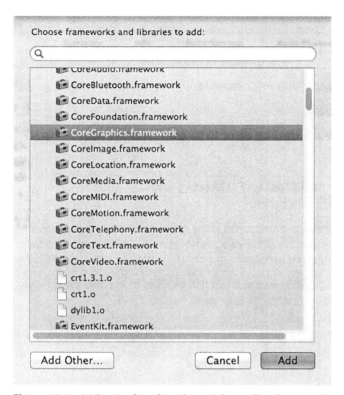

Figure 15–2. *Adding the Core Graphics and Quartz Core frameworks*

Next, create a new file called "MyView" using the "Objective-C class" template. When you enter the name, make sure the "Subclass of" field is set to "UIView".

In the header file of this new class, add the required two import statements for your extra frameworks.

```
#import <QuartzCore/QuartzCore.h>
#import <CoreGraphics/CoreGraphics.h>
```

Now, to provide a simple view displaying a drawn rectangle and square, you will implement the -drawRect: method as such:

```
- (void)drawRect:(CGRect)rect
{
CGContextRef context = UIGraphicsGetCurrentContext();

CGRect drawingRect = CGRectMake(0.0, 20.0f, 100.0f, 180.0f);
const CGFloat *rectColorComponents = CGColorGetComponents([[UIColor greenColor]
CGColor]);
CGContextSetFillColor(context, rectColorComponents);
CGContextFillRect(context, drawingRect);

CGRect ellipseRect = CGRectMake(140.0f, 200.0f, 75.0f, 50.0f);
const CGFloat *ellipseColorComponenets = CGColorGetComponents([[UIColor blueColor]
CGColor]);
CGContextSetFillColor(context, ellipseColorComponenets);
```

```
CGContextFillEllipseInRect(context, ellipseRect);
}
```

This method makes use of the following steps to draw basic shapes:

1. Obtain a reference to the current "context," represented by a `CGContextRef`.

2. Define a `CGRect` in which to draw.

3. Acquire color components for the desired color to fill each shape with.

4. Set the Fill Color.

5. Fill the specified shape using the `CGContextFillRect()` and `CGContextFillEllipseInRect()` functions.

In order to actually display this in your pre-configured view, you must add an instance of this class to your user interface. This can be done programmatically or through Interface Builder (the latter of which you will demonstrate).

In your view controller's XIB file, drag a `UIView` out from the utilities pane into your view, placing it with 20-point margins on each edge, as shown in Figure 15–3.

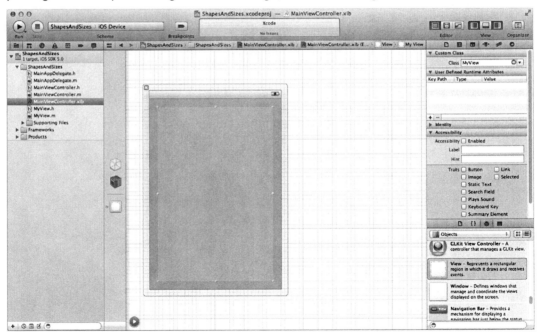

Figure 15–3. *Building your XIB file with a* `UIView`

While your `UIView` is selected, navigate to the third tab in the right-hand panel. Under the Custom Class section, make sure the Class field is changed from "UIView" to "MyView", in order to specify the custom `UIView` subclass to be used, resembling Figure 15–4.

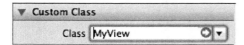

Figure 15–4. *Configuring the class of your UIView to MyView*

Upon running this application, you will see the output of your drawing commands converted into a visual display, resulting in your simulated view in Figure 15–5.

Figure 15–5. *Your simple application drawing a rectangle and an ellipse*

Thankfully, you are not at all limited to drawing only rectangles and ellipses! You are able to use a few other functions to draw custom objects by creating "paths." These paths consist of a movement from point to point, connected by lines, in order to draw a custom shape. Add the following code to your -drawRect: method to draw a gray parallelogram.

```
CGContextBeginPath(context);
CGContextMoveToPoint(context, 0.0f, 0.0f);
CGContextAddLineToPoint(context, 100.0f, 0.0f);
CGContextAddLineToPoint(context, 140.0f, 100.0f);
```

```
CGContextAddLineToPoint(context, 40.0f, 100.0f);
CGContextClosePath(context);
CGContextSetGrayFillColor(context, 0.4f, 0.85f);
CGContextSetGrayStrokeColor(context, 0.0, 0.0);
CGContextFillPath(context);
```

It is important to note that when creating these paths, you do not have to add a final line back to your last point. By calling the CGContextClosePath() function, your shape will automatically be closed between its ending point and starting point.

When you run your application now, you will see your view with a new parallelogram created from your path, as in Figure 15–6.

Figure 15–6. *Your application with a shape created from a custom path*

Programming Screenshots

Just as you are able to put things into a CGContext, you are also quite easily able to take them out. By making use of the UIGraphicsGetImageFromCurrentImageContext() function, you can extract an image from whatever is currently drawn.

In the MyView class, add a UIImage property, making sure to synthesize it.

```
@property (nonatomic, strong) UIImage *image;
```

Now at the end of your -drawRect: method, append the following code to draw the image if it is non-nil.

```
if (self.image)
    {
        CGRect imageRect = CGRectMake(200.0f, 50.0f, 100.0f, 300.0f);
        [image drawInRect:imageRect];
    }
```

Add the same two import statements as earlier to your view controller, as well as a third for your MyView class.

```
#import <QuartzCore/QuartzCore.h>
#import <CoreGraphics/CoreGraphics.h>
#import "MyView.h"
```

You will also need to reference your MyView object, so connect the one you already added into the user interface to your view controller's header file with the property customView.

```
@property (strong, nonatomic) IBOutlet MyView *customView;
```

Add a UIButton labeled "Snapshot" to the bottom of your user interface. Connect it to an IBAction method called -snapShotPressed:.

```
- (IBAction)snapshotPressed:(id)sender;
```

This method will then be implemented like so:

```
-(IBAction)snapshotPressed:(id)sender
{
//Acquire image of current layer
UIGraphicsBeginImageContext(self.view.bounds.size);
CGContextRef context = UIGraphicsGetCurrentContext();
    [self.view.layer renderInContext:context];
UIImage *image = UIGraphicsGetImageFromCurrentImageContext();
UIGraphicsEndImageContext();

self.customView.image = image;
    [self.customView setNeedsDisplay];
}
```

This method makes use of the -setNeedsDisplay method in the UIView class to instruct a UIView to re-call its -drawRect method in order to incorporate any recent changes.

Now, after testing the application again, upon pressing the Snapshot button, you should see a smaller screenshot of your own screen appear on the right side of the view, as in Figure 15–7.

Figure 15–7. *Your application having taken a screenshot, then scaled it into the view*

While most of the functionalities you've built into this application have been pretty basic, you will see a variety of them come back in more complex forms in the later, more complex image recipes.

Recipe 15–2: Using UIImageViews

The absolutely simplest way of displaying an image in your application is by use of the UIImageView class. You will start off by creating a simple application that can display an image chosen by the user, and then build on top of it to take full advantage of iOS's image processing power.

In order to enhance the functionality of your application, you will specifically design it for the iPad, and then make use of the UISplitViewController. Create a new project, and select the Master-Detail Application template. On the next screen, after entering the project name "ImageRecipes", make sure the application's device-family is set to "iPad", and that the box marked "Use Automatic Reference Counting" is checked. No other boxes should be marked, so that your dialog resembles Figure 15–8.

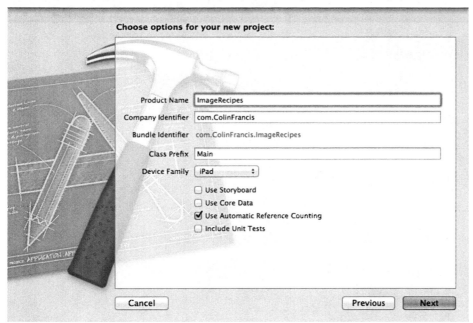

Figure 15–8. *Configuring project settings*

Upon creating your application, you will be given a nicely configured project with a UISplitViewController already set up with master and detail view controllers. If your simulator or device is in portrait mode, you will see only the view of the detail view controller, but if you rotate to landscape then you will get a nice mix of both views. You will not see both views when working in Interface Builder, but if you simulate the app, the generic view will resemble Figure 15–9.

Figure 15–9. *An empty* `UISplitViewController`

Now, you will configure the detail view controller to include a bit more content. Add a `UIImageView`, as well as two `UIButtons` to your XIB's interface so that your simulated application will look like Figure 15–10.

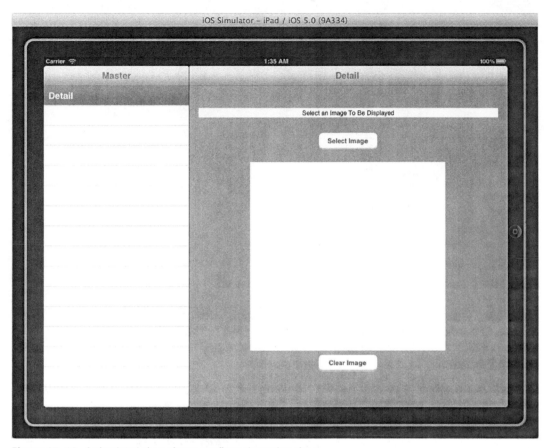

Figure 15–10. *A simulated view of your configured user interface*

In order to make sure that both your buttons and image view will be correctly centered in your final display, first set them to the center of your XIB's view as you normally would. Then, you will set the "autosizing" options for each element. Open up the utilities pane on the right side of your screen, and navigate to the fifth tab where you can set an element's frame, shown in Figure 15–11.

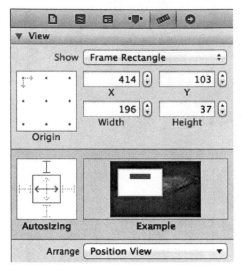

Figure 15–11. *Configuring autosizing to customize resizing behavior*

Make sure that for each element, the Autosizing box, with its various red lines and arrows, is configured exactly as shown in Figure 15–11. This will specify that each element will, if the view changes, maintain its relative position to the top of the view and stretch horizontally to maintain its general position.

Connect each element to your header file using the property names selectImageButton, clearImageButton, and imageViewContent. Each UIButton will have its respective action, -selectImagePressed: and -clearImagePressed:.

You will be configuring your application to display a UIPopoverController containing a UIImagePickerController in order to allow users to select an image from their phone. To do this, you will need your detail view controller to conform to several extra protocols: UIImagePickerControllerDelegate, UINavigationControllerDelegate and UIPopoverControllerDelegate.

```
@interface MainDetailViewController : UIViewController<UISplitViewControllerDelegate,
UIImagePickerControllerDelegate, UINavigationControllerDelegate,
UIPopoverControllerDelegate>
```

You will also create two extra properties in order to store your selected image, as well as a reference to your UIPopoverController that you will use. Make sure both of these are properly synthesized, as well as properly nullified in the -viewDidUnload method.

```
@property (strong, nonatomic) UIPopoverController *pop;
@property (strong, nonatomic) UIImage *selectedImage;
```

At this point, with your basic user interface configured, your overall detail view controller's header file should resemble the following.

```
#import <UIKit/UIKit.h>
```

```
@interface MainDetailViewController : UIViewController<UISplitViewControllerDelegate,
UIImagePickerControllerDelegate, UIPopoverControllerDelegate,
UINavigationControllerDelegate>

@property (strong, nonatomic) id detailItem;

@property (strong, nonatomic) IBOutlet UILabel *detailDescriptionLabel;
@property (strong, nonatomic) IBOutlet UIButton *selectImageButton;
@property (strong, nonatomic) IBOutlet UIButton *clearImageButton;
@property (strong, nonatomic) IBOutlet UIImageView *imageViewContent;
-(IBAction)selectImagePressed:(id)sender;
-(IBAction)clearImagePressed:(id)sender;

@property (strong, nonatomic) UIPopoverController *pop;
@property (strong, nonatomic) UIImage *selectedImage;

@end
```

Now you can implement your -selectImagePressed: method to present an interface to select a saved image to display.

```
-(void)selectImagePressed:(UIButton *)sender
{
UIImagePickerController *picker = [[UIImagePickerController alloc] init];
if ([UIImagePickerController
isSourceTypeAvailable:UIImagePickerControllerSourceTypePhotoLibrary])
    {
        picker.sourceType = UIImagePickerControllerSourceTypePhotoLibrary;
        picker.delegate = self;

self.pop = [[UIPopoverController alloc] initWithContentViewController:picker];
pop.delegate = self;
        [pop presentPopoverFromRect:sender.frame inView:self.view
permittedArrowDirections:UIPopoverArrowDirectionAny animated:YES];
    }
}
```

You can then implement your UIImagePickerControllerDelegate protocol methods to properly handle the selection of an image or cancellation.

```
-(void)imagePickerControllerDidCancel:(UIImagePickerController *)picker
{
    [self.pop dismissPopoverAnimated:YES];
}
-(void)imagePickerController:(UIImagePickerController *)picker
didFinishPickingMediaWithInfo:(NSDictionary *)info
{
UIImage *image = [info valueForKey:@"UIImagePickerControllerOriginalImage"];
self.selectedImage = image;
self.imageViewContent.image = image;
self.imageViewContent.contentMode = UIViewContentModeScaleAspectFill;

    [self.pop dismissPopoverAnimated:YES];
}
```

As you can see, you configure your selected image to be displayed in your UIImageView by using the image property. You also set the contentMode property to

UIViewContentModeScaleAspectFill, in order to ensure that the bounds of your UIImageView are always filled by at least most of the image.

Finally, you can implement a simple method for -clearImagePressed: to allow your view to be reset:

```
- (IBAction)clearImagePressed:(id)sender
{
self.selectedImage = nil;
self.imageViewContent.image = nil;
}
```

At this point, you can run your application, select an image, and display it in a UIImageView, as in Figure 15–12!

Figure 15–12. *Your application displaying an image in a UIImageView*

If you are testing this application on the iOS simulator, you will need to actually have some images saved to display. The easiest way to save images to the simulator's photo library is to use the Safari app on the simulator, navigate to your desired image, and then click and hold the mouse on the image. You will be given an option to save the image, and after this you can use it in your application.

Recipe 15–3: Scaling Images

Often the images that your applications have to deal with can come from a variety of sources, and usually will not fit your specific view's display perfectly. To adjust for this, you can implement methods to scale and resize your images.

You will configure your application to overall have a single image selected in your first detail view controller. Upon selecting different rows in your master view controller's table, you will change the display in your detail view controller to a variety of images. For now, you will configure your views to display your images as they are resized differently.

You will start off by creating a method to fully adjust the content of your detail view controller. Add the following handler to your detail view controller's header file.

```
-(void)configureDetailsWithImage:(UIImage *)image label:(NSString *)label
showsButtons:(BOOL)showButton;
```

You will implement this method like so:

```
-(void)configureDetailsWithImage:(UIImage *)image label:(NSString *)label
showsButtons:(BOOL)showsButton
{
self.selectedImage = image;
self.imageViewContent.image = image;
self.detailDescriptionLabel.text = label;
    if (showsButton == NO)
    {
self.selectImageButton.enabled = NO;
self.selectImageButton.hidden = YES;
self.clearImageButton.enabled = NO;
self.clearImageButton.hidden = YES;
    }
else if (showsButton == YES)
    {
self.selectImageButton.enabled = YES;
self.selectImageButton.hidden = NO;
self.clearImageButton.enabled = YES;
self.clearImageButton.hidden = NO;
    }
}
```

You will add a reference to the master view controller to your detail view controller to allow your chosen image to be passed back. Add the following import statement (or your own class name for the master view controller):

```
#import "MainMasterViewController.h"
```

Add the master view controller property, and make sure to synthesize it.

```
@property (strong, nonatomic) MainMasterViewController *masterViewController;
```

Add the following line to your -viewDidUnload method.

```
[self setMasterViewController:nil];
```

Next, you will add a property to your master view controller class to store the chosen image. Make sure to properly synthesize and handle it as usual.

```
@property (strong, nonatomic) UIImage *mainImage;
```

Back in your detail view controller, you will update your -imagePickerController:didFinishPickingMediaWithInfo: method to also send the chosen image back to the master view controller.

```
-(void)imagePickerController:(UIImagePickerController *)picker
didFinishPickingMediaWithInfo:(NSDictionary *)info
{
UIImage *image = [info valueForKey:@"UIImagePickerControllerOriginalImage"];
self.selectedImage = image;

//New Line
self.masterViewController.mainImage = image;

self.imageViewContent.image = image;
self.imageViewContent.contentMode = UIViewContentModeScaleAspectFill;

    [self.pop dismissPopoverAnimated:YES];
}
```

You will also adjust the implementation of your -clearImagePressed: method accordingly.

```
- (IBAction)clearImagePressed:(id)sender
{
self.selectedImage = nil;
self.imageViewContent.image = nil;
self.masterViewController.mainImage = nil;
}
```

In your master view controller, you will later implement code to utilize your images in the actual table, so you will implement a custom setter method for the mainImage property to reload the UITableView's data.

```
-(void)setMainImage:(UIImage *)image
{
mainImage = image;
NSIndexPath *currentIndexPath = self.tableView.indexPathForSelectedRow;
    [self.tableView reloadData];
    [self.tableView selectRowAtIndexPath:currentIndexPath animated:YES
scrollPosition:UITableViewScrollPositionTop];
}
```

Next, you will create two different methods to resize an image. Add the following two handlers to your detail view controller's header file.

```
+ (UIImage *)scaleImage:(UIImage *)image toSize:(CGSize)size;
+ (UIImage *)aspectScaleImage:(UIImage *)image toSize:(CGSize)size;
```

The first method will simply recreate the image within a specified size, completely ignoring the aspect ratio of the image.

```
+ (UIImage *)scaleImage:(UIImage *)image toSize:(CGSize)size
{
```

```
UIGraphicsBeginImageContext(size);
    [image drawInRect:CGRectMake(0, 0, size.width, size.height)];
UIImage *scaledImage = UIGraphicsGetImageFromCurrentImageContext();
UIGraphicsEndImageContext();
return scaledImage;
}
```

The second will, with a little calculation, determine the best way to resize the image in order to both preserve the aspect ratio and fit inside the given size.

```
+ (UIImage *)aspectScaleImage:(UIImage *)image toSize:(CGSize)size
{
UIGraphicsBeginImageContext(size);
if (image.size.height< image.size.width)
    {
float ratio = size.height/image.size.height;
        [image drawInRect:CGRectMake(0, 0, image.size.width*ratio, size.height)];
    }
else
    {
float ratio = size.width/image.size.width;
        [image drawInRect:CGRectMake(0, 0, size.width, image.size.height*ratio)];
    }
UIImage *aspectScaledImage = UIGraphicsGetImageFromCurrentImageContext();
UIGraphicsEndImageContext();
return aspectScaledImage;
}
```

To make sure your view controllers are properly interacting, add the following two lines to your application delegate's -application:didFinishLaunchingWithOptions: after both view controllers have been created.

```
detailViewController.masterViewController = masterViewController;
masterViewController.detailViewController = detailViewController;
```

Now, to finish configuring the behavior of the master view controller, modify the following delegate methods:

```
- (NSInteger)tableView:(UITableView *)tableView numberOfRowsInSection:(NSInteger)section
{
if (self.mainImage == nil)
    {
return 1;
    }
else
    {
return 3;
    }
}
- (UITableViewCell *)tableView:(UITableView *)tableView
cellForRowAtIndexPath:(NSIndexPath *)indexPath
{
static NSString *CellIdentifier = @"Cell";

UITableViewCell *cell = [tableView dequeueReusableCellWithIdentifier:CellIdentifier];
if (cell == nil) {
        cell = [[UITableViewCell alloc] initWithStyle:UITableViewCellStyleDefault
reuseIdentifier:CellIdentifier];
```

```
        }
    if (indexPath.row == 0)
            cell.textLabel.text = NSLocalizedString(@"Selected Image", @"Detail");
    else if (indexPath.row == 1)
            cell.textLabel.text = NSLocalizedString(@"Resized Image", @"Detail");
    else if (indexPath.row == 2)
            cell.textLabel.text = NSLocalizedString(@"Scaled Image", @"Detail");
    return cell;
    }
    - (void)tableView:(UITableView *)tableView didSelectRowAtIndexPath:(NSIndexPath
    *)indexPath
    {
    if (self.mainImage != nil)
        {
            UIImage *image;
            NSString *label;
    BOOL showsButtons;
    if (indexPath.row == 0)
            {
                image = self.mainImage;
                label = @"Select an Image to Display";
                showsButtons = YES;
            }
    else if (indexPath.row == 1)
            {
                image = [MainDetailViewController scaleImage:self.mainImage
    toSize:self.detailViewController.imageViewContent.frame.size];
                label = @"Chosen Image Resized";
                showsButtons = NO;
            }
    else if (indexPath.row == 2)
            {
                image = [MainDetailViewController aspectScaleImage:self.mainImage
    toSize:self.detailViewController.imageViewContent.frame.size];
                label = @"Chosen Image Scaled";
                showsButtons = NO;
            }
            [self.detailViewController configureDetailsWithImage:image label:label
    showsButtons:showsButtons];
        }
    }
```

Your original image, as shown previously, ended up expanding beyond the frame of the UIImageView in order to maintain its aspect ratio. Since this can cause some issues in blocking other elements, you would most likely want to use one of your resized images. Upon running this application, you can see the quite vast differences in your options in presenting differently sized images.

Figure 15–13 displays an example of the same image used previously, but resized simply to fit within your image view's frame.

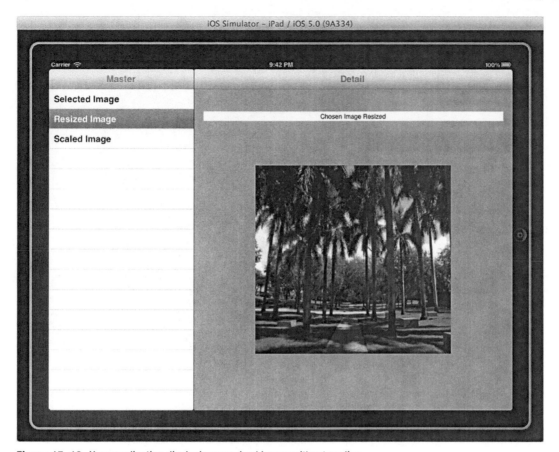

Figure 15–13. *Your application displaying a resized image without scaling*

As you can see, you have managed to fit the entire image into a smaller space, ensuring that no other view elements are obstructed by your image. The issue with this option, however, is that your image's dimensions have been changed, resulting in a slightly deformed picture. This may not be quite obvious with this particular image, but when dealing with images of people, the distortion of physical features will become quite obvious and unsightly. To solve this, you make use of the "aspect-scaled" image, as displayed in Figure 15–14.

Figure 15–14. *An alternative method of scaling to remove distortion, resulting in clipping*

Compared to the previous and original images, you can see that this image is clearly of higher quality, as it lacks any distortion of size. Unfortunately, since you have chosen to have your image "fill" the UIImageView, you end up with an image cropped from your original. This kind of resizing works incredibly well if you need to create small thumbnails from larger images, as the issue of cropping the image becomes fairly negligible with more miniscule sizes.

Obviously, if you are not dealing with thumbnails, but instead with presenting large pictures, then the above cropping is significantly less than ideal. You can hone your image scaling method to allow your image to "fit" the image view, and simply give the rest of the view a black background. With this change, your previous "thumbnail creation method" will no longer be functional, so be sure to save a new copy of your project if you want to keep a copy of the previous setup.

First, adjust your configuration method to the following code in order to change the contentMode property of your UIImageView.

```
-(void)configureDetailsWithImage:(UIImage *)image label:(NSString *)label
showsButtons:(BOOL)showsButton
```

```
{
self.selectedImage = image;
self.imageViewContent.image = image;
self.detailDescriptionLabel.text = label;
/////BEGIN NEW CODE
if ([label isEqualToString:@"Chosen Image Scaled"])
    {
self.imageViewContent.contentMode = UIViewContentModeScaleAspectFit;
self.imageViewContent.backgroundColor = [UIColor blackColor];
    }
else
    {
self.imageViewContent.contentMode = UIViewContentModeScaleAspectFill;
    }
/////END NEW CODE
if (showsButton == NO)
    {
self.selectImageButton.enabled = NO;
self.selectImageButton.hidden = YES;
self.clearImageButton.enabled = NO;
self.clearImageButton.hidden = YES;
    }
else if (showsButton == YES)
    {
self.selectImageButton.enabled = YES;
self.selectImageButton.hidden = NO;
self.clearImageButton.enabled = YES;
self.clearImageButton.hidden = NO;
    }
}
```

Your image scaling method will require a slightly different method of calculation to correctly scale your images this way. The following code shows the new implementation. Pay careful attention to the fact that you have changed the CGSize with which you are creating your image context.

```
+ (UIImage *)aspectScaleImage:(UIImage *)image toSize:(CGSize)size
{
if (image.size.height< image.size.width)
    {
float ratio = size.height/image.size.height;
CGSize newSize = CGSizeMake(image.size.width*ratio, size.height);

UIGraphicsBeginImageContext(newSize);
        [image drawInRect:CGRectMake(0, 0, newSize.width, newSize.height)];
    }
else
    {
float ratio = size.width/image.size.width;
CGSize newSize = CGSizeMake(size.width, image.size.height*ratio);

UIGraphicsBeginImageContext(newSize);
        [image drawInRect:CGRectMake(0, 0, newSize.width, newSize.height)];
    }
UIImage *aspectScaledImage = UIGraphicsGetImageFromCurrentImageContext();
UIGraphicsEndImageContext();
return aspectScaledImage;
```

}

With the newest changes, your images can now appear scaled down in size without being clipped! By adding the black background to your UIImageView, you provide a simple backdrop for your images to go on, allowing a very general, all-encompassing functionality for displaying resized images, as in Figure 15–15.

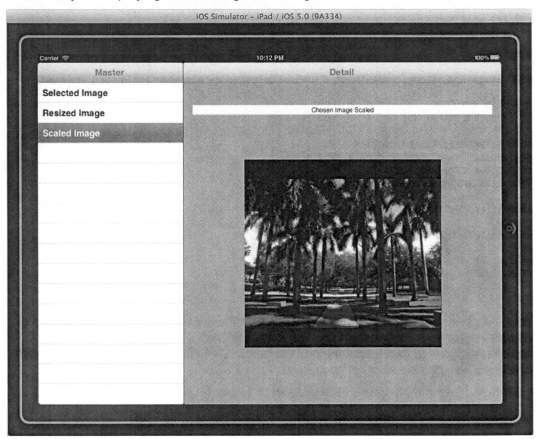

Figure 15–15. *Fitting your scaled image helps avoid clipping, but introduces background visibility of the* UIImageView.

In Review

You have covered three simple yet different methods for resizing a UIImage, each with their own advantages and issues.

1. Your first method simply resized the image to a given size, regardless of aspect ratio. While this kept your image from obstructing any other elements, it ended up giving you a fair bit of distortion.

2.　By using a little math, you were able to scale down your image to a size while manually maintaining the aspect ratio. The issue with this approach was that it tended to crop out parts of your image in order to fill its given space. If you need to create small thumbnails of images to be displayed together, this is a decent way to implement it.

3.　After reconfiguring your aspect resizing method, you were able to display an aspect-locked, smaller image to fit entirely within your UIImageView. Since this would, of course, leave blank space around the image, you applied a black background. This is an especially useful technique to use when displaying large images in an application that has no control over the original image size. It allows for any image to be comfortably fit in a given space, yet maintains a visually appealing black background no matter the case.

Recipe 15–4: Manipulating Images with Filters

The Core Image framework, a group of classes entirely new in iOS 5.0, allows you to creatively apply a great variety of different types of "filters" to images.

Start by importing the CoreImage.framework library into your project. Navigate to your application's Build Phases tab, and then click the + button under the Link Binary With Libraries area. In the dialog resembling Figure 15–16, find the Core Image framework, and add it.

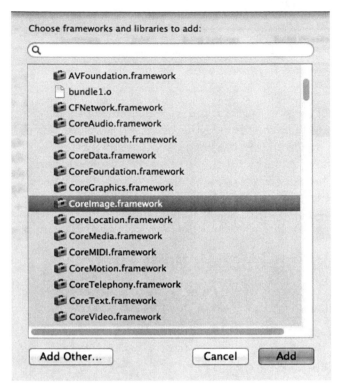

Figure 15–16. *Adding the Core Image framework to your project*

Add an import statement for this framework to your main view controller's header file.

```
#import <CoreImage/CoreImage.h>
```

Next add an NSMutableArray property to the same controller in order to store the filtered images you will display. Make sure to properly synthesize and handle it as usual.

```
@property (strong, nonatomic) NSMutableArray *images;
```

This property will also need a custom getter to ensure it is properly initialized.

```
-(NSMutableArray *)images
{
if (!images)
    {
images = [[NSMutableArray alloc] initWithCapacity:3];
    }
return images;
}
```

Now, you will modify your -setMainImage: method again to include proper handling of this array.

```
-(void)setMainImage:(UIImage *)image
{
    [self.images removeAllObjects];
if (image != nil)
```

```
    {
        [self.images addObject:image];
        [self populateImagesWithImage:image];
    }
```

```
mainImage = image;
NSIndexPath *currentIndexPath = self.tableView.indexPathForSelectedRow;
    [self.tableView reloadData];
    [self.tableView selectRowAtIndexPath:currentIndexPath animated:YES
scrollPosition:UITableViewScrollPositionTop];
}
```

This method, -populateImagesWithImage:, which will contain most of your Core Image code, will be implemented as follows. Remember to place the method declaration in your header file as well.

```
-(void)populateImagesWithImage:(UIImage *)image
{
CIImage *main = [[CIImage alloc] initWithImage:image];

CIFilter *hueAdjust = [CIFilter filterWithName:@"CIHueAdjust"];
    [hueAdjust setDefaults];
    [hueAdjust setValue:main forKey:@"inputImage"];
    [hueAdjust setValue:[NSNumber numberWithFloat: 3.14/2.0f]
forKey:@"inputAngle"];
CIImage *outputHueAdjust = [hueAdjust valueForKey:@"outputImage"];
CIContext *context = [CIContext contextWithOptions:nil];
UIImage *outputImage1 = [UIImage imageWithCGImage:[context createCGImage:outputHueAdjust
fromRect:outputHueAdjust.extent]];
    [self.images addObject:outputImage1];

CIFilter *strFilter = [CIFilter filterWithName:@"CIStraightenFilter"];
    [strFilter setDefaults];
    [strFilter setValue:main forKey:@"inputImage"];
    [strFilter setValue:[NSNumber numberWithFloat:3.14f] forKey:@"inputAngle"];
CIImage *outputStr = [strFilter valueForKey:@"outputImage"];
UIImage *outputImage2 = [UIImage imageWithCGImage:[context createCGImage:outputStr
fromRect:outputStr.extent]];
    [self.images addObject:outputImage2];
}
```

As you can see from this method, creating a CIImage requires the following steps:

1. Obtain a CIImage of the intended input image.

2. Create a filter using a specific name key. The name defines which filter will be applied, as well as its various parameters that can be used.

3. Reset all parameters of the filter to defaults for good measure.

4. Set the input image to the filter using the "inputImage" key.

5. Set any additional values related to the filter to customize output.

6. Retrieve the output CIImage using the "outputImage" key.

7. Create a `UIImage` from the `CIImage` by use of a `CIContext`.

Here, you have chosen to apply two different filters: a "Hue Adjustment", and a "Straighten Filter". The former will change the hue of your image, while the latter is used to rotate an image to straighten it out.

> **NOTE:** There are an incredibly large number of filters that can be applied to images, all with their own specific parameters and keys. In order to find details for a specific filter, use the Apple documentation at
> `http://developer.apple.com/library/ios/#DOCUMENTATION/GraphicsImaging/Re ference/CoreImageFilterReference/Reference/reference.html`.

Now, you can specify these newly created filtered images to your view controller by modifying your `-tableView:didSelectRowAtIndexPath:` method again.

```
- (void)tableView:(UITableView *)tableView didSelectRowAtIndexPath:(NSIndexPath *)indexPath
{
if (self.mainImage != nil)
    {
        UIImage *image;
        NSString *label;
BOOL showsButtons;
if (indexPath.row == 0)
        {
            image = self.mainImage;
CGSize contentSize = self.detailViewController.imageViewContent.frame.size;
            image = [MainDetailViewController aspectScaleImage:image
toSize:contentSize];
            label = @"Select an Image to Display";
            showsButtons = YES;
        }
    else
        {
            image = [self.images objectAtIndex:indexPath.row];
CGSize contentSize = self.detailViewController.imageViewContent.frame.size;
            image = [MainDetailViewController aspectScaleImage:image
toSize:contentSize];
            showsButtons = NO;

if (indexPath.row == 1)
            {
                label = @"Hue Adjustment";
            }
    else if (indexPath.row == 2)
            {
                label = @"Straightening Filter";
            }
        }
        [self.detailViewController configureDetailsWithImage:image label:label
showsButtons:showsButtons];
    }
}
```

As you can see, you have updated all of your displays to, instead of showing differently resized examples of the same image, show the original image with its different filters. You have adopted your third method of resizing images for all these to be displayed.

You will also update your -tableView:cellForRowAtIndexPath: to include your newest implementation.

```
- (UITableViewCell *)tableView:(UITableView *)tableView
cellForRowAtIndexPath:(NSIndexPath *)indexPath
{
static NSString *CellIdentifier = @"Cell";

UITableViewCell *cell = [tableView dequeueReusableCellWithIdentifier:CellIdentifier];
if (cell == nil) {
        cell = [[UITableViewCell alloc] initWithStyle:UITableViewCellStyleDefault
reuseIdentifier:CellIdentifier];
    }

if (indexPath.row == 0)
        cell.textLabel.text = NSLocalizedString(@"Selected Image", @"Detail");
else if (indexPath.row == 1)
        cell.textLabel.text = NSLocalizedString(@"Hue Adjust", @"Detail");
else if (indexPath.row == 2)
        cell.textLabel.text = NSLocalizedString(@"Straighten Filter", @"Detail");
return cell;
}
```

Back in your detail view controller, you must make a few extra changes to fully configure your new functionalities.

You will adjust your configuration method to a more general case, now that you are formatting all of your display images similarly.

```
-(void)configureDetailsWithImage:(UIImage *)image label:(NSString *)label
showsButtons:(BOOL)showsButton
{
self.selectedImage = image;
self.imageViewContent.image = image;
self.detailDescriptionLabel.text = label;
self.imageViewContent.contentMode = UIViewContentModeScaleAspectFit;
self.imageViewContent.backgroundColor = [UIColor blackColor];
if (showsButton == NO)
    {
self.selectImageButton.enabled = NO;
self.selectImageButton.hidden = YES;
self.clearImageButton.enabled = NO;
self.clearImageButton.hidden = YES;
    }
else if (showsButton == YES)
    {
self.selectImageButton.enabled = YES;
self.selectImageButton.hidden = NO;
self.clearImageButton.enabled = YES;
self.clearImageButton.hidden = NO;
    }
}
```

Finally, your `UIImagePickerControllerDelegate` protocol method will also require some adjustment. The new code will resemble the following:

```
-(void)imagePickerController:(UIImagePickerController *)picker
didFinishPickingMediaWithInfo:(NSDictionary *)info
{
UIImage *image = [info valueForKey:@"UIImagePickerControllerOriginalImage"];
self.selectedImage = image;

self.masterViewController.mainImage = image;
CGSize contentSize = self.imageViewContent.frame.size;
self.imageViewContent.image = [MainDetailViewController aspectScaleImage:image
toSize:contentSize];
self.imageViewContent.contentMode = UIViewContentModeScaleAspectFit;
self.imageViewContent.backgroundColor = [UIColor blackColor];

    [self.pop dismissPopoverAnimated:YES];
}
```

Upon running your application now, you will be able to see the outputs of your two types of filters used.

Shown in Figure 15–17 is the example of your hue adjustment. Your chosen input angle of 3.14/2.0 will drastically change the hues of your image.

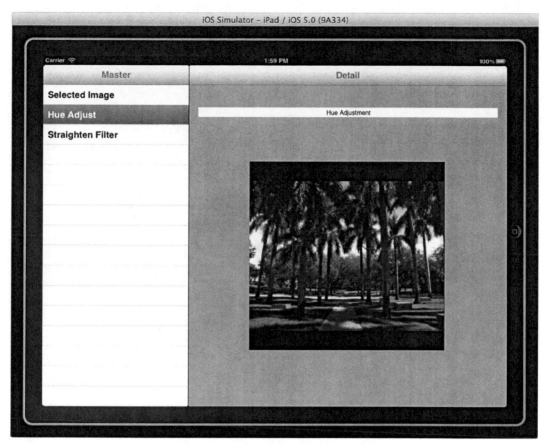

Figure 15–17. *Your new application applying a hue adjustment filter*

In the same application, your second filter, with its specified input angle of 3.14, will rotate your given image by 180 degrees, as is done in Figure 15–18.

Figure 15–18. *Applying a straightening filter to rotate an image*

You are also quite easily able to combine multiple filters in series by simply specifying the output image of one filter as the input image of another. Add the following code to the -`populateImagesWithImage:` method to create a combination filter.

```
CIFilter *seriesFilter = [CIFilter filterWithName:@"CIStraightenFilter"];
[seriesFilter setDefaults];
[seriesFilter setValue:outputHueAdjust forKey:@"inputImage"];
[seriesFilter setValue:[NSNumber numberWithFloat:3.14/2.0f] forKey:@"inputAngle"];
CIImage *outputSeries = [seriesFilter valueForKey:@"outputImage"];
UIImage *outputImage3 = [UIImage imageWithCGImage:[context createCGImage:outputSeries
fromRect:outputSeries.extent]];
[self.images addObject:outputImage3];
```

Update your -`tableView:numberOfRowsInSection:` method to show a fourth cell.

```
- (NSInteger)tableView:(UITableView *)tableView numberOfRowsInSection:(NSInteger)section
{
if (self.mainImage == nil)
    {
return 1;
    }
else
```

```
    {
return 4;
    }
}
```

Add a fourth case to your -tableView:cellForRowAtIndexPath: method to display the name of this fourth cell.

```
else if (indexPath.row == 3)
    cell.textLabel.text = NSLocalizedString(@"Series Filter", @"Detail");
```

Finally, add another case, directly after the others used to set label for rows 1 and 2, to your -tableView:didSelectRowAtIndexPath: to correctly set the UILabel.

```
else if (indexPath.row == 3)
{
    label = @"Series Filter";
}
```

Now, upon testing the application, your new double-filter will combine the effects of your previous two, resulting in a hue-adjusted and rotated image, as in Figure 15–19.

> **NOTE:** The majority of the processing work, when dealing with the Core Image framework, comes from when the UIImage is created from the CIImage using the CIContext. The creation of a CIImage itself is a very fast operation. In your application, you have chosen to create all of your filtered images at once in order to allow for quick navigation between each display. This is why, upon selecting an image, your simulator may take a couple seconds to actually display your images and refresh. If you were building this application for release, you would want to convey in some way to the user that work is being done through a UIActivityIndicatorView or UIProgressView.

Figure 15–19. *A series combination of hue adjustment and straightening filters*

Now, you will make use of your earlier resizing functionality to create a thumbnail for each filtered image, so that it can be displayed in your master's UITableView.

Since you ended up taking your thumbnail-resizing method out of your previous recipe, here is the method again that you will use.

```
+ (UIImage *)scaleImageThumbnail:(UIImage *)image toSize:(CGSize)size
{
UIGraphicsBeginImageContext(size);
if (image.size.height< image.size.width)
    {
float ratio = size.height/image.size.height;
      [image drawInRect:CGRectMake(0, 0, image.size.width*ratio, size.height)];
    }
else
    {
float ratio = size.width/image.size.width;
      [image drawInRect:CGRectMake(0, 0, size.width, image.size.height*ratio)];
    }
UIImage *aspectScaledImage = UIGraphicsGetImageFromCurrentImageContext();
UIGraphicsEndImageContext();
```

```
return aspectScaledImage;
}
```

Make sure also to place this method's handler in the detail view controller's header file, so that your master view controller is able to call it.

```
+ (UIImage *)scaleImageThumbnail:(UIImage *)image toSize:(CGSize)size;
```

Now, you just need to modify your -tableView:cellForRowAtIndexPath: again to include the selection of an image for the cell's imageView. In entirety, the method should resemble the following code.

```
- (UITableViewCell *)tableView:(UITableView *)tableView
cellForRowAtIndexPath:(NSIndexPath *)indexPath
{
static NSString *CellIdentifier = @"Cell";

UITableViewCell *cell = [tableView dequeueReusableCellWithIdentifier:CellIdentifier];
if (cell == nil) {
        cell = [[UITableViewCell alloc] initWithStyle:UITableViewCellStyleDefault
reuseIdentifier:CellIdentifier];
    }

/////NEW THUMBNAIL CODE
if ([self.images count] >0)
        {
CGSize thumbnailSize = CGSizeMake(120, 75);
UIImage *displayImage = [self.images objectAtIndex:indexPath.row];
if (displayImage)
        {
UIImage *thumbnailImage = [MainDetailViewController scaleImageThumbnail:displayImage
toSize:thumbnailSize];
            cell.imageView.image = thumbnailImage;
        }
    }
/////END OF THUMBNAIL CODE

if (indexPath.row == 0)
        cell.textLabel.text = NSLocalizedString(@"Selected Image", @"Detail");
else if (indexPath.row == 1)
        cell.textLabel.text = NSLocalizedString(@"Hue Adjust", @"Detail");
else if (indexPath.row == 2)
        cell.textLabel.text = NSLocalizedString(@"Straighten Filter", @"Detail");
else if (indexPath.row == 3)
        cell.textLabel.text = NSLocalizedString(@"Series Filter", @"Detail");
return cell;
}
```

When you test your application now, your master view controller's cells will each have a scaled thumbnail version of the larger image they refer to, as in Figure 15–20.

Figure 15–20. *Your application with scaled (clipping) thumbnails*

Recipe 15–5: Detecting Features

Along with the incredibly flexible use of filters, the Core Image framework has also brought to iOS 5.0 the possibility of feature detection, allowing you to effectively "search" images for key components, such as faces.

We will develop a new, smaller project to implement your new facial detection application, rather than continuing on with your previous recipe. Create a new project for the iPhone device family, making use of the Single View Application template, shown in Figure 15–21.

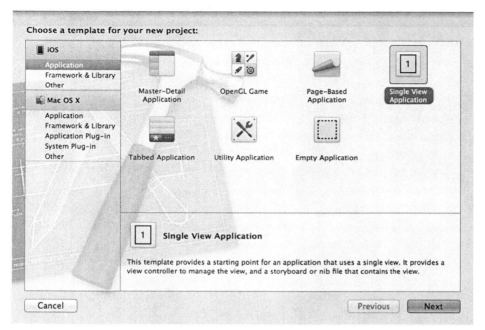

Figure 15–21. *Creating a single view application*

Once your project is created, add the Core Image framework to your project, just as in the previous recipe.

Add two instances of UIImageView and a UIButton to your view, so as to resemble Figure 15–22.

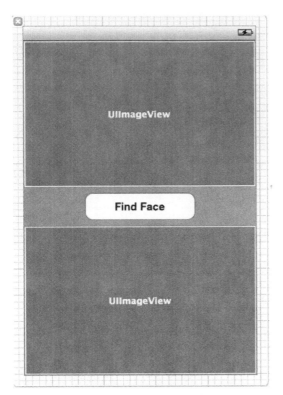

Figure 15–22. *Your view controller's XIB setup*

Connect each of the elements to your view controller. Your UIButton should have the property name findFaceButton, and perform the action -findFacePressed:. Make your upper UIImageView imageViewMain, and your lower one imageViewAlt.

```
#import <UIKit/UIKit.h>

@interface MainViewController : UIViewController

@property (strong, nonatomic) IBOutlet UIImageView *imageViewMain;
@property (strong, nonatomic) IBOutlet UIImageView *imageViewAlt;
@property (strong, nonatomic) IBOutlet UIButton *findFaceButton;
- (IBAction)findFacePressed:(id)sender;

@end
```

Next, find an image to be displayed in your application, and add it to your project. You can do this by dragging the file from the Finder into your project's navigation pane. When the dialog for adding files appears, make sure the box marked "Copy items into destination group's folder (if needed)" is checked, as it is in Figure 15–23. In order to properly test this application, try to find an image with an easily visible face.

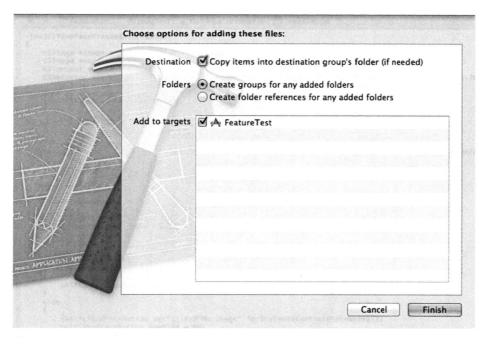

Figure 15–23. *Pop-up dialog for adding files into your project*

Now, you can build your -viewDidLoad method to configure your UIImageView elements, as well as set the initial image to your main image view. Make sure to change the name of the image ("testImage.JPG" in the following code) to your own file name.

```
- (void)viewDidLoad
{
    [super viewDidLoad];

self.imageViewMain.backgroundColor = [UIColor blackColor];
self.imageViewMain.contentMode = UIViewContentModeScaleAspectFit;
self.imageViewAlt.backgroundColor = [UIColor blackColor];
self.imageViewAlt.contentMode = UIViewContentModeScaleAspectFit;

UIImage *image = [UIImage imageNamed:@"testImage.JPG"];
if (image != nil)
    {
self.imageViewMain.image = image;
    }
else
    {
        [self.findFaceButton setTitle:@"No Image" forState:UIControlStateNormal];
self.findFaceButton.enabled = NO;
self.findFaceButton.alpha = 0.6;
    }
}
```

Finally you can implement your -findFacePressed: method to do your feature detection. You will have this method determine the location of any faces in your given image, create a `UIImage` from the last face found, and then display it in your alternate image view.

```
-(IBAction)findFacePressed:(id)sender
{
UIImage *image = self.imageViewMain.image;
CIImage *coreImage = [[CIImage alloc] initWithImage:image];
CIContext *context = [CIContext contextWithOptions:nil];
CIDetector *detector = [CIDetector detectorOfType:@"CIDetectorTypeFace"context:context
options:[NSDictionary dictionaryWithObjectsAndKeys:@"CIDetectorAccuracyHigh",
@"CIDetectorAccuracy", nil]];
NSArray *features = [detector featuresInImage:coreImage];

if ([features count] >0)
    {
CIImage *faceImage = [coreImage imageByCroppingToRect:[[features lastObject] bounds]];
UIImage *face = [UIImage imageWithCGImage:[context createCGImage:faceImage
fromRect:faceImage.extent]];
self.imageViewAlt.image = face;

        [self.findFaceButton setTitle:[NSString stringWithFormat:@"%i Face(s) Found",
[features count]] forState:UIControlStateNormal];
self.findFaceButton.enabled = NO;
self.findFaceButton.alpha = 0.6;
    }
else
    {
        [self.findFaceButton setTitle:@"No Faces Found"forState:UIControlStateNormal];
self.findFaceButton.enabled = NO;
self.findFaceButton.alpha = 0.6;
    }
}
```

This method contains the following steps:

1. Acquire a `CIImage` object from your initial `UIImage`.

2. Create a `CIContext` with which to analyze images.

3. Create an instance of `CIDetector` with type and options parameters.

   a. The `type` parameter specifies the specific feature to identify. Currently, the only possible value for this is `CIDetectorTypeFace`, which allows you to specifically look for faces.

   b. The `options` parameter allows you to specify the accuracy with which you want to look for features. Low accuracy will be faster, but high accuracy will be more precise.

4. Create an array of all the features found in your image. Since you specified the `CIDetectorTypeFace` type, these objects will all be instances of the `CIFaceFeature` class.

5. Create a `CIImage` using the `-imageByCroppingToRect:` method with the original image, as well as the bounds specified by the last `CIFaceFeature` found in the image. These bounds specify the `CGRect` in which the face exists.

6. Create a UIImage out of your CIImage (done exactly as in the previous recipe), and then display it in your UIImageView.

Upon running your application, you will be able to detect any faces inside your images, the latter of which will be displayed in your lower UIImageView, as in Figure 15–24.

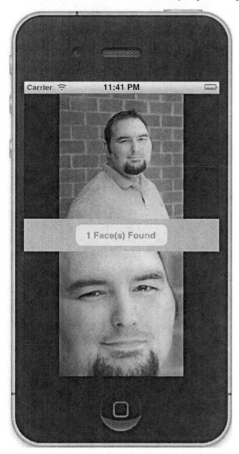

Figure 15–24. *Your application detecting and cropping a face from an image*

Summary

Images create our world. From the simplest of picture books that children love to read to the massive amounts of visual data transmitted around the Internet through Twitter, e-mail, Facebook, Tumblr, and every other web service, pictures and images have certainly become one of the key foundations of modern culture. As such, by learning to create, handle, manipulate, and display images in your applications, you are able to acquire a significantly greater connection with your users, imparting a more powerful emotional response and interacting with more flexibility and control than ever. From building colored shapes to displaying photographs, to even the newest iOS 5.0 additions of manipulating images, you are able to create more interesting and useful applications. The Core Image framework even furthers this ability with the addition of image filters, to create wildly different images, and facial detection software, to provide more in-depth information from your application. At this point of technological development, it seems quite fair to say that a picture being worth a thousand words is a vast understatement.

Chapter 16

Game Kit Recipes

In this chapter, you are going to use a simple Hangman game and integrate it with Game Center. Game Center allows you to enhance your game by providing easy methods for implementing social features such as high scores, game achievements, and multiplayer gameplay. Adding these features can not only provide more value to your game but also extend the "replay factor" of your game.

You will start by adding high scores and achievements and ultimately finish by making your game multiplayer. You can find the start of this project at https://github.com/shawngrimes/HangmanMP.

Recipe 16–1: Starting with Game Center

Before you can start using Game Center, you will need to use iTunes Connect. If you have already submitted an app or game to the iTunes App Store, you already know what iTunes Connect is. For those who haven't, iTunes Connect is where you manage the apps that you are publishing. You will enter your apps metadata (description, keywords, support URL, etc.) as well as any Apple-provided features that it will use, such as iAds, In App Purchase, or, in this case, Game Center.

In order to use Game Center, you will need to tell iTunes Connect about your game so you can start using the Game Center sandbox. The Game Center sandbox is a development area where developers can test their Game Center integration without impacting production scores or achievements.

iTunes Connect Setup

The first step to enabling Game Center integration is to create a bundle identifier in the iOS Provisioning Portal if you have not done so for your app already. The bundle identifier is used to identify all the related data for an app. For instance, if you have a free and a paid version of your game and you want them to use the same high score table, you would give them the same bundle identifier.

Visit the iOS Provisioning Portal on developer.apple.com, and click App IDs. Create your new bundle identifier. The information shown in Figure 16–1 is the app information you will use for this game.

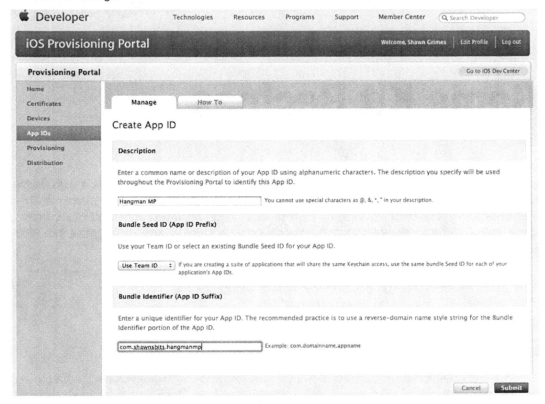

Figure 16–1. *Configuring your App ID*

Now go to itunesconnect.apple.com, and click Manage Your Applications. If you have not already submitted your app for review, click the Add New App button, revealing a page resembling Figure 16–2. Enter the information for your new app, and click Continue.

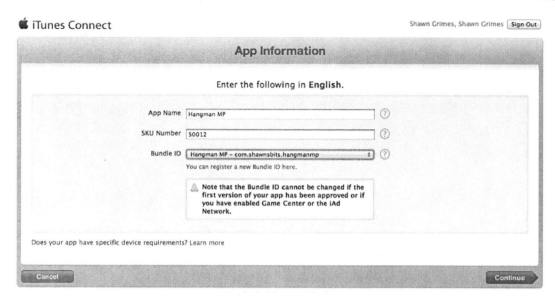

Figure 16–2. *Entering your application information*

Once you've entered all of the metadata about your app, including the screenshot and app icon, you can enable Game Center. Click the Manage Game Center button, shown in Figure 16–3, and then click Enable.

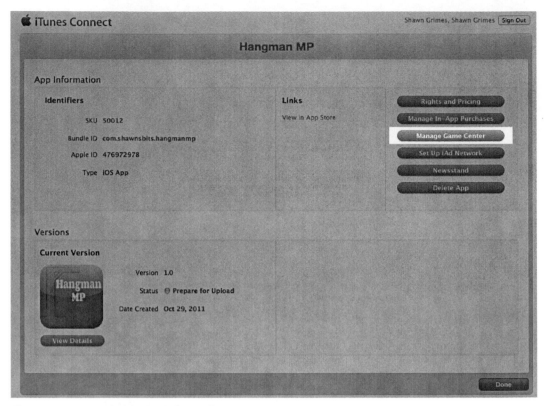

Figure 16–3. *Accessing the Game Center Management page*

Once enabled, you can configure leaderboards and achievements (more on those to follow).

Project Setup

Now get your game code set up to use Game Center. Open your project (or the one provided for this chapter) in Xcode.

Once Xcode is open, click your project name in the project navigator and select the desired target. Go to the Build Phases tab, and expand the Link Binaries With Libraries area. You want to add the Game Kit framework, so click the + button highlighted in Figure 16–4.

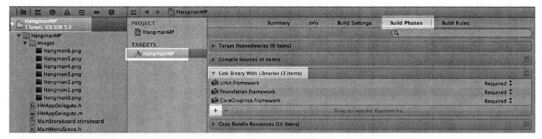

Figure 16–4. *Build Phases tab for adding frameworks*

In the resulting pop-up resembling Figure 16–5, search for Game Kit and click Add.

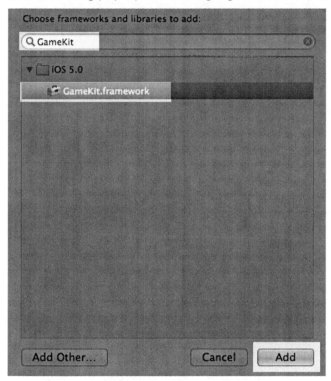

Figure 16–5. *Adding the Game Kit framework to a project*

If your game can work without Game Center, then you'll want to make this an optional framework rather than a required one, in which case your frameworks list will resemble Figure 16–6.

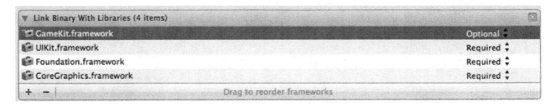

Figure 16–6. *Configuring the Game Kit framework to be optional*

If you want to require Game Center, then feel free to leave it as required, but you'll need to do one other step to require Game Center. Open the Info tab of your target, and add "gamekit" to the list of required device capabilities, as in Figure 16–7.

Figure 16–7. *Adding "gamekit" as a required device capability*

While you are editing the Info tab, make sure your bundle identifier matches what you put in iTunes Connect, as in Figure 16–8.

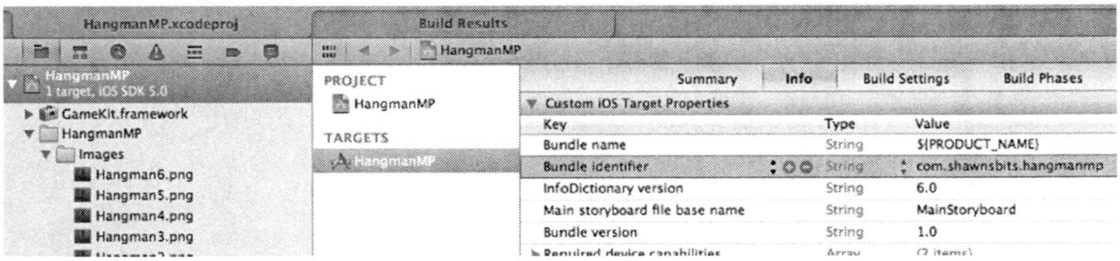

Figure 16–8. *Confirming the correct bundle identifier in your app to be the same as was used in iTunes Connect*

You can now include Game Center functionality in your code by adding the statement `#import <GameKit/GameKit.h>` to your code. Start by making sure Game Center is available on this device.

Checking for Game Center Support

First, create a method for checking for Game Center support. I'll add it to the app delegate so that you can check the state at any point in the game. Start by importing

Game Kit into the implementation file (.m), and create a method for checking the availability of Game Center:

```
#import "HMAppDelegate.h"
#import <GameKit/GameKit.h>

@implementation HMAppDelegate
@synthesize window = _window;

+(BOOL) isGameCenterAvailable
{
    // Check for presence of GKLocalPlayer class.
    BOOL localPlayerClassAvailable = (NSClassFromString(@"GKLocalPlayer")) != nil;

    // The device must be running iOS 4.1 or later.
    NSString *reqSysVer = @"4.1";
    NSString *currSysVer = [[UIDevice currentDevice] systemVersion];
    BOOL osVersionSupported = ([currSysVer compare:reqSysVer
                                       options:NSNumericSearch] !=
NSOrderedAscending);

    return (localPlayerClassAvailable && osVersionSupported);
}
```

In your interface file (.h), add a declaration for isGameCenterAvailable so other classes can use it and autocomplete will see it:

```
#import <UIKit/UIKit.h>

@interface HMAppDelegate : UIResponder <UIApplicationDelegate>

@property (strong, nonatomic) UIWindow *window;

+(BOOL) isGameCenterAvailable;

@end
```

Player Authentication

You want to authenticate your player as soon as possible. This is best done as soon as your game is finished launching, so you'll add a method to your app delegate didFinishLaunchingWithOptions: method. First, though, switch to your interface file and add a property for your local player to your app delegate so you can access it whenever needed.

Since you imported GameKit.h into the implementation file, you'll need to tell your interface file that a class of GKLocalPlayer exists. You can do this with the following line under the import statements in the interface file:

```
@class GKLocalPlayer;
```

Then add a property for GKLocalPlayer:

```
@property(strong, nonatomic) GKLocalPlayer *localPlayer;
```

The final app delegate interface file looks like this:

```
#import <UIKit/UIKit.h>

@class GKLocalPlayer;

@interface HMAppDelegate : UIResponder <UIApplicationDelegate>

@property (strong, nonatomic) UIWindow *window;
@property(strong, nonatomic) GKLocalPlayer *localPlayer;

+(BOOL) isGameCenterAvailable;

@end
```

Switch over to the implementation file and synthesize your new property:

```
@synthesize localPlayer;
```

Change your `didFinishLaunchingWithOptions:` to look like the following. This will authenticate the player and set the `localPlayer` property to the `localPlayer`:

```
- (BOOL)application:(UIApplication *)application
didFinishLaunchingWithOptions:(NSDictionary *)launchOptions
{
    // Override point for customization after application launch.
    if([HMAppDelegate isGameCenterAvailable]){
        //If GameCenter is available, let's authenticate the user
        GKLocalPlayer *_localPlayer=[GKLocalPlayer localPlayer];
        [_localPlayer authenticateWithCompletionHandler:^(NSError *error) {
            if(localPlayer.isAuthenticated){
                self.localPlayer=localPlayer;
            }
        }];
    }
    return YES;
}
```

Some notes on this: you should always check the property isAuthenticated rather than checking to see if there is an error. If there is an error, Game Kit may be able to authenticate the user with cached data and authenticate anyway. You shouldn't display the errors to the user—Game Center will do that for you. The errors are mostly for debugging.

That's pretty much all there is to authenticating a user. When you run your app, it will prompt you to log in or create a new account, as in Figure 16–9. Authenticated users can be passed between apps, so if you or a user have authenticated to Game Center in another app, this can be passed to your app without prompting you to log in again.

Figure 16–9. *Your application prompting for a Game Center account*

Recipe 16–2: Leaderboards

You are now able to authenticate your user. Let's start storing some high scores. Leaderboards, a.k.a. high scores, are a great way to increase replay value of your game and encourage competition among friends. You first need to create a leaderboard in iTunes Connect, so head over to `itunesconnect.apple.com`.

Setting Up iTunes Connect

Click Manage Your Applications, and then click your app that has Game Center enabled. On the App Information page, click Manage Game Center, highlighted in Figure 16–10.

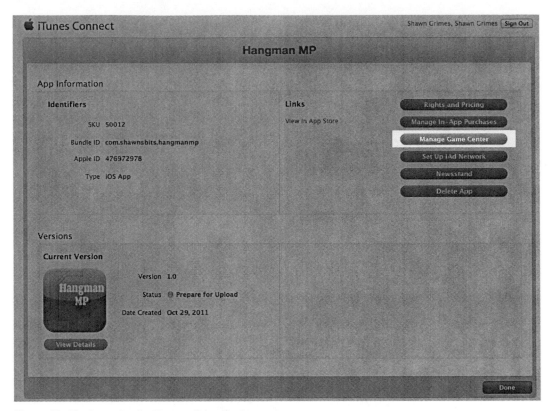

Figure 16–10. *Accessing the Manage Game Center screen*

Click Setup under the Leaderboard heading, shown in Figure 16–11.

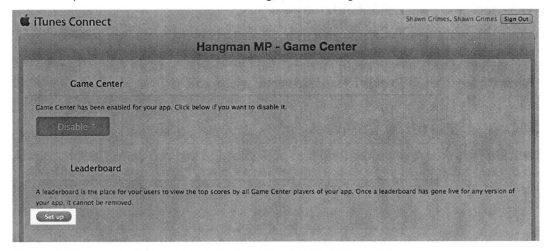

Figure 16–11. *The Game Center screen, from which you can set up a leaderboard*

Once a leaderboard has gone live for an app, it cannot be deleted, so create them with some thought. You can have up to 25 leaderboards per app. This allows you to create multiple leaderboards for different difficulties or even one for each level of your game, whatever makes the most sense. In your simple app, you are going to create only one leaderboard.

Click the Add Leaderboard button, marked in Figure 16–12, to begin.

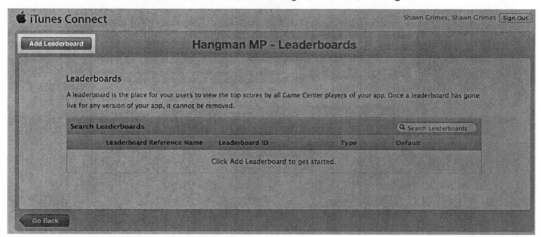

Figure 16–12. *Your app's list of leaderboards to be added to*

Click the Choose button under Single Leaderboard, marked in Figure 16–13, to continue with a stand-alone leaderboard.

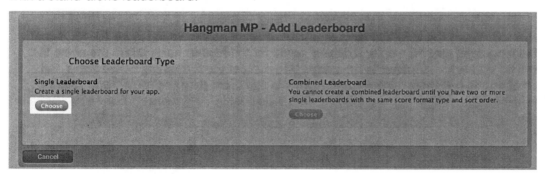

Figure 16–13. *Choosing leaderboard type*

Fill in a name for the leaderboard and an identifier. The name is an internal name for tracking purposes and will not be displayed to the player. (The display name is configured in the next step when adding a language.) Now select the score format type; in this case, I'm going to use a simple integer, but you can also use time-based, floats, and currency. Select the sort order for your leaderboard. If you want high scores at the top (typical), then sort "High to Low"; if you want your low scores at the top (for instance in a golf game), then sort "Low to High".

You will need to set up at least one language for the leaderboard. To do that, click the Add Language button, shown in Figure 16–14.

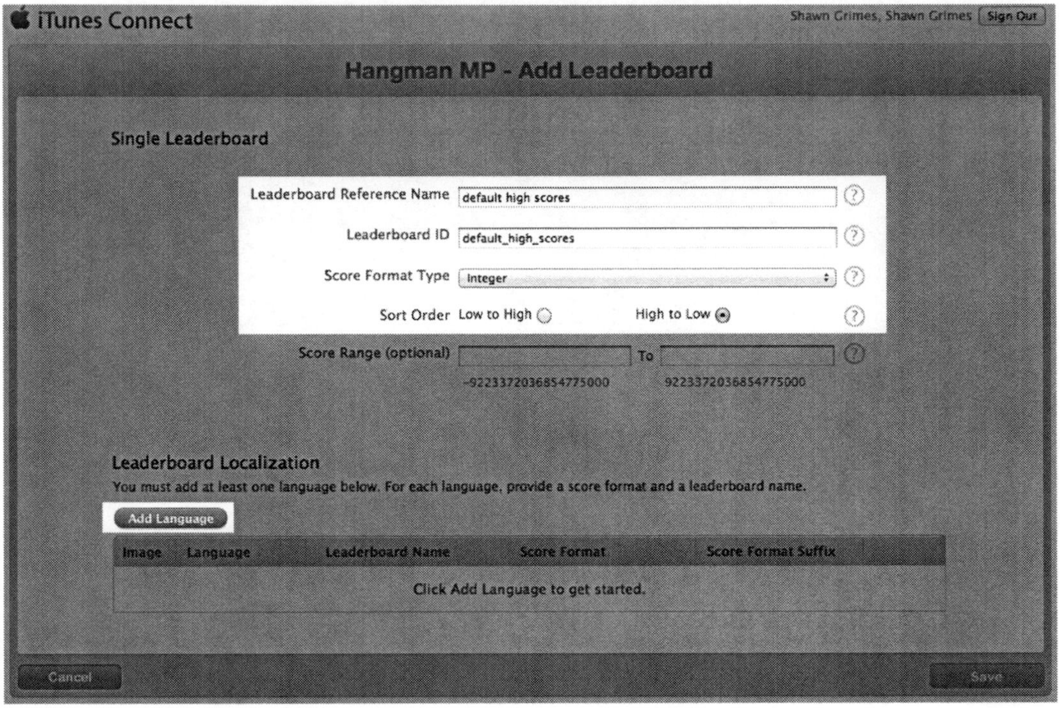

Figure 16–14. *Configuring a leaderboard*

Now configure the localized language for that score as shown in Figure 16–15. Select the language, and then enter a display name for the leaderboard; this is the name that will be visible to the player in the game. You can set the formatting of the score and what unit to call them (singular and plural); in this case, they are "point" and "points."

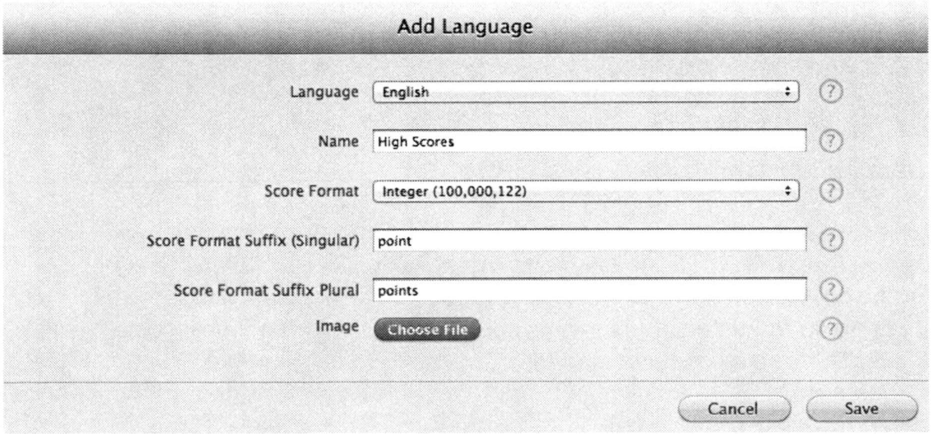

Figure 16–15. *Language display settings for a leaderboard*

Once complete, click Save and then click Save on the leaderboards page as well.

Now, let's dive into some code.

Setting Up Your Code

Open the HangmanMP project, and go to the GameScene.m file. Add the import statement at the top of the file: #import <GameKit/GameKit.h>.

Let's add a method to report the score under the @synthesize and instance variables:

```
- (void) reportScore: (int64_t) score forCategory: (NSString*) category
{
    GKScore *scoreReporter = [[GKScore alloc] initWithCategory:category];
    scoreReporter.value = score;
    [scoreReporter reportScoreWithCompletionHandler:^(NSError *error) {

        NSArray *paths = NSSearchPathForDirectoriesInDomains(NSDocumentDirectory,
NSUserDomainMask, YES);
        NSString *scoreFilePath = [NSString stringWithFormat:@"%@/scores.plist",[paths
objectAtIndex:0]];
        NSMutableDictionary *scoreDictionary=[NSMutableDictionary
dictionaryWithContentsOfFile:scoreFilePath];

        if (error != nil)
        {
            //There was an error so we need to save the score locally and resubmit later
            NSLog(@"Saving score for later");
            [scoreDictionary setValue:scoreReporter forKey:[NSDate date]];
            [scoreDictionary writeToFile:scoreFilePath atomically:YES];
        }
    }];
}
```

This method will try to report the score, but if it fails, it will save the score to a dictionary and write that dictionary to a file so you can load the scores later. You can call this method anywhere that you want to report the score to Game Center with a call similar to this:

```
[self reportScore:playerScore forCategory:@"default_high_scores"];
```

You should also try to report any saved scores when you start the app, so switch over to your app delegate implementation file (.m).

Add the following to the end of didFinishLaunchingWithOptions, before the line that reads "return YES;".

```
NSArray *paths = NSSearchPathForDirectoriesInDomains(NSDocumentDirectory,
NSUserDomainMask, YES);
    NSString *scoreFilePath = [NSString stringWithFormat:@"%@/scores.plist",[paths
objectAtIndex:0]];
    NSMutableDictionary *scoreDictionary=[NSMutableDictionary
dictionaryWithContentsOfFile:scoreFilePath];

    for (NSDate *dateID in [scoreDictionary allKeys]) {
        NSLog(@"Reporting old score: %@", dateID);
        GKScore *scoreToReport=(GKScore *)[scoreDictionary objectForKey:dateID];
```

```
        [scoreToReport reportScoreWithCompletionHandler:^(NSError *error) {
            NSArray *paths = NSSearchPathForDirectoriesInDomains(NSDocumentDirectory,
NSUserDomainMask, YES);
            NSString *scoreFilePath = [NSString
stringWithFormat:@"%@/scores.plist",[paths objectAtIndex:0]];
            NSMutableDictionary *scoreDictionary=[NSMutableDictionary
dictionaryWithContentsOfFile:scoreFilePath];

            if (error != nil)
            {
                //There was an error so we need to save the score locally and resubmit
later
                [scoreDictionary setValue:scoreToReport forKey:scoreToReport.playerID];
                [scoreDictionary writeToFile:scoreFilePath atomically:YES];
            }
        }];

    }
```

This will take a look at the old scores written to file and try to send them to Game Center.

Showing High Scores

High scores are no fun unless people see them. Your users can see the High Scores for your game from within the Game Center app, but you can also give them a direct link to the high scores very easily. Switch over to MainMenuScene.h.

You'll want to import GameKit.h and also set MainMenuScene as a GKLeaderboardViewControllerDelegate.

```
#import <UIKit/UIKit.h>
#import <GameKit/GameKit.h>

@interface MainMenuScene : UIViewController <GKLeaderboardViewControllerDelegate>

@end
```

Now go to the implementation file (.m), and add two new methods to the top. The first method will dismiss the GKLeaderboardViewController when you click Done:

```
- (void)leaderboardViewControllerDidFinish:(GKLeaderboardViewController*)viewController
{
    [self dismissModalViewControllerAnimated:YES];
}
```

The other method you need to add will show the actual GKLeaderboardViewController view:

```
- (void) showLeaderboard
{
    GKLeaderboardViewController *leaderboardController = [[GKLeaderboardViewController
alloc] init];
    if (leaderboardController != nil)
    {
        leaderboardController.leaderboardDelegate = self;
```

```
        [self presentModalViewController: leaderboardController animated: YES];
    }
}
```

Now you can create a UIButton on the main menu scene and connect it to the showLeaderboard method to display the leaderboards for your game. You can create the button in the -viewDidLoad method:

```
- (void)viewDidLoad
{
    [super viewDidLoad];
    UIButton *buttonShowHighScores=[UIButton buttonWithType:UIButtonTypeRoundedRect];
    [buttonShowHighScores addTarget:self action:@selector(showLeaderboard)
forControlEvents:UIControlEventTouchUpInside];
    buttonShowHighScores.frame=CGRectMake(104, 302, 112, 44);
    [buttonShowHighScores setTitle:@"High Scores" forState:UIControlStateNormal];

    [self.view addSubview:buttonShowHighScores];
}
```

Recipe 16–3: Achievements

Achievements in games are similar to badges and other unlockables in other apps and games. You provide your players with a notification when they reach certain milestones. In the HangmanMP game, a good achievement might be if they get all the letters right in a word without any mistakes. Let's take a look at how you would implement that.

Setting Up iTunes Connect

As with other things you've done with Game Center, it all starts in iTunes Connect, so head over there: itunesconnect.apple.com. Click Manage Your Applications, and then click the app you have set up for Game Center. Now click Manage Game Center.

In the Game Center management page, click Set Up under Achievements, shown in Figure 16–16.

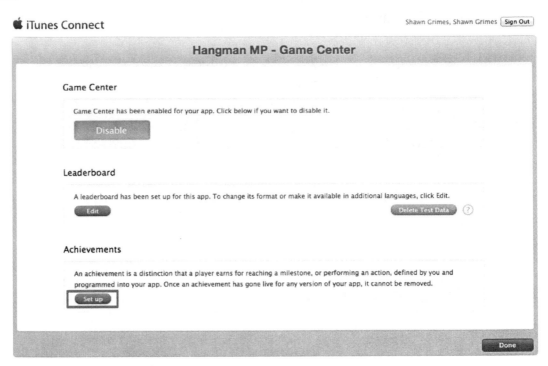

Figure 16–16. *Accessing the Achievements section from the Game Center screen*

Each game can have up to 1,000 achievement points. These points can be assigned to different achievements as you see fit, but each achievement can have a max of only 100 achievement points.

For now you are going to create a 50-point achievement, so go ahead and click Add New Achievement, as in Figure 16–17.

Figure 16–17. *Adding a new achievement for your app*

This achievement will be for getting all the letters and no mistakes in a small word (six letters or less). Your configuration is shown in Figure 16–18.

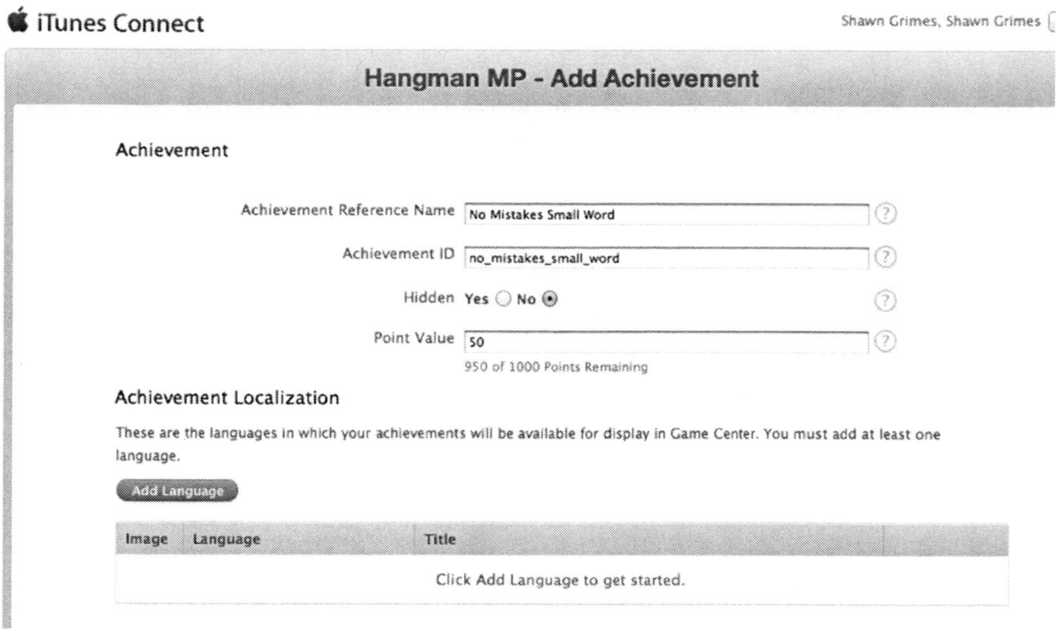

Figure 16–18. *Configuring an achievement's details*

You can't save an achievement until you add at least one language to it, so click Add Language now. The resulting view will resemble Figure 16–19. Here, you can set the achievement title as well as the "pre-earned" description. The pre-earned description should detail how the achievement is earned. There is also an earned description, which is the description shown after the achievement is earned. Finally, you will need an image to represent the achievement. This should be a 512x512 72 ppi .png file.

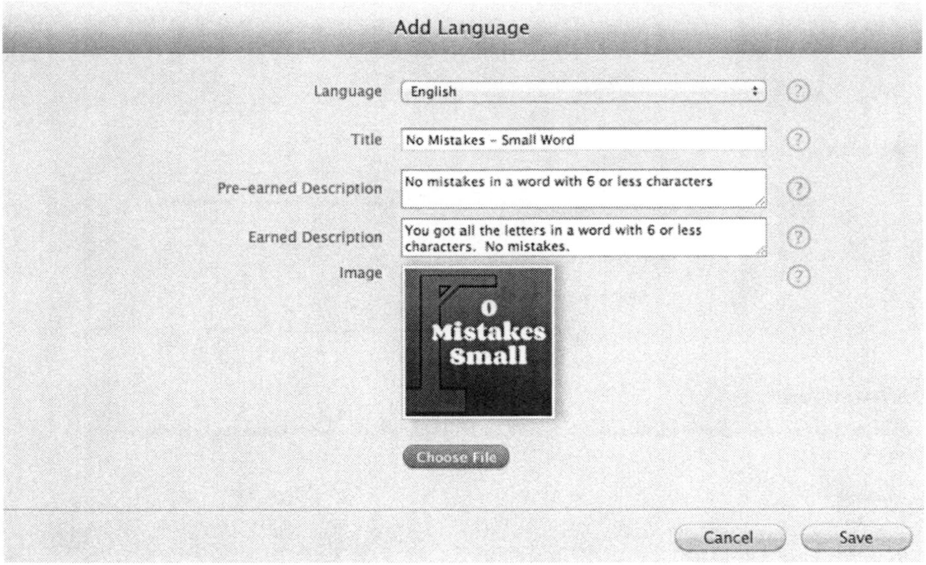

Figure 16–19. *Configuring achievement details in a specific language*

Click Save and then Save again on the Achievement info page. And let's write some code…

Setting Up Your Code

This is going to be very similar to setting up leaderboards. Open up GameScene.m, and add the following method:

```
- (void) reportAchievementIdentifier:(NSString*)identifier percentComplete:(float)
percent
{
    GKAchievement *achievement = [[GKAchievement alloc] initWithIdentifier:identifier];
    if (achievement)
    {
        achievement.percentComplete = percent;
        [achievement reportAchievementWithCompletionHandler:^(NSError *error)
        {
            if (error != nil)
            {
                //There was an error so we need to save the achievement locally and
resubmit later
                NSLog(@"Saving achievement for later");
                NSArray *paths =
NSSearchPathForDirectoriesInDomains(NSDocumentDirectory, NSUserDomainMask, YES);
                NSString *achievementFilePath = [NSString
stringWithFormat:@"%@/achievements.plist",[paths objectAtIndex:0]];
                NSMutableDictionary *achievementDictionary=[NSMutableDictionary
dictionaryWithContentsOfFile:achievementFilePath];

                [achievementDictionary setValue:achievement
forKey:achievement.identifier];
```

```
                [achievementDictionary writeToFile:achievementFilePath atomically:YES];
            }
        }];
    }
}
```

Now you just need to call this method with your achievement and the percentage complete. Since in this case, you either have the achievement or you don't, the percentage complete will be 100 or 0, but you can use this snippet to report on the completion of any achievement. This bit of code goes just after you report the score in the -processGuess method.

```
if(unfoundLetters.location==NSNotFound){
            [self reportScore:playerScore forCategory:@"default_high_scores"];
            if(self.badGuessCount==0 && self.stringHiddenWord.length<=6){
                NSLog(@"Reporting achievement");
                [self reportAchievementIdentifier:@"no_mistakes_small_word"
percentComplete:100];
            }
….
```

Similar to how you reported saved scores in the app delegate, you should do the same with achievements. So go to HMAppDelegate.m, modify your friend the didFinishLaunchingWithOptions method, and add the following code before your return statement.

```
    //Report saved achievements
    NSString *achievementFilePath = [NSString
stringWithFormat:@"%@/achievements.plist",[paths objectAtIndex:0]];
    NSMutableDictionary *achievementDictionary=[NSMutableDictionary
dictionaryWithContentsOfFile:achievementFilePath];
    for (id achievement in [achievementDictionary allKeys]){
        GKAchievement *achievementToReport=(GKAchievement *)[achievementDictionary
objectForKey:achievement];
        [achievementToReport reportAchievementWithCompletionHandler:^(NSError *error)
        {
            if (error != nil)
            {
                //There was an error so we need to save the achievement locally and
resubmit later
                NSLog(@"Saving achievement for later");
                NSArray *paths =
NSSearchPathForDirectoriesInDomains(NSDocumentDirectory, NSUserDomainMask, YES);
                NSString *achievementFilePath = [NSString
stringWithFormat:@"%@/achievements.plist",[paths objectAtIndex:0]];
                NSMutableDictionary *achievementDictionary=[NSMutableDictionary
dictionaryWithContentsOfFile:achievementFilePath];

                [achievementDictionary setValue:achievementToReport
forKey:achievement];
                [achievementDictionary writeToFile:achievementFilePath atomically:YES];
            }else{
                NSLog(@"Achievement reported");
            }
        }];
    }
```

Showing Achievements

This section is going to seem like déjà vu if you followed the "Leaderboard" section. You'll want to show players the achievements they've earned in your game, and the easiest way to do that is to tie a button in your app to the GKAchievementsViewController. Head over to MainMenuScene.m, and add the following method:

```
-(void)achievementViewControllerDidFinish:(GKAchievementViewController *)viewController{
    [self dismissModalViewControllerAnimated:YES];
}
```

This will dismiss your GKAchievementViewController. To display it, you'll add the following function into MainMenuScene.m:

```
- (void) showAchievements
{
    GKAchievementViewController *achievements = [[GKAchievementViewController alloc]
init];
    if (achievements != nil)
    {
        achievements.achievementDelegate = self;
        [self presentModalViewController:achievements animated: YES];
    }
}
```

Connect a UIButton action call to that method, and then don't forget to add GKAchievementViewControllerDelegate to the MainMenuScene.h file:

```
//
//  MainMenuScene.h
//  HangmanMP

#import <UIKit/UIKit.h>
#import <GameKit/GameKit.h>

@interface MainMenuScene : UIViewController <GKLeaderboardViewControllerDelegate,
GKAchievementViewControllerDelegate>

- (IBAction)actionShowHighScores:(id)sender;

@end
```

Now test the application by launching it in the simulator. You will be able to view your newly created achievement, as in Figure 16–20.

Figure 16–20. *Your application displaying your earned achievement*

Recipe 16–4: Multiplayer

Adding a multiplayer option to your game greatly increases the replay factor of your game because now the player can go outside the bounds of the computer and play against real-life players on the Internet.

> **NOTE:** You can't test multiplayer in the simulator. Instead you'll need two devices to test with, so borrow a friend's or pick up an old iPod touch somewhere.

Setting Up Your Code

For this recipe, you can skip right over the iTunes Connect portion because if you've enabled Game Center, multiplayer is automatically made available as long as your game supports it. So let's jump right into some code.

The first thing you are going to do is update your MainMenuScene.h file. You'll need to set it as a GKMatchmakerViewControllerDelegate and also add a new action to host a multiplayer game. It should look like this:

```
// MainMenuScene.h
// HangmanMP
//
#import <UIKit/UIKit.h>
#import <GameKit/GameKit.h>

@interface MainMenuScene : UIViewController <GKLeaderboardViewControllerDelegate,
GKAchievementViewControllerDelegate,GKMatchmakerViewControllerDelegate>

- (IBAction)actionShowHighScores:(id)sender;
- (IBAction)actionShowAchievements:(id)sender;
- (IBAction)actionHostMatch:(id)sender;

@end
```

Now switch over to the MainMenuScene.m file. You'll create two standard methods required by the GKMatchmakerViewControllerDelegate protocol, matchmakerViewControllerWasCancelled and matchmakerViewController:didFailWithError:

```
- (void)matchmakerViewControllerWasCancelled:(GKMatchmakerViewController*)viewController
{
    [self dismissModalViewControllerAnimated:YES];
}

- (void)matchmakerViewController:(GKMatchmakerViewController *)viewController
             didFailWithError:(NSError *)error
{
    [self dismissModalViewControllerAnimated:YES];
    [[[UIAlertView alloc] initWithTitle:@"Error" message:error.description delegate:nil
cancelButtonTitle:@"OK" otherButtonTitles:nil] show];
}
```

One final delegate protocol method you'll need to add is matchmakerViewController:didFindMatch:, and this is how you start to load a multiplayer game.

```
- (void)matchmakerViewController:(GKMatchmakerViewController *)viewController
                 didFindMatch:(GKMatch *)match
{
    [self dismissModalViewControllerAnimated:YES];
//Set up our game scene from the story board
    GameScene *gameSceneVC=[self.storyboard
instantiateViewControllerWithIdentifier:@"GameScene"];
//Set the match property on GameScene to the matchmaker match
    gameSceneVC.match=match;
//Set the delegate of the match to GameScene, more on this to come…
    match.delegate = gameSceneVC;
[self.navigationController pushViewController:gameSceneVC animated:YES];
}
```

Now you will create the action to actually start looking for matches with the matchmakerViewController:

```
- (IBAction)actionHostMatch:(id)sender {
    if([GKLocalPlayer localPlayer].isAuthenticated){
        GKMatchRequest *request = [[GKMatchRequest alloc] init] ;
        request.minPlayers = 2;
```

```
        request.maxPlayers = 2;
        GKMatchmakerViewController *mmvc = [[GKMatchmakerViewController alloc]
initWithMatchRequest:request];
        mmvc.matchmakerDelegate = self;
        [self presentModalViewController:mmvc animated:YES];
    }
}
```

This will get us to start looking for matches, but if you want to be able to respond to invitations, you'll need to add an invitation handler. This should be added as soon as the player is authenticated so that it can handle invitation requests as soon as possible. This block of code will handle invites you send out and invites that you receive. Add the following code in the -viewDidLoad method of MainMenuScene.m:

```
- (void)viewDidLoad
{
    [super viewDidLoad];
    [GKMatchmaker sharedMatchmaker].inviteHandler = ^(GKInvite *acceptedInvite,
                                                      NSArray *playersToInvite) {
        // Insert application-specific code here to clean up any games in progress.
        if (acceptedInvite)
        {
            GKMatchmakerViewController *mmvc = [[GKMatchmakerViewController alloc]
initWithInvite:acceptedInvite];
            mmvc.matchmakerDelegate = self;
            [self presentModalViewController:mmvc animated:YES];
        }
        else if (playersToInvite)
        {
            GKMatchRequest *request = [[GKMatchRequest alloc] init];
            request.minPlayers = 2;
            request.maxPlayers = 2;
            request.playersToInvite = playersToInvite;
            GKMatchmakerViewController *mmvc = [[GKMatchmakerViewController alloc]
initWithMatchRequest:request];
            mmvc.matchmakerDelegate = self;
            [self presentModalViewController:mmvc animated:YES];
        }
    };
}
```

Now you'll want to implement multiplayer game controls into your GameScene. Open GameScene.h, and set it as a GKMatchDelegate. You can also set it as a UIAlertViewDelegate (for later). Finally, you will add two new properties, GKMatch *match and BOOL matchStarted. GameScene.h should now look like this:

```
// GameScene.h
// HangmanMP

#import <UIKit/UIKit.h>
#import <GameKit/GameKit.h>

@interface GameScene : UIViewController <UITextFieldDelegate, GKMatchDelegate,
UIAlertViewDelegate>

@property (weak, nonatomic) IBOutlet UITextField *textFieldGuess;
@property (weak, nonatomic) IBOutlet UITextView *textViewGuesses;
```

```
@property (weak, nonatomic) IBOutlet UILabel *labelGuessedLetters;
@property (weak, nonatomic) IBOutlet UIImageView *imageViewHanger;
@property (weak, nonatomic) IBOutlet UILabel *labelLettersInWord;
@property (weak, nonatomic) IBOutlet UIScrollView *scrollViewContent;
@property (weak, nonatomic) IBOutlet UIActivityIndicatorView *activityIndicator;


@property(strong, nonatomic) NSMutableArray *arrayGuesses;
@property(strong, nonatomic) NSString *stringDifficulty;
@property(strong, nonatomic) NSString *stringHiddenWord;
@property(nonatomic) int badGuessCount;
@property(strong, nonatomic) GKMatch *match;
@property(nonatomic) BOOL matchStarted;

-(NSString *) getMagicWord;

@end
```

Switch to GameScene.m, and you have a few more changes to make to ensure that your game can handle multiplayer sessions. First, you need to synthesize the two new properties you created, so at the bottom of the @synthesize list, add this:

```
@synthesize match;
@synthesize matchStarted;
```

Now, you'll create a method in GameScene.m for sending data to all users in your game. This is just a generic function that will encode an NSDictionary and send it as an NSData object.

```
- (void) sendData:(NSDictionary *)dictionaryToSend
{
    NSError *error;

    NSMutableData *dataToSend = [[NSMutableData alloc] init];
        NSKeyedArchiver *archiver = [[NSKeyedArchiver alloc]
initForWritingWithMutableData:dataToSend];
        [archiver encodeObject:dictionaryToSend forKey:@"DataDictionary"];
        [archiver finishEncoding];

    [match sendDataToAllPlayers:dataToSend withDataMode:GKMatchSendDataReliable
error:&error];
    if (error != nil)
    {
        NSLog(@"Error sending data: %@", error.description);
    }
}
```

Note this line:

```
[match sendDataToAllPlayers:dataToSend withDataMode:GKMatchSendDataReliable
error:&error];
```

You could also send the data withDataMode:GKMatchSendDataUnreliable if you didn't need to know every update of the player (for instance, if the player were moving on the screen, you need to know only the current position, not where the player has been). In this case, you do need to know that players receive your data (the word they are trying to guess), so you will send with GKMatchSendDataReliable.

Before I show how to receive data, let's take a look at setting up the match. Add the following delegate method to notify your game whenever a player's state changes. Once all the players are in the game, the expectedPlayerCount will equal 0 and you are ready to start your game. You need to know who is going to go first, so have each player generate a random number with arc4random() between 0 and 999. Then send this random number using your previous sendData method.

```
- (void)match:(GKMatch *)match player:(NSString *)playerID
didChangeState:(GKPlayerConnectionState)state
{
    switch (state)
    {
        case GKPlayerStateConnected:
            // handle a new player connection.
            break;
        case GKPlayerStateDisconnected:
            [[[UIAlertView alloc] initWithTitle:@"Warning" message@"Opponent left the
game" delegate:nil cancelButtonTitle:@"OK" otherButtonTitles:nil] show];
            break;
    }
    if (!self.matchStarted && match.expectedPlayerCount == 0)
    {
        self.matchStarted = YES;
        // handle initial match negotiation.
        randomPlayerStartKey=arc4random() % 1000;
        NSDictionary *dictionaryRandomStart=[NSDictionary
                                        dictionaryWithObject:[NSNumber
numberWithInt:randomPlayerStartKey]
                                        forKey:@"randomStartKey"];
        [self sendData:dictionaryRandomStart];

    }
}
```

So now you have your first piece of data to receive, the random number that was generated. You'll start by decoding the NSData received back into a dictionary. Then you'll check for the key randomStartKey; if it exists, you'll check if it is larger than the random number you generated. If your number is greater, then you will prompt for a word that you will send to the opponent to guess. There are a few other handlers added to complete the implementation: WordToGuess, gameWon, and gameLost.

```
- (void)match:(GKMatch *)match didReceiveData:(NSData *)data fromPlayer:(NSString
*)playerID
{
    NSKeyedUnarchiver *unarchiver = [[NSKeyedUnarchiver alloc]
initForReadingWithData:data];
    NSDictionary *myDictionary = [unarchiver decodeObjectForKey:@"DataDictionary"];
    [unarchiver finishDecoding];
    NSLog(@"Received Dict: %@", myDictionary);

    if([myDictionary valueForKey:@"randomStartKey"]!=nil){
        NSNumber *otherRandomStartKey=[myDictionary valueForKey:@"randomStartKey"];
        if([otherRandomStartKey integerValue]>randomPlayerStartKey){
            //If their random key is larger than mine, then they will send the word

        }else{
```

```
                    //My random key is larger so I will send the word
                    UIAlertView *wordPrompt=[[UIAlertView alloc] initWithTitle:@"Enter Word:"
message:@"Type the word they must decode" delegate:self cancelButtonTitle:@"Cancel"
otherButtonTitles:@"OK", nil];
                    wordPrompt.alertViewStyle=UIAlertViewStylePlainTextInput;
                    [wordPrompt show];
            }
        }else if([myDictionary valueForKey:@"WordToGuess"]!=nil){
    //if they sent the word to guess
            [self setWord:[myDictionary valueForKey:@"WordToGuess"]];
            [self.activityIndicator stopAnimating];
        }else if([myDictionary valueForKey:@"gameWon"]!=nil){
    //if they won the game
            int guessCount=[[myDictionary valueForKey:@"gameWon"] integerValue];
            [[[UIAlertView alloc] initWithTitle:@"Your Opponent Won!" message:[NSString
stringWithFormat:@"Better luck next time.  %i bad guesses", guessCount] delegate:nil
cancelButtonTitle:@"OK" otherButtonTitles:nil] show];
        }else if([myDictionary valueForKey:@"gameLost"]!=nil){
            [[[UIAlertView alloc] initWithTitle:@"You Win!" message:@"They didn't guess your
word" delegate:nil cancelButtonTitle:@"OK" otherButtonTitles:nil] show];
        }
}
```

Since you prompt for the word to send, you should check your dictionary and make sure
it is a legitimate word. Since you set your class as a UIAlertViewDelegate in the .h file
and you set the delegate of the alert view prompt to self, you can add the following
method to process the submitted word before you send it to your opponent:

```
- (void)alertView:(UIAlertView *)alertView
didDismissWithButtonIndex:(NSInteger)buttonIndex{
    if(buttonIndex==1){
        NSLog(@"Alert View Text: %@", [alertView textFieldAtIndex:0].text);
        NSString *potentialWord=[alertView textFieldAtIndex:0].text;

        NSString *path = [[NSBundle mainBundle] pathForResource:@"wordlist"
                                                    ofType:@"txt"];
        NSString *content = [NSString stringWithContentsOfFile:path
                                                encoding:NSUTF8StringEncoding
                                                error:NULL];

        NSArray *lines = [content componentsSeparatedByString:@"\n"];

        BOOL wordMatch=NO;
        while(wordMatch==NO){
            for (NSString *word in lines) {
                if([word isEqualToString:potentialWord]){
                    NSDictionary *myDictionary = [NSDictionary
dictionaryWithObject:[alertView textFieldAtIndex:0].text forKey:@"WordToGuess"];
                    [self sendData:myDictionary];
                    wordMatch=YES;
                    break;
                }
            }
            if(wordMatch==NO){
                UIAlertView *wordPrompt=[[UIAlertView alloc] initWithTitle:@"Word Not
Found" message:@"Your word was not found in the dictionary, please enter a new word for
```

```
your opponent to decode:" delegate:self cancelButtonTitle:@"Cancel"
otherButtonTitles:@"OK", nil];
                wordPrompt.alertViewStyle=UIAlertViewStylePlainTextInput;
                [wordPrompt show];
        }
    }
  }
}
```

Now that you have data going back and forth, you can send the game notifications (e.g., winning and losing) using the sendData method, but you should first see if you are in a match. The following sample code shows how to check if you are in a match:

```
if(self.match){

            NSDictionary *dictionaryGameWon=[NSDictionary
                                             dictionaryWithObject:[NSNumber
numberWithInt:self.badGuessCount]
                                             forKey:@"gameWon"];
            [self sendData:dictionaryGameWon];

        }
```

The foregoing code would be placed toward the end of the -processGuess method in GameScene.m.

```
-(void) processGuess:(NSString *)guessedLetter{
...

        if(unfoundLetters.location==NSNotFound){
            [self reportScore:playerScore forCategory:@"default_high_scores"];
            if(self.badGuessCount==0 && self.stringHiddenWord.length<=6){
                NSLog(@"Reporting achievement");
                [self reportAchievementIdentifier:@"no_mistakes_small_word"
percentComplete:100];
            }

            [[[UIAlertView alloc] initWithTitle:@"WINNER!" message:[NSString
stringWithFormat:@"You Win!\nScore:%i", playerScore] delegate:nil
cancelButtonTitle:@"OK" otherButtonTitles:nil] show];
            if(self.match){

            NSDictionary *dictionaryGameWon=[NSDictionary
                                             dictionaryWithObject:[NSNumber
numberWithInt:self.badGuessCount]
                                             forKey:@"gameWon"];
            [self sendData:dictionaryGameWon];

        }
    }
  }
}
```

This is the start of a multiplayer game and shows the sending of player information, moves, and other data back and forth. If you have trouble with any of the foregoing code, you can find the completed project at https://github.com/shawngrimes/HangmanMP-Complete.

Summary

In this chapter, you've learned how to extend your game with Game Center and Game Kit. You should be able to include high scores in your games to encourage competition among players and establish bragging rights. You should also be able to implement achievements that can give your players a feeling of accomplishment during long levels or even easily provide mini-games within a game. Finally, you implemented basic multiplayer functionality into the game to encourage even more social game play against live opponents.

Developing iOS applications is a multifarious process: a combination of visual design and programmatic functionality that requires a versatile skillset, as well as significant dedication. Thankfully, Apple provides an excellent development toolset and programming language to work with, both of which are constantly updated and improved upon. With such a flexible language, tasks ranging from organizing massive data stores, to complex web requests, to image filtering can be simplified, designed, and implemented for some of the most widely used and powerful devices of our generation. Whether you use this book as a simple reference or a full guide, we hope that you are able to use these recipes to build stronger applications to help improve and contribute to the world of iOS technology.

Index

▪ E

▪ F

N, O

P, Q

R

U

CPSIA information can be obtained at www.ICGtesting.com
Printed in the USA
LVOW100459250412

279042LV00007B/1/P